THE HISTORICAL CREDIBILITY

OF HANS KUNG

THE HISTORICAL CREDIBILITY

OF HANS KUNG

An Inquiry and Commentary

By

JOSEPH F. COSTANZO, S.J.

THE CHRISTOPHER PUBLISHING HOUSE
NORTH QUINCY, MASSACHUSETTS

Imprimitur: Francis J. Green
                   Bishop of Tucson
                   August 15, 1978

Nihil Obstat: Robert C. Trupia
                   Diocese of Tucson

Imprimi Potest: Martin F. Mahoney, S.J.
                   Provincial
                   New York Province
                   July 13, 1976

PRINTED IN

THE UNITED STATES OF AMERICA

In memory of my Mother and Father—
who by their lives
nurtured within me
a deep and abiding love
of our Catholic Faith.

ACKNOWLEDGMENTS

I am very grateful for the services of the librarians of the Pius XII Memorial Library, St. Louis University, for providing me with photostat copies of R. A. Verardo's own *Editoris Introductio* to the Text of St. Thomas Aquinas' *Contra Errores Graecorum ad Urbanum IV Pontificum Maximum*, and of the Thomistic text itself. Also, I am indebted to the librarians for a photostatic copy of *Assertio Septem Sacramentorum or Defense of the Seven Sacraments* by Henry VIII, King of England. It is hardly possible to measure my indebtedness to Sister Mary Ruth Murphy, of the Congregation of the Sisters of Charity of the Incarnate Word, who generously undertook the task of preparing my manuscript for publication, and for her patient and valuable guidance. And not least, I wish to express my thanks to my relatives and friends who encouraged me to persevere in this critical study despite cumbersome difficulties of health.

J. F. C.

TABLE OF CONTENTS

Because I believed
I spoke out
(*2 Cor. 4:10*)

A PERSONAL RESPONSE

Every priest must, whether he wills it or not, come face to face with the novelties of theologizing in some quarters. He can either defer to the Church's claim of divine credentials, as the generality of the faith do, and turn back upon the innovators (*eversores*, St. Augustine called them—*up-rooters*). Or, he may undertake to respond as best he can in terms of a personally lived Catholic faith by the grace of God and his own intellectual and spiritual resources. I have chosen to do the latter.

In 1970, Hans Kung's *Unfehlbar? Eine Anfrage* appeared (English translation, *Infallibility? An Inquiry*, 1971), which challenges a basic dogma of the Catholic faith. *The Credibility of Hans Kung: An Inquiry and Commentary*[1] is devoted exclusively to this book. We hope that some may find it a helpful companion study to Kung's own book and perhaps conclude, as does the writer, that Kung's book raises far more disturbing questions about his credibility as a scholar learned in history and theology and, alas, about his orthodoxy of Catholic belief than he raises valid questioning of orthodox Catholic ecclesiology.

---

[1] In preparation are Part II, *Catholic Ecclesiology and Kung's Ecclesial Paradeigma*, and Part III, *The Theological Gnoseology of Hans Kung*.

Part I

THE HISTORICAL CREDIBILITY OF HANS KUNG

Anima et Animus

"A Candid Preface" (K. 11-30). The pages ache intensely here (and not infrequently throughout the entire book) with a teutonic neuralgia: "Rome," "Bishop of Rome," "Roman Pontiff," (never "Vicar of Christ"). As early, if not earlier, as 495 when the Roman synod hailed Pope Gelasius eleven times, "Vicarium Christi te videmus," cf. Council of Florence (Dz. 694), "verum Christi vicarium"; Vatican I (Dz. 826), "verum Christi vicarium"; so, too (Vatican Council II, *Lumen Gentium*, n. 18), never "His Holiness" (even members of the diplomatic corps representing non-Catholic countries use this term); "Roman canon law," (not simply canon law), "Roman ghetto," "Vatican ghetto," "curial ghetto," "Roman central administration," "traditional curial policy and theology" (not Catholic theology), "Roman curia," "Roman reaction," "narrow Roman theology and ideology," "not very ecumenical Romanism," "Roman system," "Roman textbooks" (notwithstanding that many of their authors were German and French), "Roman theory," "non-Roman readers," "Roman teaching," "Roman claim," "Roman-minded prelates," "Roman teaching office" (not the teaching office of the Catholic Church), "Roman mentality" (many of the professors of theology in Rome were non-Italians)—is it a theological discredit to teach according to the Bishop of Rome, the Roman Pontiff?); "Church of the Roman Imperial Capital," "centralized, juridicized, romanticized," "Rome at the time of the Counter Reformation" (*not* the Catholic Church), "Roman ecclesiastical policy and theology," "polarization of German and Roman theology" (*there* is the rub!), "increasing Roman influence," "Roman ideas," "as an army in battle array under Rome's command," "romanizing of the whole Church," "Roman influences," "Roman absolutism," "Roman view,"—and so on and on.

11

The author anticipates charges of "lack of faith or charity," "of arrogance," of being "sharp" and "harsh," but he pleads that such impressions are but a reflection of the way he responds to events of the Church, to the Holy Father, to the Curia, to other theologians, and above all, to matters of dogma and moral doctrine. What actually emerges is Kung's own sort of faith and charity. There is not much to distinguish between this anti-Roman *animus* and his academically avowed purpose. This reader for one, concluded his study of this volume with the firm conviction that Kung's book was certainly not an "Inquiry" as he proposed. What "faith and charity" justifies his acerbic attack upon Pope Paul VI, his frequent sardonic referrals to the Curia, his ungracious comment upon "theologians like Danielou, formerly persecuted by the Inquisition, but now, themselves bringing an aura of scholarship to the role of Grand Inquisitor, are nominated as Cardinals of the Holy Roman Church" (22), his misdirected bias for the "Dutch Church" and the Dutch Catechism, his call for the repeal of priestly celibacy, of the regulations on mixed marriage and the doctrinal pronouncements of Pope Paul's encyclicals on the *Church*, on the *Eucharist*, his myopic considerations of ecclesiastical history?

The monotonous frequency and variations on Romanism and neo-scholasticism reveals not only a psychological alienation but also an intellectual turning of the worm. When Kung berates Roman centralization, he is ignoring the necessity for it in the past as a unifying defense and systematization against medieval imperial pretensions and interventions and later against the dictations of the modern states of the last three centuries; or if he speaks of the present, he chooses to minimize the regional and national episcopal conferences and the enormously increased clergy and religious consultations and participations encouraged by Rome itself. This writer cannot entirely suppress the suspicion that Kung is really after that institutional hierarchical structure of the Church which the Dogmatic Constitution on the Church (*Lumen Gentium*, c. III) and the Decree on the Bishops' Pastoral Office in the Church (*Christus Dominus*, c. I) so unabashedly reaffirm. Since Pope Paul VI has internationalized the College of Cardinals and the Roman Curia, Kung's deprecations of what is Roman must mean simply papal government of the Bishop of Rome and universal pastor of the Church. When he speaks reproachingly of Roman doctrine and Roman textbooks he surely cannot have Italians in mind, since so many illustrious teachers and authors of "Roman" doctrine were non-Italians, and among them eminent German theologians must be numbered. He must, then, mean that theology and those textbooks, whether taught in Rome or elsewhere (geography has nothing to do with the designation "Roman"), that are in accord with the official and authoritative teaching of the ecclesial magisterium. His undisguised scorn and repetitive downbeat on "textbooks," whether of theology or neo-scholasticism, overlooks the original question. Were not the content of these berated "textbooks"—not excluding the *Enchiridion Symbolorum Definitionum et Declarationum De Rebus Fidei et Morum* (which Kung also disdains as workable theological sources, first edited by Henry Denziger and succeeded by later editions of Clement Bannwart, Karl Rahner, S.J. and Adolph Schonmetzer, S.J.,— all German)—originally in extensive scholarly works of the master theologians through the centuries—Patristic, medieval and modern— and in expansive documentary tomes of the Roman Pontiffs and Councils; and were not their economical contraction into "textbooks" but the thoughtful accommodation to assist students of theology on their way to the larger horizons of greater competence and gradually deeper learning which their pastoral duties of the future might permit in the interstices of free time?

And now my personal commentary on the particularities of Kung's resentments and objectives born of his own theological and historical prepossessions.

Mary, Mater Ecclesiae

Against the express will of the majority of the Council, Pope Paul VI proclaimed for Mary the misleading title, *Mater Ecclesiae*, which aroused great hostility and doubt about the Pope's genuine desire for ecumenical understanding and not only outside the Catholic Church. (K. 17)

It is difficult to see how calling the Mother of God (*theotókos*, Ephesus 431), Mother of Her Divine Son's Church can be misleading. When we recall the unique prerogatives affirmed of Mary and her central role in the economy of salvation in the writings of the Church in the East and West, the ecclesiastical writers, and by the great theologians (and recalled with such passion by Cardinal Newman), Pope Paul's acclamation is a well-founded development.

In the final hours of the Council of Ephesus, Cyril, Patriarch of Alexandria, began his sermon with, "Hail Mary, Mother of God"— and continuing with titles and eulogies unsurpassed through the centuries, he concluded with a startling statement: "May we...reverence the undivided Trinity, while we sing the praise of the ever-virgin Mary, that is to say, the holy Church, and of her spotless Son and Bridegroom." (*Homiliae diversae* 4) Perhaps this remarkable statement is but the resonance of the earlier thoughts of St. Ambrose, when he hailed Our Lady, "Mary is type of the Church." (*Expositio evangelii secundum* Lucam 2, 7)

What did the Fathers of the Second Vatican Council actually say? After discoursing about "the glorious and perpetual Virgin Mary, Mother of God and Lord Jesus Christ" (*Lumen Gentium,* c. 8 n. 52, hereafter *L.G.*), "Mother of the Redeemer. . .favorite daughter of the Father and the temple of the Holy Spirit," (n. 53) they continued:

> At the same time, however, she belongs to the offspring of Adam, she is one with all human beings in their need for salvation. Indeed, she is *"clearly the mother of the members of Christ*. . .since she cooperated out of love *so that there might be born in the Church the faithful*, who are members of Christ, their Head." (St. Augustine, *"DeS., Virginitate,"* 6:PL 40, 399). Therefore, she is also hailed as a pre-eminent and altogether singular member of the Church and as the Church's model and excellent exemplar in faith and charity. Taught by the Holy Spirit, the Catholic Church honors her *with filial affection and piety as a most beloved mother.* (n. 53, italics supplied)

Note: The Second Vatican Council was conducted under Mary's tutelage. Pope John's call to convoke the Council was on the Feast of Our Lady of Lourdes, February 11, 1961. The actual opening of the Council was on the Feast of the Maternity of the Blessed Mother, October 11, 1962. Earlier, Pope John made a pilgrimage to the Shrine of our Lady of Loretto to pray for the Council's success. After his address to the Council Pope John asked the faithful to pray to Our Lady, Queen of Heaven. Pope Paul closed the Council on the Feast of Our Lady, the Immaculate Conception, December 8, 1965. At the close of the Council's third session, on the Feast of the Presentation of Mary in the Temple, November 21, 1964, the Holy Father concelebrated Mass in her honor with twenty-four Council Fathers, each of whom had a major shrine of Our Lady within his jurisdiction. Pope Paul proclaimed Mary *Mater Ecclesiae* with these words: "For the glory of the Virgin Mary and for our own consolation, we proclaim Mary, the Mother of the Church, that is, of the whole People of God, of the faithful as well as the pastors, and we wish that through this tribute the Mother of God should be still more honored and invoked by the entire Christian people." (So much for those who say the Council muted devotion to the Mother of the Son of God.)

The Fathers of the Council all but called Mary explicitly "Mother of the Church," and most appropriately in the concluding chapter of the Dogmatic Constitution on the Church.

As for *Mater Ecclesiae*, it is a metaphor with a basis in reality, as the scholastics would say. Mary gave birth to the Head from whom flows the existence and life of the Church, and now, assumed into Heaven, she accompanies the life of the community of faithful by her fruitful intercession. The transparently symbolic character of the Fourth Gospel allows the interpretation that the words of Jesus on the Cross, "Woman, behold Thy Son," and "Son, behold Thy Mother," (Jn. 19:25ff) may go beyond the purely historical and point to the relationship between Mary and the Church. Pope Paul simply explicitated the traditional thinking of the Church, including that of the Council Fathers of Vatican II.

Reforms of the Roman Curia

Pope Paul's reform of the Curia would be more generously appraised by Kung (p. 20) if he shared the Pontiff's intentions and objections. In announcing the reform of the Roman Curia in 1967, His Holiness recalled his words opening the second session of the Council in 1963:

> The reform at which the Council aims is not a turning upside down of the Church's present way of life or a breaking with what is essential and worthy of veneration in her tradition. It is, rather, an honoring of Tradition by stripping it of what is unworthy or defective so that it can be rendered firm and faithful.

Declaring that "certainly there can be no doubt about the need for the Roman Curia," Pope Paul said that his objective was to make it "better adapted to the needs of the time." His many reforms of the Curia have been hailed by commentators on his pontificate to be among his major achievements. The necessary services were certainly not to be cancelled, and the assumption of additional apostolates in response to the Council v.g. Commission on Justice, the Council of the Laity, the Vatican Secretariat for non-Christians, the General Secretariat of the Synod of Bishops, *et alii*, have obviously necessitated an expansion of curial offices, not their diminution.

Dutch Catechism (K. 22)

Kung's resentment of the Church's objections (and finally, rejection of the Dutch Catechism, October 13, 1972) and his caustic remarks of Pope Paul's *Credo* are cut from the same cloth, namely, his apparent fascination with that "new" theology that is at variance with the solemnly defined beliefs from Nicaea to Vatican I and reaffirmed by Vatican II, many of which go back to the most ancient, Western and Eastern *Symbola Fidei*.

The "New Catechism," *"De Nieuwe Katechismus,"* was published in Holland in 1966. Because of protestations on the part of the faithful against the suspected heterodoxy of the catechism either by what it said in part, by omission (deemphasis by misleading explanations and ambiguous statements), three theologians selected by the Holy See and three by the Dutch hierarchy were to convene and make a study of the disputed points in accordance with the express wishes of Pope Paul (April, 1967). The theologians chosen by the Holy See asked that certain emendations be made for the sake of clarity and precision. Nothing came of these proposals, not even those particular points which the Holy Father himself had indicated: the virginal conception of Our Lord and the satisfactorial and sacrificial character of the redemptive act which Christ offered to His Eternal Father. A commission of Cardinals (Frings, Lefebvre, Jaeger, Florit, Browne and Journet) appointed by Pope Paul studied the Catechism together with theologians familiar with the Dutch language (June, 1967). They decided that the Dutch Catechism was to be revised before new editions and translations were made and they also selected a group of theologians from seven different nations to make their study of the new catechism and report on it. Every one of the evaluations and proposals of this group were unanimously approved by each of the theologians.

The commission of Cardinals reconvened (December, 1967) and decided what was to be changed and in what manner in the Dutch Catechism. With the cooperation of Cardinal Alfrink, two theologians of their choosing and two of the Dutch hierarchy were assigned to bring about the corrections. English, German and French translations of the Dutch Catechism were appearing in the meantime without any emendations. Almost with a touch of malice, disclosures were made to the public in a newspaper and in a book of the confidential transactions concerning the catechism, opinions were falsely ascribed to the theologians chosen by the Holy See, and the required corrections were cloaked over by deceptive glosses and ambiguous restatements which left the substance untouched under a novelty of verbal reconstruction. And, to top this, a distortion of the views of some modern exegetes on the Matthean and Lucan narration of the birth and infancy of Jesus (contrary to the actual belief of these theologians) is given to mislead the faithful—to suppose they are not bound to believe in the virginal conception of Our Lord in both its spiritual and corporal reality, but they are free to accept it only in symbolic signification.

All of this is a summary of the torturous frustrations visited upon the Church by the authors and editors of the Dutch Catechism. In an article in *Civilta Cattolica*, June, 1971, Father Jean Galot charged that the New Dutch textbook betrayed a tendency to reject the divinity of Christ, to challenge Catholic ecclesiology and to seem to protestantize articles of the Catholic Faith. After six years of insufficient, unsatisfactory and ingeniously contrived emendations to guard orthodoxy in the Dutch Catechism, both the prefect of the Sacred Congregation for the Doctrine of the Faith, Franjo Cardinal Seper, and the prefect of the Sacred Congregation for the Clergy, John Cardinal Wright, publicly ordered two Roman Catholic bishops to withdraw immediately as "gravely deficient," the Dutch Catechism. (October 12, 1972) So much for the "inquisitional processes against troublesome theologians" (K. 22), by the long-suffering and persevering Church

"Unhistorical Saints"

> It is true that the Church's calendar has been "reformed"— in the clumsiest way—at the expense of some unhistorical saints. (K. 23)

The thrust of this statement is unmistakable even if not explicitly expressed—the credibility of the Church on the cult of saints. Kung is much too much in a hurry to explain the action of the Church in removing the "unhistorical saints."

In the first six centuries of the Church, the sanctity, at first of martyrs, then of confessors of the faith, and later of those of heroic Christian virtue and of those exemplary in their apostolic zeal for the Church—doctors, bishops, missionaries—was so acclaimed by the *vox populi* of the faithful. From the sixth to the tenth century the definitive pronouncement of approval on the part of the local bishop gradually became a necessary culmination of a process of inquiry into the validity of such a veneration, the cult of *doulia* on the part of the faithful. By 973 formal approval of the Roman

Pontiff was deemed a matter of greater prestige for the veneration of a venerated saint, St. Udalricus. Under Gregory IX (1234) papal canonization became the only and exclusive legitimate form of inquiry into the saints' lives and miracles according to newly established procedural forms and canonical processes. In 1588 Pope Sixtus V, by his *Immensa Aeterni Dei*, entrusted the process of papal canonization to the Congregation of Rites. In 1642 Urban VIII ordered all the decrees and studies of canonizations during his own pontificate to be published in one volume—and a century later, Benedict XIV systematized in a clear and definitive manner the basic expectations of heroic virtue and the indispensable requirements of the canonical processes according to the evidences of the Congregation of Rites. In our own time, Pius X (1914) divided this Congregation into two sections: one, the liturgical section, and the other assigned entirely to the causes for canonization. In 1930, Pius XI established the historical section devoted to the critical-historical scrutiny of the evidences put forth in the causes for canonization.

The Church is infallible when she officially canonizes the beatified. The solemn act by which the Pope, with definitive sentence, inscribes in the catalogue of saints a person who has been antecedently beatified reads in part: "We decide and define that they are saints, and inscribe them in the catalogue of saints, stating that their memory should be kept with pious devotion by the universal Church." *De facto*, most likely in accordance with the "hierarchy of truth" (Decree on Ecumenism, *Unitatis redintegratio*), the Church herself does not teach authoritatively that infallibility includes such matters as the so-designated secondary objects of infallibility, the "Catholic truths" which are closely connected historically, logically or practically with the truth of faith—dogmatic facts, theological conclusions, canonizations, etc.—though they are of great importance within the context of the ordinary magisterium. *But* theologians are known to think that canonizations must be infallible, a judgment with which this writer concurs, ultimately on the grounds that the Holy Spirit would not allow the Church to venerate an unholy soul. Kung, in speaking of "some unhistorical saints," does not pause to alert his readers to the not insignificant differentials that can intervene between the popular acclamations of sanctity by the faithful in the early centuries of the Church, episcopal canonizations from the sixth to the thirteenth centuries and papal canonizations since the thirteenth century in which ecclesial and papal infallibility is squarely put on the line, at least by some theologians.

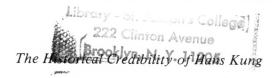
"Against the Council's wishes, the position of nuncios was strengthened by a *motu proprio*." (K. 23)

The history of papal nunciatures in modern times discloses that the accentuation on the diplomatic role of papal nuncios, that is to say, of the Roman Pontiff whom they personally represent, has been a historical response of the Holy See to the insistent call and high expectations of the international community for the Christian leaven for peace and order in the family of nations. The manifest urgency with which the new emergent nations in Europe and in Africa after each of the two world wars sought diplomatic accreditation with the Holy See belies the eventuality of the abandonment of papal nunciatures for the foreseeable future. The majority of states today maintain diplomatic relations with the papacy—"Catholic states," "Concordat," "non-Catholic," "non-Christian," "separatist," "laicist." There is no inherent confessional note in the fact of having diplomatic relations with the Holy See, and only a small number of them have concordats with the papacy. Since the relations between the Holy See and the political States are reciprocal in most cases, there is correspondingly apostolic, nuncio, internuncio or charge d'affaires accredited at the seat of the civil governments.

The Roman Pontiffs have always dispatched their own authorized representatives to all corners of Christendom and beyond from time immemorial—occasional emissaries on specific, limited missions. These special legates, *legati missi*, who were deputed for some papal commission, were not diplomatic agents, and neither were their assignment nor their office permanent. Called *apocrisarius*, in the fifth century this papal agent acted for the Pope on matters touching upon religious and ecclesiastical matters and as an on-the-spot observer of public events of importance. In time, it seemed advisable that these papal agents be *legati nati*, residential bishops of a region who, in addition to their functions as local ordinaries, were empowered with special faculties from Rome to serve as the permanent delegates of the Roman Pontiff. About the eleventh century Rome resorted to its former practice of sending its own specially chosen representatives, *legati missi* to distinguish them from the antecedent residential legates. The principal type of the *legatus missus* was the *legatus a latere*, because he came from the papal court, literally from the Pope's side. Today the *legatus a latere* performs ceremonial functions such as representing the Pope at international Eucharistic Congresses. The emergence of the papal envoy as a diplomatic agent, as a matter of historical record, was in reciprocity to representation at the papal curia already introduced by the Italian cities and by the need of negotiations with the royal courts of the modern sovereign independent states. The urgency for them, however, grew in the sixteenth century with the grave challenge to religious unity posed by the Protestant revolt in a concerted effort to secure the support of princes against the Lutheran rebellion. Today nuncios perform a double function: they represent the Roman Pontiff before the civil governments and preside over the state of the Church in the region assigned to them and report to the Bishop of Rome thereon. It is the secular side of this history that bears a significance which apparently Kung has overlooked. It is to the first separatist-laicist state of modern European history, the First Republic of France, that we must turn for paradoxical insistence that the Holy See continue to maintain the same reciprocal diplomatic relations as before the French Revolution, when the ruler of France was the "eldest son" of the Church. The First Republic, while bold to declare its state of rebellion against the spiritual authority of the Roman Pontiffs, insisted through the explicit instructions of the Directory that the Treaty of Tolentino of February 19, 1797 stipulate (Art. 5) that the French Republic continue to enjoy reciprocal diplomatic relations with the Holy See on the ambassadorial level as formerly as a "Catholic" state and not merely recognized as were traditionally the envoys of Protestant states as "residents" of Rome. For the first time, under military force, Rome was required to consent to accord at its Court the full diplomatic honors of ambassadors to the envoys of a government that was not officially Catholic—and France, in turn, has accorded to the papal nuncio assigned to France the deanship of the diplomatic corps, be it only for ceremonial occasions, a practice followed without challenge in other countries. This history of diplomatic missions at Rome reveals the full spectrum of *legationes obedientiae* (connoting a religious affiliation and political dependence upon the Papacy), ordinary missions, resident agents, special, temporary and permanent envoys, legations, ordinary and extra-ordinary ministers, vice consuls, consuls, ministers, ministers plenipotentiary, ambassadors—with the effort on the part of the foreign government to advance from one diplomatic status to another to its own advantage, tangible and intangible.

The second historic event on diplomatic relations with the Holy See was the Congress of Vienna which upset the Reformation's settlement of *cuius regio illius et religio*, the principle of the Peace of Augsburg that was confirmed at Westphalia, by a modern sense of *real politik* on political allegiance and religious confession consequent to a process of the secularization begun in 1803 that profoundly transformed relationships with the Holy See by severing diplomatic from religious relations while at the same time employing the former in the service of the latter. Will it or not, the Papacy was forced by circumstances and historical exigencies to be a participant for a variety of complex reasons in international intercourse. It was the society of sovereign states, rather than the Papacy, which was the prime motor for the inclusion of the Papacy *as a spiritual power* and all its attendant and consequential incidents in war and peace in the public community of mankind, with high expectations of service to the advantage of each state and presumably to the overarching higher advantage of the community of nations.

Pope Paul has an intimate personal concern about the substantive value of papal diplomacy. From 1944 to 1955 the then Monsignor Giovanni B. Montini was the prosecretary of State of Pope Pius XII, in frequent contact with foreign envoys accredited to the Holy See. On the occasion of the 250th anniversary of the founding of the *Pontificia Accademia Ecclesiastica*, April 25, 1951, Monsignor Montini addressed the young ecclesiastics trained for the papal diplomatic service. He defined diplomacy as "an art of creating and maintaining international order, that is to say, peace." The objective of this art is to strive perseveringly for the humane, rational and juridical relations among the people of the world, superseding both force and the calculating balancing of material interests by open and responsible settlements mindful of one another's needs.

If civil diplomacy tends to the unification of the world by making reason prevail over force, and to the growth of individual states in the harmonious concert of an ever larger international organization, it finds in ecclesiastical diplomacy almost a model towards which it can look with assurance; not so much because of any technical proficiency that the Church might display, or any success attending its efforts (for both of these elements may be lacking), as because of the ideal from which it takes its departure and towards which it tends, the universal brotherhood of men.

This is a firm persuasion that has been manifestly prevalent among the numerous states who have sought and been accredited to the

Holy See, whether the Papacy was in possession of Papal States or none at all or of a tiny geographic enclave stipulated by the Lateran Treaty of 1929, whether by major powers, small states, "Protestant," "Catholic," "Islamic," "Oriental," etc.   Prosecretary Montini was simply articulating the viewpoint and expectations of national states from the Papacy as a religious and spiritual power in the international order.

The unique status of the Holy See in general international law consists in the fact, that it is precisely as a spiritual sovereign that she enjoys the rights of sovereignty ordinarily accorded to national political sovereignty and that no other Church or religion has ever been accorded the same status in the world community of states. Sovereignty and international personality is vested with the Holy See precisely as a spiritual authority, independently of the existence of a Papal state. The reason for the existence of the State of Vatican City is wholly derivative and contingent upon the presupposition that the free exercise of a supranational spiritual sovereignty by the Holy See is better ensured by an independent territorial jurisdiction of its own. Prior to 1870 and subsequent to 1929, there have been two subjects of international law: the Papal States or the State of Vatican City, and the Holy See. The Pope united in his own person these two distinct subjects of international law, and of the two, obviously, the more important and primary is the Holy See. Papal nuncios and apostolic delegates are accredited by the Holy See, not by the Papal State. Diplomatic relations by the states of England, the Netherlands, Finland, Japan, Egypt, India, Indonesia and others are established with the Holy See and not, as it popularly supposed, with the Papal States. Their diplomatic representatives are accredited to the spiritual sovereignty and not to the temporal sovereignty. The Holy See is a non-territorial international personality. Papal nuncios are *nuntiaturae pacis*—a reciprocation of this expectation of a peace mission in the community of nations. The *motu proprio* to which Kung alludes (K. 23), *Apostolic Letter on Papal Representatives*, grounds Papal diplomacy in ecclesiology. In its introduction, the Holy Father lays stress on the bonds existing in the universal Church between the visible center of her unity, the Roman Pontiff and the churches and the faithful spread all over the world. Papal diplomacy is the Church's presence throughout the world. The nuncios are the vicars of the Vicar of Christ among the faithful of the local churches. Nuncios are personal representatives of the Pope, not of anyone else. In the *motu proprio* the Holy Father has conjoined the function of papal diplomacy in the world as he had explained it as prosecretary of State to a dynamic ecclesiology. The Papal representative is directed to the Church of the country to which he is accredited; he brings the presence of him whom Vatican Council I (*Pastor Asternus*, Ds 1821) and Vatican II (*Lumen Gentium*, n. 18) called "the permanent and visible source and foundation of unity of faith and fellowship" into the midst of all the faithful in matters of doctrine and pastoral care. It is as an overflow of the dynamism of Catholicity that the Papal representative to civil societies brings the presence and the testimony of him who is the depositary, guardian and dispenser of the truth and grace of Christ. There is no other way to explain the phenomenon after each of the two world wars, when newly emerging nations in Eastern Europe and the African states vied with each other to establish diplomatic relations with the Holy See.

Lex Fundamentalis (K. 23)

> And a Papal Commission for the reform of Canon Law—in which there was *no representation of public opinion in the Church*, not even of progressive specialists like those of the *Canon Law Society of America*—was allowed to work out a "basic Law of the Catholic Church" which would use the words of Vatican II to strengthen the hold of *Roman absolutism*. (K. 23, italics supplied)

During the Council a number of bishops and leading churchmen proposed that a fundamental law of the Church be included with the reform of the Canon Law. The benefits as envisaged were a common law, theological-juridical in character, underlying, unifying and giving life to the diversity of theologies, liturgies and ecclesiastical disciplines of the Latin and Oriental Churches of the one universal Catholic Church. Since 1965 the preliminary questionnaires, the first and second amended draft (*Schema legis Ecclesiae Fundamentalis, Textus emendatus*) of the proposed basic law, were reviewed by various ecclesiastical agencies, the Commission for the Code, by a Group of Consultants, Theologians and Canonists, the International Theological Commission, the Sacred Congregation for the Doctrine of Faith and by worldwide consultation with all the bishops of the Catholic Church for their opinions, criticisms, amendments for acceptance or rejection or acceptance *secundum modum*. All the bishops were informed in writing that they could consult learned priests and laymen, that the faithful be heard according to the explicit wishes of Pope Paul, expressed in His address to the Cardinals on June 23, 1970. Non-Catholic observer-consultants attended by invitation the meetings of committees of revision.

Kung's neurasthenic eagerness to portray the Church as darkly as possible, clandestine, conspiratorial, á déju, forever trying to put something over the faithful succeeds here to inspire him with no more than such flaccid resentment as "no representation of public opinion." Would Kung have a Gallup poll in a matter calling for theological and juridical expertise? As for the Canon Law Society of America, the Bishops in the United States can consult whom they will. Actually, Cardinal Pericle Felici, President of the Commission for the *Lex Fundamentalis*, visited the United States the Fall of 1972 in order to consult in person with groups of canonists in different regions of the country. So much for Kung's charge of Roman absolutism.

Women Religious Orders (K. 23)

> The reform of women's orders had been demanded, but in America, where it had been most seriously attempted, it was stopped by the Congregation for Religious. (K. 23)

Let us turn to the Decree on the Appropriate Renewal of the Religious Life (*Perfectae Caritatis*, October 28, 1965) and take note of what the Council Fathers meant by "religious renewal."

> Since the religious life is intended above all else to lead those who embrace it to an imitation of Christ and to union with God through the profession of the evangelical counsels, the fact must be honestly faced that even the most desirable changes made on behalf of contemporary needs will fail of their purpose unless a renewal of spirit gives life to them. (n. 2, e)

> The hope of renewal must be lodged in a more diligent observance of rule and of constitution than in a multiplication of individual rules. (n. 4)

> To live for God alone by dying to sin (cf. Rom. 6:11) but also by renouncing the world . . . share spiritually in Christ's

self-surrender (cf. Phil. 2:7-8) and in His life (cf. Rom. 8:1-13) . . . to develop a life hidden with Christ in God (cf. Col. 3:3) . . . cultivate the spirit of prayer . . . think with the Church to an ever-increasing degree. (n. 5)

The lay religious life, for both men and women, constitutes a life which of itself is one of total dedication to the profession of the evangelical counsels. (n.10)

That chastity which is practiced "on behalf of the heavenly kingdom" (Mt. 19:12), and which religious profess, deserves to be esteemed as a surpassing gift of grace. For it liberates the heart in a unique way (cf. I Cor. 7:32-35) and causes it to burn with greater love of God and all mankind . . . let them practice mortification and custody of the senses . . . a certain spiritual instinct should lead them to spurn everything likely to imperil chastity. (n. 12)

Religious poverty requires more than limiting the use of possessions to the consent of superiors; members of a community ought to be poor in both fact and spirit . . . . (n. 13)

Through the profession of obedience, religious offer to God a total dedication of their own wills as a sacrifice of themselves. . . . (n.14)

Compare the above with the entrapment with semantics: "love" ("as *I* have loved you"), "presence" (religious?), "relevance" (His?), "involvement" (His Father's business?), "self-fulfillment." This last is the facile heresy: it is so patently false and yet so beguiling. What of the defective—physical and mental: the maimed, the hopelessly frustrated, the eternal incompatibles, the casualties of war, of accident, of assault, the diseased, etc.? There is not the dimmest intimation of "self-fulfillment" in the entire New Testament (nor in the Old Testament, for that matter): Gospels, Acts, Epistles. The Christians are forewarned to the contrary on earthly expectations— for the sake of the "kingdom," and "in His name." There is only one fulfillment—to grow in the likeness of Christ. The Johannine prologue is a blunt rejection of such overweening humanist pretensions—"born, not of blood, nor of the will of the flesh, nor of the will of man". . . . And as for that eternally irresistable appeal to "reform," the Roman Catholic Church has never wanted for conscientious critics of the human failings and abuses within the Church which her Divine Master had foretold would be the stumbling block of scandal to the faithful and to the world: St. Peter, St. Paul, St. Gregory the Great, St. Bernard of Clairvaux, St. Francis of Assisi, St. Catherine of Siena, St. Theresa of Avila, St. John of the Cross, St. Ignatius Loyola and a glorious etceteration. *These saintly Christians reformed the Church first by reforming themselves and then the faithful, and not by leading themselves and others out of the Church, nor by defecting from their solemn vows nor least of all, by assaulting the unity of the Mystical Body of Christ by denigrating the Vicar of Christ and the hierarchy.*

"By their fruits shall you know them."

One of the official appraisals of the reform, notably on the "Atlantic," has been given by the late French Jesuit Theologian Jean Cardinal Danielou, a member of the Congregation for Religious and Secular institutes, of which the late Ildebrando Cardinal Antonuitti was prefect. On the occasion of a plenary session of the Congregation in mid-October, 1971, Cardinal Danielou not only addressed the assembled Religious but he also gave an interview on a Vatican radio broadcast:

Question
   Is there a real crisis in the Religious Life, today, and if so, what are its dimensions and symptoms?

Answer
   There is a very grave crisis in the Religious Life today. Indeed, we can no longer speak of "renewal" but must speak of "decadence." This crisis is especially acute in the Atlantic world. Eastern Europe and the people of Africa and Asia are in a much healthier state. Where it exists, the crisis exists across the board, not merely in this or that aspect of Religious Life. Evangelical Counsels are no longer seen as consecration to God but are viewed merely from a psychological or sociological viewpoint. A great effort is made not to appear middle class, yet individual poverty in the Christian sense is no longer practiced. Group dynamics are substituted for religious obedience. A regular prayer life is abandoned on the pretext that religious formation is to be avoided. The consequences of this confused

state of affairs can be seen pre-eminently in the growing scarcity of vocations. Young people require a serious formation if they are to take up the Religious life. These consequences can also be seen in the numerous defections from the Religious Life which give scandal to the Christian people because the breaking of actual vows is involved.

Question

What are the basic causes of this crisis which you have described?

Answer

The basic cause of this crisis in the Religious Life can be found in a false interpretation of Vatican Council II. The directives of the Council for the Religious Life were very clear: *a greater fidelity to the demands of the Gospel* to be expressed in the constitution of each Religious order, and an adaptation of these constitutions to the conditions of modern life. Those Religious orders which have followed the directives of the Council are experiencing a truly radical renewal and are attracting many new vocations; but *in too many cases the directives of Vatican II have been displaced by the erroneous ideologies which are today purveyed by so many journals, conferences and theologians.* Among the principal errors of these ideologies may be counted:

a. *Secularization*—Vatican II said that human values needed to be taken seriously. The Council never said that we should be immersed in a secularized world in which the religious dimension could no longer be taken seriously as a component of civilization. Nevertheless, in the name of such a false secularization, both male and female Religious have abandoned their habits; they have given up their specifically evangelical work in favor of secular-type work, thus substituting social or political action for the worship of God. What is remarkable is that these Religious should embrace secularism at the very moment when the world's need for a deeper spirituality has never been greater.

b. *A False Conception of Liberty*—This false conception of liberty manifests itself in a veritable contempt for rules and institutions and in an exaltation of improvisation and what is called spontaneity. This attitude is especially absurd considering that it comes at the very moment when Western society has lost its sense of true freedom, freedom with discipline. The restoration of an ordered rule is a necessity for the Religious Life.

c. *A Mistaken Conception of Evolution*—This mistaken conception is seen whether it is a question of the "evolution" of men or of the Church, for even if the things around us change, *the permanent natures of man and of the Church remain unchanged.* One of the fundamental errors of today's mistaken evolutionism is to call into question the very basis of any Religious Life or Religious Order.

Question

What are the remedies for this crisis in the Religious Life which you have described?

Answer

The simple and urgent remedy is to turn away from the mistaken road which has been travelled in the reform of so many Religious Orders. We must put an *end to experimentation* and to initiatives which are contrary to the directives of the Council. We must sound a clear warning against the books, journals and conferences which continue to disseminate erroneous notions of renewal. We must restore in their integrity the practice of the Religious Life in accordance with rules *modified only as the Council truly required.* Where it appears impossible for some to retrace the steps which have been taken, at the very least it is unjust not to allow those Religious who do wish to remain faithful to the constitutions of their orders and to the directives of Vatican II, to form their own separate communities. Superiors are obliged to respect the wishes of such Religious, and the community must be allowed to have houses for the proper formation of novices. Experience has demonstrated that vocations are more numerous in houses of strict observance than in those where discipline is neglected. In cases where superiors oppose legitimate requests, an appeal to the Holy Father for recourse would be justified. The Religious Life is called to carry out its task, the Religious Life must rediscover its true meaning and break radically with the secularization which is undermining it today and preventing it from attracting new vocations. (Italics supplied).

Each reader may judge for himself the justice of this appraisal and whether the action of the Congregation for Religious that Kung has in mind (p. 23) was necessary or not, as touching the women's orders in America.

Indulgences (K. 23)

Indulgences (have been) "reformed," but not abolished. (K. 23)

Why should they be? It is an ancient practice of the Church rooted in Scripture and repeatedly reaffirmed by papal and ecclesial teaching until its definition at the Council of Trent as an article of faith against Wycliffe, Hus and the Reformers. Old Testament texts establish the distinction between the forgiven sin (*culpa*) and the enduring consequences of guilt (*poena*), punishments due to sin, notably in the personal and original sin of our first parents (Gen. 3: 17-19; Wis. 10:2), the "sin" of Moses and his exclusion from the land of promise (Num. 20:12; 27:13f.), the fall of David (2 Sam. 12:10-14). There are consequences to guilt that are not effected by penitence and conversion and which serve even as penalties as means of spiritual regeneration and rehabilitation. (cf. I Cor. 5:5; 11:32; I Tim. 1:20; Rev. 2:22f.) The Church as minister of redemption assists in this recovery into perfect charity through her efficacious intercessory prayers in virtue of the infinite merits of Christ's Redemption and the abundant merits of the saints which constitute the Treasury of the Church (Clement VI, *Unigenitus Dei Filius*, January 25, 1343). Recapitulating Church practices and theology, especially since the thirteenth century, and ecclesial affirmations and condemnations of Wycliffe, Hus, Luther and Michael du Bay, Catholic doctrine teaches that indulgences are the remission before God of a temporal punishment for sins of which the guilt has been forgiven (at least by the end of the work to which the indulgence is attached), granted by ecclesiastical authority out of the Treasury of the Church to the living, *per modum absolutionis*, to the dead, *per modum suffragii.*

While bearing in mind this doctrinal summary, this much certainly has been defined as an article of the faith by the Council of Trent: that the Church has authority (*potestas*) to grant indulgences and that they are salutary for the faithful (DS 989). Now, why should Kung ask for the cancellation of a solemnly defined doctrine unless he thinks of indulgences in a theologically frivolous and exaggerated way? This writer, for one, sees indulgences understood as they ought to be, according to the mind of the Church; that is as a spiritual event that integrates the tragedy of sin with the ineffable wonder of Redemption, of the mercy of repentence and conversion, and the compassion of the Church made holy by her Redeemer to assist efficaciously by her intercessory prayer all who sincerely seek charity without reservation—that is God. And what of the bond of the communion of saints and the souls in Purgatory? Recall, too, the requirements of recourse to the Sacraments, life of grace, works of mercy or prayer, visits to the Blessed Sacrament, etc. in a genuine effort to purify and sanctify the spiritual life. Abolish the indulgences?

And what of the charity for the living and the dead expressed through vicarious satisfaction because of the solidarity of all Christians in the Mystical Body of Christ and the doctrine of the Communion of Saints? The first had its genesis in the words of the Risen Savior:

> "Saul, Saul, why are you persecuting me?" "Who are you, Lord?", he asked, and the voice answered, "I am Jesus, and you are persecuting Me." (Acts 9:4-5)

Paul discourses about the Body of Christ in *I Corinthians* and *Romans* only occasionally, but at length in the later captivity epistles, *Colossians* and *Ephesians*, with new developments of "Head" and "plenitude." He spoke of his own vicarious suffering for the Christians at Colossae as "filling up what is wanting in the sufferings of Christ *for the sake of His body, the Church*" (Col. 1:24) and of his "fellowship of Christ's sufferings" (Phil. 3:10), which Christians must bear in order to bring the Body of Christ to fullness. *Credo in . . . sanctorum communionem.* This unison of supernatural life and sensibilities whereby the Christians who became "partakers of the divine nature" (2 Pt. 1:4, cf. Jn. 14:6-24) contribute vicarious satisfaction to the well-being of an ailing member of the Body of Christ encompasses the present and passing world and the world to come. The theology and practice of indulgences for the living, and especially for the souls in purgatory, presupposes this living faith in a shared existence with Christ and with one another, known and unknown in Christ.

(The non-recognition of the state of Israel is an odd theological exertion of Kung [K. 24] to enlarge his resentment against the papacy—but without a whimpering whisper about the outrageous plight and inviolate rights of the Palestinian Arabs.)

Pope Paul's Encyclicals

Kung's reaction to Pope Paul's encyclicals is imbued with a politicizing mentality. Here in this matter, both in language and content, the *animus* of "Candid Preface" hardens into an adversary theologizing:

> Papal doctrinal statements seem to be party documents inspired by narrow Roman theology and ideology ... (apart from *Populorum Progressio*). The remaining important doctrinal statements, however, in essentials display a reactionary character. (K. 25)

Let us look to the encyclicals that Kung specifically lists as "reactionary."

1. Ecclesiam Suam (1963)

Pope Paul VI wrote:

> We are indeed living members of the Body of Christ, that we are the authentic heirs of the Gospel of Christ, those who truly continue the work of the Apostles. There dwells in us the great inheritance of truth and morality characterizing the Catholic Church which today possesses intact the living heritage of the original apostolic tradition. (n. 48)

> If, as we have said before, the Church has a true realization of what the Lord wishes it to be, then within the Church there arises a unique sense of fulness and a need for outpouring, together with the clear awareness of a mission which transcends the Church, of a message to be spread. It is the duty of evangelization. It is the missionary mandate. It is the apostolic commission. (n. 66)

> The desire to come together as brothers must not lead to a watering down or subtracting from the truth. Our dialogue must not weaken our attachment to our Faith. On our aposto-

late, we cannot make vague promises about the principles of faith and action on which our profession of Christianity is based. (n. 91)

Of *Ecclesiam Suam* Kung writes: "disappointing because of its not very ecumenical Romanism and its defective biblical interpretation." We may here recall what the Fathers of the Council declared in the Decree on Ecumenism (*Unitatis Redintegratio*) November 21, 1964.

> For it is through Christ's Catholic Church alone, which is the all-embracing means of salvation, that the fulness of the means of salvation can be obtained. It was to the apostolic college alone of which Peter is the head, that we believe Our Lord entrusted all the blessings of the New Covenant, in order to establish on earth one Body of Christ into which all those should be fully incorporated who already belong to any way to God's People. (n. 3)

> This unity, we believe, dwells in the Catholic Church as something she can never lose . . . the Catholic Church has been endowed with all divinely revealed truth and with all the means of grace . . . . (n. 4)

> Nothing is so foreign to the Spirit of ecumenism as a false conciliatory approach which harms the purity of Catholic doctrine and obscures the assured genuine meaning. (n. 11)

So spoke the Fathers of the Second Vatican Council, whose renewal of the Catholic Church Kung invokes with so much spirited frustration.

2. Mysterium Fidei (1965) (K. 25)

Were the Council Fathers of Vatican II "reactionary" when they confirmed the doctrine which the Church has always held and taught and which the Council of Trent solemnly defined?

> At the Last Supper, on the night when He was handed over, Our Saviour, instituted the Eucharistic Sacrifice of His Body and Blood, to perpetuate the Sacrifice of the Cross

throughout the ages until He shall come; and so entrusted to the Church, His beloved spouse, the memorial of His death and resurrection: a sacrament of devotion, a sign of unity, a bond of charity, a paschal banquet in which Christ is received, the soul is filled with grace and there is given to us a pledge of future glory. (*Constitution on the Sacred Liturgy.*) (n. 47)

In the encyclical, *Mysterium Fidei*, Pope Paul VI wrote:

Those who partake of this sacrament in Holy Communion, eat the Flesh of Christ and drink the Blood of Christ, receiving both the beginning of eternal life, and the "medicine of immortality," according to the words of the Lord, "He who eats my flesh and drinks my blood has life everlasting, and I will raise him up on the last day." (n. 5)

Indeed, we are aware of the fact that, among those who deal with the Most Holy Mystery in written or spoken word, there are some who, with reference either to Masses which are celebrated in private, or to the dogma of transubstantiation, or to devotion to the Eucharist, spread such opinions as disturb the faithful and fill their minds with no little confusion about matters of faith as if every one were permitted to consign to oblivion doctrine already defined by the Church, or to interpret it in such a way as to weaken the genuine meaning of the words or the approved import of the concepts involved. (n. 10)

To corroborate the point with examples: it is not allowable to put such emphasis on what is called the "communal" Mass as to disparage Masses celebrated in private; or so to insist on the sacramental sign as if the symbolism, which all most certainly admit in the Eucharist, expresses fully and exhaustively the manner of Christ's presence in this Sacrament; or to discuss the mystery of transubstantiation without mentioning the marvelous changing of the whole substance of the bread into the Body and the whole substance of the wine into the Blood of Christ as stated by the Council of Trent, so it consists in "transignification" or "transfinalization" as they put it: or finally, to propose the opinion and put it into practice according to which Christ the Lord is no longer present in the consecrated hosts which are left after the celebration of the Sacrifice of the Mass is ended. (*Mysterium Fidei*, n. 11)

Of this encyclical on the *Eucharist*, Kung wrote:

> Paul VI, to the scandal of many bishops, published just before the assembly of the Council for its fourth session, with an eye on Holland—also shows the Pope tied to a textbook theology on which neither the exegesis nor the historical studies of the last decades have made any sort of impression." (K. 25)

Again, Kung invokes the memory of Pope John.

> "John XXIII's statement that the clothing of formulas of faith may change, while the substance of faith remains the same, is disowned." (K. 25)

This is less than honest. The substance of faith was being subverted by the new formulas and if Kung thinks Pope John XXIII would have objected to *Mysterium Fidei* of his successor, he is presuming wildly beyond reasonable expectations.

It seems that *der Heilige Geist* which has been featured so prominently in Kung's earlier works is pitted so hopelessly against the irrepressible *Lo Spirito Santo*.

3. Sacerdotalis Caelibatus (1967)

Kung objects to this encyclical (p. 25); but was Pope John XXIII, whose memory Kung repeatedly invokes—a "reactionary" when in his Second Allocution to the Roman Synod on January 26, 1960, he declared:

> It deeply hurts us that . . . anyone can dream that the Church will deliberately or even suitably renounce what from time immemorial has been and still remains, one of the purest and noblest glories of her priesthood. The law of the ecclesiastical celibacy and the efforts necessary to preserve it always recall to mind the struggle of the heroic times when the Church of Christ had to fight for and succeeded in obtaining her threefold glory: always an emblem of victory, that is, the Church of Christ, free, chaste, and Catholic. (ASS 52, 1960. PP. 235-236) . . . ."

Of this "emblem of victory," Pope Paul VI wrote:

> Jesus, who selected the first ministers of salvation, wished

them to be introduced to the understanding of the mysteries of the kingdom of heaven (Mat. 13:11; Mark 4:11; Luke 8:10), to be co-workers with God under a very special title, and His ambassadors (2 Cor. 5:20). He called them friends and brethren (John 15:15; 20:17), for whom he consecrated Himself so that they might be consecrated in truth (John 17:19). He promised a more than abundant recompense to anyone who should leave *home, family, wife and children for the sake of the kingdom of God.* (Luke 18:29-30) More than this, in words filled with mystery and hope, He also commended, an even more perfect consecration to the kingdom of heaven by means of celibacy, as a *special gift.* (Mat. 19:11-12) The motive of this answer to the divine call is the kingdom of heaven (*ibid.* v. 12); similarly, the ideas—of this kingdom (Luke 18:30), of the Gospel (Mark 10:29), and of the name of Christ (Mat. 19:29), are what motivate those invited by Jesus to the difficult renunciations of the apostolate, by a very intimate participation in His lot. (cf. Mark loc, cit. Italics supplied. S.C. n 22)

This biblical and theological vision associates our ministerial priesthood with the priesthood of Christ; it is modeled in the total and exclusive dedication of Christ to His mission of salvation, and makes it the cause of our assimilation to the form of charity and sacrifice proper to Christ, our Savior. This vision seems to us so profound and rich in truth, both speculative and practical, that we invite you, Venerable Brothers, and we invite you, eager students of Christian doctrine and masters of the spiritual life, and all priests who have gained a supernatural insight into your vocation—to persevere in the study of this vision, and to go deeply into the inner recesses and wealth of its reality. In this way, the bond between the priesthood and celibacy will be seen in an ever improving union, owing to its clear logic and to the heroism of a unique and limitless love for Christ the Lord and for His Church. (n. 25, Italics supplied)

This encyclical is said by Kung to "distort the supreme truths of the Gospels" (K. 25). National episcopal synods have reaffirmed priestly celibacy and the third episcopal synod held in Rome, 1971, has confirmed it. Even the Committee headed by Belgian Cardinal Leo Suenens, who had been an advocate of optional celibacy, voted unanimously against it. More significantly, the Synod Fathers voted against the ordination of mature married men, with the strongest

opposition on the part of the bishops of the very areas where it
had been thought such married priests might serve.

15th. Vote: (n. 5)

Lex coelibatus sacerdotalis in Ecclesia latina vigens integre
servari debet. Placet 168. Non placet 10. Placet justa modum
21. Absentions 3.

Formula A:

Without prejudice to the right of the Supreme Pontiff, the
priestly ordination of married men is not admitted, not even in
particular cases . . . . Placet 107.

Formula B:

It pertains to the Supreme Pontiff alone, in particular cases,
to permit for reasons of pastoral necessity, and "bearing in
mind the good of the universal Church the priestly ordination
of married men, of mature age, and of approved moral character. . . .Placet 87.
(On this ballot there were 2 abstentions and 2 invalid votes.)

Is Karl Rahner, whom Kung extols on many occasions for widen-
ing the horizons of theological vision, a "reactionary" for defending
sacerdotal celibacy and exposing the pretentious fallacies of its
opponents? (cf. *The Furrow* [Maynooth College], May, 1968), cf.
too, Bernard Haering's defense of the Church's legislation on sacerdotal celibacy, *National Catholic Reporter*, July 6, 1966). The
idea that priests who have already taken the vow of celibacy should
be freed from the obligations of their vows and allowed to marry
was rejected so completely that even those bishops who had advocated
its consideration recognized the overwhelming disapproval of the
concept. One bishop said that to speak of this as optional celibacy
was a misnomer, suggesting what was asked was optional adherence
to solemn vows.

Was the Holy Spirit not at work at the Third Synod of Bishops
(1971), or were they wholly bereft of those charisms that Kung
repeatedly speaks of in the latter part of his book? Why does the
author treat with complete silence the explanations which the Second

Vatican Council gave with the greatest care on the values of "celibacy in view of the Kingdom of God" in four documents—no less—that very Council to which he had looked so hopefully for the renewal of the Catholic Church? (K. 11).

Lumen Gentium (Dogmatic Constitution on the Church):

... that precious gift of divine grace which the Father gives to some men (cf. Mt. 19:11; 1 Cor. 7:7) so that by virginity or celibacy, they can more easily devote their selves to God alone with undivided heart (cf. I Cor. 7:32-34). This total abstinence embraced on behalf of the kingdom of heaven has always been held in particular honor by the Church as being a sign of charity and stimulus towards it, as well as a unique fountain of spiritual fertility in the world. (cf. n. 42)

Perfectae Caritatis (Decree on the Appropriate Renewal of the Religious Life):

That chastity which is practiced "on behalf of the heavenly kingdom" (Mt. 19:12), and which religious profess, deserves to be esteemed as a surpassing gift of peace. For it liberates the human heart in a unique way (cf. 1 Cor. 7:32-35) and causes it to burn with greater love of God and all mankind .... As a result they will not be influenced by those erroneous claims which present complete continence as impossible or as harmful to human development. In addition a certain spiritual instinct should lead them to spurn everything likely to imperil chastity. (n. 12)

Optatam Totius (Decree on Priestly Formation):

By it (priestly celibacy) they (seminarians) renounce the companionship of marriage for the sake of the kingdom of heaven (cf. Mt. 19:12); they devote themselves to the Lord with an undivided love which is profoundly proper to the new covenant; they bear witness to the state which the resurrection will bring about in the world to come (cf. Lk. 20:36); and they gain extremely appropriate help for exercising that perfect and unremitting love by which they can become all things to all men through their priestly ministrations, etc. (n.10)

Presbyterorum Ordinis (Decree on the Ministry and Life of Priests):

For it (perfect and perpetual continence) simultaneously signifies and stimulates pastoral charity and is a special fountain of spiritual fruitfulness on earth . . . . Celibacy accords with the priesthood on many scores. For the whole priestly mission is dedicated to that new humanity which Christ, the conqueror of death, raises up in the world through His Spirit. This humanity takes its origin "not of blood, nor of the will of man, but of God." (Jn. 1:13) Through virginity or celibacy observed for the sake of the kingdom of heaven, priests are consecrated to Christ in a new and distinguished way. They more easily hold fast to Him with undivided heart. They more freely devote themselves to Him and through Him to the service of God and man. They more readily minister to His kingdom and to the work of heavenly regeneration etc.

. . . This legislation, to the extent that it concerns those who are destined for the priesthood, this most holy Synod again approves and confirms. (Italics supplied) (n. 16)

Was the Council of *aggiornamento* singularly at fault on sacerdotal celibacy?

Renewal of Vows (K. 26)

Despite the frequently expressed mind of the Ecumenical Council in *Lumen Gentium, Perfectae Caritatis, Optatam Totius* and *Presbyterorum Ordinis*, despite Pope John's unequivocal support of sacerdotal celibacy and Pope Paul's encyclical, *Sacerdotalis Caelibatus* (and reaffirmed unanimously by the Third Episcopal Synod at Rome, 1971), Kung can write most ungraciously of Pope Paul:

Also betraying an abysmal lack of confidence, he attempted to impose on all the clergy that repressive measure—the annual renewal of priestly *promises* in connection with the Maundy Thursday liturgy. (K. 26, Italics supplied)

Renewal of vows, not merely promises, has always been a traditional practice of seminarians and religious, and even after the final vows, their renewal is not uncommon on the occasion of a yearly retreat. To speak of the papal call for the renewal of priestly vows as an imposition, as "repressive," "betraying an abysmal lack of confidence," "lack of intelligence" is an inexcusable act of rashness.

Humanae Vitae (1968) (K. 25)

The kernel of Kung's argument is that the moral doctrine of *Humanae Vitae*, which Kung readily admits (35-36) was the constant and universal authoritative teaching of the Church—tantamount to an *infalliblis ex ordinario magisterio*—is wrong (according to Kung), and therefore belies the doctrine of infallibility of the Church. At this moment, suffice to observe that if such a universal, centuries old moral doctrine of the Church can be wrong and the faithful gravely deceived in a matter of eternal salvation, then *cui bono* Kung's theory of indefectibility? (K. 181-193)

Credo (1968) (K. 25)

Pope Paul VI's *Credo* recapitulates the Nicene-Constantinopolitan Creed and subsequent doctrinal definitions: God the Creator; Three Divine Persons, *coaeternae sibi et coequales*, unity in the Trinity and Trinity in the unity; the Incarnation and the economy of Redemption; the Resurrection and eternal life; the Blessed Virgin, Mother of God, Immaculate and her glorious Assumption; Original Sin, transmitted with human nature, "not by imitation, but by propagation," and that it is thus "proper to everyone"; regeneration through Baptism; the divine institution of the "one, holy, catholic and apostolic Church"; infallibility; the Mass and Transubstantiation; eternal life and the resurrection of the dead.

Kung (25) speaks of this *Credo* as a "typical Roman gesture of identification, without consulting the Church." On the contrary, the successor of Peter did, indeed, consult the solemn definitive teachings of the ecumenical councils, and the Roman Pontiffs of the preceding 2000 years.

Conclusion to the Belittling of Pope Paul's Encyclicals (K. 13)

It seems to this writer that anyone who calls into discredit Pope Paul's encyclical on the true identity of the Catholic Church as the Church which Christ instituted and its authentic mission to evangelize all the people of God into the unity of its fold, (*Ecclesiam Suam*), on the traditional and unwavering belief of the Church in the Eucharist, (*Mysterium Fidei*), on the undivided and total dedication of the priest symbolized by sacerdotal celibacy in the likeness of His Divine Lord (*Sacerdotalis Coelibatus*), on the reaffirmation of the centuries-old constant and universal teaching of the Church on the morality of marital communion (*Humanae Vitae*), on Pope Paul's *Credo*, which is in substance a repetition of the Nicean Constantinopolitan Creed— goes a very long way toward raising questions about Kung's own articles of faith.

On October 11, 1962, the first day of the Council, Pope John said that his intention of convoking the Council was "to assert once again the magisterium (teaching authority), which is unfailing . . . ." (Abbott, pp. 710-719) To what purpose?

> The greatest concern of the Ecumenical Council is this: that the sacred deposit of Christian doctrine should be guarded and taught more efficaciously. (cf. Abbot, p. 713)

To "guard" is to keep and defend, and the principal purpose is precedent to and a necessary prerequisite to the teaching of the articles of the faith more efficaciously.

This the late Pontiff repeated at greater length.

> (But) from the renewed, serene, and tranquil *adherence to all the teaching of the Church in its entirety and preciseness, as it still shines forth in the Acts of the Council of Trent and First Vatican Council*, the Christian, Catholic, and apostolic spirit of the whole world expects a step forward toward a doctrinal penetration and a formation of consciousness *in faithful and perfect conformity to the authentic doctrine*, which however, should be studied and expounded through the methods of research and through the literary forms of modern thought. The substance of the ancient doctrine of the deposit of faith is one thing, and the way in which it is presented is another. (italics supplied)

Kung's frequently expressed enthusiastic veneration for the late Pontiff seems to stop short of Pope John's unmistakable intention and meaning.

Mixed Marriage (K. 15)

Kung speaks of Pope Paul's *Motu Proprio* of March 31, 1970, the

Apostolic Letter Determining Norms for Mixed Marriages, as displaying "fundamentally unecumenical attitude of the Roman central administration." (K. 25-26)

Now surely an ecumenical perspective of mixed marriages does not mean mixed churches nor mixed credal faiths nor mixed morality of marriages. The Council Fathers did not intend that the Decree of Ecumenism (*Unitatis Redintegratio*) was to work at cross purposes with the Dogmatic Constitution on the Church (*Lumen Gentium*), both of which were not without marked significance, promulgated on the same day, November 21, 1964. The Council Fathers taught nothing that would in any way mute Pope John's exhortation for the renewal of the Catholic Faith in the personal lives of the faithful; the married, no less, than the unmarried, nor in any way give encouragement to that false conciliatory approach (*irenismus*) which, on the contrary, the Council Fathers explicitly condemned on several occasions.

The Apostolic Letter set down the minimum but indispensable requirements in a matter of divine law, the safeguarding of the faith of the Catholic and the promise to do all that is reasonably possible to ensure that children are baptized and educated in the Catholic Faith. This promise is no longer required of the non-Catholic, and the canonical form may be dispensed with by permission of the local ordinary for exceptional reasons. What more ecumenical norms can be forged for mixed marriages which do not play false to the Catholic Faith? The generality of Protestants have acknowledged the ecumenical spirit of charity of the pontifical document. The American Lutheran Church Council, to speak of one, approved the Apostolic Letter, and its implementation by the National Conference of Catholic Bishops (January 1, 1971), was equally received with manifest gratification. Dr. Carson Blake, then Secretary General of the World Council of Churches, perceptively observed that the perfect solution will be achieved only when Christian unity is recovered.

In his haste (or in deliberation), Kung never explains to the faithful the teaching and "mind" of the Church on mixed marriages, neither in *Inquiry* (Gr. 1970; Eng. 1971) nor, for that matter, in subsequent publications.

Firstly, realistically, what are the facts about mixed marriages, and secondly, the Church teaching on the grave obligation to safeguard the Catholic faith of the Catholic party and of the progeny.

Statistically, seventy percent of mixed marriages now end in divorce or separation. (C. Adams, Marriage Counsellor, Pennsylvania)

Sixty percent of Catholics in mixed marriages turn away from their religion in some significant way. (U.S. Bishops Committee on Mixed Marriages)

At least forty percent of children born to such unions are not reared as Catholics. Forty percent of Catholics who marry non-Catholics do not marry before a priest. (Rev. J. L. Thomas, S. J.)

Between two and three times as many marriages result in divorce and separation in Catholic-Protestant unions than when the couple is of the same faith. (Landis Study of 28,184 cases)

Is it then surprising that the U.S. Bishops should declare in *Basic Teachings For Catholic Religious Education* (n. 13):

> It should be made clear that the Church discourages the contracting of mixed marriages in order to encourage a full union of mind and life in matrimony.

From *Instruction On Mixed Marriages* issued by the Congregation for the Doctrine of Faith on March 18, 1966, a little more than three months after the solemn closing of the Second Vatican Council on December 8, 1965, we excerpt the following:

> That the sacrament of Matrimony, established by Christ as a sign of His union with the Church, may fully exert its sacred power and really be for the spouses a great Mystery (Eph. 5:32) by which in the intimate union of their life they symbolize the love by which Christ gave Himself for men, there is the greatest demand for full and perfect harmony of the spouses, especially in matters pertaining to religion.

> The Catholic Church considers it her most serious duty to safeguard and protect the welfare of the faith both in the spouses and the children. Consequently, the Church strives with the greatest care and vigilance that Catholics contract marriage with Catholics.

> Let all the shepherds teach the faithful the religious importance and value of this sacrament (of Matrimony). Let them gravely warn the faithful of the difficulties and dangers which are inherent in contracting a marriage with a Christian non-Catholic, and much more with a non-Christian (unbaptized). By all suitable means let them bring it about that young people contract marriage with a Catholic party.

The *Instruction*, however, points out that today communications, acquaintances and contacts of Catholics with non-Catholics are more frequent, and so the bonds of friendships are more easily established between them which, as is evident from experience, are wont to bring on more frequent occasions of mixed marriages:

> Accordingly, the pastoral solicitude of the Church today even more demands that in mixed marriages the sanctity of Matrimony in keeping with Catholic teaching and the faith of the Catholic spouse be completely safeguarded and that the Catholic education of the children be cared for with the greatest possible diligence and effectiveness.

> This pastoral care is, therefore, more necessary because, as is known, there are found among non-Catholics diverse opinions both concerning the essence of marriage and its qualities, especially in regard to indissolubility, and consequently about divorce and contracting marriage after divorce. The Church, therefore, considers it her duty to protect the faithful that they may not endanger the faith and suffer harm either spiritual or material. Therefore, those who intend to contract marriage are to be instructed accurately about the nature, qualities and obligations of matrimony and the dangers that must be avoided.

> The grave obligation of the Catholic spouse to guard, preserve and to profess his (her) own faith and to baptize and to educate in that faith the offspring that may be born must be made known to the non-Catholic party.

> Let Catholic spouses, however, take care to strengthen and increase in themselves the gift of faith, and, ever following the paths of Christian virtues in their family, let them also continually give the non-Catholic party and their children a shining example.

If we recall that the Dogmatic Constitution on the Church (*Lumen Gentium*) and the Decree on Ecumenism (*Unitatis Redintegratio*) were both promulgated by the Fathers of the Second Vatican Council on the same day, November 21, 1964, there was never any intention to compromise the inviolabilities of the Catholic Faith for salvation under the guise of a misleading irenicism against which the Decree on

Ecumenism explicitly warned—"a false conciliatory approach, *iren-ismus*, which harms the purity of Catholic doctrine and obscures its assured genuine meaning." (n. 11)   It is in that same Decree on Ecumenism that the Fathers of the Second Vatican Council declared without hesitance or equivocation:

> For it is through Christ's Catholic Church alone which is the all-embracing means of salvation, that the fulness of the means of salvation can be obtained. It was to the apostolic college alone, of which Peter is the head, that we believe our Lord entrusted all the blessings of the New Covenant, in order to establish on earth the one Body of Christ into which all those should be fully incorporated who already belong in any way to God's People.
>
> ... the Catholic Church has been endowed with all divinely revealed truth and with all means of grace . . . . (n. 4)

From Pope Paul VI's Apostolic Letter on Mixed Marriages (March 31, 1970) in which Kung sees "the fundamentally unecu-menical attitude of the Roman central administration" (K. 25, 26) we excerpt the following:

> There are many difficulties inherent in a mixed marriage, since a certain division is introduced into the living cells of the Church, as the Christian family is rightly called, and in the family itself the fulfillment of the gospel teachings is more difficult because of diversities in matters of religion, especially with regard to these matters, which concern Christian worship and the education of the children.
>
> For these reasons the Church, conscious of her duty, dis-courages the contracting of mixed marriages, for she is most desirous that Catholics be able in matrimony to attain to perfect union of mind and full communion of life.
>
> The Church vigilantly concerns herself with the education of the young and their fitness to understand their duties with a sense of responsibility and to perform their obligation as mem-bers of the Church, and she shows this both in preparing for marriage those who intend to contract a mixed marriage and in caring for those who have already contracted such a marriage.

Nevertheless, one cannot ignore the difficulties inherent even in mixed marriages between baptized persons. There is often a difference of opinion on the sacramental nature of matrimony, on the special significance of marriage celebrated within the Church, on the interpretation of certain moral principles pertaining to marriage and the family, on the extent to which obedience is due to the Catholic Church, and on the competence that belongs to ecclesiastical authority. From this it is clear that difficult questions of this kind can only be fully resolved when Christian unity is restored.

The faithful must, therefore, be taught that, although the church somewhat relaxes ecclesiastical discipline in particular cases, she can never remove the obligation of the Catholic party, which Divine Law, namely, the plan of salvation instituted by Christ, is imposed according to the various situations.

The faithful should, therefore, be reminded that the Catholic party has the duty of preserving his or her own faith; nor is it ever permitted to expose oneself to a proximate danger of losing it.

Furthermore, the Catholic partner in a mixed marriage is obliged, not only to remain steadfast in the faith, but also, as far as possible, to see to it that the children be baptized and brought up in that same faith, and receive all the aids to eternal salvation which the Catholic Church provides for her sons and daughters.

To obtain a dispensation from the bishop from an impediment (of mixed religion) the Catholic party shall declare that he (she) is ready to remove dangers of falling away from the faith. He (she) is also gravely bound to make a sincere promise to do all in his power to have all the children baptized and brought up in the Catholic Church.

At an opportune time the non-Catholic party must be informed of these promises which the Catholic party has to make, so that it is clear that he (she) is cognizant of the promise and obligation on the part of the Catholic.

Both parties are to be clearly instructed on the ends and essential properties of marriage, not to be excluded by either party.

Even after the truly ecumenical concessions of Pope Paul's Apostolic Letter which removed the former exaction of promises from the non-Catholic party and provided modifications in the *pro forma matrimonii* with the consent of the ordinary, there is nonetheless a continuity of doctrinal substratum with antecedent papal teaching. One need only consult Pope Pius XI's celebrated Encyclical on Marriage promulgated December 31, 1930 from which we choose these passages:

> The religious character of marriage, its sublime signification of grace and the union between Christ and the Church, evidently require that those about to marry should show a holy reverence toward it, and zealously endeavor to make their marriage approach as nearly as possible to the archetype of Christ and the Church.

> They therefore, who rashly and needlessly contract mixed marriages from which the maternal love and providence of the Church dissuades her children for very sound reasons, fail conspicuously in this respect, sometimes with danger to their eternal salvation. This attitude of the Church to mixed marriages appears in many of her documents, all of which are summed up in Canon 1060 of the Code of Canon Law: "Everywhere and with the greatest strictness the Church forbids marriages between baptized persons, one of whom is a Catholic and the other a member of a schismatical or heretical sect; and if there is, added to this, the danger of falling away of the Catholic party and the perversion of the children, such a marriage is forbidden also by the divine law."

So wrote the Roman Pontiff who was the first to speak of "separated brethren." We continue:

> If the Church occasionally, on account of circumstances, does not refuse to grant a dispensation from these strict laws (if the divine law remains intact and the dangers above mentioned are provided against by suitable safeguards), it is unlikely that the Catholic party will not suffer some detriment from such a marriage.

> Whence it comes about not infrequently, as experience shows, that deplorable defections from religion occur among the off-

spring, or at least a headlong descent into that religious indifference which is closely allied to impiety. There is this also to be considered that in those mixed marriages, it becomes much more difficult to imitate by a lively conformity of spirit the mystery of faith of which we have spoken, namely, that close union between Christ and His Church.

Assuredly, also, there will be wanting that close union of spirit which, as it is a sign and mark of the Church of Christ, so also should it be the sign of Christian wedlock, its glory and adornment. For where there exists diversity of mind, truth and feeling, the bond of union of mind and heart is wont to be broken, or at least weakened. From this comes the danger lest the love of man and wife grow cold and the peace and happiness of family life, resting as it does on the union of hearts, be destroyed.

A close review of the rationale underlying the doctrinal affirmations of Pope Pius XI and those given on mixed marriages after the Second Vatican Council discloses a continuity of a sense of realism of the hazards of mixed marriages and an unambiguous reaffirmation of the doctrinal integrity of marriage and the grave obligations to safeguard the Catholic faith of the Catholic party and of the offspring in mixed marriages.

Kung's own brand of ecumenism (as it bears on mixed marriages) is vastly at variance both with the Dogmatic Constitution on the Church (*Lumen Gentium*) and with the Decree on Ecumenism (*Unitatis Redintegratio*) which the Fathers of the Second Vatican Council promulgated. This is another instance where Kung's referral to the spirit of Vatican II is tragically at odds with what the Fathers of that Ecumenical Council actually taught. The Council Fathers placed the Decree on Ecumenism *within* the context of the Dogmatic Constitution on the Church, and not, as this writer surmises Kung does—outside of or in challenging parallel to the text and context of *Lumen Gentium*.

In 1972 Monsignor Jozef Tomko, an aide to Franjo Cardinal Seper, prefect of the Sacred Congregation for the Doctrine of the Faith, published his 223-page book, *Matrimoni Misti* (Ital.). It is the first systematic study of the vexed problem of mixed marriage. It examines the problem under its historical, scriptural, sociological, pastoral, ecumenical and theological aspects. His book traces the problem of mixed marriage from its earliest treatment in the Old Testament, into the New Testament and among the Fathers of the Church, through the Middle Ages and the Protestant Reformation down to the present ecumenical age.

Monsignor Tomko draws on his experience as secretary for the mixed-marriage debate at the 1967 Synod of Bishops and as secretary of the commission that prepared Pope Paul's 1970 *Motu Proprio Matrimonia Mixta*. The author reviews the public debate that helped forge the Vatican's present regulations on mixed marriages, and recalls the bitter controversy occasioned by publication of the regulations. Central to the book is a defense of the canonical form, the law (which at present allows dispensation by the bishop) that invalidates any marriage involving a Catholic that is not witnessed by a Catholic priest. In defending the canonical norm, the author acknowledges that the Church's decision in the sixteenth century to require a priest's presence for validity was based on a reason that hardly exists today: to combat secret marriages and the bigamy that often resulted from them. Marriage laws in most countries today make secret marriage a rarity, but he insists that other reasons justify the Church's decision to keep that requirement in force, although the Church has at the same time made dispensation from it easier. He retells the pro and con debate on the question of canonical form at the 1967 Synod of Bishops. His own arguments for its retention come under four headings: to safeguard the sacred and sacramental character of marriage, to guarantee the indissolubility of marriage, to offer greater certainty of the validity of marriage, and to give the Church a broader opportunity to help prepare for marriage and help sustain them.

In a chapter on the right of freedom of conscience, the author maintains that there can be no solution to the dilemma of conscience created by the choice of a religion for the children of mixed marriages. He blamed this widespread drama of conscience not on the Catholic Church's insistence that children be raised as Catholics, but rather on "the reality of divisions and contrasting convictions among religious and among Christian confessions themselves."

The religious education of the offspring is the obligation of both spouses, while at the same time it is in practice impossible that such an education follow the dictates of the well-formed consciences of both.

Primacy of Jurisdiction and Primacy of Service

> Kung writes: "His (the Pope's) primacy is not a primacy of ruling but a primacy of service." (p. 27)

As the statement stands, it applies to all Popes, including the first, Peter. This issue must ultimately find its resolution in revelational data, in the teaching of Christ Jesus as it was repeated in the *kerygma* and preserved in *paradosis*, the earliest oral traditions, which were then incorporated under apostolic supervision into the gospels, and in the self-awareness of the Church of its own true identity as His Church, its mission and empowerments. His Church cannot be deceived nor be capable of deceiving the faithful in so fundamental a claim as primatial authority.

We now state some prefatory reflections. The Catholic Church is by divine ordination a *teaching* Church. "Everything" that He commanded to be taught was, as He promised, to be understood more clearly and more fully by the operation of the Holy Spirit in the course of time. The God of revelation is not a rationalist God, nor is His teaching Church a rationalist Church. From the beginning the Church was in possession of the *depositum fidei* as its apostolic patrimony, but not in the fulness of human articulation and formal particularity. All articles of faith: the Incarnation, the Trinitarian mystery, Original Sin, Redemption, Grace, Sacraments, etc., were formally defined in the course of time. Hence, a relative or comparative tardiness of formal definition imports no doctrinal defectibility. To teach His salvific word to all men, to administer the sacraments, regulate the liturgy, requires governmental discipline with the right to demand obedience. The primacy of service to teach His message of salvation and to administer His means of sanctification—requires by a principled necessity primatial authority in order to realize unity of fellowship in the unity of faith. Let us note as a caution that, historically, the manner and extent of the exercise of primatial authority, while identical with its original endowment, hardly constitutes a continuum with its actualities in medieval, Renaissance and modern papacy. Primitive Christianity, unique and normative for the Church and her teaching to the end of time, as recipient of the definitive salvific event of Christian revelation is in view of Christ's promise for a deeper and greater understanding of His word by the assistance of the Holy Spirit, and in the development of institutional forms in accordance with its original endowment of empowerments historically just that—primitive.

If we were to gather together all the Scriptural evidences of Simon Peter's prominence and preeminence, the special marks of predilection shown him by Jesus, his role as spokesman of the Twelve—of no other Apostle is so nearly a character biography given by the evangelists—and after Pentecost (*Acts* cc. 1-15), Peter's authoritative leadership in the primitive Church in Jerusalem and his missionary preaching (*Acts* 2:14-39; 3:12-26; 4:8-12; 5:29-32; 10:34-43), all this would not by itself constitute nor provide the grounds for inferring a grant of primacy of jurisdiction, *iure divino*. For this we must find an actual historical transaction of such a commission in the Scriptural *loci classici*, the Petrine texts.

> Mt. 16:17-19, "But you," He said, "who do you say I am?" Then Simon Peter spoke up, "You are the Christ," he said, "the Son of the living God." Jesus replied, "Simon, son of Jonah, blessed are you! Because it was not flesh and blood that revealed this to you, but my Father in heaven. So, I now say to you: "You are Peter, (Kepha) and on this rock (kepha) I will build my Church. And the gates of the realm of death can never hold out against it. I will give you the keys of the kingdom of heaven: whatever you bind on earth, shall be considered bound in heaven: and whatever you loose on earth, shall be loosed in heaven."

The genuineness of this Matthean pericope is universally upheld by Catholic biblicists as textual critics apart from as well as consequent to its canonicity. Among Protestants, thanks to the learned argumentation of Oscar Cullman, the eminent Swiss Lutheran theologian, and the critical studies of others before him, many have come to acknowledge that Jesus did speak these words against those who claim they are spurious. Those who say that the Matthean verses 18 and 19 are a second century retrojection of a Romanizing process will have to contend with its Palestinian antiquity, its Semitic linguistic characteristics—*bar-yona*, "flesh-blood," "bind-loose," the ancient gravity of *rock* as a divine title and its prophetic antecedents in the Old Testament *usage*, the *qahal* of God (Gr. ΣKKESIA), "gates of Sheol," "Keys" of the steward and the Aramaic Greek strophic rhythm of three lines each that are not alien to the Matthean literary construction. (cf. Mt. 11:7-9; 25-30)

As on the occasion of the "living bread" discourse (Jn. 6:67-69), Simon Peter speaks for the Twelve and identifies Jesus to be the Messiah, the coming deliverer, "He who is to come" (Mt. 11:3), even though all of the Apostles do not yet understand clearly the true nature and mission of the messianic kingship (cf. Mt. 16:22-23; 20:20-24; Mk. 10:42-44; Lk. 22:24). *"Therefore, I say to you"*; that is, because of Simon's confession, "You are Kepha and on this Kepha I will build my Church." From the first days of His public ministry, Jesus chose the Twelve as a group apart, the Isaianic "remnant" (Isa. 4:3), which accepted the proclamation of the "kingdom," and He now provides for its continuance in the Church (*ekklesia, qahal*), of the new covenant (Lk. 22:20; 1 Cor. 11:25) an organized religious community whose leader He now appoints. The Matthean —*qahal-ekklesia* should be studied with the Danielic (7:13) "Son of Man," in mind, a title which Jesus applies to himself when He speaks of His lowliness (8:20), His humanity (11:19), His humility (20:28), generally in His references to the humiliation of His forthcoming betrayal, passion, death, resurrection and exaltation. In *Daniel* (c. 7), there is the mysteriously more than human reality conceived both as an individual (v. 13) and in its collective sense an extension of the individual sense (vv. 18, 22), where the "son of man," and "the saints of the Most High" are apparently identified, the "Son of Man" being leader, representative and exemplar of "the saints of the Most High." Just as in *Daniel*, the triumph of the "Son of Man," who includes in some fashion in his person the Saints of the Most High, follows upon the destruction of the pagan empires, so in *Matthew* a new, the messianic, community is set up from the "remnant" foretold by the prophets and receives the promise of victory over the realm of death and the rule of malign powers. The word *ekklesia* appears only twice in the four gospels, and both in *Matthew* (16:17; 18:18). But the promise to build His Church is not exclusively contained in these Matthean verses but is clearly discernible in the teaching of Jesus: in His ecclesial parables and metaphors, particularly, the Shepherd and His flock, (Jn. 10); in His private instructions to the Twelve and the worldwide commissions laid upon them to the end of time. A Messiah without a messianic community would have been unthinkable to any Jew. In the Pauline epistles, all of which, let us reflect, appeared before the first extant written gospel, *ekklesia* (Hb. *qahal, edah*), appears sixty-five times to designate every usage, the local church, the severalty of local churches, the universal Church (cf. to 3 Jn. 6, 9, 10, and in Apc. 20 times; also Jn. 5:14).

Jesus confers upon Simon His place in that messianic community by changing his name and using the only Aramaic word that would serve His purpose, *kepha*, as apparently He had promised earlier to do (Mk. 3:16; Lk. 6:14; Jn. 1:42), but only here is the explanation given for the change. In biblical usage a name did not merely indicate; rather, it made a thing what it is (Jn. 3:20; Mt. 1:21; Lk. 1: 13, 31), and a change of name meant a change of destiny (Jn. 17:5). What is unique about Simon's change of name is that there is no evidence that *kepha* (aram) or *Petros* was ever used as a person's name before Jesus conferred it to symbolize Peter's place and role in the Church as its rock-foundation. The words of Jesus are spoken in response to Simon's faith; but it is the person of the one confessing who is addressed—"*You are Kepha and upon this Kepha I will build my Church.* Any attempt to deny the identity of the one and same predicate—*Kepha*—twice repeated of the one and same predication, the person, Simon Peter, must be construed as a prepossession of confessional interpretation.

Petros, the masculinized Greek of *Petra*, appears quite commonly alone in the Gospels and *Acts*, more than 150 times. Conjoined with Simon the double name occurs about twenty times, mostly in John. In the Pauline epistles, all of which appeared before the first canonical gospel, Peter is regularly referred to as *Kephas*, the Grecized form of the Aramaic, *Kepha* (1 Cor. 1:12; 3:22; 9:5; Gal. 1: 18; 2:9, 11, 14), and twice *Petros* (Gal. 2:7, 8). And John, nearly the last of the New Testament writers, introduces Simon (1:42) as the one whose name will be changed to *Kephas*, explaining "meaning rock." These repetitive usages of *Petros* and *Kephas* stressed upon the Greek-speaking Christians the unique role and function of Peter in the primitive Church.

In the Old Testament *Rock* appears as a divine title to connote invincibility against any assault and as the surest haven of security and salvation.

> Be my Rock of refuge,
> A stronghold to give me safety,
> For you are my rock and my fortress,
> O my God, rescue me from the hands of the wicked.
>
> (Ps. 71:3-4)

God, the *Rock*, appears frequently in *Deuteronomy, Samuel* 1 and 2, *Psalms*, occasionally in first and second *Isaias*, once in *Habakkuk*.

Abraham was the rock from which Israel was hewn (Isa. 51:1). The "stone of witness" which Yahweh will lay in Zion; "a precious cornerstone"; a foundation stone" (Isa. 28:16); the "stone that grew into a great mountain, filling the whole earth" (Dn. 2:34, 35, 44, 45), where the stone stands for the new kingdom, as Daniel interpreted Nebuchadnezzar's dream; "the stone rejected by the builders that proved to be the keystone" (Ps. 118:22), (this stone Jesus identifies with Himself [Mt. 21:42]): this same symbolic rock-foundation of the messianic community which the Messiah will institute by a new testament Jesus now applies to Simon Peter alone, in the presence of the other Apostles and thus implies that Peter is more than a mere foundation as the other "apostles and prophets" are (Eph. 2:20). Christ is the "main cornerstone" (Mt. 21:42; 1 Cor. 3:11; Eph. 2:20), but this foundation appears visibly in Peter.

And the Gates of Hades Shall Not Prevail Against It

The gates of ancient cities were their stronghold both as impregnable defenses and as a vantage point for counterattack and assault. The "gates" are symbolic of the power of the realm of death (*Hb.* Sheol, *Gr.* Hades: cf. Jb 17:16; 38:17), *passim*; "gates of death" (Ps. 9:13; 107:18; Isa. 38:10, *passim*)—an underground abode of the dead, the just and the unjust—the complete negation of life, thought, love, of all spiritual activity except the mere consciousness of nothingness, a neuter terminal existence for all from which there is no possible deliverance except by Yahweh. This hopefulness appears in *Psalms* 30:3; 49:15; 86:13, *passim;* (cf. also 1 Sam. 2:6; Jn. 2:3f). Against this enigmatic Old Testament conception of death must be projected these words of Jesus:

> I am the Resurrection and the life,
> If anyone believes in me, even though he dies,
> He will live, and whoever lives and believes in me,
> Will never die.   (Jn. 11:25)

The Petrine commission and the promise of invincibility is given by Him who *is* life, the Giver of life by whose conquest over death and His own resurrection life is renewed on earth and recovered in the realm beyond, the just and the unjust according to judgment. The Risen Savior has the "keys of death and hades," the power to release souls (Apoc. 1:18). He "lord of the living and dead"

(Rm. 14:10), has deprived death of its power of paralyzing captivity by proclaiming life and immortality (2 Tm. 1:10) by descending into hell (Acts 2:27, 31; 1 Pt. 3:10; cf. Apostles Creed). In its extreme brevity, this Matthean pericope is a compendium of Christian revelation—that men may have eternal life through the Church, on earth and beyond, that the powers of evil cannot foreclose redemption and the works of salvation. The "triumphalism" of the Church, to this purpose derives from the Risen Christ, conqueror of death and Lord of life, who is the "main cornerstone" of His Church of which Peter is the visible presence. *Ubi Petrus ibi Christus.* In these Matthean verses the historical Jesus identifies himself as the author of the Church. There is no other historical explanation for its origin for what is human life but a divine invitation to eternal life (Jn. 3: 15). To the fulfillment of this salvific end the Risen Christ instituted His Church for pilgrim mankind (Jn. 21:15-17) as He had promised (Mt. 16:18, 19)—the Church of the Resurrection that cannot err about His way, His Truth, His Life, for so He mandated His Apostles and what with His abiding presence to the end of time, (Mt. 28:20 and parallel places) and the divine assistance of the "Spirit of Truth" (Jn. 14:16, 26; 15:26; 16:12, 13).

I Will Give You the Keys of the Kingdom of Heaven

In keeping with the figure of speech "build," "gates," which symbolize the two citadels of life and death, Jesus confers (promises to do so in the future) on *one* man, Peter, the "keys," the symbol in antiquity of supreme authority of the steward in place of the master over his royal household or of a ruler over his kingdom (cf. Roland de Vaux, *Ancient Israel*, tr. by John McHugh, New York, 1961, 129 ff). Yotham as regent was "master of the palace and ruled the country" (2K. 15:5); "master of the palace" is the title on the official seal of Godolias, the man whom Nebuchadnezzar installed as governor of Judah after the capture of Jerusalem (2K 25:22); the "steward, Shebna, the master of the palace" under Ezechias (Isa. 22:1-5); Elyaqim receives the keys of the royal palace and is thereby invested with the same authority as Hickial (Isa. 22:21, 22):

> I lay the key of the house of David
>   upon his shoulder;
> If he opens, none will shut;
> If he shuts, none will open.

The kingdom of heaven must be understood according to its customary Matthean usage: namely, that kingdom which is announced and instituted by Jesus by His own presence, preaching and the remnant He has gathered around Him for special and private instructions and mandates—the Church looking to an eschatological term, the *ekklesia* with its Greek connotation of the free born, a notion to which Paul was to give a profound theological signification. Accordingly, Peter's authority to govern is only over the pilgrimage Church; that is to say, he is appointed steward of that means to salvation which is His Church. How this rule will be exercised is expressed in rabbinical terminology to "bind and loose." A comparison is here intended with the disciplinary and doctrinal authority of rabbis who in Jesus' time interpreted the Old Testament for the faith and conduct of the people. A specific determination of "bind and loose" is the power to forgive sins which Jesus granted in a postresurrectional scene (Jn. 20:22, 23). The power of the "keys," the supreme and all inclusive power conferred upon Peter, must not be confused with the power of "binding and loosing." This latter power Jesus also grants to other apostles and disciples, but in regard to this wider circle, Jesus makes no mention of the power of the "keys" neither before (Mt. 18:18) nor after His resurrection. (Jn. 20:22, 23) The power of the "keys" is given exclusively to Peter, and with it the full power of binding and loosing. The grant of authority to others (Mt. 18:18; Jn. 20:22, 23), in no way diminishes nor impinges upon Peter's primatial authority to which all other authorities are subject. Herein lies the distinction by divine design between the authority of the supreme pastor, Peter and his successors, and the supreme pastoral authority which the apostolic college and its successor, the episcopal college, united with its Head, *kepha*, the bearer of the "keys" and the supreme shepherd, possess and exercise in unison. The metaphors "rock" and "keys" embody an exactitude of meaning whose boundaries the operations of the Holy Spirit and the presence of Christ in His Mystical Body (Jn. cc 14-17) will declare in and through the experiential history of the Church. The decisions of the key-bearer will be ratified with a permanent character "on earth, in heaven."

Whether or not Matthew has given us the actual history and geography does not call into question that Jesus *did* speak these *logia*. Yet its suitability at Caesarea Philippi remains in possession as long as the alternatives, the Last Supper or a post-resurrectional scene, hardly rise above conjectures, hypotheses and assumptions, and labor under difficulties of their own. (For a critique of Cullmann's Upper Room thesis, of Robert H. Gundry, *The Narrative Framework of Matthew* xvi:17-19, NovT., 1964-65, pp. 1-9.) Further, Simon Peter is prominently featured (Mt. 24:28, 29; 15:15) prior to this pericope and immediately following (17:24-27). And the ecclesial discourse (c. 18) appropriately follows upon the Petrine commission. The text is genuine-*e'vero* ("there is no scientific justification for this denial," Cullmann, *Peter*, etc., tr. Floyd Filson, London, 198), and its chronology and topography in *Matthew* is, at the least, *ben trovato*. The doctrinal and historical significance of the Matthean text is that it was written after Peter had long since left the Jerusalem community and been martyred in Rome. So evident (if not so manifest) and enduring even in his absence was Peter's primacy in Palestinian Christianity that the Matthean text was contested by no contemporaries.

Luke 22:31-34

At the Last Supper, shortly after instituting the new covenant, Jesus addresses Himself directly to Peter in the presence of the other Apostles, and warning him that Satan had obtained leave to try the faith of all the Twelve (as he had in the case of Job 1:12; 2:6)—"you all"—the Greek word for "you" here is plural; in verse 32, it is singular—"to sift as wheat" (Satan had already proceeded against Jesus through Judas, Lk. 22:3-6), Jesus promises to pray for Peter, choosing to strengthen the faith of the others through the mediation of the one whom He had called *kepha*. The Lucan pericope contains a commission which confers leadership, the commission to Peter to strengthen his fellow disciples. In a context which speaks of faith, the strengthening is best understood of faith, and the passage suggests the rock metaphor in the name of Peter (Mt. 16:18; cf. Lk. 6:48). In the same breath, as it were, of the prediction of Peter's thrice repeated denial of Jesus later that same evening we are divinely reassured that whatever the human frailties of Peter (and of his successors), the Petrine office here, as in *Matthew* 16:16-19 and *John* 21:15-17, is to be "the permanent and visible source and foundation of unity of faith and fellowship" (Vatican Council I, *Pastor Aeternus*, Dz. 1821 (3050); Vatican Council II, *Lumen Gentium*, III, 18).

(This Lucan text was cited by Vatican I [Dz. 3070] as a scriptural basis for papal infallibility.)

John 21:15-17

The Fourth Evangelist begins and ends his gospel with a truly significant focus on Peter. In 1:42 Jesus accosts Simon; "You are Simon, son of John; you are to be called 'Cephas'—meaning Rock." According to form history this must have been a calculated prolepsis. The gospel concludes with Peter as supreme pastor. From fisherman to "rock," "bearer of the keys," "steward of the kingdom of heaven," "strengthener" (teacher) of his brethren, to "universal shepherd of His flock."

The imagery of the Shepherd is one of kindly and protective providence. He leads his sheep to pasture and to water, leads them to shelter in inclement weather and defends them against beasts of prey and thieves in the night at the risk of his own life. The sheep recognize their shepherd's voice and follow him wheresoever he leads them. The shepherd keeps his flock together and seeks out the strayed sheep (Jn. c. 10; cf. Gn. 31:38-41; 1 Sm. 17:34-37). In the Old Testament the people of God are represented as the flock of Yahweh, and Yahweh Himself and His representatives (Moses, David, etc.) as shepherds, and evil rulers of Israel are denounced as unworthy (the hirelings of the Johannine Scriptures). Jeremias excoriates the shepherds, i.e., the rulers of the people; indeed, all who have authority for faulting their flock, their people (2:8; 10:21; 23:1-2; 50:6), and prophesies dire punishments for them in particular. Ezechiel is no less forceful in his denunciations of the shepherds, of men of authoritative responsibilities for failing their flock (34:2-10). Isaias scores them for their senselessness and aggrandizement of their self-interest (56:11ff). But Jeremias prophesies that in the messianic restoration Yahweh will give his people shepherds after his own heart (3:15; 23:4), and Ezechiel foretells that the people of Israel will be reunited under one shepherd (34:23; 37:22, 24 cf Jn. 10:16). From "(Bethlehem) Ephrathah . . . will be born the one . . . who will feed his flock with the power of Yahweh" (Mi. 5:3; cf. Mt. 2:6). In the *Old Testament* Yahweh as shepherd is a recurrent messianic theme and finds its classic expression in Ps. 23:1-4 (see, too, Ezk. 34:11-22). In the *New Testament* Luke's narrative (2:8-20) of the angelic announcement of the birth of the Savior to the shepherds and the shepherds' visit to the cave sheepfold in Bethlehem, city of David, to pay homage to the descendant of David, the shepherd-king, contrasts with silent emphasis with the conduct of the religious and royal rulers (also denoted shepherds in the *Old Testament*). Jesus calls himself the *good* shepherd (mindful of the faithless and devoted shepherds that Ezechiel and Jeremias distinguished) who lays down his life for his sheep "so that they may have eternal life and have it to the full" (Jn. 10). On the way to Gethesemani Jesus foretells in the words of *Zacharias* (13:7) the dispersion of the apostles with their shepherd is struck (Mt. 26:31ff; Mk. 14:27ff). During his last years in Rome Peter wrote of His Lord as the "chief shepherd" (1 Pt. 5:4). The epilogue of *Hebrews* (13:20) concludes with the greeting about the "great Shepherd" of the sheep whose blood sealed an eternal covenant, a greeting formulated by a conflation in the patterns of thought and language of the *Old Testament* texts (cf. Isa. 63:11; Zc. 9:11; Ezk. 37:26). In Jn. 21:15-17 Peter is not simply given the office of shepherd—officers in the primitive Church were considered shepherds, (Acts 20:28; Eph. 4:11)—Peter is appointed in Jesus' place, supreme and universal shepherd over all His flock including the other apostles, an office which is not shared by any of the other Apostles. Only by understanding Our Lord's role as Shepherd as He describes it and by acknowledging that Peter has been appointed to take His place on earth in His visible absence—and to consider (in a mixture of metaphors) the pastor's office and authority in terms of the commission of the "keys" by a ruler of a kingdom or by the master of a royal household to his vizier—can we see that Jesus confers upon Peter supreme, plenary and universal authority over His Church.

"The Lord is my Shepherd." Peter is now shepherd in His place over His flock. Jesus is both shepherd and "gate," the giver of life and the way into life (cf. Jn. 14:6). Peter, as rock foundation of His Church and key bearer, is now also "the gate" to His sheepfold in the sense that he dispenses the sacramental means of/for eternal life.

The First Vatican Council cited Jn. 21:15ff. in defining that the Risen Savior had conferred on Peter the jurisdiction of the supreme shepherd and the ruler of the whole flock.

Simon, the fisherman (cf. Jn. 21:11 which symbolizes the apostolic mission under Peter's leadership) is divinely appointed the visible correspondent to Christ Jesus, the main foundation (1 Cor. 3:11)—the *kepha* of the new people of God (*ekklesia, qahal/edah* Mt. 16:18), the key-bearer of Christ's household (v. 19), the strength for faith (Lk. 22:33), supreme pastor (shepherd) of His flock, the universal Church, supreme over all the faithful including other shepherds, over all other authorities within the Church (Mt. 18:18; Jn. 20:21-23), not excepting the other Apostles (Jn. 21:15-17).

Kung does not do full justice to the New Testament idea of authority. He has failed to grasp the deeper understanding of Church jurisdiction as it is uniquely and preeminently situated in *Kepha*.

That there was jurisdictional authority in the early Church, Petrine and apostolic, is evident in the *Acts of the Apostles.* Peter decides upon the full complement of the Twelve (1:15ff.). He speaks for the apostolic college (2:14), and summarily presents in public the earliest apostolic *kerygma* (2:14-39; 3:12-26; 4:8-12; 5:29-32; 10:34-43); defends Christianity before the Sanhedrin (4:8ff); and before the decisions of the Council of Jerusalem (15:7-11, 14), Peter, by authority of a special heavenly vision, receives the first heathen, Cornelius, into the Church without requiring obedience to Judaic law, and without prejudice to food, nor does he submit him and his household to circumcision. Religiously and socially the Church is opened to the Gentile world, and Peter's teaching prevails at the Council of Jerusalem (11:1-8). Luke obviously intends a parallel between Jesus and Peter in describing the crowds of infirm pressing about their persons seeking miracles (Acts 5:15-16; Mk. 6: 56). And Peter is saved for the primitive Church by a miraculous deliverance from the prisons of Herod. (12:1-12) Both Luke (24: 35) and Paul (1 Cor. 15:5) say that the Risen Jesus appeared first to Peter, and it is not beyond the legitimate bounds of exegesis to reason that in accordance with the mandate of the Petrine texts this special apparition concerned Peter's mission as primate. And Paul, when as yet he had not known Peter, journeyed to Jerusalem for the express purpose of visiting Cephas for fifteen days. (Ga. 1: 18)

Apostolic authority is manifest in the teaching, formation and supervision of the Christian community (2:42), and their conduct is stamped by divine approval by the many miracles they work (1: 43). The Twelve end the dispute between the Hellenists and the Hebrews and settle upon the seven deacons (6:1ff.). They consult the congregation but they themselves make the final decisions. (v.g. Acts 15:22) At the Council of Jerusalem, the much agitated question about the requirements to be imposed upon the Gentile Christians is decided by apostolic authority in union with and in accordance with the magisterial authority of Peter:

> After much discussion had gone on a long time, Peter stood up and addressed them . . . . This (Peter's speech) silenced the entire assembly. (Acts 15:7, 12)

Ordinances were prescribed and certain Jewish Christians rebuked for acting "without any authority from us" (v. 25).

We have stated earlier that there is a principled necessity between the primacy of service of Christ's teaching Church and the primacy of jurisdiction to ensure that the salvific message and the sacramental means of salvation and sanctification be preserved intact and inviolate by His delegated authority with the right to demand obedience of conscience and conduct. The primitive Church insisted on obedience to apostolic authority (Acts 15:25) in what is required of Gentile converts; on faithfulness to the "Good News of Christ" (Ga. 1:8), even for Paul (2:1-7); the insistence "in maintaining the traditions," i.e., the teaching of Christ and the apostles (1 Cor. 11:2), in preserving intact "what I received from the Lord, and in turn passed on to you" (1 Cor. 11:23, cf. 15:3, 11). In the *First* and *Second Epistle to the Corinthians* Paul fulfills his apostolic mission by teaching Christ Jesus and the moral law and Christian regulations touching many phases of conduct: on incest, fornication, marriage, virginity; on recourse to the pagan courts, on food offered to idols, on decorum in public worship; directives for the celebration of the Lord's Supper, on the controlled exercise of extraordinary charisms (and their subjection to Church authority, 1 Thess. 5:12; 19-21). Paul warns the faithful against deceitful teaching and lapses into paganism (Eph. 4:14, 15, 21; cf. Col. 2:7, 8). He repeatedly reassures the faithful that what he has taught them is truly Christ's message "on the authority of the Lord Jesus" (1 Thess. 2:12; 3:10; 4:2, 15; 5:12; 2 Thess. 2:15; 3:1, 3, 6). The Pastoral Epistles, *Timothy* 1 and 2 and *Titus* declare with indisputable clarity that the successors are endowed with the same authority of jurisdiction and teaching to correct distortions of the Christian truths and moral doctrine and if need be, to reprimand and punish. The insistence on the unaltered retention of the deposit of faith is repeatedly expressed in the strongest accents (1 Tm. 2:5-7; 3:15; 4:6; 3:20; 2 Tm. 1:13, 14; 2:2; 3:1-9; 4:1-5), "expounding the sound doctrine" (Tit. 1:9); "make them sound in the faith" (v. 14), "whether you are giving instruction or correcting errors; you can do so with full authority, and no one is to question it" (2:15; cf. 3:8-11, not the congregation, but the authorized representatives of the apostles are to be obeyed). And in the universal or Catholic epistles, cf. 2 Pt. 1:12; 2:2; 3:2; 1 Jn. 2:24, 26; 2 Jn. 9-11. For excommunication, cf., v.g., 1 Cor. 5:5; 1 Tm. 1:20; 2 Tm. 2:17). The postapostolic Church makes manifest this self-awareness of its divinely endowed power of jurisdiction. In the concluding decade of the first century Pope St. Clement, the third successor of St. Peter as Bishop of Rome from A.D. 90 to 99, in his *First Letter to the Corinthians* intervened authoritatively and forcefully in the internal affairs of the Corinthian Church without being requested to do so. Clement insisted that the delegation of three men who brought his letter to Corinth were not to return without confirmation of a settlement of the schism. The ancient history of the Church shows no similar letter of rebuke and reproval sent by one Christian community to another, and we judge that none would have been received except from Rome. (More of this *letter* later in our discussion of apostolic succession.)

In the opening years of the second century St. Ignatius of Antioch, the third Bishop of Antioch (Eusebius, *Hist. Eccl.* 3:36), writes of the authority of jurisdiction within the local Christian community, that of the bishop:

> Obviously the one whom the master of the household puts in charge of domestic affairs ought to be received by us in the same spirit in which we would receive our master himself. Plainly then, one should look upon the bishop as upon the Lord Himself. (*To the Ephesians 6*)

> There are those who invoke the name of bishop while their actions are without regard for him. Such men, it seems to me, are lacking in good conscience, for they do not assemble regularly as enjoined. (*To the Magnesians 4*)

> For it seems to me that, when you are obedient to the bishop as you would be to Jesus Christ, you are living, not in a human way, but according to Jesus Christ . . . . (*To the Trallians 2*)

The primacy of jurisdiction and the lower levels of jurisdictional authority is no less inherent in the Church as the authority to teach and the power of Orders. Indeed, the primacy of jurisdiction exists by Christ's ordination for the sake of service of the teaching and salvific Church for the unity of the faithful in the unity of faith. This is indisputably evident in the New Testament. History discloses its larger dimensions and outer boundaries and the diverse modes of operation with the expansion of the Church's apostolic mission in its preservation of doctrine in Scripture and Tradition against heresies with the development of sacramental theology and in the universal supervision of Catholic liturgies. Throughout ecclesiastical history the Holy Spirit was no less operative in the greater and deeper understanding of primatial authority as in other dogmas of the Catholic deposit of faith. Reason itself can discern that there is a principled necessity between primacy of jurisdiction and the primacy of service of the teaching and saving Church. The history of the proliferation of Christian sects, churches, creeds at variance with one another in the understanding of Christian revelation and even in doctrinal contradiction of one another, especially since the Reformation is a tragic confirmation of this discernment.

The promise made to Peter in Mt. 16:18-19 is fulfilled by the Risen Jesus in Jn. 21:15-17, fittingly, it seems, in the complementary conclusion of the Johannine evangel just as it had begun with the promise of the change of name from "Simon, son of John," to "Cephas—meaning Rock" (Jn. 1:42). If Form Criticism attributes this very early promise of change of name, prophetic of the role that is made explicit in Mt. 16:18, 19, to a retrojection in view of subsequent events, then this arrangement to suit the theological purpose of the authors/author of John points to a significance of a calculated intention that enlarges as it is related to the last recollection. The Johannine pericope reaffirms the Matthean singularity of Peter as the supreme and universal caretaker,—steward-keys, shepherd-tend-feed-gate (cf. Jn. 10), each of these figures of speech signify the authority of governance related, of course, to the divinely ordained mission of teaching and sanctifying.

St. Paul, Freedom, and the Law (K. 27, 48, 49)

We will have occasion to observe again and again that Kung tries to dichotomize when he can:

> The holder of the Petrine ministry may not set himself up either as Lord of the Church or—still less—as Lord of the Gospel. (K. 48)

> While "gospel" appears only twice and then as "law of the gospel" (as if Paul had not contrasted "law" and "gospel"). (K. 48)

> About thirty times in different ways, there is talk (in *Humanae Vitae*) of the "law" that the Church upholds and

proposes, while freedom of will and civic freedom are mentioned, but not the "freedom of the children of God" (as if Paul had not taught that Christ liberated us from the law into this freedom). (K. 49)

This sudden parenthetic aside into a Lutheran interpolation of Pauline theology breaks out into a depressing vision of the Church:

In this document (*Humanae Vitae*) law counts for more than Christian freedom, the ecclesiastical teaching office for more than the gospel of Jesus Christ, papal tradition for more than Scripture. (K. 49)

Neither in the entire corpus of Pauline writing nor in its theological reconstruction is there any evidence of any such contrast between law and freedom, nor in the letters of Peter and James. No opposition is set between "law" and the "gospel" by any of the scriptural depositories of Christian revelation. There are contrasts of expression to express spiritual and supernatural contrasts and a variety of contextual considerations.

The first contextual consideration is the manner by which God's justice has been made known—the same justice has been revealed through the Law and the Prophets, which as a norm of behavior made sin manifest rather than eliminated it (Rm. 3:21). The Law served as a negative, protective pedagogue (Gal. 3:24). The Law of the Jews had no power in itself to save. Let there be no misunderstanding; the Mosaic Law is God's Law: sacred, just, good and spiritual (Rm. 7:12-14). But this Law recognized deeply within us as good is rendered "unspiritual" by man's selfishness. The Law only made man more conscious of his conduct as a formal transgression, thus aggravating the offense and serving as an instrument of sin. That "same justice of God" which now comes through *faith* to everyone, Jew and pagan alike, who believes in Jesus Christ (Rm. 3:22-23), this "same justice" Paul calls the "*law of faith,*" and constitutes the first Pauline contrast of expression and spiritual reality. The contrast is in their efficacy not in their antithesis, because the "law of faith" gives the "Law" its true value (Rm. 3:31).

In the Gospels Jesus attacks the Scribes and Pharisees and denounces them for their meticulous interpretations of the Law which rendered it unbearable and inoperative, omitting what matters most—

justice and mercy (Mt. c. 23); they heap up meaningless obligations and make people pay taxes on the grass of the fields. While it is true that in the Sermon on the Mount (Mt. 5:1-10; Lk. 6:20-23) Jesus maintains a certain distance from the articles of the Law, He does so in order to go to the very heart of it and map out the road which leads to its perfection. Jesus had said that His mission was not to annul the law but to fulfill it; that is, to bring it to perfection by bestowing on that law a new and definitive form by raising it to a higher place through the spirit of the Gospel. When He was asked how one is to attain eternal life He answered, "Keep the commandments." He summarized the whole law in the commandment of love of God and of one's neighbor, as Paul was twice to do (Rm. 13:8-10; Gal. 5:6-14). The "law" of the commandments and the "law of faith" are but one and the same revealed will of God and those who accept this revelation cannot make it an excuse for rejecting the fullness of the revelation of God to which all laws of God are directed. Those who think they can be saved by works of the law without faith (in Christ) are no better than the unbelieving Gentiles (Rm. 2:14). The contrast of hopeful expectation in the Old and New Dispensation is illustrated by Our Lord's answer to a question of the Jews. "What must we do to be doing the works of God?" the Jews asked of Jesus. "This is the work of God," Jesus answered, "That you believe in Him whom He has sent" (Jn. 6:28-29). Faith in the Messiah, the Son of God, the Redeemer, carries with it the obligation and "works" of His own made manifest by the moral teaching of Jesus and the exemplar of His own life. Law gives information; it does not give spiritual strength.

The second contextual consideration is Christian Faith and the law. Paul proclaims that the Gospel (principally a Pauline term) is God's saving activity as constantly revealed and manifested in Christ's redemptive sacrificial crucifixion and triumphant exaltation over sin and death. The Judaizers posed the Law, both moral and ceremonial, as a cause of salvation and the Gentiles placed their confidence in the self sufficiency of reason as a saving power (1 Cor. 1:17-25). Paul points to their historical and theoretical sterility; even Abraham was justified by his faith, not by his works. (Rm. 4:3, Gal. 3:6) It is the Redeemer who through His Spirit writes the new law in man's heart (Heb. 8:10). Through a living faith He gives man a spiritual understanding of the law. Hence, on the one hand, the interchangeability; and on the other, an explicitation of doctrine of such expressions as "law of the faith" (Rm. 3:27); "law of the Spirit"

(Rm. 8:1); "law of Christ" (Gal. 6:2); "law of God" (Rm. 7:24); "God's Law"; "law of Grace." Renewed in mind by the gift of the Holy Spirit, the Christian freely accepts wholeheartedly the law of faith. He tries constantly to live ever more in accordance with the liberating truth of the Gospel and all that it entails in justice and charity, and all those works of the law which love demands. One must obey the whole law, which by divine ordination and effect constitutes the "perfect law of freedom" (James 1:25). This must be kept in mind when it is said spiritual freedom means being "not under the law but under grace" (Rm. 6:14). Only those who are led by the Spirit of Christ can love one another as Christ has loved them. And what shall we say of those awesome solemnities: "Amen, amen, I say unto you,—thou shalt, thou shalt not"; "It was said of old, but I say unto you, whoever..."; "If you love Me keep My commandments"; "Not everyone who cries out 'Lord, Lord,' will be saved, but he who does the will of My Father"; and what of the commandments explicitly reaffirmed and subsumed within the higher Christian economy of sanctification and salvation?

The third contextual consideration is Baptism and the law of freedom. The greater number of contrasts appear within this Pauline doctrinal purview. By its solidarity, mankind participated in the original fall of Adam, and the power of sin was made manifest by personal sins; and with sin, death entered into the world; death, spiritual and eternal, which separates man from man, of which physical death is the symbol. Within this order of sin and death, our "unspiritual" selves put our "bodies" at the service of vice and immorality, "slaves of sin," guilt oppressed by knowledge of the law. Against the background of familiar experience, social and political slavery and legal emancipation on the one hand, and on the other, the Christian slave converts who thought their spiritual liberation to have freed them from subjection to their masters, Paul speaks of our ransom by a great price, from the old order of servitude by the death and resurrection of Christ Jesus. "God dealt with sin by sending His own Son in a body as physical as any sinful body, and in that body, God condemned sin. He did this in order that the law's just demands might be satisfied in us, who behave not as our unspiritual nature, but as the spirit dictates." (Rm. 8:3-4)

By the Incarnation we have a new solidarity that supersedes the old one; by Baptism we share in the Paschal Mystery, in the death and resurrection of Christ. Baptism symbolizes and effectuates not only regeneration, so that our spiritual selves can contend now more confidently in the struggle with our unspiritual selves, with the law of the flesh (Rm. 7:22-24); not only does Baptism incorporate the Christian into the life of Christ (Gal. 3:27), but also effects his union with his fellow Christians as members of the one body of Christ (1 Cor. 12:13), and thereby eliminates all differences from spiritual freedom for slaves and freemen, between the Jews who boasted of their descent from Abraham and the Greeks who trusted in "philosophic wisdom."

"But now in Jesus Christ, you that used to be so far apart from us have been brought very close, by the blood of Christ. For He is the peace between us, and has made the two into one and broken down barriers which used to keep them apart, actually destroying in his own person the hostility caused by the rules and decrees of the Law."

The Spirit of Christ, for He is sent by Christ, becomes the inward principle of the new life and men can now, because they have the inward *power*, overcome sin and death by their own resurrection in virtue of Christ's redemptive death and resurrection. So follow the Pauline contrasts of expression and spiritual realities; "freed from the slavery of sin," we now become "slaves of righteousness"; once at "the service of vice and immorality" our bodies now can be put "at the service of righteousness" for our sanctification. "Free from sin," we are made "slaves of God." By faith in Christ Jesus, in what He claims to be and in what He said He did for us so that we may have eternal life, and by Baptism—the two go together and have the same effects—the Christian is freed from the old law which "worked unto the wrath of God" and from our sinful servitude to a new and higher service, wherein the new servants, the new slaves, obey the new master freely and faithfully. We now have the obedience and freedom of the Sons of God—also a Johannine theme. The destiny of law as the will of God, as revelation, was not to save man but to lead him to Jesus the Savior, and then to keep men in His ways: "If you love Me, keep my commandments."

The fourth contextual consideration of contrast of "law" and "gospel" is to be found in the *Epistle to the Hebrews* which, if not Paul's, surely, Pauline, wherein the ineffectiveness of the old sacrifices of the Levitical priesthood and the insufficiency of its cultic-ritual law of the old dispensation is contrasted with the higher and efficacious priesthood of Christ which fulfills and surpasses the priesthood of the Mosaic Law. This writer, for one, is quite at a loss to understand how Kung can write that Paul contrasted "law" and "gospel" (48). Any supposition that the "Good News," the "Law of Christ," the "Law of the Spirit," the "law of faith," the "law of grace" liberates from divine commandments and precepts of the natural law, negates obedience to civil law and authority and—much to the point —precludes all obligations of ecclesiastical law and governance in the ecclesial community is entirely and diametrically at variance with the written depositories of Christian revelation, the four evangels, *Acts*, the corpus of Pauline writing, the Epistles of Peter and James, with nothing else scriptural of the new dispensation excepted. The unmistakable contrast is with the "law of sin and death":

"...the law of the spirit of life in Christ Jesus has set you free from the law of sin and death." (Rm. 8:2)

The freedom that Paul speaks of is the *freedom of redemption*; freedom from the dominance of sin because of the "law of grace"; freedom from death, which we will overcome one day, through our resurrection—thanks to the faith and Baptism by which we share in the Paschal mystery of the death and resurrection of our Divine Redeemer. We were freed from the old Mosaic Law and circumcision, and that is why we speak of the old and the new law. The New Law (Christian responsibilities, duties) does not diminish the new Christian freedom of redeemed men; nor does the new freedom diminish the New Law—a new freedom and a new subjection (law), a new obedience of adopted Sons of God.

Liberty and Law

The Pauline problematic on "law and liberty" may to a considerable extent, though surely not entirely, be attributed to a surprising repetition of the same, identical terms, i.e., "law," "servitude," "obedience," "subjection," "liberty," in a paradoxical conjunction that at times are manifestly antithetical in their substantive meaning which the text and context reformulates. The *loci classici* are to be found in St. Paul's earlier Epistle to the *Galatians*, where the Pauline doctrine is put forth with the shocking impact of an impassioned polemical tone, and in his Epistle to the *Romans*, where his more reasoned and controlled dialectic forges a greater precision to his balance of paradoxes and antitheses.

If you are led by the Spirit, you are not under the Law. (Gal. 5:18)

> Sin shall not have dominion over you, since you are not
> under the Law, but under grace. (Rm. 6:14)

Repeatedly this theme is presented, now congruently and paradoxically and at other times antithetically. It matters then what
meanings "law" has for Paul. By "law" Paul surely means the
Mosaic legislation in all of its comprehension, not only its complicated ritual specificities, its all encompassing social, dietary, hygenic
minutiae but principally, as the Epistle to the *Romans* makes clear,
its moral content to the extent that it was a positive expression of
the natural law of human nature. This Mosaic Law, as an expression
of God's will, is "holy, just, and good" (Rm. 7:12), for God could
not will evil to be the way of life for men. Yet Paul writes that because of the Law we are under the domination of sin (Rm. 5:12, 13,
20; 6:14; 7:1, 6, 9-11, 21). How so? Law gives knowledge of what
is good and evil, forbidden by God. And this knowledge of what is
forbidden provides the awareness of the occasion for sin. Paul's
line of thinking is clarified when projected against the fall of Adam
and Eve as narrated in the biblical account of cc. 2 and 3 of *Genesis*,
which upon comparison with *Roman* 7 strongly suggests that
Romans 7:7-12 was written with the drama of *Genesis* 3 vividly in
mind. History in Scripture begins with man's creation, and the
occasion for the first sin occurs after the divine ban—against eating
from the tree of knowledge of good and evil. (Gn. 2:9, 17; 3:1, 3,
5; cf. Rm. 7:8-12) "Once upon a time I was living without Law"
(Rm. 7:9), applies to anyone who has not yet faced the question of
the meaning of life and its normative exigencies. The source or
author of sin is neither God, "God forbid," nor the Law itself
(Rm. 7:12), but deception of the serpent (Gen. 3:13), who is condemned to the worse punishment (Gn. 3:14; 2 Cor. 11:3; 1 Tm.
2:14), or the devil, sin personified. (Rm. 7:11) Strictly speaking,
the law provokes by its knowledgeable awareness of what is forbidden not sin but transgression. The serpent did not transgress
God's injunction, but he sinned grievously (Gn. 3:14); our first
parents both transgressed and sinned. Transgression is the exterior-
ity of a much deeper radical ambivalence in man—meant for God,
he is driven by a self love, *amor sui*, that contests over against *amor
Dei* (in Augustinian terms) but which St. Paul designates connaturally and distinctively in terms of the concupiscence that is carnally
weighted (Rm. 8:7). What then can be so salutary in the Mosaic Law
which as God's will is "holy, just, and good" that provides the
occasion and provocation to sin which is spiritual death?

Paul, Liberty, Law

Law reveals man's true helplessness to himself, his true identity. He cannot save himself, redeem himself. This is the wise providence of a merciful God, that man comes to know himself truly as not self-sufficient, that he must have need and turn to the Divine Savior. But what Paul says of the Mosaic law applies to any law—even the evangelical law, church law, to civil law—to the extent that it is merely a legal exaction on the low level of constraint and coercion. But Paul is anything but an antinomian. He speaks of the commandments of God, of the law of Christ, of obedience to Church law and to civil law. What Paul is saying is that the salvific force which the Jews attributed to the actual fulfillment of the prescriptions to the Mosaic Law is misplaced, that salvation is through Christ Jesus. Deliverance from the flesh, from sin, from death comes not through the Law, but from deliverance also from the Law. It is because of our faith, in worship and love of Christ Jesus as the Son of God and truly our redeemer, that we fulfill His law and all other derivative laws whereby they are binding on us that we are freed from the coercion, constraint and inefficacies of law merely as law. Hence the primacy of the charity of Christ (which "urges us on") in all our obediences frees us from the constraints and coercions of a legal exaction. (Jesuits will recall the promptitude of charity which distinguishes Ignatian obedience. The exterior is an overflow of the interior Christian spirit.)

Had not Jeremiah, in prophesying the new covenant (31:33), spoken of the law in radically different terms: "I will place my law within them, and write it upon their hearts." (31:33) It is the indwelling Spirit of Christ Jesus which was so superabundantly in public evidence on Pentecost that replaces the Law, any law precisely as and no more than law:

"There is therefore now no condemnation for those who are in Christ Jesus. For the law of the Spirit—(identified either with the person of the Holy Spirit or with the activity of that same Spirit in us)—giving life in Christ Jesus has delivered me from the law of sin and death." (Rm. 8:1-2)

It is this Spirit of Christ Jesus that replaces the Old Law, that supersedes any law, as the Law of the love (charity of Christ) that prompts us freely to be subject to, to obey, to enter, as it were, a new servitude where we obey what we ought (binding), without constraint and coercion. "Love therefore is the fulfillment of the Law." (Rm. 13:8-10) Let us recall with what complete oblation the Incarnate Word obeyed the will of His Father. No law, neither old nor new, saves without the inward presence of the healing grace of faith, the enriching graces that make the profession of Christian life by faith a supreme gift of grace in itself—to be one with Christ. "For me to live is Christ and to die is gain." (Yet even the constraints and coercions of law have a salutary limited utility in that in this earthly life of faith, of imperfect charity, the law reminds our consciences in our occasional presumptions of our insufficiency and that we can still fall under the domination of sin and incur the wages of sin, spiritual death.)

It is the inpouring of the Holy Spirit of Christ, whom he had promised to send, who works in us the love that is the fullness of the law (Rm. 13:8-10), not primarily as a norm of conduct but as a spiritual energizing force inspiring us to live as Christ and therefore in His way (His law), whereby, as if by instinct, the spiritually new man shies away from the carnal (Rm. 5:19-21) and reveals his Christian transformation by an exterior manifestation of Christian virtues. (1 Cor. c. 13)

> The law of faith is faith itself, which obtains the grace for action, whereas the law of works is satisfied with commanding the same.
>
> The law of works is the letter that kills and the law of faith is the Spirit who gives life.
>
> From this it follows that not only the law of Moses, but even the law of Christ, to the extent that it commands something, is the law of works, whereas the law of faith is the spirit of faith, by which not only we who are Christians, but the patriarchs as well, and the prophets, and all just men, have obtained the free gift of God's grace, and once justified by that grace, have kept the commandments of the Law." (St. Robert Bellarmine, *De justificatione impii*, Liber I, caput XIX, *Opera Omnia*, Naples, 1856-62, IV, 492. cf. too St. Thomas Aquinas masterful *Commentary on St. Paul's Epistle to the Romans.*

In a word, it is Christ who takes the place of the law—for it is He—not our works, nor the works of any law! And because of His love for us and our love for Him which the Spirit of Christ operates in us, we obey freely that which is lived in His likeness. "To live is Christ and to die is gain." It is faith which works through charity. (Ga. 5:6)

The classic Pauline opposition between law and liberty is actually between the law and efficacy of works of themselves for salvation and the law of faith and the salvific works it produces as its first fruits through Christ's saving grace. Paul was anything but an anti-nomian. He repeatedly refers to the Decalogue; to the precepts of the natural law; to church law, many of which he himself promulgated; and to the obligation to obey civil law and authorities, and not above obeying, even within the Christian dispensation, some requirements of the Old Law. (*Acts* 16:3, concerning Timothy's circumcision; Paul's compliance with the instructions of *James*, 21:24; as a subsidiary obedience to a higher purpose, 1 *Cor.* 9:20.)

But pointedly, as Paul incisively introduces the subject of faith and works:

"Do we mean that faith makes the Law pointless? Not at all; we are giving the Law its true value." (Rm. 3:31)

"If we can be justified through the law, then Christ's death was needless." (Gal. 2:21)

In a conflation of the three synoptic evangelists (Mt. 19:16-19; Mk. 10:17-20; Lk. 18:18-21), we may read:

And there was a young man who came to Him and asked, "Master, what must I do to attain eternal life?" Jesus said to him, "If you wish to attain eternal life, keep the commandments. You know the commandments. You must not kill. You must not commit adultery. You must not bear false witness. You must not steal. You must not defraud. Honor your father and mother, and you must love your neighbor as yourself."

Jesus himself enumerates at least six of the commandments, and as presuppositions even within His own economy of salvation to Christian discipleship, and beyond, to the Christian counsels of perfection. The old economy has come to an end and the new age has dawned, but the Law, as a norm of morality, still stands intact, which shows that the gospel has not abrogated the Law but has instead brought out the spirit of the Law. There is nothing in the whole of Christian revelation, of which the Pauline epistles are a part, that gives credence to the Kungian notion of Pauline morality. (K. 27, 48, 49)

The Law-Freedom (gospel) contrariety that Kung affirms is seen in more intelligible light if the Incarnate Word, His whole life, salvific message and redemptive sacrifice—a context within which St. Paul discusses the question—is the objective and motive for our worship, love and obedience. This is the understanding of St. Augustine, St. Thomas and St. Robert Bellarmine. St. Paul declares Christians to be "not under the Law, but under grace" (Rm. 6:14), that "if you are led by the Spirit, you are not under the Law." (Ga. 5:18) Yet he is careful time and again to list directives for Christian morality, and he (Rm. c. 1) makes one of the harshest indictments of all time against "unnatural" sins. The response to Kung's antithesis is resolved only by a truly Christian life directed by the grace of the Spirit of Christ, the Holy Spirit, who leads us to put on the "mind" of Christ, a life which becomes a living Law within us, a law truly binding, no less, but whose motivation the Person of Christ by far transcends a mere imperative requirement. "If you love Me, keep my commandments." Or, because you love Me, you will keep my commandments.

Nor did the Fathers of the Second Vatican Council underwrite any such Kungian contrast between law and gospel and freedom. Suffice here:

> All this corresponds with the basic law of the Christian dispensation. For though the same God is Savior and Creator, Lord of human history as well as salvation history, in the divine arrangement itself the rightful autonomy of the creature, and particularly of man is not withdrawn. Rather, it is reestablished in its own dignity and strengthened in it.

> Therefore, by virtue of the Gospel committed to her, the Church proclaims the rights of man. She acknowledges and greatly. esteems the dynamic movements of today by which these rights are everywhere fostered. Yet these movements must be penetrated by the spirit of the gospel and protected against any kind of false autonomy. For we are tempted to think that our personal rights are fully ensured only when we are exempt from every requirement of divine law. But this way lies not the maintenance of the dignity of the human person, but its annihilation (*Gaudium et Spes* n. 41)

We concluded with a passage from a talk given to a general audience by Pope Paul VI on May 5, 1971:

Christ freed us from the Mosaic Law of the Old Testament. This subject is developed broadly and repeatedly in the writings of the New Testament, so much so that we are accustomed to defining these two phases of the religious relations of man with God as the Old Law and the New Law. What does this mean? It means that in Christ was fulfilled and completed the religious economy set up with the first liberation of the elect people from Pharaonic slavery and with the promulgation of the Law of Sinai (in which natural law and positive law are united). This was a good law, but it was insufficient. It was a command, a teaching, but not a sufficient force, not a new animating principle, a supernatural principle, to live in the true justice of God. Another system was necessary to make man good, just and pleasing to God. What was necessary was the law of grace, the law of the spirit, which was obtained and conferred on us by Christ, who died and rose again for us (cf. *Romans* 4:25). This is the liberation that came to us from the paschal mystery. (we are not speaking now of civil freedom)

Quotations from the scriptures could be multiplied here: "Where the spirit of the Lord is, there is freedom" (2 *Cor.* 3:17). This freedom refers to exemption from observance of Jewish and Pharasaical legality (cf *Gal.* 2:4; 4:31; 5:13). It refers to the progress of moral life: from obedience to the exterior, formal norm to the inner, person alone. Let us recall the fundamental message of the Gospel teaching: "Think not that I have come to abolish the law and the prophets; I have come not to abolish them but to fulfill them . . . . You have heard it said to the men of old . . . but I say to you . . . . (Mt. 5:17ss). It refers to the summing up of our duties in those supreme duties of love of God and of our neighbor (Mt. 22:37ss).

But let us be careful. Precisely because of this supreme requirement of the law of the spirit, the word "freedom" might deceive us into thinking that we have no longer any obligations, either to ourselves or to others, or as regards an orderly life in the ecclesial community. Yes, we must feel free, as if borne by the way of the spirit; but St. Peter warns us (1 Peter 2:16), without using our freedom as a pretext for evil; we are always servants of God. The Christian is bound more than ever to God's will, to respect for natural and civil laws, to obedience to those who have hierarchical and pastoral functions in the church; precisely because he is a Christian. And this experience of the harmony between the blessed freedom that Christ obtained for us, and the joy of faithfulness to the order willed by Him is among the most beautiful and original experiences of our Christian election, never to be renounced.

The magistral voice of the Apostle Paul and that of Pope Paul VI, supreme teacher of the Universal Church, are on this matter in conformity with the "mind of Christ."

CHAPTER ONE

Chapter One opens with a glissade of "errors of the ecclesiastical teaching office," and immediately the author begins inauspiciously with the historical error of his own, which he incautiously repeats later on.

> The excommunication of Photius, the Ecumenical Patriarch of Constantinople and of the Greek Church, which made formal the schism with the Eastern Church, a schism which is now almost a thousand years old. (K31; 121)

In his hasty, uncritical use of history, Kung is at fault here. Perhaps prompted by his distempers toward Rome and ever eager to reach out to whatever may bear the semblance of embarrassment for the Roman Pontiff, he confuses the "schism"(?) between Byzantium and the West under the Patriarch Michael Cerularius in the year 1054 with the excommunication of Photius two hundred years before. Let us disengage the two historic events and in a summary review of the salient issues and facts, endeavor to ascertain in what way, if at all, there is involved an error "of the ecclesiastical teaching office" that can be justifiably subsumed under the heading "Infallible Teaching Office." (Inquiry, 31)

The Photian Affair

The drama of disunity which has endured to our own times broke out during the pontificate of Pope Nicholas I over the canonical regularity of the elevation of a layman, Photius, to the patriarchate of Constantinople. Photius was a leading figure in the Byzantine intellectual renaissance of the ninth century. His brother married Irene, the sister of the Empress Theodora, and in this adventitious circumstance (but not without great personal merit), he was appointed director of the imperial chancery and a member of the senate.

75

Bardas, the brother of the Empress Theodora, with the connivance of the young emperor Michael III, terminated the regency of his sister and made himself regent. Because Ignatius gave credence to the slanderous reports about the private life of Bardas and was also numbered in the conservative party of the deposed Theodora, he was removed from the patriarchal office or resigned under the insistence from the bishops, who were anxious to avoid a conflict with the new government. In December 858 Photius, a layman, was raised to the patriarchal office by the Emperor Michael or by his uncle Bardas. Because the new partiarch had to function during the approaching feast of the Lord's Nativity, he obtained all the degrees of Holy Orders in a week. Pope Nicholas I objected to the elevation of a layman to the patriarchal office. In response to Photius' invitation to the new council to be convened in Constantinople, Pope Nicholas sent Bishop Radoald of Porto and Zacharias of Anagni with instructions to reexamine the religious situation in Constantinople, while reserving to himself the definite and final decision concerning the canonical regularity of Photius' elevation. The imperial government and Photius were willing to allow the papal legates to make their investigation but on the condition that they would pronounce their verdict in the name of the Pope at the council. (At this point let us note parenthetically that the historical course of scholarly research on the Photian affair has been brilliantly challenged by the works of Francis Dvornik: *The Photian Schism. History or Legend*, Cambridge, 1948; in French, *Le Schisme de Photius. Histoire ou légende*, Unam Sanctam, 19, Paris, 1950: *Byzance et la Primauté Romaine*, Unam Sanctam, 49, Paris, 1964. The main argumentation of these more recent works are presaged in earlier publications over a period of twenty years preceding. Confer, for example, *Les Slaves, Byzance et Rome au IXe Siécle*, Paris, 1926.)

According to Dvornik, the papal legates saw in the proposed compromise the confirmation by the Byzantine Church and State of the supreme jurisdiction of the Pope over the universal Church and accordingly were well disposed to accept it. After their interrogation of Ignatius in the Synod of 861, the papal legates reaffirmed the decision of the synod of 859, which had declared, on the request of Bardas, that the whole patriarchate of Ignatius was illegitimate because he had not been elected by a synod but had been simply appointed by Theodora. Dvornik maintains that the declarations of the bishops and legates that the Byzantine Church, when allowing the legates to reexamine the Ignatian-Photius affair, had accepted the canons of Sardica (343) and so thereby showed their recognition of the right of bishops to appeal to the Pope as the supreme judge in the Church. The circumstance does lend itself to such an interpretation and inference. But the specific fact is that Ignatius had not appealed to Rome nor intended to, as he declared after the verdict: *Roman non appellavi nec appello.* Yves Congar holds, and rightly so, that the legates exceeded their explicit instructions in accepting the compromise and deposing Ignatius (*L'ecclésiologie de haut moyen-age* Cerf, 1958, p. 217). Pope Nicholas condemned and excommunicated Photius at a Roman Synod of 863 and recognized Ignatius as the legitimate Patriarch, perhaps provoked in part by Photius' silence to the papal request for further inquiry, and partly because of the pro-Ignatian reports of Abbot Theognostus and his group of monks who had travelled from Constantinople to Rome, giving the semblance that Ignatius was appealing to Rome. Unfortunately, the East-West religious situation took a turn for the worse because of a new conflict over Bulgaria. Boris I, disappointed that Photius would send only missionaries and refused to provide an archbishop or patriarch, thereupon turned to Rome. Pope Nicholas obligingly sent two bishops, Formosus and Paul, and a long letter, *ad consulta Bulgarum*—responses to the hundred inquiries that Boris had forwarded to Rome. These responses won Boris over to the Pope and to Western Christianity. Photius sharply resented Roman intrusions into Byzantine domain, the latinizing of the Greek rite and the introduction of *Filioque* into the Creed. He addressed an encyclical to the Eastern Bishops in which he, in turn, vehemently attacked Latin practices and the doctrinal formula *Filioque*, and even went so far as to call for the condemnation and deposition of the Pope in the Eastern Synod of 867. There is no need here to recount the alternating fortunes of Photius under Emperor Basil I (who murdered Bardas, the Emperor's uncle and regent, and then also his benefactor, Michael III, who had promoted him to be co-emperor), his condemnation and excommunication by Pope Adrian (869), and at the eighth ecumenical council of Constantinople (IV) in 869-870, the submission of the Greek Bishops to the formula of Pope Hormisdas (518) in acknowledgment of the Roman primacy, the restoration of Bulgaria to the Byzantine rite under the leadership of Ignatius, no less—the recall of Photius to the patriarchal office, his conditional acceptance by Pope John VIII. Dvornik maintains that Photius died in communion with Rome, and on the basis of the council of 861 admitted to a Roman primacy that left the Oriental churches in administrative and canonical autonomy. For additional evidence Dvornik points to the letter of Pope John VIII to the "union" council of 879-880 which was partially altered with the consent of the papal legates who had been convinced that Rome had been mis-informed about the true situation in Constantinople. Whatever the changes, the main scriptural arguments by which Pope John VIII confirmed his primacy in the Church were left in the Greek version, a circumstance that Dvornik says shows that Photius, although defend-ing the autonomy of his church, did not deny primacy of the Pope. Dvornik maintains that the alleged writing against the Roman pri-macy by Photius cannot be ascribed to him because the legendary tradition that St. Andrew the Apostle was the founder of the Byzan-tine bishopic, which this writing contained, was not officially listed in the Typicon of the Patriarchal church that Photius himself had re-edited. It was not until the tenth century that this legend won general acceptance in Byzantium and in the East. (See F. Dvornik, *The Idea of Apostolicity in Byzantium and the Legend of the Apostle Andrew*, Cambridge, Massachusetts, 1958; *The Patriarch Photius in the Light of Recent Research*, Munich, 1958.) But there have been demurrers to Dvornik's reappraisal of Photius. Confer, for example, E. de Moreau, "La réhabilititation de Photius" in *Nouvelle Revue Théologigue*, January, 1950, p. 180ff; Walter Ullmann, *The Growth of Papal Government in the Middle Ages*, 1963, p. 199, n. 2; Yves Congar, *op. cit.*, pp. 221, 363-370. As Congar has pointed out (pp. 216-221), there are questions to which something can be validly said for both sides: the universal applicability and binding force of canon law on the Oriental Church, and in particular, the 13th canon of the council of Sardica (341) and of Nicaea, which Photius did not admit; the legitimate diversity in ecclesiastical regu-lations and whether the Photian election was a permissible exception that can withstand even papal authority to the contrary; the under-lying motivation of Pope Nicholas' charge of canonical irregularity namely, the gradually increasing Roman resistance to the laic deter-minative insertion into the hierarchical affairs of the Byzantine Church, a historically conditioned tradition that had been firmed up by the nomocanons since the 4th century. Beneath the canonical rivalry there were implications for the primacy of divine institution. Did Rome see this clearly as touching upon the implications or the consequences in the same light? Was not Pope Nicholas' content of the primacy, enveloping at its core Pope Siricius' formula—*in nobis beatus apostolus Petrus*—considerably at variance with Photius' understanding of papal primacy?

Two centuries later Michael Cerularius, Patriarch of Constantinople, was excommunicated by Cardinal Humbert de Moyenmoutiers, July, 1054. A veil of obscurity envelops the train of sequent events that transformed the personal excommunication of Cerularius into a gradual deterioration and progressive estrangement in the relations between the East and the West. To begin with, Michael was such a controversial figure in his own lifetime that even the contemporary sources are contradictory. Born of a distinguished family of Constantinople, his ambition for ascendency was relentless. He was suspected of taking part in the plot against the Emperor Michael IV and accused of entering religious life to escape punishment. At the accession of Emperor Constantine IX, who had taken part in the conspiracy, Cerularius was appointed *syncellus*, virtual successor-designate to the patriarch, and the emperor's most trusted advisor. Succeeding to the See of the Constantinople in 1043, he broke with Constantine on the question of submission to Rome. Enjoying tremendous popularity, he forced Constantine to an abject surrender. He had sought reunion with Rome, but as equals, and was astounded when the papal legates, with the approval of Constantine, demanded that he acknowledge the primacy of Rome. In reaction to the latinizing of the Greek parts of Italy still under Byzantine rule, Cerularius turned upon the Latins for their "horrible infirmities" of using unleavened bread for the Eucharist, for their insistence on clerical celibacy, and for fasting on Saturdays. He closed all Latin churches in Constantinople, not even sparing the chapel of the papal legates unless they converted to the Greek rite. Pope Leo IX sent a mission under Cardinals Humbert of Silva Candida, his "secretary of state," and Frederick of Lorraine (later Stephen IX), and Archbishop Peter of Amalfi to treat of the various matters of contestation between Rome and Byzantium. Unfortunately, irresponsible acts by both Humbert and Cerularius aggravated the chronically strained relations between the churches. Personal excommunications were exchanged. In the bull composed by Humbert only Patriarch Celularius was excommunicated and its validity has since been questioned, as Pope Leo IX was already deceased at that time. The Byzantine synod excommunicated only the legates and refrained from any attack on the Pope or the Latin Church. According to Dvornik, contemporaries were not aware that a schism existed, and advances as circumstantial evidences the fact that the successors of Pope Leo IX,—Popes Victor II, Stephen IX, and Alexander II started negotiations with the Byzantine emperors soon after 1054. Gregory

VII planned to assemble an army in the West in order to assist Emperor Michael VII in his struggle against the Turks. Dvornik challenges the "Photian legend" in the West, picturing the patriarch as the father of schism and the archenemy of papal primacy. He also challenges the general supposition that the schism is dated from the year 1054. He points, rather, to the sack of Constantinople by the Crusaders (IV), the anti-Byzantine propaganda of Bohemund I of Taranto, the appointment of a Latin patriarch in Antioch, the foundation of a Latin Empire of Constantinople (1204). The appointment of a Latin patriarch in Constantinople was regarded by the Greeks as the culmination of the schism. The hostility of the Greek clergy against papal primacy and the West explains why the Union of the Council of Lyons (1274) and that of Florence (1439) were both of so short duration and why the Greeks preferred to live in schism.

Historians have found that the deeper causes of the schism go beyond Photius and Michael Cerularius, beyond the controversy over *Filioque*, the Procession of the Holy Spirit which had arisen in the days of Photius; they speak of growing cultural divergencies between East and West widened by the Old and the New Rome, made all the more acute by the appeal of the orthodox easterners (heresies?); the occupation of Sicily, southern Italy and Illyricum by the Byzantine emperor; the recovery of these territories and the latinizing of the Greek churches in these; the Bulgarian affair; the intrigues at the Byzantine court; the fluctuating fortunes of emperors (desirous of the unity of the empire) and of patriarchs (solicitous for ecclesiastical autonomy) *vis a vis* Rome; the dreadful impact of the Fourth Crusade upon the Greeks; the progressive estrangement, a basic inability to understand one another's customs and traditions; and so on and on. How all these complicated affairs with complexities bordering on contradictions, so many controversies yet unresolved can be set down by Kung as an "error of the ecclesiastical teaching office" bearing on the dogmatics of infallibility is one of the many intriguing perplexities that sparkle Kung's book with an absorbing interest.

Kung fails his readers when he does not discriminate excommunications for willful heresy and willful schism from excommunication as a corrective punishment in the exercise of authoritative discipline that is an incidence of the power of binding and loosing. The question of the excommunication of Michael Cerularius has been reconsidered in the light of the ecumenical movement growing out of the Second Vatican Council. Let the reader consult the joint statement of Pope Paul VI and Athenagoras, Patriarch of Constantinople, on December 7, 1965. (AAS 58, 1:20-21)

Galileo (K. 30)

The Galileo case illustrates what hazards are risked when the Roman Pontiff acquiesces in the findings and recommendations of an ecclesiastical commission. This aspect of the *Galileo* case and its relevance to Pope Paul's exercise of papal authority independent of the majority report has strangely been given the silent treatment by critics of *Humanae Vitae*. Further, what is generally overlooked is that the condemnation of Galileo was by virtue of scriptural interpretation then prevalent among theologians who could not tolerate Galileo's challenge of their Scriptural exegesis. It seems to this writer that when certain theologians fault the papal teaching authority in the *Galileo* case and pass over their favorite theme on the "co-responsibility of theologians" whose scriptural exegesis provided the major premise for Galileo's condemnation by the Roman commissions, they are looking to theological self-interest rather narrowly. Theologians have much too long swept the Galileo blunder under the papal rug.

Cardinals Conti, del Monte, Bellarmine and Barberini (who later became Pope Urban VIII) reassured Galileo that the literal interpretation of *Josue* 10:33ff.—then so prevalent among contemporary theologians—was not official infallible teaching of the Church.

Bellarmine acknowledged that the Copernican system saved the appearances better than the Ptolemaic and accordingly could be considered a superior hypothesis, but it still was not an established fact (*Letter to Foscarni*). The Cardinal, much in the manner of Pope Leo XIII in the nineteenth century, made clear that if Galileo's hypothesis could be "validated as a fact" it would be necessary to acknowledge that the passages in Scripture which appear to contradict this fact have been misunderstood. Had contemporary theologians and biblical exegetes heeded Thomas Aquinas' assertion that the sacred writers "went by what sensibly appeared," (S.T. I, q. 1 xx, a. 1 ad 3), and even beyond, Augustine, they would have spared the Church this enduring and annoying embarrassment.

Hence (these writers) did not seek to penetrate the secrets of nature, but rather described and dealt with things in more or less figurative language or in terms which were commonly used at the time, and which in many instances are in daily use at this day, even by the eminent men of science. (*De Genesi ad litteram* II, 9, 20)

Despite his discoveries, Galileo had no real and conclusive proof that the Copernican system was anything more than a theory. His scientific observations argued more effectively against Aristotle and Ptolemy than for Copernicus. The scientific data Galileo put forth in support of the mobility of the earth—the movement of Venus and Mercury, the inference he drew from "sunspots," the argument from the "tides"—were either disproven or judged to be inconclusive to translate a hypothesis to actuality. Thomas Henry Huxley thought that the opponents of Galileo had the better of the argument on scientific grounds.

What of the condemnation? It will not do to minimize it. It is a blunder of no small magnitude which the critics of the Church and Catholic discontents will resurrect when they find it opportune to do so. But by the same token, it would be even more misleading to see in it a failing of infallibility or an "estrangement between the Church and the natural sciences, not yet overcome today." (K. 31-32)

The Protestant astronomer Proctor wrote:

The Catholic doctrine on the subject (of papal infallibility) is perfectly definite; and it is absolutely certain that the decision in regard to Galileo's teaching, shown not to have been unsound, does not in the slightest degree affect the infallibility, either of the Pope or of the Church. The decision was neither *ex cathedra*, nor addressed to the whole Church; in not one single point does the case illustrate this doctrine of papal infallibility as defined by the Vatican Council. (*Knowledge*, Vol. IX, 274)

On biblical astronomy Galileo was a better scriptural exegete than the generality of Catholic and Protestant theologians of his time. But so entrenched was the Ptolemaic theory that scientists of Galileo's day, and many of them even after Newton had established the mobility of the earth, still clung to it that theologians may not be wholly blamed for not knowing any better.

Providentially, Our Lord established His Church upon His unfailing promises—not on personal sanctity, nor on scientific competence, nor on the primacy of human wisdom in the midst of contending forces within the Church—least of all on the "consensus" of theologians—and their unembarrassed mutability.

Usury (K. 31)

We continue with Kung's ricochet of "ecclesiastical errors."

There is no general morality nor principles of general morality, but rather general principles of morality. Morality is in the concrete, specific willful act. An act of uncharitableness is intrinsically evil, never justifiable. Usury, on the other hand, is a moral-practical term with an etymological history and variance of actual expression where the condemnation remains absolute; but specific forms of practice are exonerated because in the concrete it is divested of its historically experienced evil. If ever the *term* "situation ethics" can be plausibly used, it is about usury. Because of institutional developments and, above all, as a consequence of changes of economic systems, usury is a historically evolved practice and therein lies the sources of those distinctions and subdistinctions that have seemed an evasion of the absolute condemnation.

While the taking of interest of money loans has been permitted by the Church from the sixteenth century, if not earlier, it still remains true that the present Canon Law (Canon 1543) condemns usury as explicitly as it was condemned by Pope Urban III in 1186 or Pope Benedict XIV in 1745. The principles of morality affirmed by the Church that bear on usury and money interest were never changed, but both the understanding of economic concepts and of the objects of morality have undergone change of meaning as the economic system itself changed.

The Old Testament condemnations of interest on loans is indisputable, even though it is touched with an ethnic bias. (cf. Ex. 22: 25; Lev. 25:35-37; Deut. 15:5-10; Kings 4:1; Esdra 5:5-7; Ps. 14: 4-5; 108-11; Ez. 18:8, 13-17.) The Book of *Nehemiah* 5:1-13 vividly depicts the cruel injustices of avaricious creditors and the desperate lot of the needy and defaulting debtors in those times.

The Greek and Roman philosophers attacked it with righteous anger. The New Testament is generally silent on the specific question of money interest, except in the parable of the talents, (Mt. 25:27; Lk. 10:23)—the inventor could lend out his money to bankers and expect interest in an exercise of prudent industry. To remit payment from bankrupt debtors is an expected act of generosity (Lk.7:41ff). And the forgiveness of sins in the Lucan *Pater Noster* (Lk. 11:4) has its counterpart in the Matthean version of "debts," with a profoundly significant import. (Mt. 6:12) Both the malice and cruelty visited upon insolvent debtors are poignantly described in *Matthew* 5:25f; 18:28ff.; Lk. 12:58f.

Usury is distinguishable from money interest and excessive interest. *Usura* in its Latin origination denoted a charge for the loan of a perishable, a consumable. As money loan became the more common form of loan, usury signified an interest charge for the money loan. As Greek and Roman law repealed the laws which prohibited usury, the term came to mean extortionate interest beyond the legal rate.

Plato had denounced loan interest as divisive of society, pitting the hopelessly helpless poor borrowers against the wealthy creditors. Aristotle, while acknowledging it as a social evil, condemned it as intrinsically evil. Money, he taught, was sterile, incapable of fruitfulness, of production. Since justice requires an equivalence of exchange understood as the exchange of two equal sums, to exact interest is to effectuate a "birth of money from money" contrary to the nature of their being. The pre-Nicene Fathers condemned the oppression of the poor by usury as a violation of charity and mercy. With notable rising vehemence that suggests that the oppression of the poor had become cruel beyond human endurance, the later Fathers, condemned usurious practice as a sin against justice, *rapina* (Ambrose); *latrocinia, maleficus* (Augustine). Gregory of Nyssa, in his *Oratio contra Usurarios*, denounced the usurers as a breed of vipers that gnaw at the womb that bears them. But neither the patristic nor any ecclesiastical literature yields any carefully formulated moral philosophical doctrine on usury. The Fathers, it seems, concentrated on the greedy motivation of the lenders and on the disastrous consequences of the hapless borrowers. In the thirteenth century, St. Thomas Aquinas, by employing the Roman Law classification of creditor-debtor contractual relationships and Aristotle's philosophic concept of the sterility of money, argued: "It is in itself illicit to accept a price for the use of money loaned, which is called usury." In those times inherent utility in money was seen beyond its conventional function as a measure of exchange. Despite the emergence of commercial enterprise, the focus is still upon isolated exchange rather than on an organized market.

To take usury is contrary to Scripture; it is contrary to Aristotle; it is contrary to nature, for it is to live without labor; it is to sell time, which belongs to God, for the advantage of wicked men; it is to rob those who use the money lent, and to whom, since they make it profitable, the profits should belong; it is unjust in itself for the benefit of the loan to the borrower cannot exceed the value of the money lent; it is in defiance of sound juristic principles, for when a loan is made, the property in the thing lent passes to the borrower, and why should the creditor demand payment from a man who is merely using what is now his own?

Thus did R. W. Tawney summarize the "mind" of those times on the loan of money. (*Religion and the Rise of Capitalism*, p. 43)

Interest, however, was permissible by virtue of extrinsic titles; that is, for reasons extraneous to the "sterility," unproductiveness of money, principally, compensation for actual loss incurred (*damnum emergens*) or risk run. (I, II, 78, art. 2 ad 5) The first extrinsic title became universally accepted, but the second gained general acceptance gradually by the fifteenth century. With the development of modern industry and commerce and the evolution of complex international finance, the schoolmen justified money interest by expanding the list of titles "extrinsic" to unproductive money.

An illustration of the "sterility" of money in modern experience would be a man who is "financially set" but discovers at the airport he has forgotten his wallet at home. He asks his neighbor, whom he meets there by chance, for let's say three hundred dollars to be paid upon his return within the week. In a few days the debt is repaid. It would be usurious for the lender to demand an interest, granting, *ex hypothesi*—no extrinsic title, no loss incurred, no gain foregone, etc. Such a similar human experience is far from rare. Canon 1543 is hardly an extinct, unrealistic prohibition.

From the sixteenth century on two schools of thought develop: the first comprises some of the early reformers (Luther, Melancthon, Zwingli) and the generality of the later scholastics in continuation of the traditional theory on "sterile" money, while enlarging the number of extrinsic titles justifying interest on money loans; the second school includes an increasing fellowship of Catholic moralists as well as Protestant moralists (Calvin, Beza, *et alii*), who reject the absolutism of their predecessors on the unproductivity of money so that interest can be justified on intrinsic grounds as well as by extrinsic titles.

What remained to the end unlawful, was that which appears
in modern textbooks as "pure interest"—interest as a fixed payment stipulated in advance for a loan of money or wares without risk to the lender . . . . (Tawney, *op. cit.*, 54)

It was in the name of justice that philosophers and theologians
elaborated the fencing restrictions with which to contain the growing
and exploitative power of money. Belatedly modern governments
became responsive to the outraged cries of the disadvantaged without
hope of recovery because they had no recourse to remedial legal
action. (It is a sad commentary on human behavior that justice
which is the most basic of human aspirations has been the most
sluggish of human achievements in all areas of human relations,
i.e. in economy, social intercourse, in matters of political rights,
criminal law, etc.) Legislators have endeavored to circumstance and
restrict the economic vulnerability of the debtors with regulatory
states on a variety of interest transactions—loan sharking, pawn-
brokers, banks, licensed lenders, small loan companies, installment
repayments, checks upon the open market, bankruptcy laws, etc.
The Church's teaching on usurious practices and its moral theories
on extrinsic titles are not a compromise of moral principle, Kung
notwithstanding (31). On the contrary, Canon 1543 is enduringly
operative on the Christian conscience; it is part and parcel of social
justice of which interest, the just price and commutative justice are
moral components.

Rites

The condemnation in the Rites controversy, . . is one of the
main reasons for the large breakdown of the Catholic missions
of modern times in India, China, and Japan. (K. 32)

The advantages of hindsight does not warrant listing this matter
an "error of the ecclesiastical teaching office." The controversy
had its first beginnings in India, when the Jesuit Roberto de Nobili,
confronted with the caste system, chose to dedicate himself exclusively to the conversion of the Hindus by living like a Hindu, much
the same way his predecessor, Francis Xavier, had appealed to the
lower caste. To the scandal and outrage of other missionaries,
Franciscans and Dominicans, Father de Nobili permitted his converts
to keep those national customs in the religious rites he thought were

free from superstition and idolatry. In 1623 Pope Gregory XV responded to the complaints of the Dominican missionaries, decreeing that there should be two classes of missionaries in India: one for the Brahmins and the other for the lower classes. In China, the Jesuit Matteo Ricci planned to convert the populace by first winning over the class of scholarly mandarins. He, too, permitted the Chinese Christians to keep every element of their native culture that was not, in his judgment, clearly superstitious or idolatrous. He also allowed the use of various native terms for God, but whose connotations were not theologically wholly free of misconception. His successor, Father Longobardi, was strongly opposed to allowing the Chinese Christians the use of their own rites. After the advent of Dominicans in China in 1631 the rites controversy took on a disturbing magnitude. Finally the question was placed before Rome in 1643. On the basis of the Dominican representation of the religious ceremonies as betokening idolatry for the Catholic, *Propaganda* issued the first condemnation of such rites in 1645. The Jesuits then sought permission to present evidence of their understanding of these native rites. Following a report by the Jesuit Martino Martini, Pope Alexander VIII in 1656 in a decree "allowed the Chinese the said ceremonies with all superstitions removed, because it seemed that they constituted a rite purely civil and political." At the discussions held during their forced detention at Canton, 1665-68, all the missionaries of all the Orders agreed that it was imperative to practice adaptation in the matter of rites—but what adaptations: when, where and to what extent? The controversy was reopened when Bishop Charles Maigrot, Vicar Apostolic of Fukien, urged the Holy See to re-examine the question in order to ascertain what practices should definitely be forbidden. In Japan the controversy over native rites for Christian liturgy raged no less and proved just as divisive. After protracted discussion by a commission of cardinals, the Holy Office under Pope Clement XI condemned the rites in a decree of 1704, as well as the use of all Chinese terms for God except Tien-chu. On his part, Emperor K'ang Hsi, who had been the first one to issue an edict of freedom for Christianity, now ordered all missionaries to accept a *p'iao*, a certificate of imperial approval, as a condition for continuing their ministries. This was given only to those who promised to respect the rites and customs of the nation. So divided were the missionaries on Oriental symbols, language and rituals, that Pope Clement XI in the apostolic constitution, *Ex illa die* of 1715 sanctioned the earlier decree of 1704 and required the missionaries in China to take an oath of obedience to the prohibitions. Rome also sent Carlo Mezzabarba, Patriarch of Alexandria, to make some accommodations in order to save the missions from total apostasy and persecution by granting eight permissions which mitigated somewhat the rigor of the previous prohibitions. Benedict XIV issued the final judgment in his apostolic constitution *Ex quo singulari* of July 11, 1742, which revoked the "permissions" of Mezzabarba and reiterated the earlier condemnations. The European missionaries complied, but the native clergy apostasized, and the emperor declared that he could not tolerate a religion that was opposed to native customs and cultural expressions. Emperor K'ang Hai ordered by imperial decree the deportation of missionaries from the empire with the exception of those working at the court. His successors, Yung Chien and Ch'ien Lung, carried the persecution to its severest extremes of the death penalty for preaching and embracing Christianity. In the nineteenth century, at the conclusion of the Opium War, China reopened its doors to international trade and by a succession of agreements readmitted Christian missionaries, with France at first as their sole protectorate. An important decision of the Holy See that greatly facilitated mission work was the instruction of Propaganda declaring the veneration of Confucius, ceremonies in honor of the deceased ancestors and other national customs to be purely civil in character and therefore permissible to Catholics. In our times, the Communist takeover of China has paralyzed the free Christian apostolate and checked it by the kulturkampf in India.

With the "best" (?) information available from on the spot witnesses of opposing interpretation, Dominicans and Jesuits half way around the world, bearing in mind the slow means of travel and communication, Rome could do no more, no better. The decisions were *in cautela* of the orthodoxy of faith and worship. It is less than fair to equate these prudential judgments based on the earnest but nonetheless contradictory representations of western missionaries in the Far East to an "error of the ecclesiastical teaching office." The papal decisions in the Rites controversy were not exercises in doctrinal teaching but an authoritative ruling on the interpretative understanding of Oriental signs, symbols and practices in Christian belief and worship, on which the missionaries themselves were deeply divided.

This brief summary is to indicate how sharply divided were the on-the-spot theological appraisals of the Oriental rites that reached Rome.

Secular Power

The maintenance up to the First Vatican Council of the Medieval secular power of the Pope, with aid of all secular and spiritual means of excommunication, which in large measure rendered the papacy incredible as a spiritual ministry. (K.32)

Historians acknowledge that the secular power was in its origins "thrust upon the Papacy from without than assumed by its own initiative." (cf. Dawson, *The Making of Europe*, c.14)

Anyone who studies the Papal correspondence and the *Liber Pontificalis* in the eighth century will, we think, feel that the leadership of the Roman *respublica* in the West was forced upon them (the Popes) rather than deliberately sought, it was only slowly and reluctantly that they drew away from the Byzantine authority, for after all, as civilized members of the Roman state, they preferred the Byzantine to the barbarian. (Carlyle, *Medieval Political Theory I*, 289)

Papal secular power, which reached its apex in the pontificates of Gregory VII, Innocent III and Innocent IV, took two forms— the direct public governance of its own papal proprietary territories and the indirect power *in temporalibus, ratione peccati, ratione justitiae*, with practically illimitable powers of adjudication on the morality of every conceivable human activity, private and public. The Papal *cura totius christianitatis* and the *salus respiblicae christianae* melded into that unique societal phenomenon known as Christendom. When the hour for national states and later on, time for unification of Italy had come and the movement of history was irreversible, the Papal (the Church's) right to temporalities was reduced to the barest evangelical need for freedom of action, which in institutional terms meant sovereignty, and this could not be disassociated from territory. Through all those centuries there was much that was credible that would not be credible today. The Law of Guarantees of 1870 stamped with Cavour's secularizing formula, "a free church *in* a free state," was superseded by the Lateran Treaty of 1929, which provided the minimum desideratum for a free Church *and* a free state.

The spiritual powers of the modern secular states and the secular power of the churches down to the First Vatican Council were not so uncommonly acceptable in Europe and America even though their credibility was waning.

History bears its own credentials and makes no apologies or reversals for being what it is. It is for the philosopher, the theologians, sociologist—those who make a formal structured study of some selective material of history—and for historians themselves— philosophizing, theologizing, sociologizing—to seek for understanding and explanations of the origins, beginnings and motivating forces, and attendant circumstances of the evolution of centuries-old societal patterns. While the Church is in the world by divine ordination visibly active like its divine Founder, in its continuing soteriological mission, but not of this world (not worldly, i.e., merely human origination nor of its ultimate secular goals), the world (non-Catholic as well as Catholic, adversary as well as friendly) can and does force its attentions and its own self-interests upon it and even succeeds to interpenetrate the Church's ministries. The Church cannot wholly escape this envelopment, nor ought to, even as it strives to be the leaven of supernal destinies. But this unavoidable, and perhaps desirable to a significant degree, interpenetration should not be the cause for calling into question the Church's credibility as the divinely instituted and endowed society for the sanctification and eternal salvation of mankind. The prudence and wisdom, and the intemperances and miscalculations, the forced and imposed compromises of its ministers in contending with the "children of this world" can never cancel out—perhaps obscure—the Church's own original and enduring authentic credibility as God's saving presence on earth. The Church's incarnational being has suffered betrayal, flagellations, crucifixion and mockery at the hands of its implacable adversaries as well as invited by the grave and scandalous failings of its own members. Theologians and even the canonists, who are generally more cautious because of the restraints of a legal process, have had the virtuosity for extremes and exaggerations in both of the opposite directions, provoked not infrequently by historical conditions and exigencies for which the magisterial authority and the supreme pastoral concernments of the Church have been in hindsight too facilely faulted. Kung gives us an uprooted history, and his tendentious historicism has the simplicity of unreality.

Much of what he abhors *now* was abetted, approved and credible *then*. For all of the teutonic's insistence that the past be researched and understood *sitz im leben*, in its concrete situation and cultural milieu, Kung retrojects rather arbitrarily, we think, an anachronistic modernity into the past centuries of another "mind." He reads and sees in past church history only what repels him.

Like all events that history shapes little by little from chance beginnings, historic actions are limited to their immediate and partial results; the whole often remains beyond human foresight and the enlarged developments of the course of history are generally beyond human calculation. Events are decisive where a preconceived plan was wanting.

Kung never clearly distinguishes for his readers papal primatial authority and magistral infallibility from the enormous moral and actual political influence of the papacy in temporalities that historical situations (*sitz im leben*) invited for its own survival and endurance. As John Henry Newman observed:

> But, anyhow, the progress of concentration was not the work of the Pope; it was brought about by the changes of times and the vicissitudes of nations. It was not his fault that the Vandals swept away the African sees, and the Saracens those of Syria and Asia Minor, or that Constantinople and its dependencies became the creatures of Imperialism, or that France, England, and Germany would obey none but the author of their own Christianity, or that the clergy and people at a distance were obstinate in sheltering themselves under the majesty of Rome against their own fierce kings and nobles or imperious bishops, even to the imposing forgeries on the world and on the Pope in justification of their proceedings. All this will be fact, whether the Popes were ambitious or not; and still it will be fact that the issue of that great change was a great benefit to the whole of Europe. No one but a Master, who was a thousand bishops in himself at once, could have tamed and controlled, as the Pope did, the great and little tyrants of the Middle Age.

> This is generally confessed now, even by Protestant historians, viz., that the concentration of ecclesiastical power in those centuries was simply necessary for the civilization of Europe. Of course it does not follow that the benefits rendered to the European commonwealth by the political supremacy of the Pope, would, if he was still supreme, be rendered in time to come.

Newman then quotes from Dean Milman's "Latin Christianity." He is speaking of the era of Gregory I., and he says:

The Papacy was the only power which lay not entirely and absolutely prostrate before the disasters of the times—a power which had an inherent strength, and might resume its majesty. It was this power which was most imperatively required to preserve all which was to survive out of the crumbling wreck of Roman civilization. To Western Christianity was absolutely necessary a centre, standing alone, strong in traditionary reverence, and in acknowledged claims to supremacy. Even the perfect organization of the Christian hierarchy might in all probability have fallen to pieces in perpetual conflict; it might have degenerated into a half-secular feudal caste, with hereditary benefices more and more entirely subservient to the civil authority, a priesthood of each nation or each tribe, gradually sinking to the intellectual or religious level of the nation or tribe. On the rise of a power both controlling and conservative hung, humanly speaking, the life and death of Christianity— of Christianity as a permanent, aggressive, expansive, and, to a certain extent, uniform system. There must be a counterbalance to barbaric force, to the unavoidable anarchy of Teutonism, with its tribal, or at the utmost national independence, forming a host of small, conflicting, antagonistic kingdoms. All Europe would have been what England was under the Octarchy, what Germany was when her emperors were weak; and even her emperors she owed to Rome, to the Church, to Christianity. Providence may have otherwise ordained; but it is impossible for man to image by what other organizing or consolidating force the commonwealth of the eastern nations could have grown up to a discordant, indeed, and conflicting league, but still a league, with that unity and conformity of manners, usages, laws, religion, which have made their rivalries, oppugnancies, and even their long ceaseless wars, on the whole to issue in the noblest, highest, most intellectual form of civilization known to man . . . . It is impossible to conceive what had been the confusion, the lawlessness, the chaotic state of the Middle Ages, without the medieval Papacy; and of the medieval Papacy the real father is Gregory the Great. (J. H. Newman, *Difficulties of Anglicans* vol. 2. The Papal Church, pp. 206-223. Longmans, Green, 1907.)

So wrote the Protestant historian of the sociological consequents of the unique spiritual power of the papacy in the worldly affairs of men, kingdoms, and fallen empires, so much so that papal supervisory role and actual intervention became a part of the *ius publicum* of the medieval ages; that is to say, the Christian communities and their temporal rulers willed it so, or better, wanted it so. All this was very credible then. In fact, no other *desideratum* was then conconceivable by the generality of the European community known as Christendom until the French legists and anonymous authors of tracts of the thirteenth century were to challenge first papal and then imperial supremacy over the then emerging nationalist state.

Gregory the Great may be considered, under a certain aspect, as a creator of the political power of the popes. Without wish or claim on his part, he exercised in Rome a paternal power in default of Byzantium to protect its Italian territories against the Lombards and again to counter the crushing fiscal demands both from Byzantium and the Lombards. Rome and Italy could turn only to the Pope for protection. With Pope Stephen's failure of conciliation with the Lombard Astolph, human and political motives influenced the popes to turn to Frankish support. Pepin twice defeated the irreconciliable Astolph, and from the ceded territories St. Peter's partimony became a temporal State.

What was known as "the Donation of Pepin" was not then looked upon as something new nor considered questionable from the religious standpoint. There is no doubt that Pepin, when he stripped Astolph of provinces that nominally belonged to Byzantium, was able to dispose of them as he thought fit. The term "restitution to Peter" was used, since in view of the absenteeism of Byzantium there was no one but the Pope to concern himself with such provinces. Kung more than once fixes upon the *Constitutio Constantini*, the document known as the Donation of Constantine, which would later form the title to which popes and Curia referred to defend their temporal rights against the Germanic emperors. The pretended document that was first mentioned in a letter to Pope Adrian I in 788, later included in the Isidorian or pseudo-Isidorian Collection in the first half of the ninth century and finally inserted in Gratian's Decretals in the twelfth century was confirmed by events when Charlemagne ratified Pepin's donation by enlarging it to include Venetian territory down to the Duchy of Benevento. The first pope to make real and official use of the Donation of Constantine was Pope Leo IX two hundred years after its first appearance. The conjunction of the secular power of the popes over their own propriaetary domains and their spiritual authority as the supreme pastors of the universal Church in the temporalities even of the faithful was still credible in its medieval conception in the later days of royal sovereign states of the fifteenth century, when first the King of Portugal requested of Pope Callistus III, and then the King of Castile of Pope Alexander VI, for privileged grants of spheres of influence, of exclusive rights of trade and colonization, and of exclusive possession of islands and territories. They could not with any surety obtain the recognition and respect of their international rights from rival claimants and adversaries otherwise than through a papal Bull; this constituted (in those times and for those minds) a legal and religious title of the incontestable order. These pontifical grants, sought after by the royal sovereigns themselves, were an exercise of an international authority of the Papacy that developed out of medieval curialists theory in the Middle Ages, on the pontifical rights, —*naturaliter and potentialiter*, over the whole world, infidels not excluded, by virtue as it was conceived of the Church's universal apostolic mission of Christianization. Kung uproots history from the soil of history and from the minds of its contemporaries. There have been times when the Church fills a vacuum left by political society and its failure to act effectively; there have been times when temporal princes themselves turned to the papacy for adjudication; there was a time when the disengagement of the Church from the social and political fabric was unthinkable for all of its contemporaries: if past history may bear lessons for future generations, those of the future have no warrant, surely no understanding, for refashioning the past to their own image. The impact of the succeeding centuries of history—the breakup of Christendom, the post-Reformation adversary, political and religious alignments, the religious intolerances and persecutions, the State Churches, the French Revolution, the Napoleonic stirrings of European nationalism, the unification of Italy—these disengaged the Papacy from its circumstanced historical existence of the past and its spiritual authority, with merely a token territorial basis of independent sovereignty and no more than a moral directive force in the temporalities of men-endures inviolable and credible. The credibility of the papacy and of the Church is in its divine institution, its divine commission of universal evangelization in its spiritual and supernatural enpowerments and in the sanctity that it inspires and fosters. The papacy cannot escape history, nor does it dictate it; but the manner in which it touches the secular world in temporal terms and the points of contact are more often than not a requirement of forces outside its own control.

I have spoken earlier of Kung exploiting an uprooted history. In this matter Kung has not had "the mind" of those times. The deprivation of the papal territories in the twentieth century actually won world-wide sympathy for the Roman Pontiff, Pope Pius IX.

Critical-Historical Exegesis of the Bible

> Finally, at the beginning of the century, the numerous condemnations of the approach of modern critical-biblical exegesis to the authorship of the books of the Bible, to source criticism in the Old and New Testament, to historicity and literary forms, to the Comma Johanneum, to the Vulgate; etc. (K 32)

Here as elsewhere Kung enjoys the immediate rhetorical advantage of assailing the Church with a few words or sentence without, in all charity, giving the general reader the *Sitz im Leben der Kirche*, the critical historical circumstances with which the Church of Christ had to contend to safeguard the faith of its believers. To take full measure of Kung's statement it is necessary to give a summary review of the origins and development of modern biblical learning, its methodologies, the philosophical and religious presuppositions of the scholars and their significance for Church orthodoxy.

Critical studies of Sacred Scripture were very sparse before its vigorous first stirrings in the nineteenth century. Origen's *Hexapla Biblia* was the earliest attempt at biblical criticism of the Old Testament. In his *Ecclesiastical History* Eusebius has preserved for us highly significant data about the New Testament. He himself drew parallel studies of the gospels and divided them into enumerated sections that are to be found to this day in Nestle's Greek New Testament. St. Augustine in his *De consensu evangelistarum* cautioned that not infrequently strict chronology yields to topical recollections of the evangelists and that the *logia* of Jesus were always recorded faithfully, but not necessarily always *verbatim*. The Fathers of the Church met the problem of scriptural discrepancies by concordism facilitated by the allegorical exegesis of the Alexandrian school. Medieval exegesis was for the most part content to utilize four senses of Sacred Scripture: the literal or historical; the allegorical or Christological; the tropological or moral or anthropological; the anagogical or eschatological. The emergence of theology as a distinct and separate science disengaged it considerably from the prevailing allegorical exegesis. But Thomas Aquinas was to point out that metaphor is a literal sense, something Origen and the Alexandrian school failed to see because they mistakenly understood the literal sense to be only what the words expressed, without notice of the author's intent. "Nothing necessary to faith is contained in the spiritual sense that Scripture does not put forward elsewhere in the literal sense." (*Summa* 1.1.10 ad 1) Nonetheless, allegorical exegesis predominated the Middle Ages. The Reformers' *sola scriptura* and vernacular translations led actually to a more intense dogmatic and theological preoccupation, with only isolated and not insignificant instances of critical inquiry by Karlstadt, Flacius, Camerarius, Cappellius, Grotius, Cocceius.

Modern biblical criticism began in the middle of the seventeenth century with a French Oratorian priest, Richard Simon. By a critical reading of the Church Fathers and by resorting to all Oriental manuscripts available, he was the first to employ the twin critical methods of higher criticism, historical and literary (as distinct from textual or lower criticism). He undertook a historical study of the origin of the traditional form of the text of the New Testament and, at least in part, of the study of the Pentateuch and other parts of the Old Testament. On the basis of critical literary and historical analysis he concluded that Moses was not the only author of Pentateuch; that behind the supposition of unitary authors of some biblical books was a corps of writers; and most significantly for the nineteenth and twentieth centuries biblical criticism, oral tradition precedes the sources of literary history. Richard Simon's contribution to Catholic exegesis was stilled for a century, no thanks to the persecuting zealotry of Boussuet.

Father Richard Simon provided the not-too-distant spur—his proscribed works were republished and greatly acclaimed a century later—to the turn of the century search beyond source criticism, beyond the canonical and noncanonical (Lk. 1:1) Christian literature to the preliterary oral *paradosis*, the apostolic and nonapostolic traditions, and if possible, to the earliest teaching, which the primitive Church preserved in its *kerygma, didache* and liturgies. The Catholic doctor Astruc discovered that the alternate uses of *Yahweh* and *Elohim* in the Old Testament occurred in clearly distinguishable units as to constitute separate components; he maintained at least ten other separate sections were discernable. While Simon and Astruc seemingly posed a serious assault upon the Reformation, the Protestants' supreme and sole authority of Scripture, by the characteristically Tridentine "Tradition and Scripture" approach, it is to the nineteenth century liberal Protestants we are indebted for the documentary source theories, and in the following century, for their search for forms or patterns of the preliterary oral traditions that preceded the gospels and from which the authors and redactors of written canonical gospels drew and themselves regrouped forms of narration and Jesus' *logia* to accord with their own theological purpose.

From 1774-78 Lessing published posthumously the *Wolfenbuttel Fragments*, seven sections from Reimarus' unpublished *Apology* or *Defensive Writing in Behalf of the Reasonable Worshippers of God*. It was the most powerful insertion of the German Aufklarung in biblical studies. A deist, Reimarus distinguished between the historical Jesus, a Jewish revolutionary who had failed to establish an earthly kingdom and the Christ of faith, contrived by his disciples who had stolen his body from the Tomb, propagated the falsehood of his resurrection and gave enduring form to this deception in the books of the New Testament. The unwitting merit of this rationalist rejection of the supernatural was to lead to the explicit formulation of the quest of the real historical Jesus and His identity with the Risen Jesus through the Gospels. Just when the sterility of higher criticism had become too apparent because of the exhausting analyses by which the vital meaning of the texts were often spent, the future of biblical studies augured well with the new approach of *Formgeschichtliche Methode* (the history of oral patterns of tradition behind the final literary composition) and *Sitz im Leben* (the actual life situation, both brought to definition by Gunkel from his own and the discernments of his predecessors). Unfortunately, the naturalist and rationalist prepossessions of the deists who predominated in the German universities colored the interpretation of scriptural data and rendered suspect biblical criticism itself. Scripture was being dismantled, dissected, despiritualized, and the salvific events and message of Jesus were reduced to items, at best of a humanist ethic. For example, Wellhausen applied the Hegelian evolutionary postulate, thesis, antithesis, synthesis to the history of the apostolic church, setting Pauline universalism against Petrine Jewish-Christian particularism and legalism to conclude to a second century Catholicism. Semler, Schleiermacher, Ritschl, Wrede, Reiss, etc. all believed that they were liberating a beneficent way of life from "salvation history" and its dogmas to reconstruct "what really happened" within their conception of what they claimed cannot be known, the historical Christ (Schweitzer, Harnack, Bultmann).

Whatever the divergent understanding of Christianity of the biblical critics of the latitudinarian liberal Protestantism, each contributed insights, legitimate questions, an improvement of methodologies and the insistence that all the relevant disciplines be consulted: philology, textual criticism, the history of the ancient Near East, comparative literature, comparative religion, popular traditions, philosophical and cultural influences, archeology—everything that would serve the authentic understanding of the Scripture texts.

In recent years, the usefulness and misuse of form criticism has been clearly stated by V. Taylor:

> It is a mistake to suppose that Form Criticism necessarily leads to Scepticism, for this result is reached only by ignoring the limits of the method and by using historical assumptions which vitiated the inquiry from the beginning. (*The Life and Ministry of Jesus*, 21)

On November 18, 1893, Pope Leo XIII in *Providentissimus Deus* stated that the Church is the infallible interpreter of the Bible in matters of faith and morals; that divine inspiration and its consequence, inerrancy, covers the totality of scripture without exception.   Protesting against the excesses of higher criticism, the Pontiff exhorts Catholic scholars to a profound study of Oriental languages, of ancient versions of scripture and, above all, of original texts, and to a judicious study of the art of criticism.

The beneficent consequences which *Providentissimus Deus* augured were unfortunately sharply checked by the grave crisis of Modernism and by its immediate and decisive condemnation by Pope Pius X. Modernism was a movement of basic attitudes, tendencies and directions, unplanned and spontaneous, which in their daring forms, particularly in the fields of exegesis, ecclesiology, apologetics, Church governance and philosophy of religion, sought to refashion the Church, indeed, the essence, meaning and purposes of Christianity into an earthly mold; that is, draw it within the wholly human and natural, thanks to no small part, but not exclusively to the excesses of higher criticism of German liberal Protestantism and its dissolution of the supernatural.   On July 3, 1907, a decree of the Holy Office, *Lamentabili sane exitu,* approved in *forma communi* by Pius X a syllabus of sixty-five Modernist propositions condemned and reaffirmed conversely the Church's right to interpret Scripture, biblical inspiration, the historicity of the gospels, revelation, Christology, the fact of the Resurrection, the origin of the Church and of the Sacraments from Christ, the objectivity of dogma and dogma's correspondence with history. In a determined effort to trap *Modernism* in its totality, on September 8 that same year, Pius X promulgated the encyclical *Pascendi dominici gregis*, which gave the movement its name, "modernism" (the refuge of all heresies) and the appearance of doctrinal coherence which it never had but whose terminal convergences and logical development warranted. *Pascendi* concentrates on the two radical sources of Modernism: *agnosticism*, which denies the validity of rational argument in religious discourse; and secondly, *immanentism*, which derives religious truths from the intrinsic needs of life. Consequently, faith is reduced to the discernment of the stirrings of God within the human consciousness. Dogma is no more than an intellectual reconstruction of this internal religious experience and always subject to change, and the need to give it visible form created the sacraments. Scripture is a collection of the religious experiences of the Jews and of the first Christians. The Church is born from the need to embody in enduring form the collective religious experience of the followers of Christ. On September 1, 1909, in *motu proprio, Sacrorum Antistitumm*, Pius X required the clergy to take the anti-modernist oath which, in its profession of faith affirms the demonstrability of the existence of God, the value of rational and historical foundations of the faith, the institution of the Church by Christ, the unchangeability of dogmas and the role of the intellect in the act of faith. The intent of the oath was not only a solemn doctrinal and moral commitment but also to foreclose the probabilities of crypto-modernists. Of the principals of Modernism Alfred Loisy, upon his excommunication as *vitandus*, on March 8, 1908, publicly gave up his Catholic faith and all Christianity, professing a "Religion of Humanity" based on a vague agnosticism. George Tyrrell was dismissed from the Society of Jesus, suspended *a divinis* and in 1907 excommunicated, his case being reserved to the Holy See. He denied papal infallibility and considered dogma as merely protective but totally relative with no absolute value guaranteed to be true. Houtin—"there is not and has never been such a thing as a revealed religion"—rejected the whole Modernist design and became an agnostic. Hebert denied personality in God, left the Church, and taught at the Masonic University at Brussels. Turmel, unlike many modernists who wrote anonymously or under pseudonyms, wrote orthodoxy under his own name and as an unbeliever under an assumed name. Many Modernists chose to remain within the Church with the purpose of converting it to their own image; others, who had been drawn by its social and political idealism, became alarmed at its heterodoxy and remained devoted to the Church. Now it is within the historical context of this *Sitz im Leben der Kirche*, wherein the Supreme Pastor of the Universal Church, mindful to "tend and feed" the flock of the Risen Jesus, acted to guard the faith of Catholic believers, that we must weigh the misnamed "condemnations" "at the turn of the century" that Kung deprecates (32).

On the 30th of October 1902, Pope Leo XIII established by his apostolic letter *Vigilantiae* the Pontifical Biblical Commission with the instruction that:

> having first of all, rightly ascertained the trends of modern scholars in this field, should not regard as foreign to their purpose any of the recent discoveries of scholarship; rather, they should be on the alert, whenever anything has been found useful for Biblical exegesis, immediately to avail themselves of it and, by their writings, put it at the service of all. (*Enchiridion Biblicum* 137-148)

In the early years the Commission issued decrees and decisions (*responsa*); in more recent times the Commission has issued, instead, "instructions" (*instructiones*). None of the negative responses were "condemnations" as Kung unfairly calls them. They were cautionary, protective directives insisting on conclusive demonstration and sufficiency of evidence. For example, on "Implicit Citations" in Scripture, "in the negative, except . . . proved by strong arguments" (Feb. 13, 1905); on the "appearance of history in Scripture—*narrationes specietenus tantum historicae*—in the negative, except . . . it is proved by strong arguments that the sacred writer did not wish to put down true history" (June 23, 1905); on the Mosaic Authenticity of the Pentateuch, the "arguments . . . are not of such weight" to impugn his authorship (June 27, 1906); on the historical character of the earlier chapters of Genesis, allowing for metaphor, figurative language and the scientific naivete of the author, the Commission insisted on general creation, special creation, formation of the first woman, the unity of the human race, original innocence, the divine precept, the transgression, the Fall (June 30, 1909). On the *Comma Johanneum*:

> To the question: "Whether it can be safely denied, or at least called into doubt that the text of St. John in the first epistle,

c. 5, v. 7, is authentic, which reads as follows: "And there are three that give testimony in heaven, the Father, the Word, and the Holy Spirit. And these three are one?"—the response was given January 13, 1897, in the negative.

Declaration of June 2, 1927, the Holy Office:

This decree was passed to check the *audacity of private teachers* who *attribute to themselves the right* either of rejecting entirely the authenticity of the Johannine comma, or at least of calling it into question by their final *judgment*. But it was not meant at all to prevent Catholic writers from investigating the subject more fully, and, after weighing the arguments accurately on both sides, with the moderation and temperance which the gravity of the subject requires, from inclining toward an opinion in opposition to its authenticity, *provided they professed that they were ready to abide by the judgment of the Church*, to which the duty was delegated by Jesus Christ not only of interpreting Holy Scripture but also of guarding it faithfully. (Dz. 2199) (Italics supplied)

Twenty years earlier, January 11, 1906, Pius X wrote to the Bishop of La Rochelle, Le Camus:

You deserve praise for the manner in which you explain Sacred Scripture, that is, that approach which, under the governance of the Church, strives for complete dedication to truth and for the glory of the Catholic doctrine. We censure the temerity of those who attribute more to novelty than to the magisterium of the Church and who do not hesitate to employ an unrestrained freedom of criticism. *We disapprove no less those who will not deviate in any manner from the customary exegesis of Scripture, even when together with the preservation of the faith a good growth in studies requires it.* You proceed correctly between these extremes, and by your example you show that nothing is to be feared for the Sacred Books from the true progress of the science of criticism, but, on the contrary favorable light can be gained thereby. (Latin in *Civilta Cattolica*, a. 57 [1906] 11484 ff.)

For all the teutonic insistence on *Sitz im Leben*, Kung takes rhetorical advantage of the uninformed general reader by a hurried and exciting congestion of "condemnations," but it is hardly conducive to enlightenment. Actually, none of the negative responses forbade Catholic biblical scholars to pursue further investigations for stronger arguments, for a sufficiency of evidence provided they always respected the teaching authority of the Church. Had Kung recalled the *Response to Cardinal Suhard* (January 16, 1948) from the Pontifical Biblical Commission concerning the *Pentateuch* and *Genesis* 1-11, he would know that those responses "at the beginning of the century" were in no way opposed to further scientific examination of Scriptural problems. Even in our own times, after the magna charta of Pope Pius XII on Scriptural studies, *Divino Afflante Spiritu* (1943), and its further expansion in the Decree *Sancta Mater Ecclesia* (1964) on the employment of the Form-critical Method on the historicity of the Gospels, the pastoral responsibility of the Shepherd of the universal Church to guard the faith of its believers is manifest in the monitory tones of *Humani Generis* (1950), in the Holy Office *Monitum* on Historicity (June 20, 1961) and in the occasional admonitions from Pope Paul VI–"opinions in exegesis and theology often borrowed from bold but blind secular philosophies." The faithful have been alerted to the fact that in the midst of biblical scholars of eminent learning, deep piety and orthodoxy, there are not a few Babylonian theologues who take delight in theological brinkmanship and who cast the pall of distrust beyond themselves.

"Feed My lambs–tend My sheep."
(Jn. 21:15-18; cf. Jn.10)

Honorius

Kung cites the case of Pope Honorius as to how Catholic theologians "ward off any questioning of infallibility." (p. 33) It seems that Kung's *simplisme* takes advantage of the complexities of the case of Pope Honorius.

Nestorianism was condemned by the Third Ecumenical Council at Ephesus by declaring ontologically a real hypostatic union of the divine and human natures in the Incarnate Word and rejecting as heretical a merely moral union with a human personality. Twenty years later, the Council of Chalcedon (451) incorporated Pope St. Leo's *Tome* into its formula of faith:

We confess one and the same Christ Jesus, the only begotten Son, whom we acknowledge to have two natures, without confusion, transformation, division or separation between them . . . the attributes of each nature are safeguarded and subject in one person.

This formula stood as the bulwark of orthodoxy against Nestorianism on the side and Monophytism on the other. But Monophytism was to persist in the question that had not yet been explicitly or officially considered; namely, the appropriate and correct formulas to designate Christ's human and divine activity.

Sergius, Patriarch of Constantinople, wrote to Pope Honorius to settle the dispute about the formulae "one operation" and "two operations" that was then rendering Christian unity apart. Sergius recommended that both formulae be dropped, suggesting (with emphasis) that the controversy was a matter of words. He urged that silence on further disputation be imposed. Sergius' own doctrinal preference was "one will." Historically, this Christological controversy must be referred back to Eutyches, who in the middle of the fifth century held that the substantial union of the two natures, divine and human, resulted in a single *physis* (nature). He thereby ignored the terminological advance which occurred between Ephesus and Chalcedon, which explained that hypostasis (person) and physis (nature) did not denote exclusively and identically the same meaning, as had been the earlier understanding according to St. Cyril in the affirmation of the divinity and single personality of Christ against Nestorius. While adhering to the divinity of the *Logos*, Eutyches sought to avoid the dual personalities taught by Nestorius by disparaging the integral humanity of Christ and subtracting its human will and the properly human operations.

Pope Honorius' two epistles to Sergius are an embarrassing amalgam of indisputable orthodoxy and equally incongruous statements. Could it be that Honorius did not see that a matter of orthodoxy was really in issue and not merely a question of the appropriateness of formulae that threatened to divide Christians, as Sergius so ominously forbode?

(1) Epistola *"Scripta fraternitatis vestrae"* ad Sergium, patriarchae Constantinopolitae, a. 634. (2) Epistola *"Scripta dilectissimi filii"* ad Sergium, a. 634. In these two epistles of Pope Honorius to Sergius, Honorius' overall insistence is on defined dogmas of the two natures of the Incarnate Word and works proper to each nature,

and the integral distinction of each nature from the other, the divine and human, in the hypostatic unison of the divine personality.

> Duce Deo perveniemus usque ad mensuram rectae fedei, quam apostoli veritatis Scripturarum sanctarum funiculo extenderunt: Confitentes Dominum Jesum Christum, mediatorem Dei et hominum (cf. 1 Tim. 2:5) *operatum divina media humanitate Verbo Dei naturaliter* (gr.; hypostatice) *unita, eumdemque operatum humana ineffabiliter atque singulariter assumpta carne* (gr.; in) *discrete, inconfuse atque inconvertibiliter* plena divinitate . . . ut nimirum stupenda mente *mirabiliter manentibus utramque naturarum differentiis* cognoscatur (Caro passiblis divinitati) uniri (DS 487, italics supplied)

Then there follows that troublesome text:

> Unde et *unam volumtatem* fatemur Domini nostri Jesu Christi . . . .

In context patently heterodox connotation takes on orthodox meaning to the extent that Honorius discountenanced the expression "two principles of operations" (the "two wills"), which he applied to two contrarient wills *in* Our Lord's human nature—nam lex alia in membris, aut voluntas diversa non fuit vel *contraria* Salvatori, quia super legem natus est humanae condiciones. Apparently, Honorius is thinking about the Pauline two laws within our members, whose energies not infrequently work at cross purposes because of the loss of the praeternatural gift of integrity, consequent to the Fall. Sergius, on the other hand, understood the one or two operations or wills as predicates of the two separate natures, the divine and human, and within this understanding the "one will" is patently heretical. Further, Honorius' insistence that there was one operator in the Incarnate Word, may be acceptable in the light of his own explanation that he seems to be referring to the one divine personality—(was he fearing the dangers of Arianism, which had never left the Church entirely?) Quia Dominus Jesus Christus, Filius ac Verbum Dei, "per quem facta sunt omnia" (Jn. 1:3), (these are indisputably *in personam*)—ipse sit unus operator divinitatis atque humanitatis. What immediately follows explicitly makes clear that Honorius accepted Sergius' suggestion that the dispute was about words:

> Utrum autem propter opera divinitatis et humanitatis, una

an geminae operationes debeant derivatae dici vel intelligi,
ad nos ista pertinere non debent: relinguentes ea grammaticis,
Qui solent parvulis exquisita derivando nomina venditare.
(Italics added)

And so Honorius relegates the issue of "words" to the gram-
marians.

The theory of the two contrarient wills *in* Christ's human nature
as Honorius' understanding of the problem placed before him by
Sergius is not so insubstantial or ingenuous as it might appear.
Because that is precisely how Pope John IV explains the words
of Honorius about the "two wills" in his letter, "*Dominus qui
dixit*," to Constantius, the Emperor (641):

Numquam habuit contrarias voluntates, nec repugnavit
voluntati mentis eius voluntas carnis eius . . . decentur dicimus
et veraciter confitemur, unam voluntatem in sanctae ipsius
dispensationis humanitate, et non duas contrarias mentis et
carnis predicamus . . . . (DS 496)

And Pope John concludes:

So, my aforementioned predecessor said concerning the
mystery of the Incarnation of Christ, that there were not in
Him, as in us sinners, contrary wills of mind and flesh; and
certain ones converting this to their own meaning suspected
that he taught one will of His divinity and humanity which is
altogether contrary to the truth . . . .

Honorius' second letter, "*Scripta dilectissimi filii*," to Sergius
repeats his intention not to define doctrine because as he saw it,
no doctrinal matter was at issue, and within his own explanations—
the dogmas of one divine personality of the Incarnate Word and the
two natures, human and divine, in Christ, unconfusedly, inseparably,
and unchangeably performing their proper (works) for us are maintained without equivocation.

non unam vel duas operationes in mediatore Dei et hominum
definire, sed utrasque naturas in uno Christo unitate naturali
copulatas . . . *non nos* oportet unam vel duas operationes *defin-
ientes* praedicare. (DS 488. Italics supplied)

He disclaims settling definitely the question of formulae—what matters is the reaffirmation of the two natures and one divine personality—*naturarum differentias integras confitentes . . . propia operantes.*

But the problem persists—why did the Sixth General Council at Constantinople (III) include Honorius in its condemnation of all who held and taught Monothelism?   Unless we take Pope Honorius' texts by face value—what he intended to do and disclaimed to do, what dogmas he insistently repeated, how he understood the problem, etc.—then that condemnation must fall equally no less upon Pope John IV, who defended Honorius' explanation within the terms of Honorius intentions—and this no one has ever done. An examination of the council document discloses that the condemnation of Honorius faults him gravely for failing to recognize the latent heresy of his clever correspondent, for his negligence in "permitting the immaculate faith to be stained," as Pope Leo II said when he confirmed the decrees of the Sixth General Council, and again, as he wrote in a letter to the Bishops of Spain, "for not having extinguished the flame of heretical teaching, as became the Apostolic authority, and for fostering it by his negligence."   It seems that despite Pope John's saving commentary, some of the faithful had been misled or scandalized by Honorius' response, which *ex verbis* "one will," although circumstanced by orthodox premises unintentionally contributed to doctrinal ambiguity.   As far as the papal office itself is concerned, the Council Fathers gave vibrant testimony to its unique prerogatives. It received and acclaimed the dogmatic letter of Pope Agatho, "*Consideranti mihi*," on the hypostatic union addressed to the Emperors (March 27, 680):

> Summus nobiscum concertabat *Apostolorum princeps*; illius enim imitatorem et *sedis successorem* habuimus fautorem et divini sacramenti illustrantem per litteras. *Confessionem* tibi *a Deo scriptam* illa Romana antiqua civitas obtulit . . . et *per Agathonem Petrus loquebatur*, et cum omnipotenti Corregnatore pius imperator simul decernabas tu, qui a Deo decretus es." (Italics supplied)

"Chief of the Apostles . . . his successor . . . the confession (of faith) which historic Rome offered Constantius was *written* by God . . . .   *Peter spoke through Agatho*," etc. The Fathers of the Council of Constantinople sent their decrees to Pope Leo II for ratification in order to render them binding upon all the faithful and pastors. Such were the beliefs of the Council Fathers about the papal teaching office and its unique prerogative to teach divine truths (Christology) and its original authority by divine dispensation to authenticate conciliar teaching. Add to all this that Honorius, with or without a saving interpretation, was not addressing himself in his two letters to Sergius as Supreme Pastor of the Universal Church. John Henry Newman forcibly underscores how so far distant are the two letters of Honorius from the authoritative and solemn pronouncements of popes who intend to invoke their apostolic authority in matters of faith and morals. (cf. *Certain Difficulties Felt by Anglicans in Catholic Teaching* vol. II [1907] pp. 315-317)

Teaching has no sacramental visible signs; it is an *opus operantis*, and mainly a question of intention . . . . The pope cannot address his people East and West, North and South, without mentioning it . . . nor can he exert his "Apostolic authority" without knowing he is doing so . . . no words of Honorius proceeded from his Prerogative of infallible teaching, which were not accompanied with the intention of exercising that prerogative . . . .

What resemblance do these letters of his (Honorius) written almost as private instructions, bear to the "pius Episcopus, Servus Servorem Dei, Sacro approbante Concilio, *ad perpetuam rei memoriam*," or with the "Si quis huic nostrae definitione contradicere (quod Deus avertat) presumpserit, *anathema sit*", etc.

And to those who insist that at least Honorius was privately in his own person heretical, in spite of the orthodoxy that Honorius repeatedly reaffirms, in spite of the saving interpretation by Pope John of the ill-advised formula of the "one will," in spite of Honorius' disclaimer to settle definitively the verbal formulation, Newman responds:

At the utmost, it only decides that Honorius in his own person was a heretic, which is inconsistent with no Catholic doctrine. (317)

Now by what eminence of virtue, theological learning or gnostic charism does Kung justify his charge that theologians from the days of Pope John IV to John Henry Newman and since "ward off any questioning of infallibility" because in conscience they see no such question involved. Kung's *simplisme* takes advantage of the complexities of the case of Pope Honorius.

Animadversions on Kung's List of the "Errors of the Ecclesiastical Teaching Office"

A number of Kung's "errors of the ecclesiastical teaching office" (which actually began in *Candid Preface*) are nothing more than the converse of Kung's own prepossessions on artificial birth control, mixed marriages, priestly celibacy, a latitudinarian ecumenism; others betray his ill-concealed aversion for the Roman curia, for indulgences and for theologians who teach according to "Roman" doctrine; that is, papal teaching. Others are frankly crude charges that Pope Paul VI has failed the faithful by his encyclicals on the Church (*Ecclesiam Suam*), on the Eucharist (*Mysterium Fidei*), on sacerdotal celibacy (*Sacerdotalis Coelibatus*) the *Credo*, Pope Paul VI's proclamation hailing Mary, *Mater Ecclesiae*; and still other "errors" are nothing more than an exploitation of uprooted history —usury, Galileo, Rites controversy and the problematics of modern critical-historical, biblical exegesis, Honorius, Eastern church schism —not to mention his false antithesis between primacy of jurisdiction and primacy of service and, not least, his Lutheran interpolation of Pauline theology on law, the gospel and freedom, and perhaps thereby hangs the tale of Kung's ecclesiology and his acerbic assault upon papal infallibility. Let there be no doubt about it—his book is not an *Inquiry*, despite his avowal to the contrary, as each reader may see for himself.

Apart from Kung's credibility as a historian of fact and of theology, we cannot here entirely foreclose two observations. First, these alleged errors are stated categorically without any of the intellectual inhibition and incapacitations that Kung declares all propositional truths to be heir to (pp. 157-175).

> Propositions can be true or false—and add to it: propositions can be true *and* false. (cf. 169, 170)

One would suppose that Kung's theory of cognition would have tempered his complete self-assurance on the "errors of the ecclesiastical teaching office." Secondly, it is this writer's considered judgment that it is more than highly questionable that these were really errors at all; they were certainly not errors *in any way* of the ecclesiastical teaching authority touching matters of revelation, doctrinal and moral.

We conclude this summary review of Kung's credibility as a historian by examining here his use of two passages from St. Augustine's *De Trinitate* I, iii, 5, with which he introduces his work and appends at its conclusion. At the beginning:

> I ask my readers to make common cause with me when they share my convictions; to keep an open mind when they share my doubts. I ask them to correct me if I make a mistake, to return to my way of thinking if they do.

At the end of the book, the quotation continues immediately from the above excerpt:

> So shall we walk together in charity to him of whom it is said: "Seek his face at all times." I would like to join with all my readers in a pledge before God to do this, in all my books.

And then, not without telling significance on the thrust of Augustine's text, Kung leaves out the following:

> And especially in the present one where we are investigating the unity of Trinity, of the Father, the Son, and the Holy Spirit. For nowhere else is the error more dangerous, the search more laborious and the results more rewarding.

He continues after the omission, to the end of c. 3 of St. Augustine's *De Trinitate*.

De Trinitate

The excerpts from St. Augustine have a profundity deeper than the rhetoricians, *reddere benevolos.* The intellectual honesty, earnestness and sincerity of the passages is motivated by his faith and love of a defined dogma of the Catholic Church, the Most Blessed Trinity. Kung's use of St. Augustine is misapropos. St. Augustine does not under the guise of an "inquiry" proceed to cast doubt and to challenge the credal faith in the Trinitarian mystery.

His *opus*, sixteen years in composition, is essentially a response and refutation of Arian reading of Scriptures (have not all the Christian churches since, read Scripture differently?)—and by his insistence upon the Incarnation as the most appropriate manner for the redemption of mankind, he anticipates the answers to the Nestorian and Monophysite heresies which the Fathers of the Councils of Ephesus and Chalcedon were to give. He exercises himself energetically by philosophical explanations to remove any connotation of inferiority, inequality about any of the three Divine Persons from the scriptural expressions about "begotten" and "sending." He reverses the approach of Greek speculation by beginning with the unity of divine nature (this is more easily accessible to human credibility), and then argues through Scriptural data to the distinction of the Three Persons rather than begin with the Trinity of Divine Persons and then, with greater difficulty, work to the unity of the divine nature.   In a zealous discovery for human persuasions that lend themselves to dispose the human mind toward the Trinity, he discerns thirteen of the twenty-two "trinities" (to be found in his other works), those celebrated human psychological trinitarian parallelisms or analogies, i.e., memory, understanding and love, in the persevering endeavor to understand the divine processions. All in all, St. Augustine strives with every intellectual enterprise to make the Trinity credible.   His very first words stress his prejudicial zeal. "Our pen is on the watch for the sophistries of those who consider it beneath their dignity *to begin with faith."* (I, 1. Italics supplied.)

It is not so with Hans Kung.   Despite his avowed intention to make an "inquiry," his work is a relentless assault upon the credibility of a solemnly defined Church dogma.   He too, like St. Augustine, exercises his faculties and knowledge vigorously but each to opposite purpose.   Augustine to defend a Church dogma; Kung to belittle it and reject it.   Neither in intention nor objective does Kung walk in the steps of St. Augustine, though he uses St. Augustine's vocabulary.

The terminology of the political sociologist so angrily rampant in the first thirty pages contracts thereafter, perhaps through weariness, to the invariables of "conservative," "reactionary," "absolutist," and their synonyms to mark indelibly clear the identity of the dogmas, moral doctrine and church government to which Kung objects.   On the other hand, his own theological restructuring of Catholic ecclesiology is incandescently "progressive," that one word suffices.   Subject to correction, the word "orthodoxy" scarcely ever appears, if at all.
(see page 112)

Papal Magisterium and Natural Law

Kung readily acknowledges that Pope Paul VI made an "unambiguous decision"; "the encyclical (*Humanae Vitae*) is clear and unequivocal"; "it would be an illusion to think that this document might be withdrawn or revised in the foreseeable future." Kung (35) finds "the substantiation of the encyclical from the natural law not convincing," and quotes (36) with approval, Johannes Neumann of Tubingen that the doctrine "is made up of an inappropriate medley of Platonic-Aristotelian-Thomistic ideas."

My own reaction to *Humanae Vitae* was a trilogy of articles in defense of Pope Paul VI and of the doctrine of that superb encyclical: *Papal Magisterium and Humanae Vitae* (*THOUGHT*, 1969); *Academic Dissent: An Original Ecclesiology* (*THOMIST*, 1970); *Papal Magisterium, Natural Law, and Humanae Vitae* (*AMERICAN JOURNAL OF JURISPRUDENCE*, 1971). When we choose to quote from these articles on the natural law in *Humanae Vitae*, we do so in the economy of work with no other presumptuous intent.

Our comments on the use of the natural law in *Humanae Vitae*, are, we believe, more correspondent to its contextual place in Church teaching:

It has been noted in some quarters that since the encyclical makes several references to the natural moral law, might not the faithful rightly raise epistemological questions which respectfully may challenge the intrinsic validity of the natural-law reasoning as embodied in the encyclical. But, reference to the natural moral law in *Humanae Vitae* is invariably conjoined with revelation, which, as we have noted earlier (cf. p. 389, 390), has also been true in the encyclicals of preceding Pontiffs. For example, a "teaching founded on the natural law, illumined and enriched by divine revelation," (4), "human and Christian vision of marriage," (14), "the entire moral law, both natural and evangelical," (18), "natural and divine law," (23,25), "the fulness of conjugal love," as illustrated by Christ's love for the Church," (25), "to diminish in no way the saving teaching of Christ," (29), the "holiness of marriage lived in its entire human and Christian fulness," (29), and so on. This conjunction of the natural moral law with the supernatural is not merely additive in the sense that in the present frail condition of mankind it is a morally necessary corrective to the discernments of reason alone of the exigencies of the natural law. The natural moral law is part of God's will for the salvation of mankind revealed through the Incarnate Word who designated Peter and the apostles and their successors to the end of time as guardians and authentic interpreters of all the moral law. The Church then, may teach the requirements of the natural law with the assistance of Christian revelation authoritatively and provide the faithful with a more reliable moral doctrine than can be ascertained by unaided natural reason. This is not to deny that fallen man can by reason alone rationally demonstrate the existence of the natural law, nor to suggest that the Church is indifferent to the instructions of reason on the moral law. We are simply affirming that when the Church teaches authoritatively matters of natural morality, it does not do so as a master metaphysician any more than did Peter and the apostles. For centuries, the faithful were guided by the authentic and authoritative teaching of the Church without benefit of philosophical systems and the science of theology, and until the Council of Nicea, without solemn definitions. This is the profound significance of the repeated reference in *Humanae Vitae* to the Church's constant apostolic teaching through time. The validity of her teaching rests primarily on Christ's commission to her and on the abiding assistance of the Holy Spirit. The encyclical does make its appeal to reason, it discourses in part of the biological process, of demography, of the demoralizing consequences of contraceptive practices, of the nature of conjugal love. But the internal and external obedience of the faithful is directed to the doctrine propounded by reason "of the mandate entrusted by Christ" (6) to the Church. It is not dependent upon nor proportioned to the intrinsic merits of the encyclical as a philosophical argumentation, as a scientific treatise, as a sociological tract. Like his Divine Master, the Vicar of Christ does make an appeal to reason (as well as to the Christian vision and the charismatic teaching authority of the Church). But also in the manner of his Lord, he too may teach, "Amen, amen, I say unto you. Thou shalt . . . thou shalt not . . . ." (*Thought, op. cit.,* 395, 396)

All referrals to the natural moral law in *Humanae Vitae*, are, as in every Church document, not to a theory of natural law that is explicitly and exclusively identified with a particular system of philosophical speculation in the history of moral philosophy but pointedly to the existential natural law that is an integral constituent of evangelical morality, the *lex Christi*, by which man, through the redemptive merits of Christ and by the grace of God, may attain eternal life situated as he is from the moment of his being in the *de facto* supernatural status. That is why every mention of it is always in conjunction with the supernatural. It is *the* natural law (*unlike* that of the philosophers) which is within the scope of the commission of Christ to Peter and his successors to teach, interpret, and transmit to the faithful to the end of time without error. This may explain why in none of the Church official and authoritative documents, papal and conciliar, do we ever find a systematic corpus of natural law doctrine formulated, much less the development of argumentation, as to its existence, the demonstration of its general and particular principles, and the rationale vindicating the application of the principle to a particular moral act. Put into perspective, *Humanae Vitae*, propounds a doctrinal teaching which is of the natural moral law but whose certain discernment and unambiguous formulation derive principally from the abiding assistance of the Holy Spirit that has sustained the constant and universal teaching of the Church on the moral principles on marriage as they are existentially integral to the evangelical morality, the *lex Christi*, and subsequently on the unique charism of the papal magisterium which has applied these moral principles to specific acts of conjugal relations. (*The Thomist, op. cit.*, p. 651.)

There are certain discernible characteristics in the referrals to the natural law in official Church documents: (i) papal and ecclesial teaching authority (*there is no other teaching authority in the Catholic Church*) has identified a natural law precept as deriving from a natural law principle as distinguishable from the evangelical ethic: (ii) the particular concrete application is warranted by a moral obligation proceeding from that same source; (iii) the designation of the natural law invariably (as best as I have been able to ascertain) appears in context related to the *lex Christi*. This is done in one of three ways: (a) either by general all-comprehensive terms that in context preclude the exclusion of one or the other—"all his (man's) actions, insofar as they are morally good and evil," "the moral order," "the entire moral order," "moral issues," "the total deposit of truth," etc. (b) by explication—"the entire moral law, both natural and evangelical," "authentic interpreters of all moral law, not only, that is, of the law of the Gospel, but also of the natural law," etc. (c) and by conjunction: "natural law and divine law," "a teaching founded on the natural law, illuminated and enriched by divine revelation," "moral and religious," etc. (iv) in none of the pontifical and conciliar documents do we find a systematic corpus of natural law doctrine or an identification of the Church's traditional natural law with any particular system or theory of a school of natural law—(save the pontifical counsels that seminaries follow St. Thomas as a guide in philosophical and theological inquiries, not, however, as Pius XI admonished without that "honorable rivalry with just freedom from which studies make progress," (cf. Leo XIII, *Aeterni Patris*, DS 3135 Pius X, *Doctoris Angelici*, DS 3601, Pius XI, *Studiorum Ducem*, DS 3665). (v) the competence and authority to declare what is contained and the extent of the deposit of truth committed to it belongs to the magisterium solely. Private "theologians" are free to opinionate on the matter but what they say that is at variance with papal and ecclesial doctrine should have no validity with the faithful. They have received no apostolic mandate from Christ. Indeed, for centuries, theologians in the technical sense did not exist. (vi) whenever the Church teaches natural law doctrine or a specific application of it to a concrete moral issue, it does so by virtue of the Petrine commission, etc. (*The American Journal of Jurisprudence, op. cit.,* 262, 263)

The *naturalness* of our nature's moral law is unaffected by the cognitive process by which we have come to know it. It may be known by natural information (rational speculation, philosophy, synderesis) and by a divine didactic (revelation). God may reveal philosophical truths, doctrinal and moral, as well as supernatural. If the knowledge of these truths is necessary to salvation, then God must will a way by which men may come to know them with certitude and without error. It is within the boundaries of these propositions that we situate the natural law doctrine of *Humanae Vitae* as taught by virtue of the apostolic authority of the Roman Pontiff (*ibid.* 264)

Should not a natural law precept, one that is grave and necessary for salvation within the subsumption of the higher evangelical law, be demonstrable and compelling upon each conscience? Such an expectation is unfounded. In maintaining the existence, intelligibility, and obligatory force of the law of human nature, philosophers within and outside the Church, have never affirmed that all men, or the generality of men, or the majority of men are possessed of the same knowledge and convictions on the same moral precepts and on identical practical applications. Further, we may well question how many "proofs and demonstrations" which are conclusive to a philosopher are equally so for the generality of philosophers—not to mention the non-philosophizing minds. We may go yet further and ask whether there is any one "proofs" that has won general acceptance. How many proofs are there, for example, on the existence of God and personal immortality that is beyond contestation among all philosophers? We are speaking of Catholic philosophers who hold firmly to the same doctrinal propositions but who challenge one another's demonstrations. One need only recall what vicissitudes have befallen the *quinque viae* of St. Thomas. What is most intimate to our very being is not necessarily more readily evident to general acceptance. (*ibid.* 265)

It is supposed that by collective and collaborative discourse a general consensus might be reached on a moral norm and its practical application. Here the history of human experience dispels any such hopeful expectations. It is naive to believe that human consciences would be held bound in a grave matter of morality by a general consensus, that a majoritarian determination would be subscribed to and acted upon by the dissenting minority, an expectation most unlikely in an atmosphere of the inviolability of the individual conscience. (*ibid.* 265)

It borders on the facetious to object that the Encyclical bases its morality on the biological process. Should it have ignored it? The biological structures, the organic functions, and the course of the development of the natural consequences of carnal communion are a divinely designed pattern expressive of the divine will. When spouses . . . resort to the naturally infertile period, they are acting in conformity with the totality of God's will which has defined the whole ovulatory cycle of the women . . . . The morality of human sexuality is biologically grounded, very much so. But it is a biology that is human and its morality derives from man's total humanity and his eternal destiny. (*ibid.*, 275, 276)

With so much incantation of the "Spirit" of Vatican II, but with convenient disregard of the Holy Spirit that superintended its deliberations and decisions, let us recall a telling passage from the Declaration on Religious Freedom:

> In the formation of their consciences, the Christian ought carefully to attend the *sacred* and *certain* doctrine of the Church. The Church is, by the will of Christ, the teacher of truth. It is her duty to give utterance to, and authoritatively to teach, that Truth which is Christ Himself, and *also to declare and confirm by her authority those principles of the moral order which have their origin in human nature itself.* (n. 14, italics supplied)

By that same authority by which the Church is divinely called upon to teach "that Truth which is Christ Himself," she is called upon "also to declare and confirm by her authority those principles of the moral order which have their origin in human nature itself." The Council Fathers draw here no distinction between papal *ex cathedra* definitions, conciliar definitions, solemn definitions of the ordinary, i.e., constant and universal Teaching of the Church, and "the authentic teaching (authority) of the Roman Pontiff, even when he is not speaking ex cathedra." (Lumen Gentium c. 25) The Holy Spirit "breathes where He wills"—but against the literal pronouncements of the ecumenical council?

The Church does not teach the natural moral law of philosophers but that of the existential human nature, fallen and redeemed, and it does so with the pedagogy of Christ and not of the moral philosophers, which is not always certain and rarely deserving general acceptance.

For some the "spirit" of the Second Vatican Council consists in ignoring its explicit teaching and undeniable meaning in favor of some futurible Vatican III or IV.

Majority (K. 40)

Kung writes (40) that "the authority of the encyclical is seriously compromised by the fact that the Pope decided against the over-whelming majority of the commission" (K. 40). Suffice to note that Kung never tells us what constitutes one majority right and another majority wrong: (i) the near unanimity in the Galileo case (the names of ten cardinals appear in the preamble of the sentence, only seven subscribed at the conclusion) which Pope Urban VIII followed; (ii) the majority of the commission on birth control which Kung expected Pope Paul VI to follow; (iii) the unanimity of the Third Synod of Bishops in defense of sacerdotal celibacy which Kung has urged the clergy to defy. Kung never tells us how to differentiate between majorities. A close reading of the majority and minority reports on artificial birth control discloses that whereas the minority was as one in its argumentation, the numerical majority enjoyed no such unanimity of conviction except in its final recommendation for change.

Majority opinion is not in itself a guarantee of truth, not even for Kung.

Reserve to Himself (K. 40)

As a commentary on the mood of the Council Fathers, on Pope Paul's reservation to himself of the birth control question, we may consider the "mind" of Cardinal Suenens on the matter. In 1962, the year the Council opened, Cardinal Suenens declared:

> What was condemned as intrinsically immoral yesterday will not become moral tomorrow. No one should entertain any confused doubt or false hope on the point. The Church has not decided that these (contraceptive) practices are immoral; she has merely confirmed what the moral law already said about them. (*Love and Control*, Eng. trans. Robinson. Burns Oates (1962), p. 103)

And at the Vatican Council, Cardinal Suenens chose to conclude his speech on November 7, 1964, on the Schema on the Missions, pointedly to reject and dispel the misconstruction he claimed the press had placed upon his speech on marriage on the 29th of October with these unambiguous affirmations:

> Allow me to take this opportunity and this method of re-plying very briefly to some reactions in public opinion which

interpreted my speech on matrimonial ethics *as if I had said that the doctrine and discipline of the Church in this matter had changed.* So far as doctrine is concerned, my words made it quite clear that I was asking *only for research* in this whole area, *not with a view to changing anything in the Church's doctrine which has already been authentically and definitively proclaimed,* but only with a view to elaborating a synthesis of all the principles which are relevant to this domain. So far as discipline is concerned, it is clear *that the conclusions of the Commission to which I have referred have to be submitted to the authority of the Sovereign Pontiff and adjudged by his supreme authority.* I said this explicitly. It is obvious that any decisions regarding the functioning of the Commission rest exclusively with that same authority. I say these things now in order to remove all misunderstanding in public opinion. (Italic supplied)

Compare this statement of Cardinal Suenens with Kung's appraisal that this allowed the pope to decide these things "alone," "in the absolutist style that had become customary from the period of the high Middle Ages . . . without safeguarding the Church through effective control against a possible absolutist misuse of papal power." (K. 40) When has the Roman Pontiff exercised arbitrary absolutist power in matters of faith and morals? Pope Paul did not act "alone" in *Humanae Vitae.* He acted in concord with twenty centuries of Church teaching not excluding theological consensus undisturbed and uninterrupted down to 1963. By a theological (?) rhetoric (40-41), Kung tries to insert the wedge, as we had cautioned earlier, between the Bishop of Rome, "separate from the Church."

Lex Dubia Non Obligat (K. 42) and *In a State of Doubt (K. 40, 41, 42)*

Kung apparently agrees with those who thought that the *lex dubia non obligat* followed upon the suggestion of a possibility of change by the interlude of papal study and reflection and the interim intensive theological discussion (41). After examining the succession of statements made by the Holy Father, we are persuaded that there never was any personal doubt in the mind of Pope Paul on the immutability of the norms set down by his predecessors, Pius XI and Pius XII. At the same time we acknowledge that in one or some instances of categorical affirmation of the enduring obligatory force of those norms Pope Paul also gives expression to a time dimension—"as long as," "until now," "not now," "in a state of doubt." Our own conclusions are that none of the categorical reaffirmations are weakened by these temporal allusions; that the time element must be related to the interlude "of study and reflection"; that the temporal waiting period preceding *Humanae Vitae* was not expressive of any personal hesitance but a necessary incidence of and a respectful attendance upon the studies which his predecessor, Pope John, and he had initiated. The doubts that were fostered may be attributed to two principal causes: first, to the awkward, unavoidable and circumstanced conjunction of declaring firm adherence to the traditional norms and at the same time putting off the solemnity of a formal declaration until after the commission's reports were completed and studied; and second, to the excessive confidence of those who publicly foretold the novel direction of the papal teaching. It is to this latter factor that the major responsibility of engendering a practical doubt in the minds of the faithful must be attributed as well as the painful spiritual consequences that have enjured to this day:

A word is in order about the facile reference to *probabilism* and to *lex dubia non obligat*. Probabilism simply points to the lack of conclusive persuasion that an alleged law is known with such certainty as to preclude some reasonable intellectual doubts. Probabilism admits that in choosing to act contrary to an alleged law, the individual may be materially if not formally violating the law. But the saving grace of probabilism is that the moral agent who chooses to act contrary to the alleged law does so prudently, not unreasonably. If then, as we hold, Pope Paul held steadfast to the proscriptions against contraceptives set down in *Casti Connubii* and repeated by Pius XII, then reliance upon probabilism prior to *Humanae Vitae* seems to us unwarranted. A lex *dublia no obligat* is a contradiction in terms. If it is a law, it has some obligatory force. If it is doubtful, then obviously, we have no law except by extrinsic connotation. The expression, "doubtful law," is permissible in the philosophical inquest into the order of morality and its exigencies. Probabilism, on the contrary, allows that some hold to the existence of an alleged law and its substantive meaning while others are not as fully convinced. Probabilism is related to the consensus of the professional moralist. (*Thought, op. cit.,* 388)

.

A "doubtful law does not bind" presumes what it denies. Probabilism does not rely on the absolute possibility of error but rather, given the absence of certitude (which even an authentic non-infallible teaching of the Church does provide), it is an exercise of the virtue of prudence to choose between two solidly probably opinions.

> No such claim on the absence of certitude on the Church's absolute ban against artificial contraceptives may be made as existing within the Magisterium, whatever doubts some private theologians may have entertained within their own persuasion *after* 1963. (*Thomist, op. cit.*, 643)

When on October 28, 1966, Pope Paul VI in an address to the Italian National Concress for Gynecology denied that the moral issue was in doubt but only in a "state of study," not *in statu dubii* but *in statu studii*, Kung notes that (42):

> The most outstanding Catholic theologian in England gave this papal statement as the immediate occasion for his final departure from the Catholic Church in view of her general dishonesty. (*Observer*, London, January 1, 1967.)

But this is much too naive. If my recollection of the news reports are correct, the defection concurred with an announcement of bethrothal. Professed conflicts of conscience are on occasion motivated by considerations quite distanced from the avowed protest. We are reminded of the dialogue between the Lord Chamberlain, and the Dukes of Norfolk and Suffolk in Shakespeare's Henry VIII, Act II, Scene II:

> *Suf.*   How is the king employ'd?
> *Cham.* I left him private, full of sad thoughts and troubles.
> *Nor.*   What's the Cause?
> *Cham.* It seems the marriage with his brother's wife has crept too near his conscience.
> *Suf.*   No, his conscience has crept too near another lady.

Kung apparently acknowledges the chronologically circumstanced inopportuneness of Charles Davis' bethrothal and defection from the Catholic Church in his book *Truthfulness*, where he discourses for a whole chapter, pp. 51-66, on the conjunctive sequence of these actions of Davis.

Conscience (K. 44-47)

In raising the question of conscience and the teaching office Kung quotes St. Paul (Rm. 14:23), St. Thomas Aquinas (In IV Sent. dist. 38) and St. Robert Bellarmine (De summo pontifice, BK. II, c. 29, I, 607). But there is much more that is left unsaid. The objectively wrong conscience firm in its subjective sense of moral correctness may excuse from the gravity of moral culpability, but *it does not thereby transform the objective moral error into objective moral rectitude.* The question that is left untouched is whether that conscience ought not to be truthfully informed, authoritatively advised and corrected. The Incarnate Word came "to enlighten every man who comes into this world" (Jn. 1:9) to be "the way, the truth, and the life" (Jn. 14:6). He came to insert himself into human conscience, if need be, to intrude, interfere and rebuke. This is evident many times in His frequent contestations with the Pharisees, Scribes and Sadducees, and daily sermons to the people and to His own disciples. The woman at the well was quite content in her conscience with her generous distribution of affections to a number of husbands, but Our Lord corrected her conscience, and for this she went about glorifying God. This writer, for one, finds it difficult to accept invincible ignorance of *Humanae Vitae* promulgated by "virtue of the mandate of Christ" (n. 6), which has been given such world-wide publicity—except by reason of the overweening theologues who exercised themselves vigorously to interpose their spiritual counsels between the faithful and the Supreme Pastor of the Universal Church. We are reminded of the moral crisis within the Church in the sixteenth century England, when pastors of the faithful led the faithful out of, into and again out of the Catholic Church, and then sat in judgment at the heresy trial of the flock that had trustingly followed their leadership. It is then with a keen sense of the tragic lessons of history and a profound compassion for the faithful who had been misled by the doctrinal confusion, which in no small measure must be attributed to well-intentioned but ill-advised and premature predictions of the forthcoming papal pronouncement, that Pope Paul encourages marital couples to repair frequently to the sacrament of Penance, and humbly by prayer and renewed effort disengage themselves from the binding force of new-formed habits. Pope Paul VI has given the world a personal example how to enlighten and guide objectively erroneous consciences:

To diminish in no way the saving teaching of Christ constitutes an eminent form of charity for souls. But this must be
ever accompanied by patience and goodness, such as Our Lord
Himself gave example of in dealing with men. Having come not
to condemn, but to save, He was intransigent with evil, but
merciful toward individuals. (n. 29, *H.V.*)

Kung gives only half the pastoral and moral theology on objectively
erroneous consciences that act in good faith.

All of us are accountable to God and not, as it is popularly said, to
personal conscience, and (for Catholics at least) the Church's role in
the formulation of conscience is not diffused by private magisteria
of theologians, prestigious and non-prestigious. The primacy of
conscience affirms the ultimate responsibility of the moral agent, not
the superiority and autonomy of the conscience. Conscience may
speak with many tongues and not all of them are always reliable,
nor are all the persuasions of conscience above the strongest urges of
human passion, burdensome inconveniences and rationally appealing
self-interest. It is not without significance that nowhere in any of
the sixteen Council documents is there a single mention of the
vibrantly popular expression "freedom of conscience," let alone
any discussion of it.

The appeal to personal conscience may lead to opposing commitments. There is the conscience of St. Stephen and those who stoned
him to death (Acts 1:6-7), of Henry II and St. Thomas a Becket, of
Henry VIII and St. Thomas More, of Martin Luther and St. Ignatius
Loyola. The generality of mankind acknowledges the profound gulf
between objective truth and mere subjectivism, between moral right
and wrong, between the true and the false. The problematic does
not infrequently arise as to what is objectively true and false. But it
is precisely here that Catholics, at least, have the benefit of the
obligation to form a right conscience in keeping with the authentic
teaching of the Church as expressed by the supreme teacher, the
Vicar of Christ. who is guided by the Holy Spirit. It is misleading to
suggest that an incompatibility or dichotomy intervenes between a
responsible freedom of conscience and the obligation inherent in that
responsibility to abide by the authoritative pronouncements of the
papal magisterium, because, in fact, they are both gifts of God.

The continuity of Christ in His Vicars is primarily intended
as the primary informant and corrective of the conscience of

the faithful. Conscience is not the teacher of morality but the guide of personal choice, and not infrequently conscience may be its own accomplice rather than its guide. The criterion of a correct moral conscience may be known by reason alone to some extent, by reason and revelation, or by a fallible reason confirmed into certitude by revelation. This certitude, Catholics may have by the "teaching authority of the Church in its unfolding of the divine law." (Gaudium et spes., n. 51). To admit that "conscience is always binding" is not to say that a man's judgment and choice of action are invested with objective moral rectitude. Religious and civil authorities may and do contravene objectively erroneous consciences. Public law and local ecclesiastical authorities have opposed racial segregation as both immoral and illegal against those who protest their freedom to follow their consciences in racial relations. (*Thought, op. cit.*, pp. 408, 409)

Casti Connubii (K. 48)

The mention of *Casti Connubii* (K. 48) provides us an occasion to insert some comments of John T. Noonan, author of the classic work on *Contraception: A History of Its Treatment by the Catholic Theologians and Canonists*, Belknap, Harvard 1966.

On *Casti Connubii*:

How great was its authority? By the ordinary tests used by the theologians to determine whether a doctrine is infallibly proclaimed, it may be argued that the specific condemnation of contraceptive interruption of the procreative act is infallibly set out. The encyclical is addressed to the universal Church. The Pope speaks in fulfillment of his apostolic office. He speaks for the Church. He speaks on moral doctrine that he says, "has been transmitted from the beginning." He "promulgates" the teaching. If the Pope did mean to use the full authority to speak *ex cathedra* on morals, which Vatican I recognized as his, what further language could he have used? (p. 428)

On the universality of commitment of theologians to Church teaching prior to the Council, Noonan wrote:

No Catholic theologian has ever taught, "Contraception is a good act." The teaching on contraception is clear and apparently fixed forever. (p. 6)

No Catholic writer before 1963 had asserted that the general prohibition of contraception was wrong. (p. 512)

A critical study has yet to be made on theological "consensus" and "opinion" and its value before the teaching office of the Church. It is this writer's personal opinion that what is in crisis these days is the overweening pretentions of a few private theologians of what they conceive to be their role as "an intrinsic element in the total magisterial function of the Church"—as the principal author of opposition to *Humanae Vitae* in the United States has expressed it.

The Letter of the Cardinal Secretary of State, Cicognani, To the Bishops of the World, September 4, 1968 (K. 48, 49)

On pages 48, 49 we find one of the most desperate exercises in the absurdity of the association of completely dissonant human experience. We are informed of the "secret" letter of the late Cardinal Secretary of State Cicognani to the bishops of the world (September 4, 1968), of which Kung writes:

In the involved style of totalitarian party central offices, but equally unmistakable in its meaning, subordinates were required to bring to bear all their spiritual power in order "to put forward again in all its purity the constant teaching of the Church," in other words, to make it prevail. (48)

An examination of three paragraphs that Kung quotes in full discloses an appeal to the devotion, obedience and zeal of all priests that they educate the faithful "to find convincing language which will ensure its (*Humanae Vitae*) acceptance" and "by every pastoral effort" in and out of the confessional to remove doubts about it. It is the sort of language one should expect to find in the pastoral correspondence of the Head of the Church to the episcopacy, bearing all the solicitude and firm urgings "in season, out of season" (2 Tim. 4:2) that early Christians had been accustomed to read in the Epistles of Peter and Paul. Yet, Kung tartly comments:

Is it surprising then that many people inside and outside the Catholic Church drew comparisons with what happened in Czechoslavakia in 1968? (K. 49)

If the referral to Czechoslavakia is the Russian government's imposition of its will upon a freedom aspiring people by corps of the Red Star tanks, then this ludicrous parallel between the letter of Cicognani and the brute force of Soviet domination is much too preposterous to merit any further attention. It has, however, the unenviable merit of disclosing the intensity of Kung's animosity and the failure of his critical judgment.

PART II

KUNGIAN APORIAE

In his Metaphysics, Book B, Aristotle speaks of the necessity of removing the mental "road block" in order to have a clear passage to the "truth." The Greek *poros* means "passage, way, path, road." The privative *a*lpha gives the signification "lack of passage." The abstractive form "apori*a*" lends itself readily to a subjective use, just as in English a man is said to "book *his* passage" on an ocean-liner. The aporia is conceived as being operative in the reasoning process. It has a subjective sense. In an aporia the intellect has no passage; that is to say, it does function, but not on an "open road" to the "truth." In addition to this psychological aspect and relative to it, aporia also denoted the obstacles that touch upon the object of study. Aristotle speaks of "untying the knots" in the object (prāgma). They must first be located and "untied," because as the metaphorical term appropriately expresses it, these "knots" bind the object from clear discernment and in consequence bind the intellect in misunderstandings. Something in the "thing" being studied binds the intellect and prevents it from going ahead to the "truth." The term, "aporia" is applied variously to a state of the intellect, to the conceptions which caused this mental state, and to the thing itself in the manner known. Aristotle then speaks of the good or clear passage—*eúporía*—to the "truth"; but in order to have a clear way to the "truth" one must first "go through" the aporiae— *diaporesai*; that is to say, to draw up the aporiae properly. This means to become fully conscious of both the mental "knots" and of the obstacles that "bind" the object of study and to make them manifest, put them out in the open. By making manifest, by openly acknowledging these aporiae, impediments to the truth—the scholar will then have an open approach to the truth he seeks, and his *inquiry* may then be more likely than not, truly open.

We will now inquire into Kung's "state of intellect" and as Aristotle advises, "locate and draw up" the Kungian aporiae for examination.

We designate as the first aporia in Kung's *Inquiry* his acerbic resentments against *Rome*, and that is, "Romanism, papal absolutism, Vatican ghetto, Roman Curia, Roman party line, Roman intransigence, Roman reaction, narrow Roman perspective, narrow Roman theology, Roman absolutist system, power politics, Roman canon law"—and with little grace and less faith and theology, against the encyclicals of Pope Paul VI (cf. pp. 11-30). The second aporia was Kung's exploitation of an uprooted ecclesiastical history (cf. pp. 31-32). These spiritual and intellectual distempers and their pale cast of thought "bind" the intellect and place "obstacles" to an open "road to the truth" as Aristotle would say in an unembarrassed mixture of metaphors.

In our continuing study we encounter the sequent Kungian aporiae. His adversary "state of intellect" disposes him to separate, to dichotomize what are integral religious realities, inseparable constituents of the Catholic dogmas. He disjoins the institutional from the charismatic Church; the Pope, the visible Head of the Church from the Lord of Glory, the invisible Head of the Church; the Pope from the Church; the Church from the Mystical Body of Christ; the Church's teaching office from the Divine Spirit of Truth. All this is open contravention of Church doctrine:

> For Peter in virtue of his primacy is only Christ's Vicar; so that there is only one Chief Head of this Body, namely Christ. He never ceases personally to guide the Church by an unseen hand, though at the same time He rules it externally, visibly through him who is His representative on earth. After His glorious Ascension into heaven this Church rested not on Him alone, but on Peter, too, its visible foundation stone. That Christ and His Vicar constitute one only Head is the solemn teaching of our predecessor of immortal memory, Boniface VIII, in the Apostolic Letter UNAM SANCTAM; and his successors have never ceased to repeat the same.

> They, therefore, walk the path of dangerous error, who believe that they can accept Christ as the Head of the Church, while they reject genuine loyalty to His Vicar on earth. They have taken away the Visible Head, broken the visible bonds of unity, and they leave the Mystical Body of the Redeemer in

such obscurity and so maimed, that those who are seeking the haven of eternal salvation cannot see it and cannot find it. (Pius XII, *Mystical Body of Christ*, cc. 42, 43, 1943)

He severs apart the triune divine-human interrelationships of Tradition, Sacred Scripture and the Magisterium, and inserts an arbitrariness between them. The "clear passage to truth" is considerably dimmed by Kung's selective use of primary and secondary sources: he misconstrues his sources; for example, the *False Decretals*, Verardo's *Introductio Editoris*, St. Thomas Aquinas' *Contra Errores Graecorum*, and he uses authors selectively to suit his purpose and omits others whose theology is supportive of papal infallibility. Kung demands "proofs," "demonstrations," "substantiation," but he never explains what precisely would constitute "proof" in dogmatic theology on an article of faith. Kung treats of ecclesiastical history, about a supernatural history, scriptural exegesis, dogmatic theology, of philosophical and theological propositions. He does not state what method, if any, is appropriate to each science that he is following.

A Teaching Church of Divine Revelation

God in His infinite mercy willed freely a plan of salvation for fallen man to be perfectly realized in and through His Divine Son (Heb. 1:1, 2; Jn. 3:16), who came in search of His own (Jn. 1:11) to gather them to Himself and take them in Him to the Father (Jn. 17: 11, 20-26; 1 Cor. 15:28; Eph. 1:22). Jesus, the Messiah and Son of God, personally selected from the general group of disciples twelve Apostles (Mt. 10:2-4; Mk. 3:16-19; Lk. 6:13-16; AA. 1:13) to whom He entrusted His soteriological mission, first during His Public ministry (Mt. 10:1-42; Lk. 9:1-10) and then definitely after His Resurrection (Mt. 28:19-20; Mk. 16:15-18). They were sent not merely to bear witness to the truth, but to teach this truth with authority in the name of Christ (Mt. 10:40; Lk. 10:16). This authority given to them in virtue of their mission cannot be simply identified with the authority of the Word proclaimed. It is properly a pastoral authority with a moral obligation to teach and require obedience from those who believe.

"Through Him we received grace and our apostolic mission to preach the obedience of faith to all pagan nations in honor of His name." (Rm. 1:5)

Jesus identified His personally chosen apostle-disciples as His Church (Mt. cc. 16, 18). And He identified the mission He entrusted to His elect group and their designated leadership with His own. "As the Father sent Me so also I send you" (Jn. 20:21; cf. Jn. 17:18), to teach whatever He had commanded them to do (Mt. 28:19) under the primatial authority of Peter (Mt. 16:17-19; Lk. 22:31-32; Jn. 21: 15-17). Whoever heard them heard His voice. Now Petrine and papal infallibility must be understood within the context of this extraordinary supernal vocation of His Church to perpetuate His teaching to the end of time, without error, without distortion, without misconstruction. So did the Fathers of the First and Second Vatican Councils understand it:

Romanum Pontificem . . . *ea infallibilitate pollere, qua* divinus Redemptor *Ecclesiam suam in* definienda doctrine de fide vel moribus *instructam esse voluit.* (DS 3074)

This infallibility with which the divine Redeemer willed His Church to be endowed in defining a doctrine of faith and morals. . . . *This is the infallibility which the Roman Pontiff,* the head of the college of bishops, *enjoys in virtue of his office,* when as the supreme shepherd and teacher of all the faithful . . . . as the supreme teacher of the universal Church, as one in whom the charism of the infallibility of the Church herself is individually present, he is expounding or defending a doctrine of Catholic Faith.

The infallibility promised to the Church resides also . . . . (*Lumen Gentium*, c. 25)

The original requirement according to divine design for the infallibility of the Church (and of popes and councils) is that the Church is a *teaching Church of divine revelation.* Only to an infallible Church could the sacred deposit of faith be safely confided (1 Tm. 6:20-21; 2 Tm. 1:13-14). The infallibility of the Church is the work from God, the guarantee against error is from God, the unfailing efficacy is from God. The protection against error is no less a protection against the speculative pontifical "arbitrariness" and "despotism" that haunt Kung's mind. It is the Divine Spirit of Truth that "directs" the popes and councils in infallible definitions and not the pontiffs and councils who "direct" the Holy Spirit. In a word, the burden is on God, so to speak; God is to see to it that the divine *paradosis* is not distorted. The Spirit of Truth exercises His counselling and guiding power according to His pleasures, not according to papal "absolutism." And this is precisely the way in which the assistance promised to the Church by the Holy Spirit prevents the Petrine and papal office (and councils) in its ultimate doctrinal decisions from introducing human inventions into the binding apostolic witness to Jesus Christ. The unfailing assistance of the Holy Spirit to ensure the "word of the Lord," "the message of salvation," among men without error is necessarily indispensable for that purpose. That is why it was promised. Only by such a divine disposition can we know by the obedience and certitude of faith what has been divinely revealed and how it ought to be understood "by the authority of truth and by the truth of authority." (Augustine, *Contra Maxim. arian.* II, 14, 3) It is precisely at this point that Kung fails in *Inquiry*. Instead of contemplating the power of God to work through men as He wills, Kung concentrates on human capability for arbitrariness, on intellectual limitations (the many inexactitudes of human knowledge) and the liability to error. (*Inquiry*, pp. 101-105; 157-172) Kung's alternative to infallibility in the Church is indefectibility, which he explains as a "fundamental remaining of the Church in truth, which is not annulled by individual errors." (p. 181 ff.) More about Kung's theory of indefectibility in Part III, *but suffice for now to ask* if the Church erred at Vatican I for its solemn definitions on papal primatial jurisdiction and magisterial infallibility and erred again in reaffirming this dogma of faith (at Vatican II); and in the area of moral doctrine erred in reaffirming the moral inadmissibility of contraception "as it has been taught as a matter of course by all bishops everywhere in the world in moral unity, unanimously for centuries," as Kung admits (*Inquiry*, p. 58); if, according to Kung "propositions of faith participate in the problematic of human propositions in general" (p. 157) and "that they are rather fundamentally ambiguous" (p. 161), then this is so about all the solemnly defined Trinitarian and Christological dogmas. If all this be so, then we ask of Hans Kung, *cui bono*, his theological theory of indefectibility? On the contrary, any truly "fundamental remaining in truth" in divine mysteries and in the divine economy of salvation presupposes the charism of infallibility if God wills that men know His word and be faithful to it. There is indefectibility in the Church, but it cannot be severed from, much less opposed to, infallibility, as Kung maintains.

Infallibility is the inner core of indefectibility. Indefectibility concerns the Church's Constitution, sacraments, etc., as well as its doctrine on faith and morals. In the latter area, it applies to the whole historical life of the people of God above and beyond the cases of strict infallibility (which it includes). It means the indestructibility of the faith upon which and by which the Church is built. The Church will remain to the end of time. Indefectibility is bound up with the notion of the Church as the new people of God and the final covenant between God and man. Heresies and schisms have assaulted the Church of Christ, at their worst, with Arianism and at the time of the Reformation. But despite these disasters His Church continued in existence, as foretold by Christ. (Mt. 7:24-27; 16:18) Indefectibility comprehends failures, changes, reform, accommodation, and in merely disciplinary regulations, even reversals. But the nature, mission and sacraments of the Church as Christ ordained it endures inviolable.

Infallibility is the divine assurance that when the successor of Peter and of the Apostles under Peter speak in Christ's name and by His commission that their teaching is true to His salvific message, they declare with a finality beyond all challenge or recall. Ecclesial and papal infallibility is above all a question of divine providence— whether God *can ensure* inviolably and intact the faithful and unerring transmission of the apostolic kerygma of Christ to all men, through all time, *whatever the failings of men in general and even of His own specially designated ministers.* Kung's perspective is in reverse, namely, the limitations of men precludes such a divine ordination.

This writer considers the dogma of ecclesial and papal infallibility not so demanding as the Trinitarian and Christological articles of faith. And as far as Protestants are concerned, the nature and unique prerogatives of the permanent Petrine office is no more unscriptural than the doctrine of the infallibility of Scripture. (*Inquiry*, pp. 209-221) On the contrary, this writer finds it in accord with his own rational expectation about a teaching Church that has been mandated to "teach all nations whatsoever I have commanded you." The apostolic epistles of Peter, John, James and Paul are an exercise of this teaching authority.

If then, according to Kung, there is no infallibility in the Church, neither of the popes nor of ecumenical councils in union and agreement with the Roman Pontiff, if indeed Scripture is not inerrant, to whom shall the faithful turn to know "the Way, the Truth, and the Life?" Kung invites all his readers (including popes and the episcopacy) to rely on the collective expertise of learned theologians rather than on a supposed magisterial authority in the Church (*Inquiry*, pp. 230 ff.). But the manifest evidence of ecclesiastical history is far from reassuring on this sort of recourse. The generality of heretics within and without the Church have been theologians from the days of Marcion, Tertullian, Arius, Nestorius, Luther, Calvin, the Modernists of the 19th and 20th centuries, the "prestigious" and non-prestigious theologues of our own day.

Kung's Demands for Proof

On several occasions Kung denies that the definitions of the dogma of infallibility at the First Vatican Council and its reaffirmation at Vatican II can be "substantiated" or "proved" from Scripture and Tradition (pp. 108, 109, 111, 120, 198-199, 221), and just as frequently questions that "propositions which are *a priori* false" (p. 174), that "faith is dependent on infallible propositions" (pp. 150, 151, 221) can be "substantiated" or "proven." This demand for "proofs" is unexpected. To begin with, Kung denies the inerrancy of Scripture (pp. 209-221) and thereby removes the possibility of "proofs" from the New Testament books. Secondly, Kung undermines the possibility of the certitude of demonstration by his theory of cognition that "propositions of faith participate in the problematic of human propositions in general" (p. 157) and as such "they are rather fundamentally ambiguous" (p. 161). Even so, Kung's demand for "proofs" should be examined in itself apart from his own questionable postulates.

What would constitute "proof" from Scripture for all Christians to accept? Have not scriptural "proofs" divided Christians and multiplied faiths and churches at variance with one another? What article of faith has not been professed *and* denied on the basis of *sola Scriptura*? The "objective clarity" of Lutheran hermeneutics has served the non-Lutheran scriptural exegetes as well. Nor is the recourse to history more reassuring for conclusive evidences and demonstrations. It is not history that makes a person a Catholic but rather the Church's dogmatic use of history in which the Catholic believes. No doctrine can be disproved by history, but by the same token no doctrine can be proved simply by history.

This may be one of the major *aporiae* of Kung. In *Inquiry* he has not spelt out for himself a general theological criteriology that must play its part in the structure and proceedings of a demonstrative theology within the context of faith.

Our Lord did not commend Thomas for doubting apostolic testimony and for insisting on his own stated conditions (Jn. 20:21-29). Miracles, historical "evidences," even tactual evidence such as that presented to Thomas can assist the earnest search of faith, but it is in the authoritative and inviolable transmission of the apostolic witness through the unfolding centuries that the grace of God is to be found in which the issue of faith or disbelief is finally engaged (Jn. 4:48; 10:38). It was not the empirical evidences of the presence of the Risen Jesus that proved the divinity of Jesus, but rather it was the response to the gift of faith that made Thomas declare His divinity, "My Lord and my God." It is not without telling significance that it is doubting Thomas who made the most complete confession of Christ's identity to be found on the lips of anyone in the Gospel. In its beginning there is no witnessing and no Christian faith without seeing, but all Christians thereafter who can never see but do believe the apostolic witness are called blessed in the last of the beatitudes proclaimed by Christ before His Ascension.

"You believe because you see. Blessed are those who have not seen and yet believe."

These words transcend the little group present and are addressed to all Christians of all time (1 Pt. 1:8). We shall find in Scripture evidences of what is believable but never so compelling as to foreclose all resistance. All the referrals to Old Testament prophecies by Jesus left the Jewish theologians of His day on earth unmoved and even on occasion made them relentlessly hostile to Him. (Jn. 5:31-47) The evidences of Scripture and Kung's demand for proofs must be considered within the context of witness to faith. Christ Jesus was the first witness who came into the world precisely "to bear witness to the truth" (Jn. 18:37) which He had received from the Father (Jn. 8:26), to call attention not to Himself, but to the Father. And since He is God the Son as well as man, the witness He gives must be identical with that of the Father (Jn. 8:18). Jesus specifically asks His Apostles to be His witnesses even to the ends of the earth (Acts 1:8). They are the eye and ear witnesses to the Messiah—He who was to come, as the prophets of the Old Testament had foretold—testifying to the historical and saving events (Jn. 3:11; 1 Jn. 1:1-5; Lk. 24:48; Acts 1:22; 4:33; 5:31; 10:42). What is true of the Apostles as primary witnesses to Christ Jesus, is true of His Church as the permanent witness. Its mission is to continue Christ and His saving work in the World to the end of time. It is the witness to the faith by the *ecclesia* of the New Covenant built upon *kepha,* superintended by the chief stewart with the powers of the keys, called upon to confirm his brethren and to feed His flock in the Christ-faith. The faultless witness to the Faith by the Church in its fidelity to the apostolic kerygma is the basis for the Catholics' confession of faith—*Credo in . . . apostolicam ecclesiam.* I believe in ecclesial and papal infallibility because the Church of Christ teaches me so, to believe as an article of faith. This is sufficient proof for the Catholic and should be (as it had been) for Kung, in his publications prior to *Inquiry.* There is no other adequate reason for being a Catholic but that the Catholic Church is truly *the* Church of Christ, which, sustained by His Holy Spirit can teach through its authoritative magisterium what the faithful ought to believe. The teaching authority within the Church enables it to function as the living pastoral instrument of the Word of God by giving testimony to that Word of God, proclaiming in an authoritative manner what must be believed as the Word of God, what is revealed by God *by the handing on of the apostolic tradition by the successors of Peter and the other Apostles.* The dogmatic definitions of Vatican I were but the Church's own confession of faith. In this confession the Church together with the Holy Spirit testifies that the response to the Word of God is the obedience of faith (Rm. 1:5).

No convert to Catholicism ever attributed his faith to a "proof" that he could not withstand if he chose. I am reminded of the time when the late Willmore Kendall asked me if I would instruct him in the Catholic faith, adding, "You see, Father, I agree with most of what the Catholic Church teaches." I replied: "We do not become Catholics because we agree with the Catholic Church, but because by the persuasions of reason and by God's grace we come to acknowledge Her as the Church of Christ, and therefore we owe Her obedience. Of course, it helps to obey when we agree."

The witness of Faith which each and every Catholic is called upon to bear (cf. *Lumen Gentium,* cc. 30-37) is always within and in agreement with the ecclesial witness to the faith if it is to accord with the original apostolic witness.

Let us consider briefly what the demand for proof has yielded to Protestants on one scriptural text. Toward the end of the 19th century H. J. Holtzmann denied the genuinity of the Matthean *logia* to have been spoken by Jesus—Weiss, Klostermann to Dibelius, Easton, Goguel, Grill, Schnitzer, Heiler, Bultmann, Kummel, Grant, von Campenhausen, etc. Others followed Kattenbusch and Schmidt in denying that the Matthean Petrine text was spurious—Wendland, Gloege, Michaelis, Schniewind, Leenhardt, Otto Fridrichsen, Flew, Cullmann, Linton, Jeremias, etc. In 1953 Oscar Cullmann, the eminent Lutheran theologian, published his *Peter, Disciple, Apostle, Martyr: An Historical and Theological Study* (trans. by Floyd V. Filson, London, 1953). Cullmann not only maintained the genuinity of the Matthean Petrine text, but also held that Peter is promised authority over the whole Church (pp. 164-212), though he limits this authority to the brief period during which he was head of the Church at Jerusalem, yielding his primacy to James the Less. (We shall have occasion to enter into this matter when we study Petrine and apostolic succession.) Suffice at this point to ask how would Kung discriminate by his demand for proof between the variant textual criticism and scriptural exegesis of all these Protestant scholars.

In 1859, a decade before the solemn definition of papal infallibility by the First Vatican Council, John Henry Cardinal Newman published an essay entitled, *The Orthodoxy of the Body of the Faithful during the Supremacy of Arianism* in the volume, *The Arians of the Fourth Century* (Longmans, Green, 1901, pp. 445-468). Newman maintained that the doctrine implicit in the devotion and practice of the Church's faithful, the laity and with them, the parish priests and the monks, confessed the faith of the 318 Fathers of Nicaea even when the bishops and theologians of the Church, not to mention the Emperor, denied it:

> The Catholic people in the length and breadth of Christendom, were the obstinate champions of Catholic truth, and the bishops were not. Of course, there were great and illustrious exceptions; it was mainly by the faithful people that Paganism was overthrown; it was by the faithful people, under the lead of Athanasius and the Egyptian bishops, and in some places supported by their Bishops or priests, that the worst of heresies was withstood and stamped out of the sacred territory. (p. 446)

Newman summarily illustrates this contrast of the orthodoxy of the faithful with that of the generality of the episcopacy with historical data of councils. We, in turn make more concise his schema.

The Arian Assemblages

A.D. 334, 335—The Synods of Caesarea and Tyre. Sixty bishops accuse and formally condemn Athanasius of rebellion, sedition, and ecclesiastical tyranny; of murder, sacrilege, and magic. Athanasius is deposed, banished from Alexandria and sent to Gaul for life. These Synods receive Arius into communion.

A.D. 341—Great Council of the Dedication at Antioch attended by approximately one hundred bishops ratified the proceedings of Caesarea and Tyre, and install an Arian in the See of Athanasius. Four creeds which abandoned the formula of "consubstantial" were adopted.

A.D. 345—Council of the Creed called Macrostich. This creed too suppressed the doctrinal word "consubstantial." The eastern bishops forward a copy of it to the bishops of France who rejected it.

A.D. 347—Council of Sardica with approximately three hundred bishops divided on the question whether Athanasius should be admitted to the Council. Seventy-six "seceders" set up their own council at Philippolis. They excommunicated the pope and the Sardican Fathers and composed another creed.

A.D. 351—The Bishops of the East met at Sirmium. The semi-Arians separate themselves from the Arians. They composed a new creed embodying the language of some of the Ante-Nicene writers concerning Christ's divinity, and eliminated the word "substance."

A.D. 353—The Council of Arles. Several bishops attend as papal legates. All but one—the Bishop of Treves—voted for the condemnation of Athanasius and he alone confessed the Nicene faith.

A.D. 355—The Council of Milan was attended by more than three hundred bishops of the West. Nearly unanimously, they subscribe to the condemnation of Athanasius. Only the Pope's four delegates and St. Dioysius, Bishop of Milan remain firm. An Arian is put in Athanasius' See. St. Hilary is banished to Phrygia.

A.D. 357-9—Arians and Semi-arians construct new creeds at Sirmium.

A.D. 359—The Councils of Seleucia and Arminium, being one bipartite Council, representing East and West respectively. There were 150 bishops at Seleucia, of whom only 12 or 13 (from Egypt) espoused the Nicene "Consubstantial." At Arminium, Arians adopt the tactic of exhausting delays until approximately 400 bishops finally submit through weariness to the ambiguous formula which the heretics had substituted in place of "Consubstantial."

A.D. 361–St. Jerome Grimly observes: *"Ingemuit totus orbis et se esse Arianum miratus est."*

Let this much suffice to indicate, more summarily than does Newman (pp. 445-468), the all pervasive suffusion of Arianism by Arian bishops.

Of these times, Newman wrote:

> The episcopate, whose action was so prompt and concordant at Nicaea on the rise of Arianism, did not, as a class or order of men, play a good part in the troubles consequent upon the Council; and the laity did (p. 445).

Now, of the *Nicaean assemblages*:

A.D. 325–To begin with, the great Council of Nicaea of 318 bishops, the generality of them from the eastern provinces of Christendom, under the presidency of Hosius of Cordova. It is the first ecumenical Council, and recognized at the time its own authority as the voice of the infallible Church. The Council had convoked against Arianism, which it condemned and anathematized, and inserted into the Creed the fundamental dogma which Arianism impugned—the formula of "Consubstantial."

A.D. 326–St. Athanasius, the foremost champion of the *homoousios* formula was elected Bishop of Alexandria.

A.D. 341–At the Council of Rome, attended by 50 bishops who had been exiled by Arian councils, declare Athanasius to be innocent of the charges levelled against him.

A.D. 347–Council of Sardica. After the "seceders" departed, bishops from Italy, Gaul, Africa, Egypt, Cyprus, and Palestine confirmed the action of the Council of Rome, and restored Athanasius and the other exiles to the Sees from which they had been removed.

Newman observes of these turbulent times with its multiplication of creeds (by the Arians) and hostile encounters even to the point of actual physical violence that it was the "people," the "laity," "inclusively of their parish priests," "the monks," and some bishops who adhered to orthodoxy. It was the zeal and perseverance of the faithful people rather than the strength of the heresiarchs and their followers that finally prevailed in Christendom. What of Rome? Newman quotes the fifth century historian Sozomen:

> With respect to the doctrine no dissension arose either at Rome or in any other of the Western Churches; the people

unanimously adhered to the form of belief established by Nicaea.

What matters in the ultimate outcome of those distressing times is that those who stood with Rome or where Rome stood on Nicaea and Arianism were orthodox.   Whatever may be said about who convened the Council of Nicaea, the Roman (papal) adherence to Nicaea and Athanasius is the highest and most significant form of papal approbation of a council considering the vehemence of the heretical forces with Byzantian imperial power to promote and strengthen their cause.   One need only recall Hosius, Bishop of Cordova, who had presided at the Council of Nicaea, how he was "broken" and in 357 made to sign the Arian Second Formulary of Sirmium, a forced submission that he recanted on his deathbed. And what of Pope Liberius who withstood emperor Constantius' insistence that he abandon Athanasius and to reject the Nicaean doctrine of *homoousios* or consubstantiality of Father and Son.   In a letter to the Emperor, Liberius wrote:

> God is my witness that it is in spite of myself that I have accepted this office, but I want to live in it as long as I am in this world without offending God. It is not my own decisions (*statuta*) but those of the Apostle (Peter) that I am to conserve and guard. Following the tradition of my predecessors I have added nothing to the episcopal power of the Bishop of Rome; but neither have I allowed it to be diminished in any way. In preserving the faith handed down by the succession of bishops, many of them martyrs, I hope it will always remain intact (*Ad Constant.*, Jaffe 212).

Yet weakened by infirmity, age, and the rigors of exile he was forced to sign the first formula of Sirmium of 351. This symbol was not in itself offensive to the Creed of Nicaea but it was void of the doctrinal terminology that characterized the Nicaean faith, i.e., *homoousios*. It is remarkable, however, that despite his flagging energies he did resist endorsing the second formula of Sirmium (357) with its patently subordinationist tendency. But once back in his papal office, he required as a prerequisite for communion with Rome acceptance of the Nicaean creed and condemned anyone who adhered to the Arian displacement of orthodoxy. Upon his return to Rome, the Romans with their sense of Latin realism saw through the

duress by which Liberius had been coerced and hailed him enthusiastically. St. Jerome has captured this paradoxical event. *Liberius,
taedo victus exilii, et in haereticam praevitatem subscribens, Roman
quasi victor intraverat* (*Chron.* et Val. p. 797).

This inadequate brief hardly suggests the extensive hold of Arianism on so many Eastern bishops. How would Hans Kung, with his
demands for "proof," have recognized the orthodox doctrine on the
divinity of Jesus at a time when so many bishops, the theologians
of their time, were Arians? Cardinal Newman gives as his explanation
for this extensive faulting of episcopal orthodoxy: "there was no
authoritative utterance of the Church's infallible voice in matter of
fact between the Nicene Council, A.D. 325 and the Council of
Constantinople, A.D. 381 . . . there was nothing after Nicaea of firm,
unvarying, consistent testimony for nearly sixty years." (pp. 445 ff)

The crucial ecclesiastical experience for Newman is the "infallibility of the *Ecclesia docens*" (p. 464). Bishops, even popes, may err,
"and yet they might, in spite of this error, be infallible in their
ex cathedra decisions." Speaking of the doctrinally contentious
fourth century, Newman distinguished between *ecumenical* councils
which cannot fail in orthodoxy and general councils which can, such
as the Arian or Eusebian Councils (p. 468). The decisive fact for
Newman is *infallibilis ecclesia docens*. What scriptural "proofs"
would Hans Kung have required to have settled on *sola scriptura* to
restore unity in Nicaean orthodoxy in the fourth century? The
historical facts are that the main arguments used by the Arians were
scriptural texts. All through the controversy with the defenders of
the Nicene Creed the Arians consistently rejected nonscriptural
argumentation. If there is a demand for proof, then the ultimate
and irrevocable determinant is the authoritative voice of the *infallibilis ecclesia docens*. It was the celebrated apostle of the Goths,
Bishop Ulfilas (b. 311; d. 382), who converted the people beyond
the Danube to semi-Arianism, and Christianity in this heretical form
prevailed for more than two centuries among the Visigoths, Ostrogoths, Vandals and Burgundians while Rome held fast to the solemn
definitions of the Council of Nicaea. Apart then from the teaching
authority of the Church and her infallible pronouncements, how
would Kung have discerned orthodoxy in those times, when the very
shepherds of the flock had wandered from the Nicaean faith? "Evidences," scriptural and historical at best can lead to credibility —
even by God's grace to the intellectual and spiritual urgency of
credentity. But this may be the personal experience of every earnest

Protestant Christian. For Catholic orthodoxy the authoritative and authentic voice of the magistral office of the Church is required. "He who hears you, hears Me." But faith is not to be confused with credulity. The Father does not draw us, any less than Peter, to His divine Son as non-rationals. There are credentials for belief as there were for Simon. When St. Augustine exhorted his contemporaries *crede ut intelligas* he was recommending faith, not as a substitute for, but as a condition of understanding. And Hans Kung had once both the faith and understanding for the infallibility of the Church (and of popes and councils). Faith nourishes faith. *Ex fide vivimus, ambulamus per fidem.* If faith precedes understanding, understanding becomes the reward of faith. It seems to this writer that the Kungian spiritual crisis is not how he can retrace his steps into belief and understanding in the dogma of infallibility, but rather how he can explain his loss of both. Could it be that he shredded the *preambula fidei* and the *actus fidei* into quotients of a historicist's analysis of human forces?

The definition of papal infallibility was largely decided before the Council itself voted for it (p. 89).

And then there follows five pages (pp. 89-94) of a succession of historical "ifs," thereby reducing a dogma of faith to a dialectic of human activity to the complete exclusion of the supernatural event. *"Would papal infallibility ever have been defined in 1870 if*:

the majority of the Council Fathers had not grown up in the period of the political restoration and of the antienlightenment and antirationalist romanticism of the first half of the century: a time when people in Europe, after the confusion and excesses of the great and of Napoleonic times, had an irresistible longing for peace and order, for the good, old times—in fact, for the Christian Middle Ages—and when nobody better than the pope could offer the religious foundation for the maintenance of the political-religious status quo or the restoration of the status quo ante? (p. 89).

And so on and on of *"Would papal infallibility had been defined in 1870 if . . . ."* Sonorously, these words are repeated with every consideration of a number of "historical constellations" (p. 90).

New Testamentary history led Heinrich Schlier into the Catholic Church. Historicism and its rationalist mentality have robbed Hans Kung of the faith he once had in *kepha*—the rock-foundation, the chief steward and key bearer, the strengthener of his brethren, the universal shepherd of His flock—and in Peter's successors.

As an aside, we cannot but reflect how amusing the thrust of the passage quoted above might have sounded to the England of Gladstone, to the Freemasonic Republic of united Italy, to the laicist Third Republic of France, to the Germany of Bismarck and of the Kulturkampf. If, on the contrary, the passage is a commentary on the Fathers of the First Vatican Council, then their inability to read the "signs of the times" must be proven not presumed—and surely not to the extent of falsifying their Catholic Faith!

After this historicist motivation behind the religious declaration of a faith-consciousness by its teaching office—as Kung sees it—the situation becomes even more hopeless in explaining the minority's acceptance of the defined dogma. For example, Kung quotes Aubert on the religious mentality of the majority and minority at the Council (and of the generality of the faithful and clergy in the universal Church):

> Even if they did not approve all the centralizing measures of the Curia, these prelates hardly saw anything unsuitable about a solemn acknowledgement by the Council of papal infallibility, *which was admitted at least in practice by their faithful and clergy and which seemed to them an obvious theological truth.* They saw in the Gallican and Febronian theses a backward step, a departure from the ancient tradition attested by some Scripture texts which seemed to them quite clear and by the totality of the great scholastic teachers from St. Thomas to Bellarmine.
>
> They considered it normal therefore to take advantage of the assembling of the Council to cut short the revival of what they regarded as completely sterile controversies on this matter. (R. Aubert, *Vatican I*, Paris, 1964, pp. 110-111, quoted by Kung, p. 122-123. Italics supplied)

Kung then quotes Aubert on the minority (*Inquiry*, pp. 123-124). Even this Kung will construe as a historical entrapment of the minority in their own religious predispositions:

> For from a theological perspective too, it cannot be overlooked that the minority itself remained largely fixed in the traditional ways of looking at questions. (*Inquiry*, p. 124)

If only the Council Fathers of the universal Church could have assembled at the First Vatican Council each with a *tabula rasa*!

For one who makes demands for "proofs," "demonstrations," and "substantiation," one might suppose that the Scriptural Petrine texts and the faith consciousness of the universal Church (which Kung acknowledges) might yield a more credible and probative force of papal primacy and magisterial infallibility than Kung's own clairvoyant probing of motives, a search for historical causes and a psychological reading of the religious predispositions of the Fathers of the First Vatican Council. Kung is a victim of the pitfalls of scientific intelligence, which proceeding as it does by way of analysis, solely (albeit unwittingly) on the level of natural monism, breaks up the concrete whole of Christian experience. An analysis is a basic method that brings to the fore information. It is not an explanation. Besides, Kung employs solely the historical (?) and psychological approach about a supernatural event, without even admitting to the theological approach, i.e., the development of a religious doctrine into a formal article of faith, the implicates of conciliar definitive judgments on Christology, Trinity, Grace in the fourth and fifth centuries. Nor does he entertain the philosophical inquiry and speculate: is it possible for God to speak in time, place, and local language the same way of salvation to all men to the end of time without the hazards of serious distortion of His word? Could Christ Jesus, true God and true man, effectively guarantee that His Gospel can be preached to all men to the end of time inviolably as He promised, whatever the language, the attendant historical circumstances, the cultural differentiation? Ultimately the question is, is God the Redeemer capable of speaking to all men through His Church? If faith seeks understanding, understanding finds the necessary presuppositions to a wider intelligibility.

Evidences, scriptural and historical, are seen, at first, dimly as a light shining in darkness, because of the indisponibility of the whole person who is divinely "drawn" to the ecclesial faith. This religious orientation gradually invests the "evidences" with credibility; they become worthy of belief. God's grace engenders the intellectual and spiritual urgency of credentity. Individuals who lose their faith feel compelled to give reasons, just as believers give reason, and the demonstrative force on either side is almost equally never conclusive to the opposing camp. The gift of Faith is the great divide. This faith in ecclesial infallibility, papal and conciliar, Kung had prior to *Inquiry*, and explained and "demonstrated" with manifest personal commitment.

But we have not yet done with Kung's demand for "proofs." It must be reviewed within the larger context of theological methodology to which we now turn.

Methodology and Proofs

Each *scientia* has its own discipline, the appropriate way to learn. The Greeks spoke of the *méthodos* from *metá*, "after," and *ódós* "road" or "way." Method is applied both to the process or art of investigation and to the treatise or body of knowledge resulting from inquiry. Plato was the first philosopher to use the term, but Aristotle gave it technical meaning. He raised the question whether there is one method of inquiry for all subject matters. He concluded that there are as many methods as there are subject matters or parts of subject matters. For the Romans method was *via* or *ratio* or *ars*. For Cicero it was *ratio diserendi*. The right course of inquiry is *recta ratio* or you are off the road—*a-poria*. The meanings of methods developed through the centuries have been as diverse as the kinds of philosophies, sciences, arts, beliefs and problems. But generally no one denies there is an appropriate way for each discipline, however understood. The appropriate method is to ensure that the right road has been taken to the benefit of the inquiry and to avoid the errors and absurdities by the incautious or overweening presumptions into alien studies. In the immediate post-Reformation period, since the days of Melchior Cano's epoch making treatise, *De locis theologicis* (1563), theologians have stressed the increasing necessity of the defined areas of each theological discipline, especially with the growing demand for interdisciplinarian theological studies, an instruction that has been much discussed in our own day by Journet, Muñiz, Fries, Thils, Congar, Lonergan.

Now Kung fails in coping with the requirements of theological methodology in two ways: first, in his hasty and uncritical referrals to matters of fundamental theology, dogmatic theology, biblical textual criticism, scriptural exegesis, ecclesiastical and secular history he makes no open acknowledgement of abiding with the methodology appropriate to each of these sciences, nor does he in fact give any evidence that he does; second, in his demands for "proofs" for the Catholic dogmas of ecclesial infallibility, of the popes and of the councils, of the divine inspiration and inerrancy of Scripture Kung withdraws from the faith-consciousness of the Catholic faithful—in a word, he will not leave the Catholic Church, and who at the same time demands the "proofs" of fundamental theology such as are offered to non-Catholics.

There are two questions that Kung does not raise. One, what would constitute a "proof" in matters of faith, and in particular, in matters of divine institution. Secondly, what would be their efficacy in the light of the theology of the act of faith—"No one can come to Me unless My Father draws him,"—and faith in Christ Jesus is faith in the apostolic faith in Christ Jesus *as transmitted to us by the Catholic Church.*

There are no mathematical Q.E.D.s in theology. The Church points out, as did John the Baptist, "Behold the Lamb of God who takes away the sins of the world." (Jn. 1:29, 30, 34) The best human demonstration can achieve is to *"give witness"* by the depth of our Catholic Faith, our intelligent persuasions, our zeal and charity for all, especially the "least of His brethren." That is what Jesus expected of His apostles—"to give witness to Him," "to be a *witness of Him.*" (Lk. 24:47; Acts 1:8, 22; 5:32; 2:32; 3:15; 10:39-43; 13:31). They gave witness not only to the historical reality of the Christ-event; they proclaimed their own Christian faith (a gift of the Father) in the divine meaning of that reality. Now the Fathers of the First Vatican Council gave witness, in accordance with the faith-awareness of the universal Church—which Kung admits (pp. 122, 123, *Inquiry*)—to the divine meaning of the historical reality of the Petrine texts and of Peter's leadership so manifest in the *Acts of the Apostles—et tu aliquando conversus.*

But the Kungian demand for "proof" situated as it ought to be within the distinct requirements of diverse methodologies cannot be uprooted from one's own spiritual and intellectual life. For the Catholic theologian the basic method remains always—*faith seeking understanding—Fides quarens intellectum*, the subtitle of St. Anselm's Proslogion, a book to support the faith of the believer. The Catholic theologian begins with faith, remains always within the faith, and the objective is a zealous search for a clearer, deeper, and greater knowledge of the mysteries of God revealed in and through history (Eph. 1: 9). The procession is *ex fide in fidem*. The *fides formata* cannot be separated from *fides informata* by a process of titration. For the cognitive process of the Catholic theologian is invested with faith and faith is never reducible to merely epistemic realities even in a systematic methodic doubt for the sake of reexamining the credentials for a solemnly defined dogma.

It is an ancient historical tradition of the Church theologians.

During the Medieval Age of faith (which was far more an age of reason than the seventeenth and eighteenth centuries)—it was a time of *quaestiones, controversiae, disputationes,* Abelard's method of inquiry, the *Sic et Non,* the Thomistic *videtur quod non,* a relentless scrutiny that challenged every theological and philosophical verity in order to plumb the full dimensions of a question and to conclude to a richer knowledge of truth that had already been professed.

Reason alone does not satisfy reason even in the very observance of theological methodologies. To the directive—*fides quaerens intellectum*—we must yet add for the sufficiency of reason even on the supernal level in the very employment of the appropriate theological method—*intellectus quarens intellectum per fidem.* (Maine de Biran) There is always the rationally incalculable, the grace of faith that is the way and the truth that leads to eternal life. Catholics are neither bound nor allowed to suspend their assent by a positive methodic doubt until they have scientifically justified their assent. The Fathers of the First Vatican Council excluded the parity of conditions for Catholics and non-Catholics in this question of positive methodic doubt.

> illi enim, qui fidem sub Ecclesiae magisterio susceperunt, nullam umquam habere possunt iustam causam mutandi aut in dubium fidem eandem revocandi. (DS 3014)

There are grave hazards to Kung's open-ended methodology. Selective Catholicism bears within itself a logic of declension in the faith that is professed. The Catholic theologian who does not accept the Church's formative role in a Catholic's faith departs from what makes faith—*recedit a formali ratione fidei* (cf. Cajetan's Commentary in the Leonine edition of *Opera S. Thomae Aq.,* Vol. VIII, p. 10, *Ad primam ergo*). St. Thomas Aquinas considers the faith consequences to a "Catholic" who departs from one article of faith—

> manifestum est, quod talis haereticus circa unum articulum fidem non habet de aliis articulis, sed opinionem quandam secundum propriam voluntatem. (II, II, q. 5, a. 3)

This declension of faith has proceeded from Kung's assault upon Catholic ecclesiology to his latest disintegration of the Nicene-Constantinople Creed by his assault upon Christology in his latest publication *Christ Sein*. The core belief of all Christianity except for liberal Protestantism is the divinity of Christ. The logical and necessitous consequences of Kung's denial that authentic and valid propositional categoriacal affirmations of revelational disclosures may be made with the protective assistance of the divine Spirit of Truth against the human capacity of errancy by the divinely instituted infallible teaching office of the Catholic Church, has led *gradatim* to the rejection of the Trinity, Incarnation (and the divinity of Christ), the Virgin maternity of Mary, the actuality of the Resurrection and Ascension, the divine constitutional structuring of the hierarchical Church, the Real Presence of the Incarnate Word by the sacerdotal consecration in the Eucharistic liturgy, etc. All this Kung has brought about by inserting, as liberal Protestants have so long done, a dichotomy between the historical Jesus and the Christ of Faith despite the evangelical insistence on the identity, and by constituting scientism and the modernity of man the *norma normans* of *relevant* religious belief, a predictable consequence of the theological gnoseology of Kung put forth in *Unfallibility? An Inquiry.* (cf. pp. 157-240) We shall have occasion to discourse in a succeeding volume on Kung's assault on ecumenism by his offensive rejection of what is essential to Catholics, to Protestants, (excluding liberal Protestantism), to Orthodox Greeks, despite his avowed purpose for ecumenicity.

Our Heavenly Father does not draw us less than Peter to His Divine Son, as non-rationals. There are, of course, credentials for belief as there were for Simon—the whole public ministry, the miracles, the Old Testament prophecies—*nullus quippe credit aliquid, nisi prius cogitaverit esse credendum.*

Perhaps no one has ever so sensitively felt and theologically probed more deeply the need for the intelligibility of the articles of faith than St. Augustine so that credibility can be distinguished from credulity on the one hand and from the incredulous on the other. And God willed it so.

> Far be it from us to suppose that God abhors in us that by virtue of which He has made us superior to other animals. Far be it, I say, that we should believe in such a way as to exclude the necessity either of accepting or requiring reason; since we could not even believe unless we possessed rational souls. (Ep: 120.3 *ad Consentium*)

Augustine would not have been satisfied with a mode of acceptance in which faith is content to remain blind, that is, to stop short with the *credo quia absurdum* of Tertullian.   Reason is not excused from accountability but rather must itself present credentials by virtue of which it presumes to operate.   And all scholars of St. Augustine will surely agree that human intelligence was never more earnestly exerted to the fullest extent of its capabilities than St. Augustine's in his *De Trinitate* in his effort to make this greatest of mysteries intelligible.   And at the same time Augustine insists that faith itself provides the conditions for understanding—*crede ut intelligas*.   And the indispensable intermediary between reason and faith is divinely constituted authority.

> And for the man that cannot see the truth, authority is at hand to make him fit for this, and to allow him to purge himself. (*De utilitate credendi* c. 34)

And once so benefited,

> Faith has its own eyes, with which, in a certain way, it sees to be true what it does not yet see, and with which it sees with complete certainty that it does not yet see what it believes. (Ep: 120. 8)

The source of faith is divine authority; the motive for faith is divine authority; the content of faith is guaranteed by divine authority; and it is preserved on earth by a magistral authority within the Church that is guaranteed by that same divine authority not to fail.   To believe is to believe with the Church and within the Church.

St. Thomas Aquinas forcibly stresses the limitations of reason and of empirical evidences for the "demonstration" of divine truths by his discussion of the apostolic belief in the Risen Jesus.

> Utrum fuisset conveniens quod discipuli viderent Christum resurgere *Ad primum* ergo dicendum quod apostoli potuerunt testificari Christi resurrectionem etiam de visu; quia Christum post resurrectionem viventem oculata fide viderent, quem mortuum sciverant. (S.T. III, q. 55, Art. II, ad lm)

Even ocular testimony must be supernaturally uplifted to recognize the Lord of Glory.   And given this *oculata fide*, Thomas could not yet have confessed the Risen Jesus to be, "My Lord and My God" (Jn. 20:28) except by the gift of faith.   How would Kung "prove" the divinity of Christ Jesus to non-Christians and nonbelievers? How would Kung prove to the modern Jews that Christ Jesus is the Messiah foretold by the prophets of the Old Testament (cf. Lk 24: 13-35).

Between the credibility of the Catholic Church as *the* Church of Christ and the inerrancy of its solemn teaching and the actual "obedience in faith" there is the great divide—the gift of faith. This is the real issue of the credibility of the Catholic Church—is this the Church of Christ Jesus?—and not whether the manner of living among some ecclesiastics or the manner of exercising authentic authority appears credible to non-Catholics. This seems to be Kung's constant refrain. On the credibility of conduct, we may recall that Our Lord's conduct turned Him off as the Messiah for the Jewish Sanhedrin. But as for us Christians in a very real sense it is an irrelevant question. Our failings are personal; they do not impugn the Church which has inspired extraordinary and general sanctity.

Years ago, I was walking with one of my graduate students, a Jew, a very good and devoted friend. He jokingly spoke of scandals, true or alleged, in the Catholic Church. He was visibly disturbed when I continued to add to his narration. In embarrassment he apologized for an unfair joke. I responded, "You see, the question is whether we are speaking of the Church which Christ Our Lord instituted or what we Christians do to it, with it."

To conclude a discussion that really deserved both on Kung's part and my own a lengthier discussion on the credentials of faith (and ecclesial and Petrine and papal infallibility are matters of faith)—and the theologizing within the faith—awareness of Church dogmas, we quote St. Paul on how he understood his problem in rendering the apostolic faith worthy of acceptance:

> As for myself, brethren, when I came to you I did not come proclaiming God's testimony with particular eloquence or "wisdom." No, I determined that while I was with you I would speak of nothing but Jesus Christ and Him crucified. When I came among you it was in weakness and fear, and with much trepidation. My message and my preaching had none of the persuasive force of "wise" argumentation, but the convincing power of the Spirit. As a consequence, your faith rests not on the wisdom of men but on the power of God. (1 Cor. 2:1-5 NAB trans.)

Kung's demand for "proofs" overlooks the real question. How did it come about that his former faith in ecclesial and papal infallibility, in the inerrancy of Scripture, is now lost despite the fact that the *material* is the same, the Scriptural texts, the historical data? Where had he failed before, where is his new evidence? In his summary and hurried discourse on infallibility in *Inquiry*, he never enters into the meaning of the abiding presence of Christ in the Church and, in particular, in the exegetical construction of the Johannine texts on the unfailing assistance of the Divine Spirit of Truth (Jn. cc. 14-17)—of the "convincing power of the Spirit" that St. Paul spoke of as his only "demonstration."

As for Protestants we respectfully suggest as an intellectual and spiritual predisposition in their study of papal jurisdictional primacy and magisterial infallibility the position of an eminent liberal Protestant theologian as Kung himself records:

> It is significant that even such a theologian as Karl Barth, who can certainly not be accused of "Catholicizing tendencies," and who has often and vigorously proclaimed his opposition to the Papacy, admits that it is impossible to establish *from the Gospel any radical* objection either to the concentration of the apostolic function in Peter or to the possibility of a primacy in the Church, which might even be that of Rome. (Kung, *The Council, Reform and Reunion*, 1961, p. 138; cf. K. Barth, *Church Dogmatics*, Edinburgh, 1936, vol. 1, pp. 106-115)

In 1961, Kung wrote this passage in an ecumenical effort to encourage Protestants to restudy the primacy—which he declared to be a matter of Catholic faith—of the pope (to whom he then referred as the "Vicar of *Christ*"). In 1961 his overiding concern was that the papacy be *spiritually* credible (p. 139). Ten years later, in *Inquiry* (1970), Kung denies ecclesial and Petrine and Papal infallibility to be rooted in Scripture. In 1970 he writes of "the absolutist monarch—the only one from the old order who has survived the French Revolution." (*Inquiry*, p. 107)

To continue with the Kungian *aporiae*. In regard to both the procedural methodology (the requirements of a theological or non-theological discipline) and the substantive methodology (the faith or lack of faith, that is, the "state of mind," from which and within which one theologizes), Kung enjoys the dubious advantages of an open-ended methodology of his own choosing in numerous considerations.

For example, Kung objects to the fact that Pope Paul VI decided against the majority report of the commission on artificial birth control. (*Inquiry*, p. 40) But Kung does not tell us what constitutes a majority right or wrong. Galileo was condemned by a near-unanimous papal commission, an "overwhelming majority" which Kung reprobates. (*Inquiry*, p. 31) The Second General Assembly of the Synod of Bishops which convened in Rome in 1971 unanimously reaffirmed the present discipline of priestly celibacy in the Latin Church. Yet, Kung called upon priests to disregard this ruling. Kung might have noted for his readers that the papal commission on artificial birth regulation was devoid of all authority human or divine. There was no misunderstanding about this in the mind of Cardinal Suenens. In 1962, the year the Council opened, Cardinal Suenens said:

> What was condemned as intrinsically immoral yesterday will not become moral tomorrow. No one should entertain any confused doubt or false hopes on the point. The Church has not decided that these (contraceptive) practices are immoral; she has merely confirmed what the moral law already said about them.

And at the Vatican Council, Cardinal Suenens chose to conclude his speech of November 7, 1964 on the Schema on the Missions pointedly to reject and dispel the misconstruction he claimed the press had placed upon his speech on marriage of the 29th of October with these unambiguous affirmations:

> Allow me to take this opportunity and this method of replying very briefly to some reactions in public opinion which interpreted my speech on matrimonial ethics as if I had said that the doctrine and discipline of the Church in this matter had changed. So far as doctrine is concerned, my words made it quite clear that I was asking *only for research* in this whole area, *not with a view to changing anything in the Church's doctrine which has been already authentically and definitively proclaimed*, but only with a view to elaborating a synthesis of all the principles which are relevant to this domain. So far as discipline is concerned, it is clear that the conclusions of the Commission to which I have referred have to be *submitted to the authority of the Sovereign Pontiff and adjudged by his*

supreme authority. I said this explicitly. It is obvious that any decisions regarding the functioning of the Commission rest exclusively with that same authority. I say these things now in order to remove all misunderstandings in public opinion.

Cardinal Suenens, had no doubt about the unchangeable validity of the Church's moral teaching on contraceptive birth control nor did he misunderstand the service of the Papal Commission.

Kung's Misconstruction of Episcopal Authority

On p. 71, Kung quotes from *Lumen Gentium*:

In matters of faith and morals, the bishops speak in the name of Christ and the faithful are to accept their teaching and adhere to it with a religious assent of soul . . . . (art. 25)

Kung's commentary on this:

Can the simple statement of one bishop—who is acknowledged to be fallible—command in this way, unconditionally, a religious submission of will and mind (in the school's question for instance, when a bishop declares it to be a matter of faith or morals)?

We observe that Kung omits the introductory sentence of the paragraph:

Bishops, *teaching in communion with the Roman Pontiff*, are to be respected by all as witnesses to divine and Catholic truth. (Italics supplied)

In this pontifical and collegial context, the sentence he quotes above can hardly be considered a mantle covering "misuse of episcopal authority" (p. 71). As for Kung's commentary, no pope, no ecumenical council, no bishop, no theologian has ever taught that "one bishop" can teach in matters of faith and morals independently from the doctrinal teaching of the Church, much less—and this borders on the facetious, can a "school's question" be a matter of faith and morals.

At the bottom of p. 71, Kung asks:

Why is the individual bishop as successor of the apostles—who, according to this theory, were infallible as individuals—not also infallible as individual bishops?

Because the extraordinary power of infallibility which each of the Twelve and St. Paul had was given to each of them by virtue of their direct personal election by Christ Jesus, their unique status is manifestly non-replaceable. The body of bishops are successors to the apostolic college not obviously as the Twelve apostles but as inheritors of the apostolic office, which is the basic constitutive element of the Church, with its original apostolic commission to teach His word to the consummation of ages and its continuance in the apostolic witness and *kerygma*. Bishops individually are fallible; but collectively (as a college) whether dispersed or gathered together in ecumenical councils they share in the infallibility of the Church because and when they act in unison and agreement with its head, the rock-foundation, the key-bearer, and the supreme shepherd of the universal Church in whom the charism of the infallibility of the Church is individually present.

Tradition, Scripture, and the Magisterium

Another Kungian *aporia* is his adversary "state of intellect" which disposes him to divorce and even set at odds with one another the multiple constituents of an indissoluble divine-human integral reality. He disjoins the institutional from the Charismatic Church; the Pope, the visible Head of the Church, from its invisible Head, the Lord of Glory; the Pope from the Church; the Church from the Mystical Body of Christ; the Church's Teaching Office from the Holy Spirit (*passim*; cf., in particular, pp. 74-79; 101-108). We will now focus upon Kung's disjunction of what the Fathers of the Second Vatican Council declared to be inseparable—sacred tradition, sacred scripture, and the teaching authority of the Church.

But when either the Roman Pontiff or the body of bishops together with him defines a judgment, they pronounce it in accord with revelation itself. All are obliged to maintain and be ruled by this revelation, which, as written or preserved by tradition, is transmitted in its entirety through the legitimate succession of bishops and especially through the care of the Roman Pontiff himself. Under the guiding light of the Spirit of truth, revelation is religiously preserved and faithfully expounded in the Church. (*Lumen Gentium*, art. 25)

Kung's commentary on this text is:

It might almost seem from this that in the last resort the teaching office of the pope and the bishops is in fact the ultimate, self-sufficient authority on what is revelation. Are perhaps the accusations confirmed here that some raise against the Catholic Church and theology: that Scripture is played down by the present day teaching office, which decides what is tradition and therefore also what is Scripture? (*Inquiry*, 76)

Again in a related passage in the Dogmatic Constitution on Divine Revelation (*Dei Verbum*), the Council Fathers declare:

It is clear, therefore, that sacred tradition, sacred Scripture, and the teaching authority of the Church, in accord with God's most wise design, are so linked and joined together that one cannot stand without the others, and that all together and each in its own way under the action of the one Holy Spirit contribute effectively to the salvation of the souls. (Art. 10)

And Kung's commentary:

Vatican II however suffered from the first day to the last from the fact that the question of what really is the ultimate, supreme norm for the renewal of the Church remained undecided. Once again the beneficiaries were that group which, for understandable reasons, was able to prevent a decision in favor of the New Testament: the Roman Curia, its teaching office and canon law.

Kung's animadversions on the solemn declarations of the Fathers of the twenty-first Ecumenical Council are *unspiritual*. The oral transmission of Christian revelation by the teaching of the apostolic Church preceded the New Testament, most of the *Epistles* and *Acts of the Apostles* by years, and the four gospels by decades. By divine ordination, this tradition was to be preserved without deformation; and fidelity to the received tradition was the ultimate assurance that the doctrine proposed was genuine. The formative role played by tradition in the composition of New Testament Scriptures attained their definitive form under the authoritative supervision of the Apostolic Church. Tradition as the living faith of the Church in Christ Jesus did not eliminate itself by the formation of the Scriptures of the new dispensation. It endures as the faith consciousness of the new people of God toward the fulness of divine truth by virtue of the abiding presence of Christ and the unfailing assistance of the Spirit of Truth. (Jn. cc. 14-17) It is of this divine *paradosis* that St. Irenaeus wrote:

> And what if not even the Apostles themselves had left us any Scriptures? Ought we not to follow the course of that tradition which they delivered to those to whom they entrusted the Churches? (*Adv. Haer.* 3.4.1)

> And to this rule consent many nations of the Gentiles, those I mean who believe in Christ, having salvation written by the Spirit in their hearts, without paper and ink, and diligently keeping the old tradition. (*ibid.* 3.4.2)

In a sense, a gospel was prior to the Gospels.

> For by no others have we known the method of our salvation than those by whom the gospel came to us: which was both in the first place preached by them, and afterwards by the will of God handed down to us in the Scriptures, to be the ground and pillar of our faith. (*ibid.* 3.1.1.)

The Council of Trent affirmed the existence of unwritten apostolic traditions. And the Second Vatican Council reaffirmed this Ireneian persuasion:

> The Church, in her teaching, life and worship, perpetuates and hands to all generations all that she herself is, all that she believes (*Verbum Dei*, art. 8)

Tradition of the Church is the living faith of the Church, which was prior to Scripture, recorded in Scripture, and accompanies Scripture in the Church's understanding of Scripture—and more; it is the living tradition of the Christian faith. Nowhere is tradition more vital among the faithful than in sacramentary liturgy. Christ speaks and acts in the liturgy, for it embodies the Scriptures and reenacts the salvific events of His life and death, His Resurrection and ascension. For example, in the Holy Sacrifice of the Mass there is reenacted the Last Supper—*This is My Body; This is My Blood;* the redemptive sacrifice of Golgotha—*which will be given up for you; will be shed for you;* the Resurrection which both validates and ratifies the Redemptive act. In addition to the Scriptural readings, the *Gloria*, and the *Credo*, the Canon of the Mass embodies all the principal articles of faith, the Trinity, the Incarnation, Virgin Motherhood of Mary, Real Presence, Resurrection, Angels, Ascension, heaven, purgatory, hell, the Church, saints, intercessory prayers—repeatedly affirmed and interwoven into an all enveloping act of faith uniting all the faithful in one Mystical Body of Christ, more real than reality— mystically. In this sense the Mass through the centuries, since the days of "the breaking of the bread" by the Apostles, was *kerygma, didache, catechesis.*

Both Scripture and Tradition need a living bearer, one who assumes the responsibility for their authenticity. This has been fulfilled by Christ Jesus in His personal selection of Peter as the Rock foundation of His Church, the key-bearer, strengthener of his brethren, universal shepherd of His flock, and head of the apostolic college. Christ also promised to send the Holy Spirit to guarantee infallibly the retention of the *depositum fidei* and its development. How else could the canonical scriptures be recognized. Since divine inspiration pertains to the realm of the supernatural the fact of inspiration can be known only through divine revelation. The proximate criterion of biblical canon is the infallible decision of the Church. St. Augustine wrote: "I would not believe the Gospel unless the authority of the Church moved me to do so." This writer cannot suppress the notion that because Scriptural inspiration requires as its complement the gift of infallibility that Kung in the latter part of his book (pp. 209-221) will deny the inerrancy of Scripture.

Scripture is the permanent *norma normans, non normata* of the Church, which is the *norma normata* of orthodoxy. But Scripture is not self-explanatory, not *sui ipsius interpres.* The Ethiopian's reply, when the apostle Philip asked him if he understood what he was reading, focuses directly on this unavoidable problematic: "How can I unless I have someone to guide me?" (*Acts* 8:31). The Catholic Church undertakes that office; she does what none else can do by virtue of her divinely endowed trust to preserve the *depositum fidei.* The passage from Scripture was *Isaias* 53:7-8, "Like a lamb that is led to the slaughter-house" etc. The Ethiopian then asked of the apostle: "Tell me, is the prophet referring to himself or someone else?" "Starting, therefore, with this text of scripture, Philip proceeded to explain the Good News of Jesus to him." (Acts 8:35). Scripture speaks God's salvific message, but not by itself alone. It needs the apostolic tradition for the authentic commentary, the inerrant interpretation. Otherwise Christians are abandoned to the "fertility of the heretical principle," as John Henry Newman called it, and the historical consequence of proliferation of Protestant sects and churches, and worse still, within liberal Protestantism to exegetical systems that are subversive of Scripture. Since the days of Marcion, Scripture has been used to support heterodoxy no less than orthodoxy. The realization that the clarity of the intelligibility of Scripture (and the illumination of the Holy Spirit) can serve contrarient claims of understanding led Tertullian to subordinate it to the "rule of faith" from which the interpretation of Scripture must never deviate. This "rule of faith" is the body of teaching handed on by the Church. Actually, as Pope Pius XII observed in *Divino Afflante Spiritu*, there is a very small number of scriptural texts whose meaning has been authoritatively settled. (AAS 35 [1945] 319) But the magisterium exercises its authoritative supervision by approving or disapproving, by reminding theologians of the requirements of *analogia fidei* (cf. Rm. 12:3) and of the "rule of faith."

Tradition, Scripture, and the Magisterium—each is supreme as each can be. Scripture has *actual* supremacy; but it is not self-explanatory. Tradition can be authentic and inauthentic. The discriminatory norm is within itself. But the discriminatory judgment, the act of recognition is magistral. The Magisterium in its abiding faith-consciousness by virtue of the divine mandate has the *practical* supremacy. It can teach authoritatively, unerringly. It explains, declares, interprets as only the Spirit-assisted Teacher can to which the interpretation of Scripture has been exclusively entrusted.

Kung's comments on the passage from *Verbum Dei*, are unspiritual. He never considers what the abiding assistance of the Divine Spirit of Truth can and does mean, what its unfailing efficacy is, to ensure that the divine intent be fulfilled in this beneficent circular interdependent relationship of Tradition, Scripture, and Magisterium. Without full acknowledgment, for the "action of the one Holy Spirit" (*Verbum Dei*, c. 10), without any apparent theological sensitivity to the divine presence of the Spirit of Truth (Jn. cc. 14-16), Kung reduces the living tradition of the Church to the exigencies of historicism and submits Scripture to arbitrary, self-serving interpretation by the teaching office of the Church (*Inquiry*, pp. 76, 77). The Fathers of the Second Vatican Council under the guidance of the Holy Spirit had an entirely different Christian vision of the living faith of the Church:

> The task of authentically interpreting the word of God, whether written or handed on, has been entrusted exclusively to the living teaching office of the Church, whose authority is exercised in the name of Jesus Christ. This teaching office is not above the word of God, but serves it, teaching only what has been handed on, listening to it devoutly, guarding it scrupulously, and explaining it faithfully by divine commission and with the help of the Holy Spirit; it draws from this one deposit of faith everything which it presents for belief as divinely revealed.

> It is clear, therefore, that sacred tradition, sacred Scripture, and the teaching authority of the Church, in accord with God's most wise design, are so linked and joined together that one cannot stand without the others, and that all together and each in its own way under the action of the Holy Spirit contribute effectively to the salvation of souls. (*Verbum Dei*, art. 10)

Kung has missed God's "most wise design."

Kung Misunderstands Pope John XXIII

We are now advancing to the more serious *aporiae* of Hans Kung. Until now, we have had to contend with his resentments to "Rome" and all that "Rome" stands for, with his exploitation of an uprooted history, of his partisan argumentations, and unwarranted assumptions, his historicist and rationalist approach to divine-human realities. We will now examine Kung's misuse of sources, primary and secondary. To begin with an uncomplicated one. Kung repeatedly holds up Pope John XXIII as his model of a pope, and of the principal reasons that he gives for this high veneration is that Pope John did not speak *ex cathedra* and that he precluded any solemn dogmatic definitions for the Second Vatican Council. Kung quotes Pope John as saying:

> I'm not infallible; I'm infallible only when I speak *ex cathedra*. But I'll never speak ex cathedra." And John XXIII never did speak *ex cathedra*. (*Inquiry*, 87)

Pope John never disclaimed papal infallibility. On the contrary, he confesses to this unique papal prerogative in the quotation above. And if he did not speak *ex cathedra*, neither did Leo XIII, Benedict XIV, Pius XI, nor to this day has Pope Paul VI. No inference, however subliminal, other than its facticity can be drawn. Certainly no prejudicial commentary on the dogma of *ex cathedra* infallible definitions.

On October 11, 1962, the first day of the Council, Pope John addressed the Fathers in Peter's Basilica. We excerpt the following:

> In calling this vast assembly of bishops, the latest and humble successor of the Prince of the Apostles who is addressing you *intended to assert once again the magisterium, (teaching authority), which is unfailing* and perdures until the end of time, in ᵣ order that this magisterium, taking into account the errors, the requirements, and the opportunities of our time, might be presented in exceptional form to all men throughout the world.

(We may note at this point that Pope John spoke "of the magisterium," "this magisterium," "this extraordinary magisterium," the "Church's magisterium," "magisterium" on this solemn occasion. Kung denies there is a teaching office in the Church. (cf. *Inquiry,* 221-240)

> The greatest concern of the Ecumenical Council is this: that the sacred deposit of Christian doctrine should be guarded and taught more efficaciously . . . from the renewed, serene, and tranquil adherence to all the teaching of the Church in its entirety and preciseness, as it still shines forth in the Acts of the Council of Trent and First Vatican Council . . . .

In the light of Pope John's intent to bring the Church's deposit of faith, intact and without any compromise (including Vatican I and not excluding its solemn definitions on papal primacy and magisterial infallibility)—"to transmit the doctrine, pure and integral, without any attenuation or distortion"—to bear upon the lives of modern men and the awesome problems that burden the world, to unite men in charity—there is no startling reflection on the fact that the Council acting in accordance with Pope John's directive did not solemnly define any doctrine, not even that of episcopal collegiality. *Still,* the teachings of the Second Vatican Council are solemn declarations of

cussion, imply the possibility that their authors had a fair chance of their works being accepted by contemporaries. To undertake all this labor of collecting and inventing documents, if there were little prospect of acceptance, would be hardly more than an exercise in mental gymnastics. To judge by the numerous manuscripts of these forgeries still extant, the assumption is not unwarranted that their authors sensed the climate of the time correctly. By forging documents they clothed the one or the other hierocratic idea in the language of a decree issued by a second—or third century pope. What the forgers did not invent was ideology: what they did forge was the decree which was to "prove" this ideology. The atmosphere of the time pervaded as it was with hierocratic ideas, together with the character of these products as useful reference works, account largely for the immediate influence which they exercised. Lastly, these great forgeries symbolize, so to speak, the coalescence of Rome and Rheims. Precisely because they had originated quite independently of the papacy, these products of the Frankish intelligentsia were to become the natural allies of the papacy. (Walter Ullmann, *The Growth of Papal Government in the Middle Ages*, 1953, p. 178)

As we have said before, these forgeries do not excel in inventing new ideas; what they did was to give certain fundamental theses, already largely accepted, a historical twist and foundation. (*ibid*. 188)

The author (of the False Decretals) wished to establish by detailed and unequivocal evidence the rights of the local episcopate to appeal directly to Rome against their metropolitans, and to safeguard the independence of the Church against the secular power. But great as was their importance for the subsequent development of canon law and for the progress of ecclesiastical centralisation in the Middle Ages, it is impossible to regard them as directly responsible for the increased prestige of the Papacy in Western Europe in the ninth century. They were a result rather than a cause of that development, which had its roots in the conditions that we have just described. (Christopher Dawson, *The Making of Europe*, 1956, p. 223)

The Isidorian Collection is a hotch-potch of authentic documents marred by interpolations of a topical nature, of manipulated passages from Greek or Latin ecclesiastical writers, reduced to the form of canons and decretals and attributed to popes, of earlier collections of dubious origin, and of pieces entirely invented. It is certain that the compilation was neither directly nor indirectly influenced by the Papacy. The overriding motive of the Frankish authors was to challenge the dominion of the metropolitan bishops over the suffragan bishops, of strengthening the central authority of the Holy See and of ending the abusive interference of laymen with the clergy. This motive drove them to insert non-existent phrases and passages into genuine documents, to create false ones and to make use of them if they had already been created. However, this may be, the *Pseudo-Isidoriana* mirrors the situation that had come into being in the Carolingean Empire and in the Frankish Church, and is an attempt at a reaction, which joined forces with that already active in both Rome and the provinces, growing steadily as under Charlemagne's heirs the Empire fell to pieces. The pretended documents were the result not the cause of an ecclesiological development strongly centered in Rome, and its provinces. The Roman claims of those times were never based on the inauthentic *Isidoriana*; rather these were based on the Roman claims. In his summary treatment of *Pseudo-Isidoriana*, Kung twice refers to *L'Ecclésiologie du Haut Moyen-Age. De Saint Grégoire le Grand à la Désunion entre Byzance et* by Y. M.–J. Congar, O. P. (du Cerf. 1968), Appendix Notes 56, 57. Having used the data-information of Congar, Hans Kung might have also have incorporated in *Inquiry* Congar's appraisal of the historic role of the *False Decretals.*

Cependant, l'utilisation formelle des FD par la Curie romaine sous Nicolas Ier et Hadrien II se réduit à peu de chose et n'a pas fondé alors un droit véritablement nouveau. n. 22. Cette conclusion est communément reçue, même par Hartmann, *Der Primat*. (p. 231)

Le Pseudo Isidore n'a nullement créé la conviction de la primauté papale; il n'a pas été sans influencer l'ecclésiologie dans le sens de la Monarchie pontificale, elle–même traduite dans un régime concret de centralisation romaine (p. 232)

From the Pseudo-Isidorian collection, the false decretals, together with numerous perfectly genuine texts were transmitted into many of the most important later collections, until the mid-twelfth century, and thus played a vital part in sustaining the doctrines of clerical and papal superiority, which received an ever more confident expression. The dubious character of these documents did not pass unnoted, and the beginnings of a critical attitude towards them appear as early as the twelfth century, in Peter Comestor, Godfrey of Viterbo and Stephen of Tournai. In the 14th and 15th centuries they were attacked by Wyclif and Nicholas of Cusa. But the falsification was proved by textual criticism in the 16th century, when first Protestants and then Febronians used it as a weapon against the Papacy, as though it constituted the title-deeds of papal authority. But it is certain that the compilation was neither directly nor indirectly influenced by the Papacy. Kung never raises the question whether any of the pretended Isidorian Decretals are correspondent to actual ecclesiastical practices and claims.

On April 19, 1961, Hans Kung received the ecclesiastical *Imprimi Potest* for the publication of his *The Council, Reform and Reunion*, scarcely four months after Pope John XXIII first announced on January 25, 1959, his intention to summon an Ecumenical Council. In this work, the Tubingen theologian discoursed on the Petrine office (132-42, 167, 171, 174, 185), papal primacy (84, 87, 133, 138-40, 161, 166, 193-201), and papal infallibility. (84, 87, 149, 161, 189, 194, 195, 197, 204)

He did not call these matters into question. For example:

> True as Catholics one can and must reply at this point that the primacy, is a matter of faith; that the Pope is indeed the Vicar of Christ but only, after all, the *Vicar* of Christ. (p. 139)

> What is called for on the Protestant side is to consider whether the words of Scripture about the abiding rock (Matt. 16:18), the guiding and ruling key bearer of the Kingdom of Heaven (Matt. 16:19), the special possessor of the power of binding and loosing (Matt. 16:19), the means of confirming the faith of others (Luke 22:32), and the deputy shepherd over the whole of Christ's flock (John 21:15 ff.)—(incidentally compare these affirmations with the diametrically different interpretations of *Inquiry*, p. 109, and elsewhere)—need to be understood more deeply, more powerfully, and with more relevance to the present day, by Protestant Christians. To ask themselves whether the Apostolic Church, united in Peter, was not meant to go on,

with the Petrine office continuing along with the pastoral office of the Apostles, for the sake of the Church (so that what was once *laid* as a foundation would continue to *function* as a foundation). (P. 140)

At no time in his book published a decade before *Inquiry* does it ever occur to Kung to challenge papal primacy and infallibility for any reason—with not even a passing reference to the *Pseudo-Isidorian* decretals of which he makes so much in *Inquiry* (pp. 115 ff.), nor of the misuse of them (in good faith) by St. Thomas Aquinas (*Inquiry*, pp. 117-119) nor the dimmest suggestion that these, historically, were the basic materials from which papal infallibility was forged and uncritically passed on *via* Aquinas-Torquemada-Cajetan-Bellamine to Vatican I. (*Inquiry*, p. 119)

We may note as an aside that Kung never before in his precedent works uses the *Pseudo-Isidorian* Decretals to the same argumentative purpose as he does in *Inquiry*.

There is not a word about the *False Decretals* to challenge papal primatial authority in *The Council, Reform and Reunion* published in 1961 where Kung writes of *the primatus jurisdictionis* as springing from the *primatus fidei* (Luke 22:32)(.133); "as a Catholic one can and must reply at this point that the primacy, too, is a matter of faith; that the Pope is indeed the Vicar of Christ but only, after all the *Vicar* of Christ" (p. 139); "What is called for on the Protestant

side is . . . ask themselves whether the Apostolic Church, united in Peter, was not meant to go on, with the Petrine office continuing along with the pastoral office of the Apostles, for the sake of the Church (so that what was once *laid* a foundation would continue to *function* as a foundation); . . . something which does indeed seem to be not the mere work of men but the work of our common Lord, promised to us and protected for us by the Word of God." (Italics in the original, p. 140)

And on pp. 167-168 Kung approvingly quotes from the writing of Otto Karrer on the *Petrine Office in the Early Church* from which we excerpt the concluding sentences:

The Petrine office is more in the nature of a breakwater against errors than a fertile source of doctrine. It is essentially regulative; but as such, according to our belief, it is willed by Christ and providentially to such a degree that, in the light of early Christian history, none of the most important of the traditional beliefs of Christendom—the canon of Scripture, Christology, the dogmas concerning the Trinity, the validity of heretical baptism—is ultimately thinkable without it.

The False decretals are not ever mentioned in 1961. In 1964 in *Structure of the Church* (pp. 289-291) Kung does speak of Pseudo-Isidore as providing the "legal Principle, that every (not only the ecumenical) lawful synod requires papal convocation and direction, that their legislative and judicial acts require papal confirmation." But as we will presently note, this very statement was in fact not forged by Pseudo-Isidore, or first discovered by him. Rather, Pseudo-Isidore is citing the unfalsified, thoroughly genuine *Historia ecclesiastica* rule which requires that no council be celebrated without the approval of the Roman Pontiff.... (CSEL LXXI. 165) Subject to correction, we point to what appears to be an anachronism. In *Structures*, (p. 289, n. 4), Kung writes:

> Pseudo-Isidore had already induced Pope Pelagius II to claim the right of convocation for the Roman See by suggesting the following: "Since the authority of the apostolic see to convoke a general synod was given to St. Peter as a singular privilege, no synod was ever ratified unless it was done by apostolic authority, etc." (Decretales Pseudoisidori, ed. Hinschius [Leipiz 1863] 721)

But the False Decretals of Isidore were written about 850 a.d. and Pope Pelagius sat in the *cathedra Petri* from 579-590.

There is vast difference in Kung's discussion of Pseudo-Isidore in *Structures* from his use of them in *Inquiry*. In *Structures*, Kung's discussion centers exclusively on the right of convocation of councils with no challenge to papal primacy and infallibility. But in *Inquiry*, Kung will argue that if the ecclesiastical practice and legislation regarding the teaching authority of the Pope is based upon "monstruous forgeries" (p. 115), then so also is theological thinking and the First Vatican Councils' dogmatic definition about this papal function. In his book, *The Church*, published in 1967 barely two years after the conclusion of the Second Vatican Council, Kung makes no mention at all of the False Isidorian Decretals, but he does, however, presage in small print the thesis on the "fundamental remaining in the truth," the "fragmentariness" and ambiguity of propositional truths (pp. 342-343) which he will espouse at greater length in *Inquiry*. (pp. 156-181) Even so we encounter an ambivalence in Kung's intellectual and spiritual "state of mind."

On p. 449 of *The Church*, Kung in small print repeats in resume what he had written in *Structures*, three years earlier. (pp. 206-223) The central sentences are:

> Since the definition of the primacy has often been misunderstood the elucidations of it emerging from the Council documents are of importance. They show that papal primacy, even in the view of Vatican I, is by no means an arbitrary absolutism, but rather that: etc.

Compare these attentive specificities with the alarums of papal absolutism in *Inquiry*. (pp. 103-108; and passim)

In concluding our reflections upon Kung's misuse of the *False Decretals*, we ask the question—what could have motivated Kung to exert himself so energetically about the Pseudo-Isidore in *Inquiry* when he had never done so before? What new knowledge had he now learned about these pretended documents in 1971 (*Inquiry*) that he had not known all along? Kung would have us think that he is playing the historical method against the dogmatic method when actually in his hands they are both casualties.

> For questions of doctrine the following claims from the forgeries were of particular importance: that the holding of any council, even of provincial council, is linked with the authority of the pope and that all more important matters in the Church are subject to the pope. (*Inquiry*, 115-116)

Actually, the Pseudo-Isidorian statement is a wholly authentic citation from the *Historia ecclesiastica tripartita* (560) of Cassiadorus:

> cum utique regula ecclesiastica jubeat non oportere praeter sententiam Romani pontificis concilia celebrari. (*Corp script eccl* lxxi, 165)

Cassiodorus' *historia* was a compendium of the ecclesiastical histories written by Theodoret of Cyr, Socrates, and Sozomen, as translated and condensed by the monk, Epiphanius. Socrates (b.c. 380; d.c. 450) was the first known layman in the field of ecclesiastical historiography. His own *Historia ecclesiastica* written between 439 and 450 and justly reputed for its objectivity, was used as a source by Cassiodorus. Writing of the absence of Pope Julius or of any papal legate at a particular synod, Socrates observes that the ecclesiastical canon requires that no ecclesiastical law may be promulgated without the concurrence of the Bishop of Rome. (M.P.G. clii. 196)   It appears then that for more than four centuries before *Pseudo-Isidore* the primatial position of the Bishop of Rome was a fact sufficiently evident to be noted by the historian, Socrates, as a general principle applicable to particular instances.

In that same Appendix—Note 56, in which Kung refers to Congar, the author also refers to an article by Horst Fuhrmann on the *Papal Primacy and the Pseudo-Isidorian Decretals.* If Kung's referral to Fuhrmann is intended to suggest the source of his data-information and the interpretation of the historic role of the Isidorian Decretals, we find that there is actually no such correspondence between the two authors. What Fuhrmann writes is the exact opposite of what Kung is trying to prove:

> What success did pseudo-Isidore actually have? Undoubtedly the forgeries of pseudo-Isidore could have generated an impulse which would have mightily furthered the strengthening and development of papal jurisdiction. To see this, a comprehensive analysis would be necessary, which however, can be pointed out: in this case the date and the development are actually less dramatic than they are commonly represented to be. *A strong acceptance of Pseudo-Isidore was not the cause, but rather the result of a development strongly centered upon Rome, and the primary influence of the forgeries must have lain completely outside the area of the rights of papal primacy.* Although the forgeries of pseudo-Isidore may because of their historical and therefore often relevant character, actually have worked as a ferment, nevertheless, in their substance—and precisely because of their freedom from temporal ties—they have not penetrated very deeply anywhere, and nowhere have they become structural elements. (pp. 335f. Italics supplied)

A comparative study of Kung's understanding of the pretended

Isidorian documents with the two authors to whom he refers, Congar and Fuhrmann, discloses no correspondence of knowledge and judgment. Kung's consistency of *Inquiry* is hardly remarkable.

Kung's Myopic Reading of Early Papal History

On pp. 111 to 114, Kung gives a cursory and jejune review of the early papacy as if to belittle the historical evidence for the papal claim of primatial authority. This is less than fair to the facts of history, to the general scenery and particular circumstances, favorable and unfavorable, and even to the silence of history which cannot be entirely ignored. Historians have been known to draw inferences, however tentative, from inaudible voices.

In what follows we point to explicit *doctrinal* claims of primacy, to *practical* claims of primacy, to events and papal conduct that proceed from such a papal authority, i.e., appeals from the East and West to Rome for final decision on matters of orthodoxy and heresy, ultimate decisions of Rome on canonical regularity of episcopal consecrations and jurisdictional disputes, the condemnations of heresies and the healing of schisms—despite an oppressive history of persecutions, imperial interference, and not least the turmoil of barbarian invasions, the sack of Rome, and the close attendance of hostile forces.

The Popes had long maintained their claim to a primatial authority in the Church as Peter's successors. The earliest recorded evidence is Pope St. Clement's *First Epistle to the Corinthians* (95) to settle a dissension in the Church at Corinth. It is to be noted that the serious religious disturbance was corrected not by St. John, the Apostle, who was still alive, but by the Bishop of Rome, Clement, whom the ancient lists of the Popes, including that found in Irenaeus (*Adv. haer.* III. 3.3) agree in showing him as the third successor of St. Peter. Of the second century popes, hardly anything is known of them—St. Evaristus, St. Alexander, St. Sixtus, St. Telephorus (martyred under Hadrian), St. Hyginus, St. Pius, St. Anicetus (who received Polycarp), St. Soter, and St. Eleutherius (a friend of St. Irenaeus). All are distinguished by the veneration for holiness they were held in by the faithful. It may be that the secrecy to which persecution drove the Church covered its official administration with a mantle of silence. And perhaps the open, public assertion of religious authority in the independence of the new Christian faith *vis-a-vis* the all enveloping one, supreme, universal, and omnipotent *potestas* of the Roman

State would be in the realm of the most unlikelihood. After all, Pope St. Clement's letter was sent and addressed to Corinth, not too far from the rim of the Roman Empire. No conclusive argument can be drawn from the silence of history. With Pope St. Julius I, 337-352, whose election to the papacy coincided roughly with the death of Constantine, papal authority in the universal Church takes on a public prominence in the great controversy over St. Athanasius and the Arians. In 341, he addressed a letter to the church at Antioch where the Arians under the forceful agitation of Eusebius of Nicomedia became part of the anti-Nicaean reaction and among others ousted Athanasius from his bishopric at Alexandria. In this celebrated letter, Pope Julius declares himself not bound by the decisions of the Council of Tyre (335), that he had the right to judge the bishoprics of Antioch or Alexandria, that the contestation over the bishopric of Alexandria should have been brought *first* to him for a just judgment. The Eusebians are charged with violating the canons by deposing Athanasius without reference to Rome. Both the Eusebians and Athanasius turned to Rome for final decision —though the Eusebians did not abide by Julius' defense of Athanasius. At the Council of Sardica (Sofia) in 343, convoked by the Emperors Constans I and Constantius, at the request of Pope Julius, after the Eusebians seceded, the remaining 100 Western bishops and six Oriental bishops confirmed the orthodoxy and legitimate consecration of Athanasius of Alexandria, of Aesclepiades of Gaza, and Marcellus of Ancyra, who had been deposed at the Council of Tyre (355) by the Semiarian Eusebians and replaced by members of the Anti-Nicene party. Each of these three had appealed to Rome for final judgment on their orthodoxy. At Sardica, several canons were passed that were intended to regulate appeals to Rome, in particular canons, 3, 4, 5. A deposed bishop who appealed to Rome should not be replaced until judgment was passed. Canon 5 acknowledged the right of the bishop of Rome to receive and judge an appeal, to send the case to be adjudicated by neighboring bishops, or to send or designate the judge. In its encyclical letter to all the churches describing its decisions, it declared among other things, the propriety of the provinces in keeping in touch with "the head, that is the See of Peter, the Apostle." Unfortunately, all these settlements were ineffective because of the secession of the Arian bishops who refused to abide by the judgment of Sardica. Nonetheless these canons manifest the prevailing mind of over 100 Western and six Oriental bishops. The Eusebian seceders numbered about eighty. These canons embody authentic evidence of the persistence of the belief that the Roman primacy was based on Peter: "in order to honor the memory of blessed Peter . . . ."(DS 133-136) The *recensio graeca* which is generally held to be the original as against the *recensio latina* is more specific in its Petrine and papal correlation:

"let us honor the memory of Peter the Apostle, and let these judges write to Julius, bishop of Rome."

What is significant about the canons of Sardica is that practices which, until then, had gathered through general acceptance the force of custom based on tradition were henceforth given a juridical basis and title. Julius received the submission of two prominent Arians, Ursacius of Singidunum (Belgrade) and Valens of Mursa (347), who withdrew their allegations against Athanasius both before a council in Milan and before the Pope in person in Rome. Unfortunately, they relapsed soon after.

Papal authority becomes most manifest in two areas of Church life, the defense of the faith against heresies, and the insistence that in areas of discipline Rome had the ultimate say. The basic strength of the authority of the papal office is seen to surface in the pontificate of Pope St. Damasus I (366-384). Among the almost overwhelming difficulties he had to confront the charge of a grave crime by Isaac, the converted Jew, the violent contestation with Ursinus, a rival claimant to the pontifical office, to be subject to a civil exoneration which the Council of Rome in 378 confirmed. He suffered slanders by the Donatist Macrobius and by Paschesius the eunich. But the forcefulness of his own awareness of the nature and functions of the office he occupied were evident in his relentless combat against the Arians despite the strong support given them by the Emperor Valens and the Empress Justina. He deposed the Arian bishops of Illyricum, Ursacius and Valens. He opposed the adherents of Lucifer of Cagliari, sending their leaders into exile. At the Council of Rome (378) one of its most significant decrees was to the effect that henceforth bishops should be tried by a court of fellow bishops and not be subject to trial in civil courts, and that this policy should be followed, above all, in the case of the bishop of Rome, a show of confident strength in the face of the imperial rescript of the same year to the contrary. The Trinitarian heresy of Marcellus of Ancyra (though firmly anti-Arian his Trinitarian doctrine savored of Sabellianism) was largely abated by his death and by the acceptance of the formulas of Damasus by the Council of Antioch (374). In 377, Damasus condemned the heretical Christology of Appollinarius of Laodicea (DS 146, 149) a verdict which two councils did not hesitate to affirm, the Synods of Alexander of 378 and Antioch of 379. He refused to accept the third canon of the Council of Constantinople I (381) which based the second preeminence of the bishop of the New Rome on a political principle—it was the residence of the emperor, *urbs regia.* He was the first of the popes to call the See of Rome the Apostolic See at the Roman Council of 382, declaring in unmistakable terms that the bishop of Rome's claim to supremacy was based exculsively on the succession to Peter. The two events are undoubtedly related. The *"apostolica sedes"* was a direct counter to the third canon of Constantinople I (381) which decreed that the bishop of the "City" should have "precedence of honor" after the bishop of Rome "because Constantinople is new Rome."

The Roman Church was not founded by a synod decree—*Sancta tamen Romana ecclesia nullis synodicis constitutis ceteris ecclesiis praelata est.*

The Roman Church owed its primatial position to the commission given to Peter by Christ—*sed evangelica voce domini nostri primatum obtinuit: Tu es Petrus . . . .*

Unique among all churches, the Roman Church was founded by two apostles, SS. Peter and Paul, while Constantinople had no warranty for claiming apostolic foundation—*Cui addita est etiam societas beatissimi Pauli apostoli vasis electionis . . . .*

Pope St. Damasus I chose St. Jerome to be his secretary in 377 and because of his knowledge of Scripture, was commissioned to revise the Latin translations of the New Testament on the basis of the original Greek. Jerome was responsible for the official canon of the Scriptures approved by the Roman Council of 382. (DS 179)

During the pontificate of Pope St. Siricius (384-399) appear the first decretals, pontifical letters with a general bearing on faith, morals and discipline. The very style of these decretals express a sense of awareness of a central and supreme authority with immediate concernment for the universal Church. *Ad Romanam ecclesiam, utpote ad caput tui corporis.* (Ep. 1. c. 15) *Quis enim infirmantur, et ego non infirmior? Quis scandalizatur, et non uror?* (*ibid.* c. 7) with obvious Pauline resonances. (cf. II Cor. XI 29) And again, *nos . . . quibus praecipue secundum Paulum instantia quotidiana et sollicitudo omnium ecclesiarum indesinenter incumbit.* But it is as heir of St. Peter that he bears in his person the cares of the universal Church

—Portamus onera omnium, qui graventur: quinimmo haec portat in nobis beatus apostolus Petrus, qui nos in omnibus, ut confidimus, administrationis suae protegit et tuetur haeredes. So wrote Pope Siricius in the first decretal ever issued by the papacy. It was sent to Spain with fifteen major dispositions, and its high significance was celebrated by Isidore of Seville who described it aptly as a *decretale opusculum.* The *decretale* is hard evidence that the supreme legislative power, the supreme right of supervision, and supreme judicial power in the Church were comprehended under the primacy of jurisdiction of the successor of Peter. Popes will refer to their predecessors, but they always refer to themselves as successors of Peter—never as successors of their precedents in office. The decretal is a *rescriptum* or *responsum* to queries submitted to the pope and his answers, proceeding from the *caput ecclesiae*, remain valid as law binding the universal Church as well as the instant case. The obvious parallel between the imperial *responsa* of earlier Roman history and the papal *rescripta* or *responsa* more than suggests a calculated imitation of legal form and the connotation of their undoubted binding force. Just as the Roman imperial *responsa* were also expressed in *epistola*, so too, did the Sirician *rescripta* take the form of letters. These queries came from all quarters of the Church. Siricius wrote to Himerius of Tarragona, who had referred several disciplinary matters to Damasus. (Epist. 1. a. 385) To the bishops of Africa he wrote of the decisions of a council that had met in Rome "above the relics of St. Peter." (Epist. 5. a. 386) To Anysius of Thessalonica he wrote about episcopal ordination in Illyricum. (Epis. 4. a. 386) *Epistola* 7 (a. 390) condemned Jovinian and the others who denied the perpetual virginity of Mary. Arians and Novatians are not to be rebaptized but reconciled by the imposition of hands (*Epist.* 1). Priests and deacons are obligated "by the everlasting law of continence" (Epist. 1). A baptized man who embraced civil office or military service could not be admitted to the clerical state (Epist. 5), etc. These letters settle pastoral problems and set down particularities of ecclesiastical discipline. They reveal the growth and development of the authority of the Apostolic See. The pope's decisions are called *Statuta Sedis Apostolicae.* The papal responses are given with complete authority, *jubemus, decernimus.* Bishops who do not obey these pontifical decisions separate themselves from the solidity of the apostolic rock, on which Christ built the universal Church (*Epist.* 1). Siricius addressed such *epistolae* to the bishops of Italy, Gaul, Spain, Africa, Illyricum, Thessalonika, and intervened in

matters of faith, morals, and discipline with full authority.

> We bear within us the burdens of all who are weighed down,
> but it is rather the Blessed Apostle Peter who bears these bur-
> dens in us, since, we trust, he protects us in all the matters of
> his administration and guides us as his heirs. (*Epist.* 1 DS 181)

Pope St. Anastasius I (399-401) wrote letters to Simplicianus,
Bishop of Milan and to his successor, proscribing Origenistic heresies.
He also wrote to the Council of Carthage (401) to urge the African
bishops to continue the battle against the Donatists. With Pope
St. Innocent I (401-417) the *auctoritas* of the Apostolic See is
frequently asserted.   Because all the Western churches take their
origin from Peter and from his successors in the Roman See, the
Roman liturgy should be observed everywhere (Epist. 25). Ecclesiastical matters should be adjusted by the provincial bishops, in accordance with the canons of Nicaea and Sardica, "without prejudice,
however, to the Roman Church, respect for which should, in all cases,
be maintained," and to which major problems should be submitted
(Epist. 2). "Each time a problem has to do with a point of doctrine,
I consider that the bishops, our brothers, should refer it to Peter, the
founder of the episcopate, to provide for the common good of all
the churches throughout the whole world." (*Epist.* 30) The African
bishops acknowledged "what was due to the Apostolic See" and while
questions can be solved in far away provinces they agreed that it was
not necessary to come to a decision before having recourse to Rome;
and that a just decision should be confirmed by its authority in order
that other churches might learn from it how to conduct themselves
(Epist. 29).   The authority of the bishop of Rome is that of the
Apostle Peter himself, who was, in Christ, the first of the Apostles
and in the episcopate. *Per quem (Petrum) apostolatus et episcopatus
in Christo coepit exordium.*   The papal claims are not discounted
but on the contrary complied with and supported. A reading of the
Innocentian letters discloses papal *auctoritas*, which is identical with
Peter's is exercised in matters of faith, morals, liturgy, and discipline.
They are addressed to bishops and councils in the West, East, and
Africa.   The Council of Carthage had condemned Pelagianism in 411.
But when a synod at Diospolis in Palestine in 415 pardoned Pelagius,
councils in Carthage and Milevis reaffirmed the excommunication of
411 and forwarded their decisions to Rome in 416.   Five bishops
including St. Augustine sent a Pelagian dossier to the Pope, requesting

the intervention of the Apostolic See, that the Pope summon Pelagius to Rome, and anathematize his errors. These African bishops asked Innocent if "their small stream of doctrine flowed from the same source" as his own. When Augustine received Innocent's reply he wrote:

> On this matter two councils have been sent to the Apostolic See and rescripts have been received in reply. The case is closed (*causa finita est*)—would that the error were likewise ended." (Serm. 131)

Innocent reiterated on several occasions the prohibition against marriage for bishops, priests, and deacons and the obligation of continence for those already married before entering the clergy. He sanctioned the vow of chastity for consecrated virgins. He made a list of the canon of the Bible and excluded several apocryphal books. After St. John Chrysostom had been deposed at the Synod of the Oak (403), Innocent refused to recognize the deposition. The matter had not been decided by a legitimately constituted council in conformity with the canons of Nicaea. Innocentian *auctoritas* was firming up the government of the universal Church as it was radically required by the Petrine primatial authority that was now his as successor. On January 27, 417, Innocent wrote to the bishops of Africa commending them for referring their action against the Pelagians for his approval in such terms as to underscore the underlying reason for their recourse to Rome, namely Roman primacy:

> Following the examples of ancient tradition . . . in your pursuit of the things of God . . . you have made manifest by your proper course of action the vitality of your religion . . . when you agreed to refer to our judgment. For you knew what was due to the Apostolic See, since all of us who are here desire to follow the apostle from whom have come this episcopate and all the authority belonging to this name. By following him we know how to condemn what is wrong and to approve what is praiseworthy. Moreover, in safeguarding the ordinances of the Fathers with your priestly zeal, you certainly believe they must not be trodden under foot. They decreed, not with human, but with divine judgment that no decision (even though it concerned the most remote provinces) was to be considered final unless this See were to hear of it, so that all the authority

of this See might back up whatever just decision was reached. (*Epist.* 29. DS 217)

Whatever the historical judgment on the merits of the short pontificate of Pope St. Zosimus (417-418), his position on Roman primacy is firmly and forcefully expressed:

> Although the tradition of the Fathers has attributed such great authority to the Apostolic See that no one would dare to dispute its judgment, and it has always preserved this judgment by canons and rules, and current ecclesiastical discipline up to this time by its laws pays the reverence which is due to the name of Peter, from whom it has itself descended . . . since therefore Peter the head is of such great authority, and he has confirmed the subsequent endeavors of all ancestors, so that the Roman Church is fortified . . . by human as well as by divine laws, and it does not escape you that we rule its place and also hold power of the name itself . . . we have such great authority that no one can dare to retract from our decision . . . . (Epist. *Quamvis Patrum traditio* to the African Bishops, March 21, 418. DS 221)

Pope St. Boniface I (418-422) in his epistle *Retro maioribus tuis* to Rufus, Bishop of Thessaly (March 11, 422) wrote: We have sent . . . to the Synod (at Corinth) and from this letter all

> the brethren may realize . . . that our judgment is not to be reviewed. For it has never been permitted to controvert a matter once it has been decided by the Apostolic See. *Numquam etenim licuit de ea rursus (re), quae semel statuta est ab Apostolica Sede, tractari.* (DS 232)

His words imply the universal recognition of Rome's supreme authority and the finality of its judgments.

Pope St. Celestine I's (422-432) vigorous assertion of the authority of the Apostolic See is very much in evidence in the Nestorian controversy. In August 430, Nestorius was solemnly condemned by a Roman synod over which the Pope presided. He sent three legates to the Council to be convened at Ephesus (431) instructing them "to execute what has already been decided by us." At the Council one of the papal legates, the priest Philip, addressed the assembled bishops exhorting them to carry out the decisions of Pope Celestine with regard to Nestorius:

No one doubts, in fact, it is obvious to all ages that the holy and most Blessed Peter, head and Prince of the Apostles, the pillar of faith, and the foundation of the Catholic Church, received the keys of the kingdom from our Lord Jesus Christ, the Savior and the Redeemer of the human race. Nor does anyone doubt that the power of forgiving and retaining sins was also given to this same Peter who, in his successors, lives and exercises judgment even to this time and forever. (DS 112)

There is no recorded objection to this assertion of the Roman primacy. The above passage is quoted verbatim by the Fathers of the First Vatican Council in solemnly declaring the perpetuity of the primacy of Peter in the Roman Pontiffs. (DS 3056)

Following the pontificate of Pope St. Sixtus III (432-40) noted for the most part for several of Rome's outstanding monuments, i.e., the Liberian Basilica of Santa Maria Maggiore, its majestic mosaics commemorated the triumph of the Church over the heresy of Nestorius—Leo, the deacon was elected pope.

Pope St. Leo I (440-461) summed up the permanent Petrine office enduring in the Roman Pontiffs in his celebrated *Sermons* and *Letters* and firmly set the course of public development of Petrine-papal primatial authority that culminated in the dogmatic definitions of the First Vatican Council.

De toto mundo unus Petrus eligitur, qui et universarum gentium vocationi et omnibus apostolis cunctisque ecclesiae patribus praeponuntur; ut quamvis in populo Dei multi sacerdotes sint multique pastores, omnes tamen proprie regat Petrus, quos principaliter regit et Christus. (*Sermo* 3.4)

And the consequent continuity of the identical mandate from Christ was that he, Leo, was the vicar of Peter, *cuius vice fungimur*, so that *principaliter* and *proprie* Christ and Peter somehow in a real way shared in his governance of the Church. "The Blessed Peter continues in the rock structure he was given; he will never abandon the government of the Church, which has been placed in his hands." And in the full awareness that he occupied the *cathedra Petri* and was invested with the *primatus Petri* he wrote on August 10, 446 to the African bishops, "Rome gives the solution to all cases which are submitted to her, these solutions take the form of judgments, and Rome declares the penalties for the future." He gave *Roma aeterna* a new meaning, "Rome, the sacred seat of the Blessed Peter, through whom she has become the queen of the universe." All that Leo says is not new but the stresses on jurisdictional supremacy has sharper edges.   He speaks of the papal *principatus apostolicus* (instead of simply apostolic authority) which can be delegated but not shared. When his vicar in Illyricum, Anastasius of Thessalonika had acted precipitously in his relations with his suffragans, Leo wrote him, "I gave you power as my vicar, but did not invest you with the *plenitudo potestatis*"—or more fully in the Latin original.

> Vices enim nostras ita tuae credidimus caritati, ut non in partem sis vocatus sollicitudinis, non in plenitudinem potestatis. (*Epist.* 14. 1)

Papal authority is plenary and indivisible and nontransferable. When he is assertive he is not self-assertive.   He acts in Peter's place or rather Peter acts through him.   "Non de nobis, sed illo praesumimus, qui operatur in nobis." (*Sermo* 3.2) The Emperor Valentinian III in the imperial edict (July 8, 445) by which he confined St. Hilary to his diocese by request of Pope Leo acknowledges papal primacy—*primatus sedis apostolicae*.   Bishops are equal in the episcopacy but guided by "Peter in the person of Peter's successor (*Serm* 3.3) who is the "primate of all the bishops" (*ibid*. 4).   He taught the universal priesthood of the faithful under the presidency of Christ, who is represented by the bishop of Rome, by taking the place of Peter.   Christ conferred such great power to him whom he made ruler (*principem*) of the entire Church so that "if anything is properly done or directed by us in our time" it is to be attributed to the activity of him to whom it was said, "And you converted, confirm your brethren." (*Serm* 4. 2-4) Leo saw Peter function in the person of the Pope. (*Serm* 5. 2-4) And as successor of Peter, the supreme shepherd over Christ's flock, Leo was relentlessly vigilant against Nestorianism, Manichaeism, Monophytism, Pelagianism, and other heresies which he condemned as false doctrines, and bearers of those doctrines.   When Eutyches recognized only one nature in Christ, Leo chided Flavian, bishop of Constantinople, for his delay in referring the matter to Rome.   When Eutyches was condemned at the *synodos endemousa* (448), he appealed to Rome for redress. Pope Leo confirmed the synod's decision. (*Epist* 23) When Eutyches was rehabilitated at the Council of Ephesus (449) Pope Leo denounced it as *illud Latrocinium*, that Robber Synod.   The anti-

Eutychian bishops were excluded, the adherents of Flavian were reduced to silence, and the request of the papal legates that the pope's letter, which came to be known as the *Tome* of Leo, be read, was evaded. The *Tome* was later adopted by the Council of Chalcedon (451), the fourth ecumenical council, as an accurate expression of the traditional teaching on the two natures and one person of Christ. By his uncompromising doctrinal insistence on orthodoxy and by his demand that the *statuta* of the Apostolic See and the decrees and authority of the canons be obediently preserved (*Epist.* 1.1), Leo gave papal primatial authority a juridical structuring through ecclesiastical law.

Pope St. Hilary's (461-468) pontificate is noted for his insistence on the moral character of royal governance, the restoration of ruins left by the Vandals, at a time of the dismemberment of the Western Empire into regional kingdoms. What may be to our particular interest, Hilary legislated to maintain, by means of frequent provincial councils, the cohesion of Christianity which could not but be disaffected by the dislocation of the Roman world. When Ascanius, Metropolitan of Tarragona in Spain, appealed to him a complaint against Silvanus of Calahorra, Hilary convoked a council (Nov. 19, 465) in the Church of Santa Maria Maggiore. The Spanish bishops were notified by a synodal letter after the rights of the metropolitan were upheld.

Pope St. Simplicius (468-483) like Leo before him rejected the request of Acacius, Patriarch of Constantinople, that the Pope acknowledge canon 28 of the Council of Chalcedon (451) which had decreed for the See of Constantinople a rank equal to that of Rome, because of the political status of the "new Rome," in which the Emperor and senate now resided. On January 9, 476, Simplicius wrote his Epistle, *Quantum presbyterorum*, to Acacius on the authority of Roman Pontiffs and ecumenical councils as having a binding force in guarding the faith which has been handed down with specific reference to the condemnation of Arius, Nestorius, Dioscorus, and Eutyches. On January 10, 476, he addresses his Epistle, *Cuperem quidem*, on the unchangeableness of Christian doctrine, to the usurper emperor Basiliscus who favored the Monophysites and had published an encyclical condemning the decrees of the Council of Chalcedon and the *Tome* of Pope St. Leo I:

Those authentic and clear truths which flow from the very pure fountains of Scriptures cannot be disturbed by any argu-

ment of vague subtlety. For this same norm of apostolic doctrine endured in the successors of him upon whom the Lord
imposed the care of the whole sheepfold (John 21:15 ff.),
whom (He promised) He would not fail even to the end of
the world (Matt. 28:20), against whom He promised that the
gates of hell would never prevail, by whose judgment He testified
that what was bound on earth could not be loosed in heaven.
(Matt. 16:18 ff.)

Let whoever, as the Apostle proclaimed, *attempts to disseminate something other, than what we have received, be anathema.*
(Gal. 1:8 f.) (DS 160)

Pope St. Felix III (483-492) though he was elected to the pontifical office by benefit of the influence of King Odoacer and, it seems,
was a friend of the Emperor Zeno, was quick to assert the independence of the Church. In a letter, *Quoniam pietas*, (Aug.1, 484)
addressed to Zeno he lectured the emperor on the Church's right to
act according to her own laws and pointedly warned him "to learn
divine things from those who are in charge of them, and not to desire
to teach them—*discere potius quam docere.* (DS 345) It was the
courtly language customarily used with Christian emperors who had
convoked councils and intervened in matters of faith. Zeno, under
the inspiration of Acacius, Patriarch of Constantinople, and in
concert with Peter Mongus, had sought to restore religious unity
between the Monophysites and those who supported the Council
of Chalcedon by issuing the *Henoticon* or Decree of Union. The
decree was rejected by both sides. Felix wrote a letter of protest to
Acacius, then excommunicated and deposed him in a Roman synod
(July 28, 484). This occasioned the first serious official estrangement
between Rome and the East, the disaffection known as the Acadian
schism which lasted for thirty-five years (484-519).

In Pope Felix, papal primatial authority in matters of faith declares
its independence of imperial dictation. The emperor's role is to learn,
not to teach. Neither the Church nor its apostolic doctrine was to be
severed according to Christ's prayer and promise.

Omnia, quae per apostolicae scita doctrinae ligarentur in terris,
nec in celestibus memoravit (scil. Salvator) absolvi. (*Epist.* 2.7)

. . . in me qualicumquo vicario beatus Petrus apostolus, et haec in illo, qui ecclesiam suam discerpi non patitur, ipse etiam Christus exposcit. (*Epist.* 15.3)

If Leo I laid the juridical foundations of papal authority, Pope St. Gelasius I (492-496) applied and developed those principles in letters and treatises that were resonant with legality. Primacy, *libertas ecclesiae*, the superiority of the religious, moral, spiritual over the temporal even in its very entanglements in the political order. The Gelasian *Duo sunt* was the papal armature against Caesaro-papism in the West. The much celebrated letter *Famuli vestrae pietatis* (DS 346) was addressed to the emperor Anastasius I in 496, reproaching him for his support of the schismatical conduct of the patriarchs of Constantinople, particularly in their attitude toward the Monophysite heresy which Rome had condemned. The Gelasian distinction of powers was a papal declaration of independence, for which the Church had been struggling since the days of Constantine, in deciding the doctrine and discipline for the faithful. It was not without some legal significance that Gelasius wrote of the sacred authority of the Popes (*auctoritas sacrata pontificum*) and the royal power (*regalis potestas*), a distinction that had been drawn by the Emperor Augustus between the imperial *auctoritas* with which he was charismatically-invested and the *potestas* of the Roman magistrate. Gelasius wrote to the emperor: "Mark this well: when the see of the Blessed Peter pronounces judgment, no one is permitted to judge that judgment"; decades before the sixth century forgery at the time of Pope Symmachus with its *prima sedes a nemine iudicatur*. At the council of Rome, 495, he declared: *Sedes apostolica, quae Christo domino delegante totius ecclesiae retinet principatum.* (*Epist.* 14.9) At the conclusion of this same synod, the episcopacy in attendance acclaimed Gelasius eleven times *Vicarium Christi te videmus*, the first occasion when the pope was hailed as Vicar of Christ. Gelasius refers to himself as the vicar of Peter with Peter's plenary powers.

Si quantum ad religionem pertinet, non nisi apostolicae sedi juxta canones debetur summa judicii totius; si quantum and saeculi potestatem, illa a pontificibus et praecipue a beati Petro vicario debet cognoscere, quae divina sunt, non eadem ipsa judicare. (*Epist.* 10.9)

And the comprehensive extent of the plenary power of the Vicar of Christ, of the vicar of Peter is as broad as Matt. XVI. 18-19:

In "quibuscumque" omnia sunt quantacumque sint et qualiacumque sint. (Tractatus IV. c. 5)

This *Tractatus* was written to rebuff the overweening pretensions of the Caesaropapists in matters of Christian faith, and in particular, with vivid recollection of Emperor Zeno's *Henoticon*.

To the disintegrating critics of evangelical Christianity who see, among other things, the papacy as the quotient of historical forces and their mastery for papal supremacy, the faith and conviction of Gelasius on the divine origination of the Petrine office and its permanency and continuity in the papal office stands in contradiction.

Post (has omnes) propheticas et evangelicas atque apostolicas (quas superius deprompsimus) scripturas, quibus Ecclesia catholica per gratiam Dei fundata est, etiam illud intimandum putavimus, quod, quamvis universae per orbem catholicae diffusae Ecclesiae unus thalamus Christi sit, sancta tamen Romana Ecclesia nullis synodicis constitutis ceteris Ecclesiis praelata sit, sed evangelica voce Domini et Salvatoris primatum obtenuit: Tu es Petrus, inquiens, et super hanc petram aedificabo Ecclesiam meam, et portae inferi non praevalebunt adversus eam, et tibi claves regni caelorum et quaecumque ligaveris super terram, erunt ligata et in caelo, et quaecumque solveris super terram, erunt soluta et in caelo. (Mt. 16, 18s; Epist. 42, 495; DS 350)

Pope St. Anastasius II's (496-498) brief pontificate is remembered for his conciliatory efforts to bring the Acacian Schism to an end by recognizing the validity of the baptisms and ordinations performed by Acacius. (DS 356. Epist. *"Exordium pontificatus mei"* ad Anastasium I imp. 496) His sincere labors for the restoration of Christian unity were compromised because the Emperor was led to believe that Rome may yet be persuaded to accept *Henoticon*. Thus failed the historic vision of a pope who thought not unwisely that Byzantine support might facilitate the spiritual assimilation of the barbarians by the Catholic West. His efforts at conciliation were misconstrued in subsequent centuries and he was unjustly immemorialized by Dante Alighieri who placed him among the heretics in the sixth circle of the Inferno. (Canto XI. 6, 10) On August 23, 498, Pope Anastasius addressed a letter *"Bonum atque iucundum,"* (DS 360, 361) to the bishops of Gaul in which he condemned traducianism.

The pontificate of Pope St. Symmachus (498-514) was sorely tried by the contestations of an anti-pope, Laurentius, (498: 501-505) who after a year of opposition ceded, and after two years, revived the challenge to Symmachus by a variety of grave charges, of which one was that Symmachus had alienated ecclesiastical property contrary to the regulations of 483 with the intention of ensuring his own election. Symmachus was willing to appear before a synod of Italian bishops that King Theodoric, who ruled Italy as the Emperor's viceroy, summoned to judge the Pope in Rome (501). But Symmachus denied that any synod had the right to judge the Pope. The *Synodus palmaris* (October 501) decreed the Pope could not be tried for the charges of which he was accused and that his case must be left to the divine judgment. A deacon in Milan, Ennodius, developed in a series of apocryphal works, the position that the cause of the bishops of Rome could be judged by God alone. The inauthentic documents pretended to be Acts of the Synod of Sinuessa in 303 under Pope Marcellinus; the *Constitutum* of Pope Sylvester I; the *Gesta* of Pope Liberius; and the Acts clearing Pope Sixtus III of the accusation by Polychronius. Actually, the "Symmachan Forgeries" expressed the Gelasian doctrine on the papacy. Walter Ullmann, in his work, *The Growth of Papal Government in the Middle Ages*, (New York, 1953), wrote of Pope Gelasius as maintaining that, "there is nobody who can sit in judgment on a verdict of the Roman Church."

Ep. 26, c. 5–Neque cuipiam de eius liceat judicare judicio . . . ab illa autem nemo sit appellare permissus.

This is a characteristic example of how unnecessary certain forgeries were: the Symmachan forger working two or three years after this was written, cococted the so-called *Constitutum Silvestri*, in which he coined the famous phrase, "Prima sedes a nemine judicatur," with which he credited Silvester. *The forger had at his disposal a perfectly genuine statement by Gelasius, which would have suited his purpose.* (p. 27 n. 6. Italics supplied)

Pope Symmachus defended himself against the charges of Laurentians in the letter," *Ad augustae memoriae*, to the Emperor Anastasius I c. 506. "Compare, O Emperor, your dignity and that of the head of the Church" and after a comparative parallel of prerogatives, *Defer Deo in nobis, et nos deferimus Deo in te.* (DS 362)

The election of Hormisdas to the papal office, (514-523), and the accession to the imperial throne of Justin, the strictly Catholic, Prefect of the Praetorian guard, brought the brightest prospects for Church reunion.   Hormisdas welcomed back into communion the remaining followers of Laurentius and sent an embassy headed by Ennodius, now Bishop of Pavia, and Bishop Fortunatus of Catina, in response to Emperor Anastasius I's request for a council, to end the Acacian schism (515). This effort failed at the time but succeeded four years later under the new Emperor on exactly the same terms as in 515.

Chalcedon

The condemnations of Nestorius, Eutyches, Dioscorus, Timothy, the parricide, Peter of Alexander, of Acacius, of Peter of Antioch, and of all who remained their disciples are reaffirmed. Chalcedon and the *Tome* of Leo are to be accepted as norms of orthodoxy. All the bishops are to make a formal profession of orthodoxy in their churches and condemn by name the leaders of the Monophysite heresy. The Bishops must sign a *libellus* of the true faith composed by the Roman legates. The Apostolic See will reexamine the cases of those bishops who had persecuted the orthodox. The subscription to the *Libellus fedei Hormisdae papae,* by approximately 250 Eastern bishops, and by the Emperor Justin, is remarkable for its complete submission.   The papal legates had come only to receive signatures. They refused to engage in discussions.

Prima salus est rectae fidei regulam custodire et a constitutis Patrum nullatenus deviare. Et quia non potest Domini nostri Jesu Christi praetermitti sententia dicentis: "Tu es Petrus et super hanc petram aedificabo Ecclesiam meam" (*Mt*. 16, 18), haec, quae dicta sunt, rerum probantur effectibus, quia in Sede Apostolica immaculata est semper catholica servata religio.

De hac ergo qua spe et fide separari minime cupientes et Patrum sequentes in omnibus (—) constituta . . . .

. . . sequentes in omnibus Apostolicam Sedem et praedicantes eius omnia constituta . . . in una communione vobiscum, quam Sedes Apostolica praedicat . . . in qua est integra et verax christianae religionis (et perfecta) soliditas. (DS 363, 364)

Pope St. John I's brief pontificate, (523-526), was marked by the extremes of hostility and devotion. When Emperor Justin I and his nephew Justinian, with the intent of consolidating and restoring the Roman Empire, decreed to eliminate Arianism in Constantinople, the Ostrogoth King Theodoric of Italy, an Arian, retaliated by reversing his own policy of tolerance toward Catholics. He ordered Pope John to go to Constantinople to induce the Byzantine ruler to allow the Arians their own churches and not to expel them from the imperial services. Pope John agreed to this request but would not comply with the second, namely, that Arians who had turned Catholics under imperial persuasion, be allowed to revert to their former faith. Upon his arrival in Constantinople, the Emperor prostrated himself before him "as if he were Peter in person." The entire populace greeted him with extraordinary enthusiasm. Justin asked the Pontiff to crown him, during the Easter festival of 526, even though he had already been crowned by the Patriarch of Constantinople. Upon his return to Ravenna, Pope John was imprisoned for not completely fulfilling the paradoxical mission that Theodoric had given him. Shortly thereafter, he died from maltreatment.

Pope St. Felix IV (526-530) is remembered for restoring to the Roman Clergy privileges that the civil authorities had taken away, namely, the custom that clergy accused of civil or criminal disorders, were to be tried by the pope or by a papal court. This restoration was facilitated by a more benevolent royal court that succeeded upon the death of Theodoric. Felix is also remembered for the doctrinal direction he gave to the Council of Orange. St. Caesarius, archbishop of Arles, had asked the Roman Pontiff for short articles (*pauca capitula*) from Scripture, the Fathers of the Church, particularly St. Augustine, which embodied the authentic teaching of the Church on grace and free-will. These papal norms were adopted as canons, (*canones*), as binding standards of orthodoxy (DS 370-397) by the Second Council of Orange (529)—*secundum admonitionen et auctoritatem Sedis Apostolica ... ut pauca capitula ab Apostolica nobis Sede ab omnibus observanda*. The *canones* of faith of the Second Council of Orange together with those of Carthage contributed to the theology of grace used by the Council of Trent. To obviate the likely disorders that had been attendant upon papal elections, shortly before his death, Felix conferred his pallium of papal sovereignty on Bonifact designating him thereby his successor at a convocation of Roman clergy and several Senators. It was Pope Boniface II (530-532) who confirmed the acts of the Second

Council of Orange which terminated the controversies over Semi-pelagianism in South Gaul. (DS 398-400)

> ut pro ambiguitate tollenda, confessionem vestram, qua vos e diverso fidem rectam in Christo . . . iuxta catholicam veritatem . . . auctoritate Sedis Apostolicae firmaremus.

> Quapropter . . . supra scriptam confessionem vestram con-sentaneam catholicis Patrum regulis approbamus. (Ep. *"Per filium nostrum."* Jan. 25, 531)

Pope John II (533-535) inherited a doctrinal Scylla and Charybdis from Pope Hormisdas. After the papal legates had obtained the submission of the Eastern bishops to the formula of Hormisdas, before leaving Constantinople, some monks from Little Scythia suggested a formula for the reconciliation for the Monophysites to the Church—"One of the Trinity suffered in the flesh"—and for that reason were called the theopaschite monks. When the legates rejected their formula because it had Monophysite associations, these Scythians went to Rome to defend their own Roman orthodoxy before Pope Hormisdas. The situation was further complicated when Emperor Justin thought that this formula could succeed to reconcile the Severan Monophysites to Chalcedon. Pope Hormisdas responded that the Council of Chalcedon and the *Tome* of Leo sufficed. As to the formula itself he gave no judgment neither approving nor disapproving but cautioned against its possible mis-interpretation. (*Epist.* 70) In 533 Emperor Justinian published a profession of faith in the form of an edict based on the theopaschite formula hoping to reconcile the Monophysites and the Catholics. But when the *Acoemeti* (sleepless) monks, the strongest opponents among the orthodox to oppose the formula, protested and appealed to Pope John, Justinian dispatched the edict to Pope John, asking that it be confirmed as orthodox and that the Acoemeti be con-demned as Nestorians. In their opposition to Justinian's formula they even went so far as to deny the title of *Theotokos* to the Virgin Mary. When the monks proved intransigent, they were excommuni-cated. John wrote to the emperor approving the use of the formula. (*Epist.* "*Olim quidem,*" March 534)

> Gloriosam vero sanctam semper virginem Mariam et proprie

et veraciter Dei genitricem matremque Dei Verbi ex ea incarnati ab hominibus catholicis confiteri recte docemus. (DS 401)

What saved the formula from misconstruction was its adherence to the Marian dogma of Nicaea. The response of the Emperor, (*Reddentes honorem*, June 6, 533), luxuriates with grateful acknowledgment of the Apostolic See as "the authority of your See." As far as the literal expressions of the imperial letter is concerned, papal primacy is widely and freely acclaimed. (Pope John II was the first pope to change his name—Mercurius.)

Pope St. Agapetus I's pontificate lasted scarcely one year (535-536). When Justinian I chose to rid Italy of Strogothic rule because King Theodatus had assassinated Queen Amalasuntha who had placed herself under imperial protection, Pope Agapetus went to Constantinople to dissuade the Emperor from his plan of conquest. Theodatus had threatened in reprisal to execute all the Roman senators and their families. While there the clergy informed him that the Patriarch of Constantinople, Anthirnus who had been installed through the influence of Empress Theodora (1), was suspect of the Monophysite heresy. Despite the fact that Agapetus was a guest of the imperial throne, he ordered the Patriarch's deposition on the grounds that he had been uncanonically transferred from the See of Trebizond to Constantinople. Agapetus personally consecrated the orthodox, Mennas, to the vacated See. During his brief stay, Justinian submitted his profession of faith to the Pope who approved of it with high commendation.

Pope St. Silverius (536-537) succeeded to the papal office upon news that Agapetus had died in Byzantium. The Council that Agapetus had requested the Emperor to convene, condemned Anthimus, Severus of Antioch, and Peter of Apamea of Monophytism. When Pope Silverius refused to accede to Empress Theodora's request that Anthimus be restored to the See of Constantinople the aged pontiff was subjected to an intrigue of false charges, disrobing, and in a monk's garb secretly banished to exile, his resignation extorted, and shortly thereafter died. Such multiple tribulations in one year were visited upon an elderly pontiff who preserved the independence of the papal office in upholding orthodoxy and in condemning heresies.

If the historical problematic of Vigilius' alleged involvement and complicity in Theodora's intrigue to bring about the forced deposition of Pope Silverius has not been conclusively solved beyond all questioning, the matter of a Pope Vigilius (537-555) reversing himself about statements of doctrine is not so challenging as it may seem.

The main issue is the preservation of the authority of an ecumenical council, that of Chalcedon (451) which defined the two natures, divine and human, in the one person of Christ. The implied but nonetheless obvious issue is the *libertas Ecclesiae*; or, the obverse terms, what effect duress can operate upon the Vicar of Christ when he is spared the ultimate and liberating trial of martyrdom. Summarily, these are the data and the attendant circumstances.

In reaction to Arianism and Appollinarianism, Nestorius, Patriarch of Constantinople (381-451), inaugurated a vast theological controversy by preaching against the title *Theotokos*, Mother of God, claiming that the Virgin Mary should be called rather the Mother of Christ. Against Arianism, Nestorius held that Christ Jesus was truly divine and against Apollinarianism that his human nature was fully human, with its own human soul. But he was only able to admit a "moral" union of the eternal Logos with the created humanity, not a real hypostatic union, i.e., real and ontological with the Second Person as its subject. Nestorianism was condemned at the Council of Ephesus (431) and the Blessed Virgin Mary was expressly accorded the title, "Mother of God," *Theotokos*. In opposing Nestorius, Cyril of Alexandria used the expression *mia phusis*, "one nature of the Incarnate Word of God," in the sense of a subsistent nature. As such, it was an exact equivalent to *hypostasis, prosopon*, —or person. When Cyril spoke of the *mia phusis* he meant the sole Person of the Word, eternally subsistent, who had extended His proper subsistence to the fully human nature to which He was united by the Incarnation. However, when the Council of Chalcedon (451) spoke of the "two natures" of Christ, distinct, unconfused, the word, "nature," was used according to an earlier tradition of the older Trinitarian terminology in which it was completely distinct from *hypostasis*, from independent existence. Eutyches, (375-454) the archimandrite of a monastery at Constantinople, feared that the "different natures . . . in a real union" (DS 250) still offered the possibilities of lapsing into Nestorianism, and so he reverted back to the formula of Cyril of "one nature of the Word God Incarnate," without acknowledging the terminological advance that took place between Ephesus and Chalcedon. While Eutyches would admit that Christ was of two natures before the union and that Christ's flesh was consubstantial with that of the Blessed Virgin, he denied that after the union there are two natures in Christ and that Christ's flesh is that of a man. Eutyches himself was condemned by Flavin, Patriarch of Constantinople, in the synod of 448. The heretical doctrine, known as Monophytism was condemned at the Council of Chalcedon in 451. Now, as to Pope Vigilius, the Imperial court at Constantinople, and Monophytism: the Byzantine court considered Monophytism as grave a divisive political force as it was religious and a formidable obstacle to the reconciliation and solidification of the East and Western Empires. In an effort to achieve religious unity in the Empire, Emperor Zeno in 482 sent an epistolary decree, the *Henotikon*, to all the bishops in the East citing the first three ecumenical councils and affirming the consubstantiality of Christ with God and with man, but skillfully avoiding the Chalcedon use of the terms "nature" and "person." It was rejected by both sides, by the Egyptian Monophysites for its admission of human carnality and created soul, and by Rome and the West as a calculated avoidance of explicit Chalcedonian orthodoxy.

Emperor Justinian's determination to achieve religious unity was reenforced by his belief that he possessed a special authority over the Church, and by his growing interest in theology. With a despot's love of uniformity, his theological approach, when not acceded to, were accompanied by harsh and repressive measures. Of all the religious dissidents, the Monophysites offered the most stubborn resistence. One of his theological approaches to the problem of reconciling the Catholics and Monophysites was to remove from Chalcedon the stigma of Nestorianism which the Monophysites attached to its "two natures" of Christ, understanding "nature" in the cyrillian sense of hypostasis. This he was persuaded he could do by condemning the Three Chapters, (*kephalia*), selected passages from the writings of Theodore of Mopsuestia, Theodoret of Cyrus, and Ibas of Edessa, all three had died nearly a century ago at peace with the Church. Theodore of Mopsuestia had been suspected by Rabula of Edessa and Proclus of Constantinople as an originator of Nestorianism. Theodoret had assailed the twelve Anathemas of Cyril and Ibas had defended Theodore of Mopsuestia and criticized Cyril's Christology. Theodore died before Chalcedon.

Theodoret and Ibas were both exonerated and rehabilitated at the Council of Chalcedon when their orthodoxy was recognized by the papal delegates. In his Edict against the *Three Chapters* (544), Justinian condemned the three men personally by name as well as the "chapters" quoted. When Pope Vigilius protested he was abducted by imperial soldiers and brought to Constantinople (547). Under Imperial pressure, Vigilius published his *Judicatum* (548), concurring in Justinian's Edict but specifically upholding the authority of the Council of Chalcedon. The outcry of the western bishops who saw in the imperial edict a dangerous derogation of the authority, competence and decisions of an ecumenical council which had settled the dogmatic question of the two natures of Christ (and had rehabilitated two of the men)—was such that Justinian had to return the original copy of the *Judicatum* to the Pope (550). In 551 the Emperor published a long theological tract, with the assistance of Theodore Ascidas, condemning the doctrinal content of the *Three Chapters*. The Pope responded by promising to excommunicate anyone who subscribed to the imperial document. Whereupon Vigilius, resisting arrest, was on two separate occasions attacked with physical force. Public outrage forced the Emperor to guarantee safety to the Pope and his entourage. The Condemnation of the *Three Chapters* was annulled and all discussion of them suspended by papal and imperial agreement. On May 14, 553, Vigilius published *Constitutum* (I) "*Inter innumeras sollicitudines*" (DS 416-420) anathematizing propositions—*prout sonat*—but not Theodore personally. The *Constitutum* also condemned certain propositions which were attributed to Theodoret and Ibas and isolated from context were heretical, but it did not reverse the council's vindication of their orthodoxy.

At Chalcedon, the Council Fathers condemned the person and writings of Theodore (canon 12; DS 434), the writings of Theodoret against Cyril (canon 13, DS 436), and Ibas' *Letter to Maris*. (canon 14, DS 437) On February 23, 554, after enduring enormous mental pressure from overbearing imperial "persuasions,"—*machinationibus imperatoris demum cedens*—Vigilius in his *Constitutum* II reversed his former decisions and in spite of himself condemned both the persons as well as the writings of the *Three Chapters*, confirming the decision of the Second Council of Constantinople (537-55, Cf. DS 421-438) in which he had refused to participate. Vigilius, despite the final capitulation, should be revered for his determination to adhere to the authority, competence, and decisions of an ecumenical council, (Chalcedon) and in keeping inviolate the pope's ultimate power of decision. But the final outcome that was due to enormous duress and physical assaults is a loud lesson in ecclesiastical history. The *libertas Ecclesiae* and fundamentally that of the successors of Peter can lose most of its effectiveness—when it is short of martyrdom—in a historical order where all conduct, including ecclesiastical affairs, are comprehended within one all enveloping juridical power that admits of no other.   At the worse, Vigilius' retraction was about facts—about the agents of heresy and their culpability—not about orthodoxy, certainly not about revealed truths.   His principal objective was to uphold, when free to do so, the validity of the decisions of the Fourth Ecumenical Council (451).

Pope Pelagius I (556-561) had been his predecessor's papal *apocrisiarius* in Constantinople and very knowledgeable with political theologizing of the imperial court. He clearly saw that the Justinian condemnation of the *Three Chapters* was an assault upon the decisions and authoritative competence of the Council of Chalcedon which had rehabilitated two of the three theologians, Theodoret and Ibas, while Theodore of Mopsuestia had died before that Council in peace with the Church.   He supported Pope Vigilius against the incessant importuning of the Emperor, assisted Vigilius in the composition of *Constitututum* I, and when Vigilius retracted under duress, Pelagius wrote a *Refutatorium* against the condemnation.   As a consequence he was taken into custody and imprisoned. During this interval, he wrote *In defensione trium capitulorum* in opposition to Vigilius' *Constitutum* II. Despite his uncompromising stance against Justinian's condemnation of the *Three Chapters*, he was designated by Justinian personally to be the new Pope.   And paradoxically because he was designated by the Emperor, Pelagius's orthodoxy was suspect among the Western bishops.   Upon his consecration to the papacy, he made a profession of faith, declared his unwavering adherence to the first four ecumenical councils, with particular reference to Chalcedon, and made a point of holding Theodoret and Ibas blameless. This distrust still persisted. To King Childebert, he protested his faith in a Letter, *"Humani generis"* (DS 44-443) and again in an encyclical *"Vas Electionis" ad universum populum Dei* (DS 444) both in 557.   And in a Letter to *"Adeone"* a bishop (559), he spoke of the necessity of union with the Apostolic See because of its primacy.

Has the truth of your Catholic mother so failed you, who have been placed in the highest office of the priesthood, that you have not at once recognized yourself as a schismatic, when you withdrew from the Apostolic See?   You were appointed to preach the Gospel to the people.   Have you not read that the Church was founded by Christ Our Lord upon the chief of the Apostles, so that the gates of hell cannot prevail against it? (cf. Mt. 16, 18) If you had read this, where did you believe the Church to be outside of him in whom alone are clearly all the Apostolic Sees. Who beside him has received in the same way the keys, the power of binding and loosing? As blessed Cyprian, the martyr, has explained it, it was first given to him alone, and then to the others also thereby demonstrating the unity of the Church. (DS 446)

In his Letter, "*Admonemus ut*" to Gaudentius, Bishop of Volterra, about the year 560, he set down that there is only one valid form of baptism. In his Letter "*Relegentes autem*" to the patrician Valerianus (595), he ruled that no local synod can pass judgment on the decisions of general councils. Any doubt about the meaning of its decrees must be resolved by the Holy See—

> Sed quotiens aliqua de universo synodo aliquibus dubitatio nascitur . . . ad Apostolocas Sedes pro percipienda ratione conveniunt. (DS 447)

Pope John III's pontificate (561-574) was enveloped by the Lombard invasion and conquest of northern and central Italy under King Alboin. This adverse circumstance hastened the end of the schism over the *Three Chapters* that had separated Milan and the northern Italian sees from the Apostolic See. Pope Benedict I (575-579) had to cope with the threat and eventually siege of Rome by the Lombards. Of Pope Pelagius II's (579-590) extant six genuine letters two are to our purpose. First, his Letter "*Quod ad dilectionem*" to the schismatic bishops of Istria (c. 585).

> You know that the Lord proclaims in the Gospel: *Simon, Simon, behold Satan has desired you to have you, that he might sift you as wheat: but I have asked the Father for thee,—that thy faith fail not; and thou being once converted, confirm thy brethren.* (Luke 22:31f.)

Consider, most dear ones, that the Truth could not have lied, nor will the faith of Peter be able to be shaken or changed forever. For although the devil desired to sift all the disciples, the Lord testifies that He himself asked for Peter alone and wished the others to be confirmed by him; and to him also, in consideration of a greater love he showed the Lord before the rest, was committed the care *of feeding the sheep* (cf. John 21: 15ff.); and to him also He handed over *the keys of the kingdom of heaven*, and upon him He promised to *build His Church*, and He testified that *the gates of hell* would not prevail against it. (cf. Matt: 16ff.)

(The faith of the Councils of Nicaea, Constantinople I, Ephesus I, and especially of Chalcedon, and the dogmatic Epistle, *"Lectis dilectionis tuae"*, of Pope St. Leo to Flavian, Patriarch of Constantinople, June 13, 449, are reaffirmed.)

In his second Epistle to the schismatic bishops of Istri, *"Dilectionis vestrae,"* the same year (DS 468-469), Pelagius again insists on the necessity of union with the Apostolic See of Peter:

For although it is evident from the word of the Lord Himself in the Sacred Gospel (cf. Matt. 16:18) where the Church is established, let us hear nevertheless what the Blessed Augustine, mindful of the Lord's words, has declared. He says that the Church of God has been established among those who are known to preside over the Apostolic Sees, through the succession of those in charge, and whoever separates himself from the communion of authority of these Sees, proves he is in schism. After some additional remarks, (he says), "If you place yourself outside (the Church), you will die even if you invoke the name of Christ. Rather for the name of Christ suffer among the members of Christ clinging to the body, fight for the head!"

The Blessed Cyprian said among other things:

"The Church" was born in unity—Exordium ab unitate profiscitur—and primacy was conferred upon Peter, so that there be one Church of Christ and one office of teacher (*cathedra*) . . . .

Does he who does not adhere to the unity of the Church believe that he has the faith? Does he who deserts and resists the chair of Peter, on which the Church was founded (cf. Mt. 16: 18) have confidence that he is in the Church?

In our cursory review of the popes of the first six centuries, we find a surprising number of short-lived pontificates, ten one-year terms, five two-year terms, three three-year terms, four four-year terms, one five-year term.   The enormous obstacles with which the Christians of those centuries had to contend were such that a religion that was not divinely revealed and whose social and corporate existence had not been guaranteed from on high, could not have survived.   From the time of Nero Christianity was treated as a forbidden religion and profession of the Christian name was sufficient grounds for proscription.   In the second century, Trajan's rescript set the public policy under the enlightened Antonines. Later persecutions made up in bitterness what they had lost in duration.   The third century was a time of relentless persecution on a wide scale beginning with Maximin's accession to power in 235, and continuing with Decius, Valerian, and Diocletian.   Popes, bishops and the faithful were martyred; Christian books and records destroyed; and the tragic and agonizing failure of apostates, bowed the Church low in her own garden of Gethsemane.   The Church's own existence was precarious and its shepherds solicitous for the perseverance of the faithful.   From Constantine to Justinian, from the fourth to the sixth century, the Church was under the superintendence of the Emperors, who directed, interfered, and even dictated in matters of the Church.   There was no *libertas ecclesiae* that set the Church apart and outside of the only juridical power conceivable at the time. With the fall of the Western Empire and the barbarian invasions, even the organism of the Church, established within the framework of the Empire, was severely shaken, and many parts of Europe found it hard to maintain contact with their chief centres and with Rome. Local churches grew up, confined within the boundaries of the occupied territories and impoverished kingdoms, and often lacking in a constant and effectual bond of discipline.   The situation of Italy, and especially the position of Rome, since the turmoil of the invasions, restricted the activity of the Popes, or directed it to tasks not directly related to the government of the Church.   In the East, the imperial power and intrigue of the Byzantine court were deeply involved in regional synods and ecumenical councils, and in endless political theologizing.   Yet, despite all these unbearable burdens, the voice of the Roman Church could be heard and the evidences of papal claim of primatial authority are unmistakable. (We will review in Part II, the nonpapal testimonies to primacy in our study of the Petrine office, its permanence and continuity, and of apostolic succession.) It would indeed have been surprising if the successors of Peter did not know the uniqueness of the papal office and its exclusive prerogatives. If, on the other hand, there had been no papal awareness of the primatial powers of the Petrine office, no profession of *cathedra Petri, Sedes Apostolica, primatus, principatus, gubernatio principalis, gubernacula Apostolicae Sedis*, and the invocation of the Petrine Texts (Mt. 16:18, 19; Lk. 22:33; Jn. 21: 15-17), if the papacy did not claim to be the ultimate settlement on matters of faith, if indeed, Rome did not receive, accept, and require appeals of ultimate recourse, if Rome were not the final arbiter, if all these claims were made by others than Rome for Rome, then a serious question might reasonably arise about these prerogatives being inherent in the Petrine papal office.

It was a quotation from Kung's volume that prompted this survey of papal claim and exercise of primatial authority in the Church— as best as the pontiffs could within the burdensome restrictions and obstacles and interferences of their contemporary history. Of Gregory the Great suffice to observe that his exercise of papal primacy was in the administrative forging together of a Christian unity in the West. He corresponded with bishops of Spain, Africa, Ravenna, Milan, Illyricum to bring an end to schism or to correct heresy. Gregory closely supervised the administration of the papal patrimonies and used their revenue to help the destitute, ransom captives, and to buy peace with the Lombards. The right of appeal to Rome over any of the partiarchs of Constantinople, Alexandria, Antioch, and Jerusalem was not only generally acknowledged but accentuated when Gregory reversed the two decisions against two priests handed down at Constantinople (595). Gregory's opposition to the Patriarch, John IV the Faster's use of the title, "ecumenical patriarch," was motivated not by personal sensitivity but by the challenge it might pose to papal prestige in the East. He wrote of his *principatus*, of his universal jurisdiction as Bishop of Rome even as he signed his letters, *servus servorum*. His deep humility did not derogate the papal prerogative just as primatial authority of the papal office did not exalt him above his own unworthiness. The Apostolic See is "the head of all the churches," the *"caput fidei,"* to whom is committed the care and primacy of the whole Church," and for this reason, "the See of Constantinople is subject to the Apostolic See." He reenforced the bonds of the ecclesiastical structure by sedulously safeguarding the jurisdiction of other churches; "My honor is the honor of the universal Church. It is also the firm authority of my brothers. I am truly honored only when the honor due to each and every one of them is not denied to them." He restored the papal vicariate at Arles and thereby linked the Church in Gaul with Rome and the Church Universal. His achievements defy summation. Suffice to say, that by his administrative genius he restored the West through the agency of the Church, its bishops, its missionaries, the establishment of monasteries, the healing of schisms, the removal or containment of heresies, the conversion of the Angles, Saxons, and Visigoths, a check upon the Lombards, by his contribution to the liturgy of the Church, the Gregorian chant, in the composition of the Mass, the Gregorian Sacramentary, by his deep Christian ascetism—(the Scriptural Homilies, the *Book of Morals, Pastoral Care* written for bishops and priests, the *Dialogues* for the simple and uneducated people), by his numerous *Letters*, the *Registrum Epistolarum*, and their enormous canonistic significance for the papal chanceries that succeeded Gregory's pontificate. His pontificate was an exercise of primatial authority. His papal primacy reached *practically* into every phase of Church life. Its effectiveness originated in the faith of the Church and its moral consequences were reenforced with ecclesiastical sanctions, with no exemptions, no immunities.

Si quis vero regum, sacerdotum, judicum atque saecularium personarum hanc constitutionem nostrae paginam agnoscens contra eam venire temptaverit, potestatis honorisque sui dignitate careat reumque se divino existere de perpetrata iniquitate cognoscat et nisi ea quae illo sunt male ablata restituerit vel digna poenitentia inlicite acta defleverit, a sacratissimo corpore ac sanguine Dei Domini redemptoris nostri Jesu Christi alienus fiet atque in aeterno examine districtae ultioni subjaceat. (Reg. xiii p. 378)

The above summary survey is inadequate in more than one way. It is restricted to formal statements of papal claims to primacy. It does not, could hardly do so, enter into the multitudinous acts of practical governance that were exercises of this Petrine authority. Papal supremacy was admitted and more often than not it took the practical form of the court of final appeal. Not that it was the court of last recourse but that its settlements whenever sought were binding and not to be overruled, certainly not in matters of orthodoxy, i.e., Trinity, Christology, virginity of the Blessed Virgin Mary, the validity of sacraments, (the baptism of heretics), on discipline, i.e., canonical regularity, celibacy, etc. And where and when schism and heresies threatened the unity of the Church, papal direct action did not await appeals. This is not to deny that imperial power did assume a superintendence over Christianity, interfere with ecclesiastical self-governance, dictate and even compel in matters of orthodoxy and heresy. That is why we have concentrated on papal claims, whatever the variant degrees of the reach and efficacy of its Petrine authority with which the popes identified their own *auctoritas* and *principatus*. This is not to deny that papal decisions and pronouncements were occasionally contested and defied. The history of schisms and heresies bears witness to this defiance of the Roman Pontiff no less of ecumenical councils.

Henry VIII on Papal Primacy and Infallibility

For what it's worth, we may recall the testimony of His Royal Highness, King Henry VIII, while he was still with his first wife.

"What plague so pernicious did ever invade the flock of Christ?" he wrote in the *Assertio VII Sacramentorum*. "What serpent so venomous as (Luther) who calls the Pope's authority tyrannous and esteems the most wholesome decrees of the universal Church to be captivity? What a great limb of a devil he is, endeavoring to tear the Christian members of Christ from their head!" Luther has "denied the Pope's supremacy to be of divine right as if this were a matter doubtful" .... Luther, in fact, "cannot deny but that all the faithful honor and acknowledge the sacred Roman See for their mother and supreme".... What punishment is too great for the man who "will not obey the Chief Priest and Supreme Judge upon earth?" "The Pope of Rome," in fact, is "the successor of St. Peter, Christ's vicar, to whom as to the Prince of the Apostles, 'tis believed Christ gave the keys of the Church, that by him the rest should enter or be kept out." It is vain, to imagine distinctions between Christ's church and the Pope's church: the Pope is "Christ's vicar in that Church over which Christ is the head," and "the whole church, not only is subject to Christ, but, for Christ's sake, to Christ's only vicar the Pope of Rome." As for the Church itself, it "has from God not only the power of discerning God's word from that of men ... but also the discerning betwixt divine and human senses of scripture ... betwixt divine institutions and the traditions of men ... Christ's care being that His Church may not err in any manner whatsoever." And the king will not hear of Luther's criterion that nothing is to be believed but what the clear witness of Scripture confirms. Were this the case, "an inexhaustible material would be furnished for battering the church at the pleasure of everyone minded to stir up new sects . . . . When, in fact, was there ever a heretic who did not claim that his new-broached opinions were confirmed by Scripture?" Thus wrote Henry VIII manifesting his faith in the papacy as the ordinary thing that it was less than a decade before he sought papal declaration of annulment of his marriage to Catherine of Aragon, for whose sacramental contraction Henry in the first place had dutifully sought papal approbation. (*Assertio Septum Sacramentorum* or Defence of the Seven Sacraments by Henry VIII, King of England.   Benziger, 1908.   Cf. pp. 188, 200, 202, 316, 398, 400, 402, 404)

In 1527, when Rome was sacked, Henry wrote to Cardinal Nicholas Ridolfi that the most wicked effect of the sack is that the imperial soldiery "should have dared to perpetrate these most terrible atrocities against our most holy Lord, the true and only Vicar of Christ on earth, so that, the head being taken away and the shepherd of the Lord's flock being stricken, holy church should collapse . . . ." All the horrors that have taken place are but a trifle in comparison with this captivity of "that great priest and supreme bishop on earth (*summo in humanis antistite*) by whose power and guidance what God has founded for the salvation of mankind is ruled" (*cuius ductu et firmitate instituta in hominum salutem moderantur.*) (Cf. Philip Hughes, *The Reformation In England*, 3 vols. Macmillan, 1951. See Vol. 1 pp. 203-204.)

Even Luther, when he appeared before the papal legate in 1518 for examination as one gravely suspect of heresy, did not deny that most men believed "we ought to hearken to the decretals of the Roman Pontiff as to the voice of Peter." Luther witnesses more directly still to the belief that it was by God's appointment that the popes rule the whole of Christ's church, when he writes, at the beginnings of the controversies:

> The first thing that moveth me to hold that the Bishop of Rome is superior to all others whom we know to bear themselves as bishops is the very will of God (*ipsa voluntas Dei*) which we see in the fact itself (of the superiority).   For without the will of God the Bishop of Rome could never have arrived at this monarchy (*in hanc monarchiam*).   Now the will of God, whatever be the way it comes to be known, is to be received with

reverence; and therefore it is not lawful rashly to resist the primatial authority of the Bishop of Rome. So great is this reason, that even were there no scripture (in support of it), or no other cause, this would be enough to stay the temerity of them that resist. Therefore, I do not see how those who, going against the will of God, withdraw themselves from the authority of the Bishop of Rome, are to be excused from the guilt of schism." (cf. Hughes, *op. cit.*, I, p. 199)

Basel—Ferrara—Florence

It would be a perversion of history to suggest the deduction that, within papal jurisdiction, there was, until the Reformation in Germany and in England, an undisturbed accord about the nature and extent of the universally admitted powers of the Roman Pontiff. In 1521, the year of the royal treatise *De Romani Pontifice*, scarcely a century intervened from the Council of Constance (1418), barely seventy years from the healing of the schism brought on by the Council of Basel (1431-7), Ferrara (1438), Florence (1439) and a scant ten years from the attempted schism of the Council of Pisa (II). The Schismatic council, the *conciliabulum* of Pisa (1511), was really the work of Louis XII and the Emperor Maximilian, whose intention was not the destruction of the papacy, but the deposition of Pope Julius II, whose Italian policies had wrecked their own schemes for that peninsula—in a word they sought the election of a pope more in accord with their own royal and imperial expectations. This ecclesiastical charade (there were only four cardinals, several bishops, and abbots present together with the envoys of the French king) was disowned and condemned by the Fifth Lateran Council (1512-1517). The Council of Basel convoked by Pope Martin V (the council proper 1431-37) the *conciliabulum* (1437-49) split in half defeating its programs of reform by its fierce antagonism to the papacy. The pro-papal group, together with the Greeks, were transferred to Ferrara by the bull *Doctoris gentium* (1437). At Ferrara, the Latin and Greek contestation over *Filoque* went unresolved. After a year the Council was translated to Florence where union with the Greeks is finally achieved on the procession of the Holy Spirit, on Eucharistic rites, on afterlife, and on papal primacy, (*Laetentur coeli*), union with the Armenians (*Exulte Deo*), with the Coptic Church of Egypt (*Cantate Domino*). After the Council went to the Lateran in Rome (1443), union was concluded with certain Syrians

(1444), with Chaldeans and Marionites of Cyprus (1445). The success and definition of papal supremacy at Ferrara-Florence dealt a grievous blow to the anti-papalists of Basel and conciliariam.   On papal primacy, Florence defined (*item diffinimus*): that the holy apostolic see and the Bishop of Rome enjoy a primacy

> (*tenere primatum*) over the whole world, and the Bishop of Rome himself is the successor of Blessed Peter, the Prince of the Apostles, and is the true Vicar of Christ, head of the whole Church (totiusque Ecclesiae caput), father and teacher of all Christians; to him in blessed Peter there was given over by our Lord Jesus Christ full power to pasture, to rule, and to govern the whole Church (pascendi, regendi ac gubernandi universalem Ecclesiam . . . plenam potestatem); as is all contained in the acts of the general council and in the sacred canons. (DS 1307)

Kung belittles the success and effectiveness of Florence. (*Inquiry*, p. 121) It is less than fair for Kung to write that the doctrine of papal primacy was "imposed on the Greeks." The facts are that 700 Greeks attended the Council; the Emperor John VIII Palaeologus and his brother Demetrius; the Patriarch of Constantinople, Joseph II, 20 metropolitans, deacons, monks, etc. There were in comparison only 118 Latin prelates from the West. For one year, 1438-1439, the Greeks at Ferrara held their ground and were prepared to return home. At Florence on two occasions they threatened to leave. At the Council sessions the Greeks spoke as frequently as did the Latins, and in all but three of the twenty sessions, there was but one constant opponent of union, Mark Eugenicus, one of the six spokesmen of the Greeks. Florence concluded to an agreement that resulted from mutual understanding.   The faith of the two churches was identical. On the Procession of the Holy Spirit, the Latin "from the Father and the Son" and the Greek "from the Father through the Son" were accepted as equivalent. *Filoque* was not "imposed" upon the Greeks, and in the Eucharistic celebration diversity of rites was accepted. The Pope is successor of St. Peter, head and teacher of the whole Church, and successor to the plenitude of power given by Christ to Peter. There is no evidence of any imposition of doctrine nor that the acceptance of any doctrine was under duress that in its absence would have allowed an alternate course of action. Undoubtedly, as at any Council there are contestations, arguments, counter-arguments, but freedom of expression and independence of decision was much in evidence at Florence. The Council's achievements were a significant success. *Laetentur coeli* is an infallible document. Nor may Kung point to the collapse of the union as a sign that it was not genuine, that it was "imposed." Of the six Greek spokesmen, Bessarion, Isidore, Dorotheus of Mitylene, Metrophanes (successor of Joseph II) patriarch of Constantinople were for union; Mark Eugenicus against union. Mark swung the populace and the poorly educated monks against "Rome" despite the pro-union profession of Patriarch Gregory III, successor of Metrophanes. With the fall of Constantinople to Mahomet on May 29, 1453, the union came to an end. Union elsewhere prevailed until Turkish arms reduced territories to Moslem predominance.

It is no invention of reflection to say that popes have been opposed and that their papal pronouncements have been challenged. Hans Kung apparently is within *this* ancient Catholic tradition. Many opponents of the papacy have left the Church to institute another and their proliferation and diversity is adumbrated under the nomenclature—Protestantism. What shall we say of the abnormal Council of Constance (1414-1418) and its peculiar circumstances, a rather singular historical situation, hardly ever repeatable. Vatican II distinguished between "conciliar" and "conciliarist." Conciliar ideas are to be found in canonical legislation centuries before Constance. Conciliarist ideas can be traced back to Marsilius of Padua. The Fathers of the Second Vatican Council allowed no dichotomy between the episcopal college and the pope, the bond between the two being inseparable, the pope, as the successor of Peter is head of the episcopal college as Peter was of the apostolic college. The Fathers gathered in an ecumenical council act in concert with the pope and no decree has any validity unless approved and ratified by the pope. This doctrinal formulation of *Lumen Gentium* (cc. 18-25) is but the authority of every council as opposed to the authority of every pope. Constance is out of accord with authentic Catholic tradition.

Council of Lyons

Kung writes (*Inquiry*, p. 121) of the Council of Lyons (1274) as he does of Florence that they were "Roman acknowledgments of the Roman primacy, composed by Romans, which one tried to impose on Greeks . . . ." Here again nonscholarly liberties are taken about Lyons as there were of Florence. Actually, the Greeks attended and participated at the Council of Lyons with manifest eagerness. Emperor Michael VIII Palaeologus had retaken Constantinople in 1261. He corresponded most cordially with Pope Gregory X and sent a deputation to the Council of Lyons. At its fourth session, Michael's *Professio Fidei* was read from his letter, (*Quoniam missi sunt*), in which his religious persuasions and those of fifty archbishops and hundreds of bishops were stated. The Greek representatives raised no objection to papal primacy, to filioque, the seven Sacraments, purgatory. Michael's letter declared his full acceptance of the Roman faith and primacy. He asked that the Greek Church be allowed to retain its *symbola fidei* and its own rites. Gregory acceded to this request. Reunion was formally effected. There is no historical evidence to support even a suggestion of the Roman imposition of primacy on the Greeks as Kung writes. (p. 121) Because of the manifest readiness of the Emperor and of the Greek representatives at Lyons to subscribe to the decrees of the Council (DS 850-861), the declaration on papal primacy bears a significance beyond Kung's narrow construction.

> The same holy Roman Church also has supreme and full primacy and jurisdiction over the whole Catholic Church. This is truly and humbly recognized as received from the Lord himself in the person of St. Peter, the Prince or head of the Apostles, whose successor in the fullness of power is the Roman Pontiff. And just as the holy Roman Church is bound more than all the others to defend the truth of the faith, so, if there arise any questions concerning the faith, they must be decided by its judgment. Anyone who is aggrieved may appeal to it in matters pertaining to the ecclesiastical court; and in all cases that require ecclesiastical investigation, one may have recourse to its judgment. Also, all churches are subject to it, and their prelates render it obedience and reverence. There is such a fullness of power vested in this Church that it admits other churches to a share in its responsibility; and many of these, especially the patriarchal churches, the same Roman Church has honored with various privileges. Yet, always its special position has remained intact, both in general councils and in some others. (DS 861)

From the ecumenical councils of the Church which principally defined articles of faith and the Sacraments and condemned heresies, we see the exercise of ecclesial infallibility, of the Church founded upon *kepha* against which the powers of hell will not prevail. (Mt. 16: 18, 19) In the unfolding of the doctrine of Petrine primatial authority as it becomes manifest in Peter's leadership in the *Acts of the Apostles*, in accordance with the commissions and mandates given him by Jesus (Matt. 16: 18, 19; Lk. 22:33; Jn. 21:15-17), there is inherent therein an exercise of infallibility in passing on the Christian *paradosis*. Whether or not Peter (and the other Apostles) spoke of infallibility, used such a word or one comparable to it, is really not much to the point. The fact is, according to *Acts,* that Peter spoke without doubts, hesitation, or reservation that Jesus was truly the Messiah foretold by the prophets of the Old Testament; that Jesus is the Savior of mankind; of the *metanoia*, of the requirements of conversion for salvation. He is never opinionated but dogmatic on matters of revelation; he does not conjecture about the Resurrection, the Ascension, and the Exaltation of Jesus but speaks in absolute terms and with an unshakable certitude. Neither the threats of the Sanhedrin, nor imprisonment, nor the dangers of death will mitigate, modify, the Petrine *kerygma* (cf. *Acts* 2:14-39; 3:12-26; 4:8-12; 5:29-32; 10:34-43; 2 *Pet.*). The primatial authority in faith and morals, whatever pertains to the deposit of faith, whatever is necessary for salvation, is exercised infallibly when it is indisputably manifest that the Church, the pope alone, and the pope and the episcopal college acting in concert, formally declare that such is its official and authoritative intention.

The infallibility of Peter is the infallibility of the Church which is built upon him, *Petrus, kepha, Rock*, against which the powers of hell will not prevail. This Matthean text applies to the Church and to Peter as inseparably one. That is the way the Fathers of the First Vatican Council expressed it:

> Romanum Pontificem, cum ex cathedra loquitur ... ea infallibilitate pollere, qua divinus redemptor Ecclesiam suam ... instructam esse voluit. (DS 3074)

That is the way the Fathers of the Second Vatican Council declared it to be:

> This infallibility with which the divine Redeemer willed His Church to be endowed .... This is the infallibility which the

Roman Pontiff, head of the College of bishops, enjoys in virtue of his office, when as the supreme teacher of the universal Church, as one in whom the charism of the infallibility of the Church herself is individually present.... This infallibility promised to the Church.... (*Lumen gentium*, c. 25)

As we shall have occasion to study in our commentary on Kung's *Inquiry*, papal infallibility is comprehended within the papal primatial authority in faith and morals as the Fathers of the First Vatican Council taught:

Ipso autem Apostolico primatu, quem Romanum Pontifex tamquam Petri principis Apostolorum successor in universam Ecclesiam obtinet, supremam quoque magisterii potestatem comprehendi....

With the unfolding of papal primatial authority in faith and morals, there emerges from within to ever greater acknowledgement among the episcopacy, the theologians, and the faithful the infallibility of the solemn pronouncements of the successors of *kepha*. Kung admits as much. "In fact, papal infallibility was already taken for granted by the majority of bishops before it was defined." (*Inquiry*, p. 122) And he quotes Rober Aubert to the same purpose:

Even if they did not approve all the centralizing measures of the Curia, these prelates hardly saw anything unsuitable about a solemn acknowledgement by the Council of papal infallibility, which was admitted at least in practice by all their faithful and clergy and which seemed to them an obvious theological truth. They saw in the ancient tradition attested to by some Scriptural texts which seemed to them quite clear and by the totality of the great scholastic teachers from St. Thomas to Bellarmine. They considered it normal therefore, to take advantage of the assembling of the Council to cut short the revival of what they regarded as completely sterile controversies on this matter. (*Vatican I*, pp. 110-111; quoted by Kung, pp. 122, 123)

We may sum up the doctrinal development of Petrine-papal primatial authority over the universal Church by a nonpapal testimony from Yves Congar's remarkable book, *L'Ecclesiologie du Haut Moyen-Age. De Saint Gregoire le Grand à la Desunion entre Byzance et Rome* (du Cerf. 1968). The general thesis of this scholarly volume is the historical and doctrinal unfolding of papal authority. While its acknowledgement throughout christendom is uneven — what Catholic doctrine has not been unevenly received? — and its understanding variant in different places as to its comprehensiveness, reach, and manner and conditions of exercise—down to Vatican I, there was never a real opposition to it within the temporal boundaries of this study. Certainly there was no actual practical opposition until the fifteenth century at the Councils of Constance and Basel, an opposition that suffered a grievous blow at the Council of Florence.

When Pope Gregory IV went into Gaul, the emperor interdicted the bishops from entering into any rapport with the pope. When the Pope hesitated on whether he should proceed, a group of French bishops from the region of Wala, encouraged him on: they sent the pope a florilegium of testimonials from the Fathers and the earlier popes, proving:

quot eius potestas, imo Dei et beati Petri apostoli, suaque auctoritas, ire, mittere ad omnes gentes pro fide Christi et pace ecclesiarum, pro praedicatione Evangeli et assertione veritatis, et in eo esset omnis auctoritas beati Petri excellens et potestas viva a quo oporteret universos iudicari, ita ut ipse a nemine iudicandus est.

And further on:

vice beati Petri . . . cuius potestas in eo vivit et auctoritas excellit. (p. 155; also n. 99)

Of this, Yves Congar comments: "Témoignage précieux et sans ambiguïté."

On p. 114 of *Inquiry*, Kung writes:

Even though the ecumenical councils—where, apart from Chalcedon, the bishops of Rome exercised scarcely any influence—would not pass any decisions on faith without or against the pope—Partiarch of the Western Church and first Patriarch of the Imperial Church—nevertheless they made their decisions in virtue of their own plenitude of power, for they had not been called by the Roman Pontiff, nor led, nor necessarily confirmed by him.

The saving clause is "would not pass any decisions without or against the pope." As for the rest of passage quoted, Kung could have responded in words that he quotes approvingly from scholars in his earlier work, *Structures of the Church.* For example:

Although the convenience and the ability of councils cannot be denied there is neither a command of Christ nor an apostolic regulation which could prove their necessity; hence councils must be described as of ecclesiastical law. (B. Kurtscheid, *Historia Iuris Canonici*, quoted in *Structures*, p. 7)

The accounts that are found in the manuals and in the treatise *De Ecclesia* propose a theology of councils that exactly follows the actual regulations of canon law. In particular, it has been asserted that a council is not ecumenical unless it has been convoked, presided over, and approved by the pope. This is perfectly legitimate and even necessary if it is a matter of stating what a council must be in order to be ecumenical in the actual state of discipline. But history shows that the norms thus posed cannot be exactly applied to a number of ancient councils, especially to the first ecumenical councils. None of these councils was convoked by the pope. Certain of them were not presided over either by him or by the legates (this, seemingly, is the case with Nicaea), and papal approbation of them did not constitute a part of the *essential structure* of the Church, as do the Sacraments or the primacy of Peter, for example. They are of ecclesiastical institution, at most of apostolic institution, and depend upon the canonical power of the Church, not strictly on "divine law." (Y. Congar, "Concile," in *Catholicisme* [Paris, 1950] II, 1439f. Quoted in footnote 13, p. 7, *Structures.* Cf. too Aubert in the same footnote.)

Within this historical, canonical, and theological perspective the thrust of Kung's remarks in *Inquiry* (p. 114) loses its intended force. What matters doctrinally is that no "authoritatively" professed article of faith is taught as binding all the faithful of the universal Church contrary to the authoritative teaching of the Roman Pontiff, the successor of Peter, that he intends to be binding officially, that is, by virtue of his apostolic authority, on the credal confession of the faithful. In *Lumen Gentium* the Fathers of the Second Vatican Council taught solemnly—though without the solemnity of infallible decision—that there is an episcopal college with the Roman Pontiff as its head, who are the successors of the apostolic college with Peter as its head. The episcopal body must act in union with and in agreement with the successor of Peter. This concert with the Roman Pontiff, the "permanent and visible source and foundation of unity of faith and fellowship" (*LG* c. 3, n. 18; cf. n. 23, *et alibi*), has found expression through two formats of concourse that are obvious and historically much experienced since the Council of Jerusalem (*Acts* 15:28, c. A.D. 52), the New Testamentary Apostolic Epistles, and subsequently, the frequent appeals from all parts of the Christian world to Rome for final adjudication and doctrinal declaration. Neither one nor the other formats of concurrence with the Roman Pontiff by the episcopal college, dispersed throughout the world or solemnly convened in ecumenical council, neither one nor the other is a format *iure divino*, at most, apostolic institution. Since Vatican II, the emergence of the Roman Synod that is virtually representative of the universal episcopacy and of national episcopal conferences, in accordance with papal directives and the instruction of the Council documents, must be counted as historical developments of the formats for the unity of faith by which agreement with and in union with the Roman Pontiff may be expressed. The fixing of canonical requirements for the legitimate convocation of ecumenical councils and for the validity of its doctrinal teaching and the promulgation of decrees ratified by the Bishop of Rome (cf. CIC 222-229) were born of the unfortunate history of councils that were schismatic, heretical, *reprobata* (v.g., the Arian councils), *partim confirmata, partim reprobata* (v.g. Council of Constance), *nec manifeste probata nec manifeste reprobata.* (v.g. Ignatian Council, 869-870). So circumstanced and regulated, the faithful of the universal Church would not be divided against themselves but held in unity in the obedience of faith by the Shepherd to whom the supreme and universal task of "feeding-tending" His flock was personally entrusted by the Risen Jesus.

Kung, Thomas Aquinas, Pseudo-Isidore-Verardo (117-119)

There is no doubt that Aquinas, basing himself—we may

assume, in good faith—on the forgeries, in this way laid the foundations for the doctrine of infallibility of Vatican I. (*Inquiry*, p. 119)

via Torquemada, Cajetan, Bellarmine. And so the theological house of cards collapses! In a word, outside the Isidorian documents and St. Thomas' use of them, there was no other faith-awareness of the primatial authority of the successor of Peter, the bishop of Rome— "certainly not on Scripture nor on the common ecumenical tradition of the Church of the first millennium" (*Inquiry*, 120).

Thomas Aquinas is said to have:

incorporated the new political-juridical development in the second half of the thirteenth century into the dogmatic system. (*Inquiry*, 117)

and this he allegedly did in two successive steps. As Kung tells it:

In his opusculum, *Contra errores Graecorum*, which he wrote in 1263, commissioned by the Curia for Pope Urban IV and the negotiations for union with the Emperor, Michael VIII Palae-logus, he presents to the weak Greeks the arguments for the Roman rights in an exorbitant way, and this had its effect also on the West. In connection with the sublime questions of trinitarian doctrine, in several chapters toward the end of the work, which positively wallow in quotations from forgeries, it is "shown" "that the same Pontiff presides over the whole Church," "that he has the fulness of power in the Church," "that in the same power conferred by Christ on Peter the Roman Pontiff is the successor of Peter, 58. In regard to papal teaching authority Aquinas demonstrates "that it is for the pope to decide what belongs to faith . . . ."

These theses resting on forgeries Thomas then takes over in the *Summa Theologiae*, where they really begin to make history. Basic for our context is the article on whether it is for the pope to ordain a profession of faith, 61 . . . . He takes as his major premise the historically correct statement: "The publica-tion of a profession of faith takes place in a general council." His minor premise is documented only from a text in the

Decretals, which again is based on the Pseudo-Isidore forgeries already mentioned and in no way corresponds to the historical truth. "But a council of this kind can be called only by the authority of the Supreme Pontiff." The conclusion then follows (*because* the publication is by a council, it is by papal authority). "Therefore the publication of a profession of faith pertains to the authority of the Supreme Pontiff."

And so, Kung concludes:

There is no doubt that Aquinas, basing himself—we may assume, in good faith—on the forgeries, in this way laid the foundations for the doctrine of infallibility of Vatican I. (*Inquiry*, 119)

Let us now examine Kung's two principal links—*Pseudo-Isidore* and St. Thomas Aquinas—in his concatenation (Torquemada, Cajetan, Bellarmine) of the doctrinal emergence of papal infallibility at Vatican I. We must bear in mind that just as Kung thought it necessary to discredit *Humanae Vitae*, (to be defectible, in error), by rejecting infallibility *ex ordinario magisterio*, so now he must, logically, challenge papal infallibility by denying papal primatial authority. In fact, in the dogmatic constitution of *Pastor Aeternus* of July 18, 1870, the definition of papal primacy of jurisdiction which precedes it (cc. 1-4) and adumbrates it as well, as Kung twice points out. (*Inquiry* pp. 94, 111) Cap. 4 *De Romani Pontificis infallibili magisterio*

Ipso autem Apostolico primatu quem Romanus Pontifex tamquam Petri principis Apostolorum successor in universam Ecclesiam obtinet, supremam quoque magisterii potestatem comprehendi . . . . (DS 3065)

The reader must bear in mind how adroitly Kung has circumstanced his argumentation with the supposition that but for the forgeries and St. Thomas' unwitting employment of them, the primacy of jurisdiction and the supremacy of magisterial authority of the Roman Pontiffs was unknown to theology. Kung also intimates that but for these, the Fathers of the First Vatican Council had no other grounds for the dogma of infallibility.

Now the key to Kung's misuse of the matter he discusses is Note 58 on p. 117. On page 256, Note 58 reads as follows:

St. Thomas Aquinas, *Contra errores Graecorum*, Pars II, capp. 32-35; the forgeries are also dealt with frankly and noted in recent Catholic commentaries, as for instance in R. A. Verardo's edition with an excellent introduction, *Opuscula Theologica* I, Turin and Rome, 1954.

I am very grateful to Mary Bires, Reference Librarian, Pius XII Memorial Library, Saint Louis University, for photostat copies of Verardo's *Editoris Introductio* (pp. 269-283); of the *Synopsis* (pp. 284-314) and full Latin text of Aquinas' *Contra errores Graecorum.* (pp. 315-346)

If Kung read Verardo's "excellent introduction," he did not read it with learned diligence.

In 1954, the Marietti firm of Rome and Turin published the *Sancti Thomae Aquinatis Opuscula Theologica* under the editorial direction of R. A. Verardo. In the First volume appears the angelic doctor's *libellum Contra errores Graecorum ad Urbanum IV Pontificem Maximum* prefaced by a truly excellent introduction by the editor, Verardo, that extends from pp. 269-314 and comprises a critical appraisal of the researches of other scholars, and Verardo's own organic construction of their findings. (pp. 269-283)

This is followed by a meticulous *Synopsis* in two parts on the *Auctoritates ab auctore libelli, "de fide S. Trinitatis," exhibitae atque a D. Thoma in opusculo "Contra errores Graecorum" adhibitae*, and a *Nota Bibliographica.*

This is what we learn from Verardo's justly celebrated *Editoris Introductio.* Pope Urban IV (1261-1264) gave to Thomas Aquinas a *libellum* entitled *De Fide Sanctae Trinitatis* by a then unknown author whose principal objective was the reunion of the Greek churches with the Roman Church by confession to the Procession of the Holy Spirit *Patri Filoque* and the acknowledgment of the Roman Primacy. P. A. Uccelli discovered the *Libellum De Fide S. Trinitatis* at the turn of the last century among the manuscript collection in the Vatican Library. Its author was then unknown, hence the title given it in Uccelli's edition, *Anonymi liber de fide Sanctae Trinitatis.* No scholar has since contested its authenticity and that it is the tract given by Pope Urban IV to St. Thomas for his appraisal of its orthodoxy of doctrine. According to the best calculations, it seems that the *libellus* was written about 1255 by Nicholas de Dyraccho, (ital. Durazzo), bishop of Crotona, of Greek origin or at least a man much cultivated in Greek culture. The most controverted matter about this *Libellum* are the many quotations from the Councils and the Greek Fathers which are not to be found in either of the alleged sources. It is no small wonder that the author should have had such self-assurance that his learned Greek contemporaries would not see through his inventions of the conciliar and patristic quotations. St. Thomas Aquinas was commissioned by Pope Urban IV to ascertain whether the contents of the treatise conformed to orthodox doctrine. The Angelic Doctor gave his judgment in his own *libellum, Contra errores Graecorum*, in which St. Thomas repeated the pretended conciliar and patristic quotations *totidem fere bervis* with but two exceptions. (Uccelli) In the section which treated of the Roman primacy (cc. 3136) in (*Contra errores Graecorum*) there is perfect concordance with the corresponding section in *de Fide S. Trinitatis* (concordantia ista perfecte, according to Reusch). In the *Synopsis*, Verardo, following the lead of Uccelli and Reusch, lists in full in parallel columns the *concordatia locorum* of the two tracts (pp. 284-309), and those on the Roman primacy in particular on pp. 305-308. Kung seizes upon the suspect documentations (*Inquiry*, 117) which St. Thomas repeated, in particular, in the sections on the primacy under these titles:

Caput 32. Quod Pontifex Romanus est primus et maximus inter omnes episcopos.

Caput 33. Quod idem Pontifex in totam ecclesiam Christi universalem praelationem habet.

Caput 34. Quod idem habet in ecclesia potestatis plenitudinem.

Caput 35. Quod in eadem potestate quae collata est Petro a Christo Romanus Pontifex sit Petri successor.

Caput 36. Quod ad eum pertinet determinare quae sunt fidei.

Kung relates Thomas Aquinas' judgment on the orthodoxy of the doctrine affirmed in the *Libellum de Fide S. Trinitatis* to the forged quotations in that tract and Aquinas' own profession of Roman primacy under each of the above titles to be dependent upon the contrived quotations repeated in his own tract *Contra errores Graecorum* cc. 32-36. This is a very hasty and rash judgment and gravely unfair to the general reader whose vocation in life is not to track down the sources and to check upon the notes of an author.

Verardo gives an entirely different understanding of the matter. We read in his *Editoris Introductio*:

> Exquirebat enim Summus Pontifex ab Aquinate *iudicium theologicum de doctrina* in quo Libello, contra Graecos confecto, tradita. (p. 269)

And Verardo quotes from Aquinas' *Prooemium*:

> Libellum ab excellentia vestra mihi exhibtum, Santissime Pater Urbane Papa, diligenter per egi, in quo inveni *quamplurima ad nostrae fidei assertionem utilis et expressa* . . . . Et ideo, ut remota omni ambiguitate, ex auctoribus in praedicto libello contentis verae fidei fructus purissimus capiatur, proposui *PRIMO* ea quae dubia esse videntur in auctoritatibus praedictis exponere, et POSTMODUM ostendere quomodo ex eis *veritas catholicae fidei et doceatur et defendatur.*

From the expressed intent of the pontiff and Aquinas' own understanding of the papal commission, it is manifest that St. Thomas is not addressing himself to the "substantiation" of the Church's teaching on Roman primacy nor to "prove" his own confession in Roman primacy.   There is only one objective to ascertain whether the libellus *de Fide S. Trinitatis* (et de primatu Romani Pontificis) affirms orthodox doctrine. What of the pretended quotations from the councils and the Greek Fathers?   On this we make two observations.   First, Verardo quotes the judgment (sapienti quidem iudicio) of Echard, who identifies himself with the opinion of other scholars on this very point:

> Recentiores quiden inter quos Alva . . . in hoc opere reprehendunt, quod pleraque Patrum Graecorum auctoritates in eo citatae, in illorum libris iam non legantur, sed *facilis responsio, nempe S. Thomam harum se vadem non dare* . . . . Thomas, in id solum incumbit, ut ad rectum sensum et ad fidei defensionem convertat. (Verardo, p. 277-8)

Verardo also quotes De Rubeis:

> Num vero sanctis Patribus, quorum nomina in oblato libello inscripta legebantur, recte fuerunt attributa, an falso supposita, quaestio est quam *minime Thomas versavit.*

Singula huiusmodi testimonia, quae supposita aut adulterata dicuntur, vocare ad examen *neque libet, neque vacat.* (Verardo, pp. 278-279)

In the judgment of at least these two scholars what really mattered to Aquinas was the concordance of these spurious texts with the orthodox doctrine on Roman Primacy. Verardo concludes on this point: Munus igitur sibi commissum ab Urbano IV rite atque absolute adimplevit Aquinas licet, bona fide, deceptus fuerit. (p. 282)

The second observation: In the text of *Contra errores Graecorum,* Aquinas points to the concordance of the inauthentic quotations with Scripture. *Hoc autem auctoritati consonat sacrae Scripturae,* quae inter Apostolos Petro attribuit primum locum tam in *Evangeliis* quam in *Actibus Apostolorum.* (*Caput* 32–Quod Pontifex Romanus est primus et maximus inter omnes episcopos, p. 340.) And again in *Caput* 33–Quod idem Pontifex in totam ecclesiam Christi universalem praelationem habet. After repeating a spurious quotation from Chrysostom, Thomas adds: *Hoc etiam trahitur ex auctoritate sacrae Scripturae*; nam Petro indistincte oves suas Christus commisit, dicens, Ioan. ult. 17: *Pasce oves meas; et Ioan.* X, 16: Ut sit unum ovile et unus pastor. At the conclusion of *Caput 34*–quod idem habet in Ecclesia potestatis plenitudinem, Aquinas, after quoting the pretended texts of Cyril of Alexandria and John Chrysostom, adds: *Hoc etiam trahitur ex auctoritate* Scripturae; nam Dominus, Matt. XVI, 19, universaliter Petro dixit: *Quodcumque solveris supra terram, erit solutum et in caelis. Caput 36*–Quod ad eum pertinet determinare quae sunt fidei–begins with an alleged quotation of Cyril that is followed by an authentic quotation from Maximus: Item Maximus in epistola Orientalibus directa dicit: Omnes fines orbis qui Dominum sincere receperunt, et ubique terrarum Catholici veram Fidem confitentes in Ecclesiam Romanorum tanquam in solem respiciunt, et ex ipsa lumen catholicae et apostolicae Fides recipiunt. Of this quotation of St. Maximus Confessor, Verardo says (p. 342, n. 2) Pars ista citationis ex S. Maximo authentica omnino est. Immediately following, Aquinas adds: Nec immerito; nam Petrus legitur primo perfectam Fidem esse confessus, Domino revelante cum dixit Matth. xvi, 16: Tu es Christus Filius Dei vivi. Unde et eidem Dominus dicit: Ego pro te rogavi, Petre, ut non deficiat fides tua. (Luc. xxii, 32) There then intervenes a spurious quotation from Chrysostom, immediately followed by Aquinas' own conclusion: item etiam hoc patet ex auctoritate Domini dicentis

(Luc. xxii, 32) Tu aliquando conversus confirma frates tuos. Cc. 32-
36 are the only chapters that treat of the papal primacy in *Contra
errores Graecorum*. We have given excerpts in direct dicourse from
Thomas' own commentary. They are all scriptural. Whatever may
be said about the inauthentic quotations from the *libello de fide S.
Trinitatis* by Nicolas Dyracco which are repeated by St. Thomas in
his own text (*C.E.G.*), for Aquinas the origination and continuing
basis for Petrine and Papal primacy, the *norma normans* for his own
faith in the universal primatial authority of the Roman Pontiff is
revelational data of the Matthean, Lucan and Johannine gospels. It
appears to this writer that just as Hans Kung misused the Pseudo-
Isidorian decretals so too Kung has misused Thomas Aquinas' *Contra
errores Graecorum* and Verardo's "excellent" *Editoris Introductio*,
to that text. For St. Thomas, the first and final word on papal
primatial authority is *consonat Scripturae ex auctoritate sacrae
scripturae; hoc autem trahitur ex auctoritate Scripturae, Domino
revelante; item etiam hoc patet ex auctoritate Domini dicentis.* If
Kung ever read *Contra errores Graecorum*, cc. 32-36 and Verardo's
"excellent" *Editoris Introductio*, he did not do so with learned
diligence. We have given Latin excerpts from the Angelic Doctor's
text and from Verardo's own introduction so that readers who may
not have access to Verardo's edition of *S. Thomas Aquinatis Opuscula
Theologica* may pause about the credibility of Hans Kung as a critical
scholar.

On p. 118, Kung states:

> These theses resting on forgeries Thomas then takes over in
> the *Summa Theologica*, where they really do begin to make
> history.

The *Contra errores Graecorum* was probably written in 1263
about three years before the *Summa Theologica* was begun and
almost a decade before it was left incomplete by Aquinas' untimely
death. Verardo observes:

> Animadvertendum tamen Aquinatem ipsum nuspiam in
> *Summa Theologica* haec testimonia Patrum et Conciliorum
> graecorum praesertim ad primatum Romani Pontificis vindi-
> candum. (*Editoris Introductio*, p. 282)

And he adds that Launoy conjectured that as Thomas grew "more mature and more knowledgeable" he sensed that these conciliar and patristic quotations employed by de Dyraccho in *De fide S. Trinitatis* (with its section on papal primacy) and repeated by Aquinas in *Contra errores Graecorum*—that they were suspect documentations.

> Verum enimvero ad maturiorem cum pervenit aetatem, factus doctor et cautior, testimonia haec pro derelicto habuit; et silentio deprehensae vel saltem olfactae falsitatis indice, suppressit. (p. 282)

And de Rubeis thought that Aquinas, factus consultior, falsitatem suboluit, quam minus consultus olim subolere non potuerat. (Verardo, p. 282)

Whatever may be the explanation for Aquinas' silence in *Summa Theologica* about the spurious quotations of *de fide S. Trinitatis* that Aquinas had repeated in *C.E.G.*, what matters is that his faith in papal primacy did not falter because it was never based—"resting on forgeries," as Kung put it—on them but on the infallible authority of Scripture and the instructions of divine revelation.

Kung's commentary on the passage he quotes from the *Summa Theologica* is as questionable as his recourse to Aquinas' *Contra errores Graecorum* and to Verardo's *Editoris Introductio*.

> Sed contra est quod editio symboli facta est in synodo generalis. Sed huiusmodi synodus auctoritate solius Summi Pontificis potest congregari, ut habetur in Decret., dist. 17, cap. 4 et 5. Ergo editio symboli ad auctoritatem Summi Pontificis pertinet. (S.T. II, II. q. 1, a. 10. ad 3.)

Kung acknowledges that the major premise is a historically correct statement; "the publication of a profession of faith takes place in a general council." But he faults the minor premise because it "is documented only from a text in the Decretals, which again is based on the Pseudo-Isidore forgeries already mentioned and in no way corresponds to the historical truths." (p. 118, n. 62) Here again Kung repeats the same error he had committed earlier. On the contrary as we have already noted, Pseudo-Isidore's declaration that there can be no synod without the authorization of the Bishop of Rome was actually not a false statement but a historically correct one in the midst of the hotch potch of inauthentic and authentic texts that owed its origin *via* Cassiodorus' *Historia ecclesiastica tripartita* to the *Historia ecclesiastica* of Socrates written before the middle of the fifth century. Kung's note 62 refers to his own *Structures of the Church*, VII, 6. On p. 289 of this latter work there is a footnote 4 which reads:

> Pseudo-Isidore had already induced Pope Pelagius II to claim the right of convocation for the Roman See, etc.

Subject to correction or enlightenment, this writer finds this statement very challenging. Pope Pelagius II reigned from Nov. 26, 579 to Feb. 7, 590, while Pseudo-Isidore, the False Decretals, were assembled at Rheims or Le Mans or in the chapel of Charles the Bald, between 847 and 852, four centuries later.

We continue with the Latin text of St. Thomas.

> Respondeo dicendum quod, sicut supra dictum est, in arg. 1. nova editio symboli necessaria est ad vitandum insurgentes errores. Ad illius ergo auctoritatem pertinet et editio symboli ad cuius auctoritatem pertinet finaliter determinare ea quae sunt fidei, ut ab omnibus inconcussa fide teneatur. Hoc autem pertinet ad auctoritatem Summi Pontificis, ad quem majores et difficiliores Ecclesiae quaestiones referuntur, ut dicitur in Decretalibus, extra de baptismo, cap. *Majores.* Unde et Dominus, Luc. 22, 32, Petro dicit quem Summum Pontificem constituit: *Ergo pro te rogavi, Petre, ut no deficiat fides tua; et tu aliquando conversus confirma fratres tuos.* Et huius ratio est, quia una fides debet esse totius Ecclesiae, secundum illud 1 Cor. 1, 10: *Idipsum dicatis omnes, et non sint in vobis schismata;* quod servari no posset, nisi quaestio fidei exorta determinetur per eum qui toti Ecclesiae praeest; et sic eius sententia a tota Ecclesiae firmiter teneatur. Et ideo ad solam auctoritatem Summi Pontificis pertinet nova editio symboli, sicut et omnia alia quae pertinet ad totam Ecclesiam, ut congregare synodum generalem, et alia huiusmodi. (S.T. II, II, q. 1, art. 10 ad 3)

Kung quotes the above passage in English but he makes no note of the Scriptural source of Aquinas reasoning—Unde et dominus, Lk. 22, 32, Petro dicit. It is a matter of no little perplexity that Kung who will insist on Scripture as the *norma normans* of Catholic ecclesiology does not do so when Thomas Aquinas does. What the Angelic Doctor held on papal primatial jurisdiction and authority was not dependent upon nor derived from the Gallican production of the pretended texts of *Pseudo Isidore* nor from the spurious quotations of the councils and Greek Fathers composed by Nicholas de Dyraccho. Would Kung say that Aquinas' faith in the Blessed Trinity was dependent upon textual forgeries in Dyraccho's libello *de Fide S. Trinitatis* which Aquinas repeats on the Trinity in his own *Contra errores Graecorum* (n. 1028-1118) just as he repeats Dyraccho's fabricated quotations from councils and the Greek Fathers in the section on papal primacy? Or are both Christian doctrines based primarily upon the revelational data of the New Testament which Aquinas quotes as the source of his own credal profession? As for that particular passage from the *Decretals*, it is historically correspondent to Church law and practice. Thomas' own faith was neither unique nor novel but within the mainstream of the faith-consciousness of the universal Church.

Kung misuses his primary and secondary sources and bends them to the direction of his dominating prepossession—his assault upon papal primatial authority and magisterial infallibility. One should stop short of inferring a deliberate, calculated intent on his part to do so, but is it beyond the bounds of fairness to suggest that his overarching purpose becomes *the* psychological aporia that diverts him from the cautious circumspection of the critical scholar.

This has been a long Kungian aporia. His use of sources, primary and secondary and of general history, is, as we have shown, but not completely, partial and partisan in a manner at variance with a truly open "Inquiry."

Rights of Conscience

Kung's discussion of "The Rights of Conscience" (pp. 134-136) *vis a vis Humanae Vitae* in particular and with papal magisterial authority in general, and with papal infallibility in particular, in a word, conscience as opposed even to a dogma is very inadequate and disappointing. There is no discussion of the place of the Catholic faith in the conscience of a Catholic nor any presentation of the role of the Catholic Church in the information and formation of conscience. Kung falls back on the inviolability of the subjective conscience. Be that as it may, Our Lord came to correct human conscience, to inform it, to enlighten it, to obligate it, and He instituted His Church to continue His magisterial mission on earth to the close of time. While not challenging sincerity, still the question of how a conscience can contest justly and justifiably a solemn teaching of the Vicar of Christ not only the *ex cathedra* but also a traditional moral doctrine which bishops everywhere taught uninterruptedly for centuries in concert with the successor of Peter, Kung does not examine the question. For the assistance of the Holy Spirit is always present to the Vicar of Christ and the other bishops and in their adherence to the Church's traditional ban on contraceptives they have relied on more than ordinary human resources. It is not left to the conscience of Catholics to subordinate the authentic and authoritative interpretation of divine moral order to their own superior determination of the morality of an act. Conscience can speak with many tongues and not all of them are reliable, nor are all the persuasions of conscience above the strongest urges of human passion, burdensome inconveniences, and rationally appealing self-interest. The objectively erroneous conscience firm in its personal sense of moral correctness may excuse from the gravity of moral culpability. But religious and civil authorities may and do contravene objectively erroneous consciences. Public law and local ecclesiastical authorities have opposed racial segregation as both immoral and illegal against those who protest their freedom to follow their consciences in racial relations. Kung has not dealt circumspectly with the question of the conscience of a Catholic vis-a-vis the teachings of the Church neither in *Structures* (pp. 341-344) nor in *Inquiry*. Faith binds us to faithfulness, to a firm and authentic adherence to the truth revealed by Our Lord before (Mt. 16:18, 19; Lk. 22:32) and after His Resurrection (Jn. 21:15-17) and guaranteed by the apostolic magisterium, and historically substantially identical with itself in the teaching authority of the Church.

PART III

KUNG'S DECLENSION OF FAITH

The most notable failure of Hans Kung is his complete silence on his former faith in the unique prerogatives of the Petrine—papal office. He never adverts to it; he never reexamines his former exegetical, theological, historical persuasion in support of it; he never tells his readers what were the faults and failings in these antecedent convictions that had eluded his detection. Nor does he inform us of any new evidences—scriptural, theological, historical, (that he had never known before), that warrants faulting his former adherence to the ecclesial faith in papal infallibility.

We cannot entirely suppress two persistent reflections. If *Humanae Vitae* had never been promulgated or—*ex hypothesi impossibili*—if a novel moral doctrine had been taught by Pope Paul VI that reversed the traditional moral teaching of the Church on contraceptives, would Kung have ever challenged papal infallibility? The second notion: is it possible that Kung's ecumenical zeal has been protestantized at the sacrifice of the papal office?

We have examined three books by Hans Kung that appeared before *Humanae Vitae* and selected passages that are unambiguously supportive of the Petrine-papal office.

In 1961, more than a year after Pope John XXIII first announced at St. Paul's Outside the Walls his intention to summon an ecumenical council, (January 25, 1959) and about a year before the Twenty-Second Ecumenical Council solemnly opened on October 11, 1962, Hans Kung published his book, *The Council, Reform, and Reunion* (Sheed and Ward, New York). Kung took his theme from Pope John's inaugural encyclical, *Ad Petri Cathedram*, of the 29th of June 1959 in which the Roman Pontiff prayerfully hopes that the revival of the Catholic faith and morality, and the adaptation of the ecclesiastical governance and discipline to the demands of the present hour might induce:

those who are separated from the Apostolic See, beholding this manifestation of unity, derive from it the inspiration to seek out that unity which Jesus Christ prayed for so ardently from his heavenly Father.

It is highly significant that in all the proposals for reform suggested by Kung, he never dimly intimates the removal of what the generality of Protestants consider the major obstacle to reunion, namely, the pontifical office.   On the contrary, he earnestly and repeatedly urges them to reconsider and shed their opposition to it.

the only Church there is, and in which we believe, is simply and always the visibly and hierarchically organized totality of the baptized, united in the external profession of faith and in obedience to the Roman Pope. (p. 33)

Of course, it is constantly happening (and often in a strange way) that a non-Catholic comes to see a greater fullness of light shining in the Catholic Church; that he comes to recognize, despite all her numerous deficiencies that she preserves the wholeness of Christianity, with the apostolic and Petrine succession, in a way that other communions, lacking the apostolic or Petrine succession, despite all the good that is in them, do not. (p. 94)

Contrast this with *Inquiry*. (pp. 82, 83, 221 ff.)

Is it not still the case that "Catholicizing" is the deadliest of all sins to a true Protestant? Is it not true that every sort of "liberalizing" is allowed, so long as one does not lead in the direction of the Catholic Church? Is one not free to deny or minimize the divinity of Christ, and "interpret" his resurrection away to nothing, so long as one does not show too much understanding of the New Testament witness to a Petrine or episcopal office? (p. 99)

Deformation of doctrine in *theology* (whether directly heretical or inclining toward heresy) is not in the least unthinkable for a Catholic; on the contrary, history shows that, because of men's deficiencies, it has happened only too often. But the situation is different when we come to the Church's dogma:

for the Church is the chosen herald and witness of Jesus Christ himself (Matt. 28:18-20; Luke 10:16; John 17:17 f; Acts 1:8), taught by the Holy Spirit (John 14:26; 16:13), the pillar and ground of the Truth. (Tim. 3:15) We cannot speak of any "deformation" in the Church's dogma, such as is possible in theology, nor, in consequence, in this sense, of a "reform" of doctrine. What the Catholic Church does recognize in her dogma is the giving of new forms or more developed forms to a doctrine which has not in every respect achieved its complete form; as the Vatican Council defined it, a growth and advance. (p. 112)

Here Kung is far more reassuring on Vatican I, dogma, and its "growth and advance" than he is in *Inquiry* where he questions the human capability in general to formulate propositional truths and, in particular, solemnly defined truths (dogma) by popes and councils even with the assistance of the Holy Spirit whose efficacy he minimizes in this context. (cf. *Inquiry*, pp. 157-181)

There is a *development* of dogma in the sense of an unfolding of what is implicit so as to make explicit, under the influence of the Holy Spirit. Although dogmatic definitions express the truth with infallible accuracy and are in this sense unalterable (as against Moderism), yet they are by no means rigid, fossilized formulae. They form part of human history, with its limitations. What they express is indeed an objective view, but it is at the same time one that is historically conditioned; hence, as human, finite statements, they can never exhaust the mystery and the fullness of the divine revelation of truth. One and the same truth of faith can always be expressed in a still more complete, more adequate, better formula. (p. 113)

Compare all these unequivocal affirmations of the "infallible accuracy," "unalterable," "objective" truth of "dogmatic definitions" thanks to the "influence of the Holy Spirit," that remain free from error even as they are, time-conditioned, imperfect, incomplete, as obviously any truthful affirmation of a divine mystery must be—with the inherent ambiguity ("fundamentally ambiguous") of human propositions in general not excluding articles of faith that Kung insists on in *Inquiry*. (pp. 157, 161) In *Inquiry*, Kung does not explain the change in his theological gnoseology. It seems that logically he is forced to maintain the human incapability of possessing any infallible knowledge even with divine help so that he can deny infallibility anywhere, in popes, councils, and scriptures in order to withstand the reasonable expectation of many, that is, apart from the divine promise, that divine revelation on the salvific event and message for all mankind should reach its auditors unadulterated with error if it is to be truly the Word of God, "whatsoever I have taught you." (Mt. 28:20)

> there is today a growing number of Protestant theologians (except for those who eliminate all the "Catholic" Scripture texts on a basis of subjective prejudice or explaining away, or say that they are theologically irrelevant, which calls in question the authority of Scripture itself) who are trying to pay serious attention once more to what the Scriptures have to say about ecclesiastical office, and to ask themselves: Is there not in Scripture, an apostolic vocation, blessing and commissioning, which confers the Spirit and is associated with prayer and the laying on of the hands—in fact, ordination, effectively communicating the grace of office and making it lawful in the eyes of the congregation? An ordination which, according to Paul's intention, was to be continued? Is there not then a succession, not only in general in the apostolic faith and confession of faith, but in a special apostolic faith—an apostolic succession? Was there not even in the Apostolic Church a visible hierarchy of bishops, presbyters and deacons? Is the present-day organization of the Protestant Church scriptural? Is not the question "By what authority" a deeply disturbing question for many who hold office in the Protestant Church today? (p. 131)

In theology too, there is more objective consideration nowadays, on the protestant side, of the question of the Papacy: books like Oscar Cullman's (*Peter: Disciple, Apostle, Martyr,* London, 1953) represent an enormous advance in clarification. The problem today is not so much concerned with the really very striking scriptural testimony to the primacy of Peter (are the promise of the primacy in Matt. 16, 18 and the conferring of it in John 21. 15 ff. authentic—and did Peter exercise a primacy?) as with the primacy of the *Pope*: must the Petrine office necessarily have continued in the post-apostolic Church?

Catholic theologians are trying to demonstrate the necessity of a Petrine office in the modern Church not only on a merely sociological basis as expedient for the preservation of unity (though this unity as displayed by the Catholic Church is something of which Protestants, even when critical, often painfully feel their own lack) but theologically, by a more profound insight into the Old and New Testaments and early Christian tradition (there is a Petrine office, not because things would not work without it, but because Christ willed it so. (p. 132)

But what we have said before of ecclesiastical office in general needs to be said even more emphatically of the Petrine office in particular, for this is a decisive factor in the discussion: Luther's denial of the Petrine office (for which this theology prepared the way, but which it did not make inevitable) did not fundamentally have a theoretical, exegetical or historical basis but was due to practical, existential forces at work in the situation at that time. Luther's opposition to the Pope did not begin from some new interpretation of Matt. 16, 18, or John 21; the new exegetical and historical interpretation was a *consequence* of Luther's opposition to the Pope; and the opposition itself has to be explained in terms of the situation of Luther, of the Church at that time and the politics of that time, especially by the obscuring of the idea of the primacy by abuses in the Curia and by the Conciliar Movement. The *concrete situation* of the Papacy at that time made it impossible to see the *nature* of the Papacy clearly—and this is why the Papacy was denied. (p. 133)

One may compare the above passages from Kung's *Reform* on ecclesiastical office, on the Petrine-papal office, the scriptural sources —"the very striking scriptural testimony," "Christ willed it so," the origin of Luther's opposition, "the new exegetical and historical interpretation was a *consequence* of Luther's opposition to the Pope—one may compare them with their contrasting studies in *Inquiry* and wonder whether Kung's opposition to the Pope's promulgation of *Humanae Vitae* did not prompt as a *consequence* Kung's present day, new exegetical and historical interpretation of the Church and the papacy in particular.

It is significant that even such a theologian as Karl Barth

who can certainly not be accused of "Catholicizing tendencies," and who has often and vigorously proclaimed his opposition to the Papacy, admits that it is impossible to establish *from the Gospel* any *radical* objection either to the concentration of the apostolic function in Peter or to the possibility of a primacy in the Church, which might even be that of Rome. (p. 138)

True, as a Catholic, one can and must reply at this point that the primacy, too, is a matter of faith; that the Pope is the Vicar of *Christ*, but only after all, the *Vicar* of Christ; that Christ did not promise us outstanding human personalities . . . . One can, in short, as a Catholic protest to the Protestant that he must not demand *too* much from the human element in the Papacy. (139)

What is called for on the Protestant side is to consider whether the words of Scripture about the abiding rock (Matt. 16, 18), the guiding and ruling key-bearer of the Kingdom of heaven (Matt. 16, 19), the special possessor of the power of binding and loosing (Matt. 16, 19), the means of confirming the faith of others (Luke 22, 32) and the deputy shepherd over the whole of Christ's flock (John 21, 15, ff.), need to be understood more deeply, more powerfully, and with more relevance to the present day, by Protestant Christians, to ask themselves whether the Apostolic Church, united in Peter, was not meant to go on, with the Petrine office continuing along with the pastoral office of the Apostles, for the sake of the Church (so that what was once *laid* as a foundation would continue to *function* as a foundation); whether it might not be possible to view the history of the popes, for all the dubious matters in it, in a somewhat more cheerful and understanding light; whether much disputing and bitterness could not now be forgotten, allowing us to recognize, across the barrier of all that is human and all too human, something which does indeed seem to be not the mere work of men but the work of our common Lord, promised to us and protected for us by the Word of God. (p. 140)

This remarkable passage sums up not only Kung's earnest invitation to Protestants to concentrate upon the divine origination and abiding intention in the Catholic Church with a compassionate understanding of the human frailties within it, but also the deep faith of Kung himself in that Church and above all in the Petrine-papal office despite all the vagaries of its history. Perhaps there is no sharper contrast between *Reunion* and *Inquiry* than the opposing scriptural exegesis of the Petrine texts. The all pervasive contrast between *Reunion* and *Inquiry* is in their respective styles, tone, temper of spiritual and intellectual responses. But the *matter* is the same, the scriptural texts and the irrevocable records of history. No new "evidence" is put forth to fault his former theology that was supportive of the papacy; no new "evidence" to discredit the scriptural exegesis he adhered to before *Inquiry*; no explanation for the reversal of his former historical interpretation. In *Reunion*, Kung called upon the Protestants "to view the history of the popes . . . in a somewhat more cheerful and understanding light." In *Inquiry*, Kung concentrates on everything in papal history that offends him and the papacy becomes the "arbitrary, autocratic, absolutist monarch." (p. 103-107) It is as if the two different minds of *Reunion* and *Inquiry* had never met in one and the same believer. It is an intellectual, spiritual, and religious experience that has not yet been explained. It may be that Kung's reaction to the traditional moral teaching of *Humanae Vitae* was so opposed or his ecumenism has been so Protestantized that there resulted a "deformation of doctrine in theology" and as a consequence conduced to a liberal Protestant rejection of infallibility, ecclesial, papal, and conciliar and scriptural.

As to the "spiritual credibility of popes" apart from the fact that it has no cancelling effect on the divine institution of the Petrine-papal office, we find appropriate the observation of Humbert, Cardinal bishop of Silva Candid to the Patriarch Michael Cerularius in the eleventh century:

> (*Papa*) *qualis Petrus officio . . . non qualis Petrus merito* —
> the Pope is like Peter by his office . . . he is not like Peter by his merits.

Primarily and principally, it is not the human credentials but its divine credentials that makes the Catholic Church credible and invite all men to its fold.

During the forty years of the Western schism (1378-1417) saints (Catherine of Siena, Bridget of Sweden, Gerard de Groote, Vincent Ferrer) and nations clung to their faith in the divine institution of the Petrine—papal office despite the scandal and even though their obediences were pledged to different claimants to the pontifical office. Less than a century earlier, Dante Alighieri had castigated Boniface VIII, the Gaetani pope, as the "Prince of the New Pharisees," who cynically boasted: "The heaven I can shut and open, as thou knowest" (*Inferno*, xxvii, 85ff); who is styled by an irate St. Peter, a person:

> usurping on earth my place, my place, my place, which in the presence of God's son is vacant (*Paradiso*, xxvii, 22f.)

whom Beatrice, in her last words to Dante, once more remembers when she predicts that Clement V will also be thrust into the earth tubes of Simon Magus and there push deeper down "him from Anagni." (*Paradiso*, xxx, 147 f.) And yet in that very village of Anagni and in the moment when William Nogaret and the agents of Phillip IV dared lay hands on Boniface to seize him, the same Pope Boniface VIII appeared to Dante, in reverence of the papal office, as the true Vicar of Christ, even as Christ himself:

> I see the fleur-de lys enter Anagni
> And in his Vicar Christ made captive.
> A second time I see Him mocked, I see
> The vinegar and gall renewed, I see
> Him slain between the living thieves.
> (*Purgatorio*, xx, 86 ff.)

Dante believed in the primatial authority of popes because of the divine commission of Christ Jesus however spiritually incredible a pope may be. He was far from denying or disregarding the effectiveness of the papal office even in a man whom he considered an unworthy incumbent. But more to the historical point. What has Kung found "spiritually" incredible about the popes of recent memory—Leo XIII, Pius X, Benedict XV, Pius XI, Pius XII, John XXIII, Paul VI? In *Inquiry* Kung regurgitates everything of past Church history that repels him but instead of focusing his criticism on individual popes in their human failings, he rejects an article of faith. In order to make popes "spiritually credible" (i.e., ecumenically acceptable, as he sees it) Kung has reformed the Petrine–papal office out of existence, that is, the existence given it *iure divino*.

In *Inquiry*, Kung does not use authors that are supportive of papal primatial authority and magisterial infallibility. Either they are excluded entirely, that is, not even listed in the *Notes* or if listed their theologizing is not incorporated into the text and context of the book—such as Thils, Rahner, Karrer, Schlier, Schelke, Ratzinger, Braun, von Balthasar, etc.—not even Oscar Cullman for his scriptural exegesis of Matt. 16: 18, 19. These scholarly theologians are repeatedly referred to and quoted in *The Council, Reform, and Reunion* (1961) and even more so in *Structures of the Church.* (1964) They are usually listed in clusters of footnotes in *The Church.* (1967) But one of the most notable omissions in *Inquiry* is the *Collective Declaration by the German Episcopate on the Circular of the Imperial German Chancellor concerning the Next Papal Election* which is discussed in *Reunion* (p. 165), quoted in full (pp. 194-199) with a Commentary by Dom Oliver Rousseau, O.S.B. (pp. 199-201), and duly summarized in a paragraph in *Structures.* (p. 212) It is, as Kung observes (*Reunion*, p. 193), an extremely important declaration of principle by the German bishops after the Vatican Council (1875) on the status of bishops in the Catholic Church." But more to our point is Kung's unchallenging approval and enthusiasm for a document that says much that he will question in *Inquiry.* For example:

According to the decisions (of Vatican I), the ecclesiastical jurisdictional authority of the Pope is indeed a "potestas suprema, ordinaria et immediata," a supreme authority, conferred upon the Pope in the person of St. Peter by Jesus Christ, the Son of God, extending over the whole Church, and so over each diocese and directly over all the faithful, for the preservation of unity of faith, of discipline and of the government of the Church, and certainly not merely consisting of a few reserved rights.

But this is not a new doctrine; it is a truth of the Catholic faith which has always been recognized, and a well-known principle of canon law, a doctrine which the Vatican Council has declared and affirmed afresh against the errors of the Gallicans, Jansenists and Febronians and in union with the pronouncements of earlier general councils . . . .

Nor do the decisions of the Vatican Council give any shadow of ground for stating that they have made the pope an absolute sovereign, more totally absolute, by virtue of his infallibility, than any absolute monarch in the world . . . the description of absolute monarch, even with reference to the Church's affairs, cannot be applied to the Pope, because he stands under the divine law and is bound by the provisions made by Christ for his Church. He cannot change the constitution given to the Church by her divine founder, as a secular legislator can alter the constitution of a state. The Constitution of the Church rests in all essential points on divine ordinances and is exempt from all human arbitration. It is in virtue of the same divine institution upon which the Papacy rests that the episcopate also exists; it, too, has its rights and duties, because of the ordinance of God himself, and the Pope has neither the right nor the power to change them . . . .

Finally, the view that the Pope is in virtue of his infallibility "a totally absolute sovereign" rests on a completely erroneous notion of the dogma of papal infallibility. As the Vatican Council expressed it in clear, precise words, and as proceeds from the very nature of the case, infallibility refers simply to the character of the supreme papal teaching authority; this covers precisely the same field as the infallible teaching office of the Church in general, and is limited to what is contained in the Scriptures and Tradition and the doctrinal decisions already made by the Church's teaching office.

The complete text was solemnly approved by Pius IX in a brief to the German bishops on March 2, 1875: ". . . Your declaraton is an expression of that true doctrine which is at once the teaching of the Vatican Council and of the Holy See," and again in his consistorial address of March 15, 1875. Now we ask why was this celebrated document of the German Bishops excluded from the theology of *Inquiry*? What led Kung (like Luther) to a "new exegetical and historical interpretation" in *Inquiry* in opposition to his former faith in papal primacy and infallibility? What new scriptural and historical knowledge which he had not known before led him to read and understand the Petrine texts (and all of the New Testament) and Church history differently? And lastly, what had led Kung to adopt Bismarck's charges of papal absolutism? (cf. *Inquiry*, pp. 104-108)

The German text of the *Declaratio Collectiva Episcoporum Germaniae*, Jan.-Feb., 1875 may be found in DS 3112-2116 together with Pope Pius IX's Apostolic Letter, *Mirabilis illa constantia* ad Germanae episcopos, March 4, 1875 (DS 3117)—cum declaratio vestra nativam referat catholicam ac propterea sacri Concilii et huius Sanctae Sedis sententiam. From Father Rousseau's commentary we abstract the following excerpt:

> Even though, in practice, the Council's clarification of the juridical position was limited to the prerogatives of the Bishop of Rome, yet it is obvious that the decisions of the Council did not, in this matter, go beyond the definition of the doctrine which had long been held in the Church, and that they changed absolutely nothing, most particularly nothing in respect of the episcopacy.

There is nothing in *Reunion* that offers a challenging criticism of any of the doctrinal affirmations made by the German Bishops nor even a mild demurrer against Rousseau's commentary. We conclude our summary review of Kung's *Reunion* with a quotation from the works of Otto Karrer:

> The idea of the Petrine office was there from the beginning. The Church was given her structure in her very foundation by our Lord. She did not sail under sealed orders, not to be opened til later on in the voyage . . . . The Petrine office is more in the nature of a breakwater against errors than a fertile source of doctrine. It is essentially regulative; but as such, according to our belief, it is willed by Christ and providential to such a degree that, in the light of early Christian history, none of the most important of the traditional beliefs of Christendom—the canon of Scripture, Christology, the dogmas concerning the Trinity, the validity of heretical baptism—is ultimately thinkable without it. (quoted in *Reform*, pp. 167-168)

Otto Karrer is a noted scholar on the petrine-papal office and his classic work is passed over in silence in *Inquiry*, namely, his response to Oscar Cullman's thesis of limited primatial authority conferred upon Peter by Christ, *Peter and the Church: An Examination of Cullman's Thesis* (Quaestiones Disputatae 8. English text, Herder. 1963). One would suppose that in a truly open *Inquiry* Karrer's exegetical and historical interpretations would be an object of study, and comment, or response.

One of our constant attentions in our study of Kung's *Inquiry* has been to ascertain *why* and *how* did he defect from an article of faith, a solemnly defined dogma of the Church? For this particular reason, we have had recourse to his earlier works to ascertain, by comparison, his reason, if any, for abandoning his former exegetical and historical interpretation for a contrary critical construction. We were prompted to this principally by the fact that the *matter*, scriptural and historical, is the same in his intellectual possession before and after *Humanae Vitae* and *Inquiry*. We have discovered no new "evidence," no new knowledge on his part for his reversal of faith on the unique prerogatives of the Petrine-papal office. Indeed, he never adverts to his former faith and theological convictions and never points out, as did John Henry Newman more than a century ago, and Heinrich Schlier, a prominent Protestant theologian, now a convert to Catholicism, what was wanting in his former faith. We were encouraged to persevere in this purpose by Kung's own reflections upon Martin Luther:

> Luther's denial of the Petrine office . . . did not fundamentally have a theoretical, exegetical or historical basis but was due to practical, existential forces at work in the situation at that time. Luther's opposition to the Pope did not begin from some new interpretation of Matt. 16, 18 or John 21; the new exegetical and historical interpretation was a *consequence* of Luther's opposition to the Pope . . . . (*The Council, Reform, and Reunion*, p. 133)

We have wondered inconclusively whether the opposition to the primacy of jurisdiction and magisterial infallibility of the pope was consequent to *Humanae Vitae*, or whether it was because of a Protestantized ecumenism, or whether the "new theology" with its rationalist criticism has appeared to Hans Kung as the catalyst of a latitudinarian christianity.

But there is a ray of light, a saving grace in all this intriguing religious experience, this crisis of faith. In *Inquiry*, Kung adopts as his own a passage from St. Augustine's *De Trinitate* from which we excerpt these sentences:

> "I ask them to correct me if I make a mistake . . . if anyone says, 'I understand your meaning well enough, but it's not true,' I ask him to state his own position and refute mine . . . I hope

God in his mercy will help me never to turn my back on teachings which I believe to be true."

We respectively suggest that Kung meditate on his own writings that have been supportive of the Petrine-papal prerogatives of office. To this purpose, we now select some passages from Kung's book, *Structures of the Church* (1964), in particular, scriptural exegesis that led Heinrich Schlier into the Church and Kung's approving repetition of Bishop Gasser's official interpretation of the decree on infallibility. (*admonitum*: what Kung puts forth as the teaching of Luther, Calvin, and Karl Barth on ecclesiastical fallibility in *Structures*, pp. 305-326, reappears as his own position in *Inquiry* with a discernible leaning toward Barth's)

The scriptural study begins with the question about the continuity and discontinuity of the Catholic Church with the apostolic church. After reviewing the variant Protestant conjectures on the beginning of "Catholic decadence," of "early Catholicism," Kung concludes with a Protestant admission that it begins with the New Testament itself.

Where does the defection from the apostolic Church, where does "Catholic decadence," begin, according to the Protestant view? Is it just coincidence that this point in time in the development of Church history is always being pushed further back under the pressure of the findings of historical research? Luther still felt himself at one with the old Church of the first millenium: for him, "Catholic decadence" begins—at least in a crucial sense—with the Middle Ages. Later Protestantism identified itself only with the Church of the first centuries. For it "Catholic decadence" had its beginning after the "*consensus quinquesaecularis*" or, even earlier, after the conversion of Constantine. A. von Harnack set the first century as the time when the apostolic Church ceased to exist: Catholic decadence begins with the influx of the Greek spirit into primitive apostolic Christendom . . . .

Hence, in the second century, we can begin to observe "the Christian religion in its development into Catholicism." (Harnack) This is the starting point for the discussion of the following decades about the Hellenistic-Catholic original sin which, after the apostolic period, ushered in the period of "early Catholicism." It is in this early Catholic period that the typical Catholic concept of ecclesiastic office began to crystallize: "The struggle with Gnosticism compelled the Church to put its teaching, its worship, and its discipline into fixed forms and ordinances and to exclude everyone who would not yield them obedience. . . .If by "Catholic" we mean the church of doctrine and law, then the Catholic Church had its origin in the struggle with Gnosticism. (Harnack)

Had not this continuous pushing back of the "Catholic decadence" practically reached the New Testament itself? Had not the borders between the New Testament and the post-New Testament writings become fluid for Harnack too? It is to the credit of the Bultmann school in particular, that the specific problem raised herewith has been discussed with an unmitigated clarity: "Catholic decadence" begins even earlier; "early Catholicism" can be found in the New Testament itself. (*Structures*, 135-136)

What follows is a presentation of the evidences of the structural order of the Church in the *Epistles* by two scholars, Ernst Käsemann, a Protestant theologian, and Heinrich Schlier, formerly a Protestant theologian, now a convert to Catholicism since 1955. As Kung points out, both Christians largely agree on the question of ecclesiastical office in the New Testament. But one prompted by the "catholic evidences" became a Catholic, and the other, despite these scriptural evidences employed a formal principle of interpretation which in effect turns out to be a material principle of selection. What concerns us here is not only the exposition of the revelational data that Käsemann and Schlier both examine (and Kung's apparent concurrence, with some explicitly expressed reservations about Käsemann's) but even more significantly, Kung's own response to Käsemann's way out of the dilemma that confronts Protestants on the early Catholicism in the New Testamentary epistles.

(Käsemann) distinguishes sharply between the different concepts of organization underlying the Church structure in the Pauline Epistles, on the one hand, and in the Pastoral Epistles and in Luke (Acts), on the other. In contrast to the charismatically determined Pauline congregation, the structural order of the congregation both in the Pastoral Epistles and in Luke is defined in terms of early Catholicism.

According to Käsemann, in the Pastoral Epistles the congregation was sorely put on the defensive by the Gnostic heresies. The resistance was led from a single centre: by the apostolic delegate and by the presbytery closely linked to him. In the *Pauline Epistles* a presbytery is never addressed, although it would have been the logical body to struggle against the heresies. Indeed there was no presbyterium of such a kind in the Pauline congregations as had probably been established in the congregations of the Pastoral Epistles.

Presumably *ordination* (I Tim. 4:14; 5:22; II Tim. 1: 6) in the Pauline congregations derived from the Judeo-Christian tradition: "It had the same meaning as in Judaism, namely, the communication of the spirit and the authorization to administer the *depositum fidei* of I Tim. 6:20, which we may well interpret to be the tradition of Pauline teaching. This means, however, that an office confronting the rest of the congregation had become the actual bearer of the spirit and the primitive Christian conception, according to which every Christian partakes of the spirit in Baptism, receded into the background and actually disappeared. Equally clear is that this no longer corresponded to the charism doctrine of Paul. The Pauline legacy receded before the Judaic, at least at a central point of the Church's message. Thus the word "Charism" appears only in I Tim. 4:15 and in II Tim. 1:6, which is illuminating in connection with statements concerning ordination and the authorization to administer the *depositium fidei*. Awkwardly but most appropriately one could speak of a spirit of office."

Thus, according to Käsemann, all references to the apostolic legates (Titus, Timothy) in fact, pertain to the monarchical bishops: "His task is the continuation of the apostolic office in the post-apostolic period. In other words, he stands in the succession of Moses and Joshua, receives and controls the doctrinal tradition and the administration of justice by divine right—namely, as empowered through the gift of the Spirit at ordination. This was how that concept of office which was to be the determining factor in the subsequent period was formed; at least, in fact, there existed a distinction between clerics and lay persons. A tacit principle of tradition and legitimacy safeguards the unmistakable foundation of congregational order vested in the authority of institutional office which, in the form of the presbytery, diaconate and widows' institutes, surrounded itself with executive organs."

The conception of the Church in the Acts of the Apostles is quite similar to that in the Pastoral Epistles. Here, too we find mentioned everywhere bishops, presbyteria, ordination, as well as the principle of tradition and legitimacy. "As far as we can see, Luke was the first to propagate the early Catholic theory of tradition and legitimacy. Even he did not engage upon this on his own but in order to defend the Church against the threatening danger. The historian can do nothing but admit that this theory proved to be the most effective weapon in the struggle against Enthusiasm and protected early Christianity from sinking into radical sectarianism. To that extent the recognition of Acts as canonical is understandable and well deserved as an expression of gratitude on the part of the Church." Hence it is no longer a cause for surprise that also the presumably latest writing of the New Testament canon, the Second Epistle of Peter, according to Käsemann, bears the stamp of early Catholicism. "From beginning to end Second Peter is a document of early Catholic views and it is probably the most dubious of all the writings of the canon." Chapter I, verse 20 may be viewed as the most characteristic utterance of the whole epistle. It means: "Personal exegesis is not permitted to the individual unless authorized and prescribed by the teaching office of the Church."

All these statements (in their positive content) are of course, not new to the Catholic theologian. What is new is that those statements are made by a *Protestant* theologian and made with the utmost clarity. The simple scriptural texts in question here were, in fact, always understood in this way by Catholic exegetes (if we here disregard certain of Käsemann's loaded formulations and their relationship to the great Pauline utterance). Indeed Catholic exegetes have repeatedly pointed out that the interpretation of early Catholic texts must be taken seriously. Actually Protestant exegetes often considered them non-existent nor did not extensively interpret them.

Käsemann, however, is soberly and clearly aware of the full

importance of these passages; courageously and perceptively he sees the provocative nature of the question which his admission entails. At the end of his chapter on Second Peter he writes: "What is it about the canon in which Second Peter has its place as the clearest testimony to early Catholicism?"

In the treatise, "Is the unity of the Church founded on the New Testament claim?", he first of all reiterates the decisive facts: "Here (in Second Peter) the Spirit no longer wields His influence also through tradition, he has become one with tradition. Hence, as already the case in the Pastoral Epistles and in the Acts, the Church's teaching office is the possessor of the "spirit of office," and every non-authorized exegesis and interpretation of Scripture is forbidden as in the almost classic monitory passage in II Peter 1:20. Here ordination is an indicator of the principle of legitimacy and succession. In short, one has stepped beyond the borders of primitive Christianity and established early Catholicism." From it is drawn the important conclusion: "The time when one could confront Catholicism with the full text of Scripture is past beyond recall. Protestantism today can no longer apply the so-called formal principle without adopting an untenable position in terms of historical analysis. The New Testament canon does not stand between Judaism and early Christianity but provides in itself scope and foundation to both Judaism and early Catholicism."

At this point, Hans Kung interposes the dilemma that confronts Protestant biblical scholars on the evidences, the "hard facts" about early Catholicism in the New Testament before continuing with Heinrich Schlier.

The dilemma of the Protestant theologian is obvious: either to accept Catholicism as an element of the New Testament and thereby definitely embark on the road to "late Catholicism," or else to reject early Catholicism as an element of the New Testament and correct the canon accordingly. It is instructive to compare Käsemann's decision with that of another prominent Bultmann scholar, with whom Käsemann's exegetical work is in a continuous latent and, in part, overt discussion.

Heinrich Schlier chose the first path. His investigation regarding the structural order of the Church according to the

Pastoral Epistles, which appeared in 1948 . . . led him to a conclusion with respect to the question of office which largely agreed with Käsemann: "(1) The structural order of the Church 'which is the Church of the living God, the pillar and mainstay of the truth' (I Tim. 3:15) rests upon the 'office.' The 'authority,' the spiritual power, lies in the hands of specific officeholders who are called thereto, provided with the grace of office, and installed in a service. Thus, they teach, and govern the Church, and transmit the office through the laying on of hands (ordination). The principle of office prevails. (2) This 'office' has its origin in the vocation and the installation of the apostles in the service of the Gospel through Christ Jesus. It is transmitted and expanded through the transmittal of the charism of office (and on the apostolic paradox) from the apostle to the disciple of the apostle and from him to the local presbyter-bishops. The principle of succession prevails. (3) The office contains specific gradations. It appears in the service of the disciple of an apostle in charge of a Church territory who, at the same time, acts there as apostolic delegate; and in the service of several 'presiding' elders or bishops in the local Church. In addition there is the service of the deacons and 'widows' both of whom exercise supporting functions. In its gradation the office exhibits a tendency towards a monarchical apex. The principle of primacy permeates it." In 1955, after his conversion to the Catholic Church, Schlier basing himself not only on the Pastoral Epistles but also on the Epistle to the Ephesians and especially on the great Pauline epistles (above all, First Corinthians) wrote: "The New Testament led me to inquire whether the Lutheran confession and more specifically the modern Protestant faith, which has so widely deviated from its original form, is in agreement with its own testimony. Gradually I became convinced that the Church which it had in mind was the Roman Catholic Church. Hence it was, if I may say so, an authentic Protestant path which took me to the Church; a path which is actually provided for in the Lutheran confessional writings, although naturally not expected. In that context I must still mention something else. What led me to the Church was the New Testament as it presented itself to unbiased historical interpretation."

And the collection of exegetical articles which was published in the same year, almost all of which derive from his Protestant period, purposed "to ask only one question" of the reader: "Whether what I have heard from the New Testament is not right and whether the New Testament therefore—in a word—is not after all Catholic, whether her Catholic principles are not after all the apostolic principles?"

Ernest Käsemann chose the second path. He insists decisively upon the "discernment of spirits."

As this writer understands it, Käsemann fixed upon a norm of selectivity similar to but not identical with that of Martin Luther. Luther put his reliance on *sola scriptura* as opposed to the Catholic "Scripture and Tradition." Since Luther's original premise of "objective clarity" served the Anabaptists at cross-purposes to Luther's —it actually made any norm for interpretation superfluous—he narrowed it to the doctrine of justification by faith alone. This private norm had the double effect of rejecting the Anabaptist's appeal to a charismatic understanding of Scripture on the one hand and on the other replaced the norm of ecclesiastical tradition. New Testament books which did not preach justification were considered as of secondary significance and placed in an appendix at the end of Luther's New Testament and thereby the principle of "the canon within the canon" was established. The use of this principle in contemporary protestant scholarship is truly alarming. Whole sections of the New Testament are rejected as examples of "early Catholicism," simply because they do not correspond to the theological prepossessions or preferences of the individual exegete. Now Käsemann's key to the understanding of Scripture is the event of justification, as distinguished from the doctrine of justification, and this constitutes the discriminating norm of the "Gospel in the canon." Only the believer by the "discernment of spirits" can submit his own history to a personal inspection in terms of the justification of the sinner. What St. Paul did with the Old Testament by his distinction between "letter and spirit" (II Corinthians 3), Käsemann applies the same discrimination to the Christian canon.

Kung clearly sees through this "Gospel in the canon" and asks the pertinent question and accurately describes the dangerous consequence.

Does not the *whole* New Testament deal with the proclamation of the justification of sinners; is it not a question of the "Gospel" in the whole New Testament? It is precisely this that Käsemann cannot admit within the framework of his chosen argument. In his view there are clearly texts which do not proclaim the justification of sinners, which are therefore not of the "Gospel." Hence Käsemann's concentration simultaneously signifies reduction or—as one might say—selection. A formal principle of interpretation is applied which then also turns out to be a material principle of selection, a principle of choice. Only thus can Käsemann declare as unevangelical, within the context of the New Testament, not only the sectarian Enthusiasm on the left and legalistic Judaism on the right, but also early Catholicism which, in the Catholic view, is already found in Paul.

Readers are well advised to read Kung's perceptive critical analysis and exposition of the principle of selectivity in Scriptural study. We choose certain excerpts that highlight his reflections.

The bold programme "canon in the canon" demands nothing but to be more biblical than the Bible, more New Testamentary than the New Testament, more evangelical than the Evangel and even more pauline than Pauline . . . .

Throughout a turbulent history of the canon it is the Church, nevertheless, which has preserved for us the New Testament as a a whole. Without the Church there would be no New Testament. The Church also maintained that all parts of the New Testament were to be regarded as positive attestations of the message, deeds, and life of Jesus Christ—and not merely as partially negative contrasting presentations—and incorporated into the New Testament canon. The concrete relationship to the Church will also be a decisive factor today as to whether a theologian will or will not be able to accept with confidence, and yet at the same time critically, the whole New Testament as handed down and vouched for by the Church. We Catholics are convinced along with the early Church that we do right to consider the whole of the New Testament as a *conclusive* testimony of revelation as an event in Jesus Christ. We are, therefore, also convinced that recognition should be granted to every single testimony—as truly, but diversely oriented towards the event of salvation in Christ—and that each one of them should be accorded its full value, theologically as well as practically.

Kung then quotes K. H. Schelkle, the New Testament authority of the University of Tübingen, on the total and indissoluble catholicity of the New Testament with an "authentic and valid process of development" of the original message to early Catholicism. "To recognize only part of it means to choose, which means heresy." And Kung then concludes this study on the ecclesiastical office in the New Testament:

> On the basis of the present-day state of exegetic problems, the Catholic view can be summarized in the following three statements (it is significant that competent Protestant witnesses can be cited in support, not of the whole, but certainly of each of the individual statements): (1) The New Testament encompasses "early Catholicism" and the "early Catholic" conception of ecclesiastical office. (2) The *whole* New Testament must be given full value, though historically differentiated and translated in terms of the present. (3) The early Catholic testimonies regarding ecclesiastical office should not be placed in direct opposition to Paul and his doctrine of justification.

All of these quotations are from *Structures of the Church*, pp. 135-151. We have quoted at length in order to disclose Kung's own theological persuasions on ecclesiastical offices in the Church and its striking contrast to a parallel study in *Inquiry* (pp. 79-87; 221-240). In *Structures* we find indisputable insistence on office, structural order, principle of tradition and legitimacy, the authority of institutional office, the Church's teaching office, the Acts of the Apostles, the Pastoral Epistles, on Schlier who found in the Catholic Church the three principles of office, of succession, and primacy that are clearly discernible in the Christian Testament. One can sense Kung's pulse beating in unison with Schlier as he explains that Schlier based himself not only on the Pastoral Epistles, but also on the Epistle to the Ephesians, and especially on the great Pauline epistles (above all, First Corinthians). One can sense Kung's dismay at Käsemann's principle of selectivity to avoid the consequences of his scriptural evidences on the ecclesiastical offices in the Church and the horn of the dilemma Käsemann chose in contrast to Heinrich Schlier—and what is more to the point, if *Inquiry* were truly an open inquiry why did Kung completely leave out all the exegetical reasonings of

Schlier as well as the positive contribution of Käsemann from the text of *Inquiry*? Why does Kung who insists with the Church in *Structures* that the whole New Testament is the Gospel, the message of salvation, omit by silence any consideration of the Pastoral Epistles in *Inquiry*? Has Schlier lost Kung or has Kung lost Schlier? Has Kung chosen in *Inquiry* to mute the "early Catholicism" in the New Testament and subtly chosen a selective principle of his own in accordance with new found preferences? Perhaps, his present "concrete relationship to the Church" has become a decisive factor as to "whether he will or will not be able to accept with confidence the whole New Testament." In ignoring the Pastoral Epistles is not Kung being less Pauline than Paul? The reader will judge for himself whether the excerpts taken physically out of the text are also taken out of context.

Kung is not accountable to himself nor to others. He does not explain why his theological persuasions on the ecclesiastical offices *iure divino* in the New Testament apparently have lost their forcefulness on his "state of intellect." John Henry Newman felt compelled to explain his conversion to Catholicism to the public, not least to his former co-faithful, the Anglicans of England, and surely to satisfy his conscience fully. Apart from (but surely under) the operation of grace, he discerned that the Church of Rome and not the Church of England was in continuity with the Church of the Fathers and through them with the apostolic Church. Heinrich Schlier, in our time, felt compelled to explain himself to his former co-religionists and to his new companions in the Catholic faith what he now saw that he had not seen before—much to the apparent satisfaction of Kung. But Kung himself feels no moral obligation to explain how and why he now reads the same material, the same revelational data, the historical and exegetical evidences of the New Testament in opposite ways. Where had he failed formerly and wherein lies the dogmatic correction. Kung never speaks of his former faith as did John Henry Newman and Heinrich Schlier. What was the historical and exegetical weakness in his former faith that he had failed to discern, what is his new found strength that he had not known before?

And now more pertinently, the Petrine and papal office. What has Kung to say of it in *Structures*; We have already noted that in this same volume there is a summary exposition of Luther's, Calvin's and, in our own day, of Karl Barth's views on infallibility, and it is our settled opinion that Kung in *Inquiry* has adopted the Barthian criticism.

It is important that we recall the temporal context of *Structures*. On January 25, 1959, Pope John XXIII, at St. Paul's Outside the Walls, first announces his intention to summon a Council. In 1961 appears Kung's *The Council, Reform, and Reunion* with its proposal that Protestant and Catholics seriously consider the valid criticisms of each by the other—and, in a word, to become more intelligible to one another without the burden of ancient animosities and antagonistic biases. The removal of mutual misunderstandings and a sincere effort at mutual understanding would pave the way for reunion at least by degrees. Kung's theological contribution was to spell out for both sides what he saw to be the major issues of encounter. On October 11, 1962, the twenty-second Ecumenical council solemnly opened. On November 24, 1964, the third session closed with the promulgation of the Dogmatic Constitution on the Church (*Lumen Gentium*) together with the Decree on Ecumenism, and the Decree on Eastern Catholic Churches. Pope Paul VI proclaims the title of Mary as Mother of the Church. In the third chapter of *Lumen Gentium*, the Council Fathers set down in doctrinal terms, the hierarchical structure of the Church, with special reference to the episcopate. Vatican I (1869-1870), after defining the primacy and infallibility of the Roman Pontiff, had intended to consider the episcopal office, but the labors of the Council were interrupted by political upheavels. The unfinished business was to resolve just how the ordinary, immediate, episcopal power of the Pope can be united with the ordinary and immediate power of the bishops. The Second Vatican Council formulated and promulgated a doctrine of episcopal collegiality under the headship of the Roman Pontiff as successors of the apostolic college under the headship of Peter. In 1963, Kung received an *imprimatur* for *Structures* which was the first published in 1964 and obviously, both its composition and publication anteceded the Dogmatic Constitution of the Church with its doctrinal promulgation of episcopal collegiality under the primatial authority of the Roman Pontiff. In *Structures*, he is espousing his own theological resolution of the relationship of bishops to the Pope by the application of the principle of subsidiarity that had been formulated by Pius XI in the Encyclical *Quadragesimo Anno*. What concerns us here are the efforts of Kung to show that there is not and should not be an opposition between papal primacy as defined by Vatican I and a doctrinal formulation of the duties and rights of the episcopal office, that the coexistence of papal and episcopal authorities can be such so that neither of the two might lose its authority, and such general harmony is reassured by the discussions and definitions of the First Vatican Council. Contrast this with the phantasmagoric fears of papal absolutism, despotic, and arbitrary rule in *Inquiry* (pp. 103-107).

We will now attend to Kung's own reassurance on the matter in 1964 by his own repetition and apparent agreement with the provisions of the First Vatican Council, reassurances and agreement which have left him by 1970 in *Inquiry*.

From the third chapter of the dogmatic constitution, *Pastor aeternus*, of the First Vatican Council (4th. session, July 18, 1870) we excerpt from the Latin text the solemn declaration of the Council Fathers on the primatial authority of the Roman Pontiff:

Docemus proinde et declaramus Ecclesiam Romanam, disponente Domino, super omnes alias ordinariae potestatis obtinere principatum, et hanc Romani Pontificis iurisdictionis potestatem, quae vere episcopalis est, immediatam esse: erga quam cuiuscumque ritus et dignitatis pastores atque fideles, tam seorsum singuli quam simul omnes, officio hierarchicae subordinationis veraeque oboedientiae obstringuntur, non solum in rebus, quae ad fidem et mores, sed etiam in iis, quae ad disciplinam et regimen Ecclesiae per totum orbem diffusae pertinent: ita ut, custodita cum Romano Pontifice tam communionis quam euisdem fidei professionis unitate, Ecclesia Christi sit unus grex sub uno summo pastore. Haec est catholicae veritatis doctrina, a qua deviare salva fide atque salute nemo potest. (DS 3060)

And so we teach and declare that, by the disposition of the Lord, the Roman Church holds the preeminence of ordinary power over all the others, and that this power of jurisdiction of the Roman Pontiff, which is truly episcopal, is immediate. Pastors and faithful, of whatever rite and dignity, individually and collectively, are bound by a duty of hierarchical subordination and of true obedience to this jurisdiction, not only in matters that pertain to faith and morals, but also in those matters that pertain to the discipline and government of the Church throughout the whole world. When, therefore, this bond of unity with the Roman Pontiff is guarded both by the unity of communion and by the profession of the same faith, then the Church of Christ is one flock under one supreme shepherd. This is the doctrine of Catholic truth from which no one can deviate without losing his faith and his salvation. (DS 3060)

(Canon) Si quis itaque dixerit, Romanum Pontificem habere tantummodo officum inspectionis vel directionis, non autem plenam et supremam potestatem iurisdictionis in universam Ecclesiam', non solum in rebus, quae ad fidem et mores, sed etiam in iis, quae ad disciplinam et regimen Ecclesiaie per totum orbem diffusae pertinent; aut eum habere tantum potiores partes, non vero totam plenitudinem huius supremae potestatis, aut hanc eius potestatem non esse ordinariam et immediatam sive in omnes et singulos pastores et fideles: anathema sit.

And so if someone says that the Roman Pontiff has only the office of inspection or direction, but not the full and su-preme power of jurisdiction over the universal Church, not only in matters that pertain to faith and morals, but also in matters that pertain to the discipline and government of the Church extending throughout the world; or that he possesses only the more important part, but not the complete plenitude of this supreme power; or that this power of his is not ordinary and immediate, be it over all the churches or over each church, be it over all and each of the pastors and the faithful: let him be ana-thema. (DS 3064)

Kung observes together with E. Amann that by declaring the jurisdiction of the pope over each of the churches "ordinary, im-mediate, episcopal," the Vatican Council certainly was making no innovation. After noting that the Council Fathers had not set down "just how the ordinary, immediate episcopal power of the pope can be united with the ordinary and immediate power of the bishops," because of the sudden suspension of the Council, Kung feels reassured that both "the discussions and the definitions of the *Constitutio prima* provide us with valuable suggestions, which we shall utilize" (p. 208). Let us note here that Kung at no time questions much less disowns the universal, supreme, plenary primatial authority of the pope as defined by the First Vatican Council (cf. pp. 206-223). In *Structures*, on its face, he appears free of the difficulties that agitate him in *Inquiry* (pp. 94-101). In *Inquiry* (p. 96), Kung summarily and all too briefly purses together the limits on papal primacy which "their spokeman at the council admitted." But in *Structures* these limits are discoursed about, yes, according to "their spokeman" but with concurrence by Kung himself and at considerable length (pp. 206-223). Adverting to the opposition in the *Deputatio Fidei* to the formulation of any limitation to the plenitude of the Pontiff's primatial authority, Kung observes that while the pope possesses the fulness of authority, "this authority is neither absolute nor arbitrary" according to the response of Bishop Zinelli to an objection of the Melchite Patriarch of Antioch and the anathema proposed by the Bishop of Verot. Bishop Bartholomaeus d'Avanzo spoke of a double limitation on the Petrine primacy, an active one, that is, the limitation set by the mission that Christ gave Peter, and a passive one, that is, Peter's commitment by Christ's prayer to "strengthen your brethren." In a word, the Petrine commission to Peter is governed by the divine mandate from which it proceeds.

There are concrete limits to papal primacy from the essential structure of the Church willed by Christ (1) the existence of the episcopate which exists *iure divino* and cannot be suspended, nor abolished by the pope. The congruity of two truly episcopal powers bearing immediately upon the pastors and faithful by both the pope and the bishops is effectuated by the subordination of the episcopal jurisdictional authority to the universal primacy of the supreme pastor. Kung is quick to point out that any misunderstanding about the absorption of the episcopal into the pontifical authority was clarified by the *Collective Declaration of the German Episcopate* to rebuff the charges of the Imperial German Chancellor, Prince Bismarck, a statement that was approved by Pope Pius IX as the authentic exposition of Catholic doctrine and of the doctrine of the Vatican Council; (2) the orderly exercise of office by the bishop is undisturbed by pontifical immediate jurisdictional authority over all without exception except *in peculiaribus* (as Kung has chosen to adopt Gustave Thils "terminology, cf. his *Primaute" pontificale et prérogatives épiscopales* Louvain, 1961), neither *extraordinarie* nor *quotidie*. Kung here inserts as a criterion for the exercise of papal universal authority the principle of subsidiarity which Pius XI has espoused in *Quadragesimo Anno* for the social order *vis-a-vis* state power. Kung makes this principle applicable also to the relationship between the Petrine and episcopal offices, encouraged to this purpose by a statement of Pius XII (AAS 38 [1946] 14f) that the principle of subsidiarity "is valid for social life in all its organizations, and also for the life of the Church without prejudice to her hierarchical structure." (3) The third concrete limit to the exercise of papal universal authority is the aim of the Roman Pontiff's use of his office. Primacy is a service, a *diakonia*, for the sake of the unity of the Church, for its edification, not for its undoing, nor for worldly aims. (4) The reasons for the actual use of papal immediate authority in the very area of a bishop's own immediate jurisdiction would be motivated by *evidens utilitas, Ecclesiae necessitas* (cf. G. Thils. *op. cit.*).

And so Kung concludes:

> According to the discussions and definitions of the First Vatican Council four borderlines circumscribe the exercise of the papal office; all are based on the nature of the Petrine office itself, the episcopal office, and also precisely on the assembled people of God who, as a priestly and royal race, are the Church, and whom the Petrine office must serve in the cause of charity and of strengthening the faith for the maintenance of unity. (*Structures*, 222)

Throughout Kung's discussion of Petrine and papal supreme and universal primatial authority in *Structures*, he never once questions its validity, nor raises scriptural difficulties about it, certainly never disowns it. On the contrary, he works energetically to explain it with the assistance of Karl Rahner, Gustave Thils, and K. H. Schelkle, Catholic scholars whose contributions he does not incorporate into the text of *Inquiry* but at most lists them inconspicuously in the Appendix Notes of *Inquiry*. Compare *Structures* (1964) on primacy of jurisdiction with *Inquiry* (pp. 101-108) scarcely six years later (1970), a work that was in preparation in the intervening years. The content, the theological reasoning, the temper and style of writing are contrasts in study. Speaking of the "Pope's high-handed encyclicals and decrees" and of the power of the Curia, he writes with tart bitterness and cynicism:

> Can anything be done about all this? Well, if we want to beat them at their own game, we would have to use all the tricks of canon law to provide collegiality in the Church also with juridical security, as the Romans have been doing so thoroughly for centuries for the papal primacy. Only in this way would the absolutist monarcy—the only one from the older order who has survived the French Revolution—become at

least a constitutional monarch, and the Roman Empire something like a Catholic Commonwealth. (*Inquiry*, p. 107)

Ah! there is the rub!—"juridical security." First as to Kung's
untheological insinuations. Which of Pope Paul VI's encyclicals—
Ecclesiam Suam (1963), on the divine constitution and unique
salvific mission of the Catholic Church, *Mysterium Fidei*, on the
Real Presence of the Incarnate Word in the Blessed Eucharist, *Sacerdotalis Coelibatus* (1967) on priestly celibacy, *Humanae Vitae* (1968)
on the inviolability of the marital communion, the *Credo* (1968)
etc., have not been in accordance with the faith of the Church?
As for the two Marian dogmas, the only two solemn papal definitions,
of the Immaculate Conception by Pope Pius IX (*Ineffabilis Deus*,
Dec. 8, 1854) sixteen years before the definition of papal infallibility
by the First Vatican Council, and of the Assumption of the Blessed
Virgin Mary by Pope Pius XII (*Munificentissimus Deus*, Nov. 1, 1950)
—both pontiffs acted after, so to speak, turning to an unassembled
ecumenical consultation, a fact Kung himself does not deny (*Inquiry*,
p. 105).

As for "juridical security," this is the placing of the pope not only
under divine and natural law as God willed it so, but also under
human ecclesiastical law. But who is to legislate this "juridical
security?" Others than the pope? That is to transpose the Kungian
problematic. For the question is one of the ultimate authority of
decision and that is what primatial authority means. Petrine and
papal primacy of jurisdiction means that the authority of the
supreme pastor and of the keys belongs to Peter *alone* and His
successor even as the supreme pastoral authority *also* belongs to the
apostolic college *under* Peter and to its successor, the episcopal
college *under* and *in union with the pope*. Primacy of jurisdiction
comprehends supreme legislative power, supreme judicial power, and
supreme right of governance in the Church. A juridical security by
others than the pope and papal supreme and universal jurisdiction are
contradictories.

Kung's phantasmagoric fears of papal absolutism in faith and
morals (and that is what we are speaking of in discoursing of papal
primacy of jurisdiction and primacy of teaching with its unique
prerogative of infallibility) are hardly for the *edificatio Ecclesiae,
salus ecclesiae*, but for its disruption in its very foundation. Kung,
unfortunately for his theologizing, confuses papal authority as
commissioned by Christ Jesus in faith and morals with its enormous

incidences of temporal authority pervasive in Christendom and which reached its most extensive envelopment under Pope Innocent III.

And now from primacy of jurisdiction to primacy of teaching with its unique prerogative of infallibility, the Petrine and papal office, as defined by the First Vatican Council:

> Itaque nos traditioni a fidei christianae exordio perceptae fideliter inhaerendo, ad Dei Salvatoris nostri gloriam, religionis catholicae exaltationem et christianorum populorum salutem, sacro approbante Concilio, docemus et divinitus revelatum dogma esse definimus. (DS 3073)

> Romanum Pontificem, cum ex cathedra loquitur, id est, cum omnium Christianorum pastoris et doctoris munere fungens pro suprema sua Apostolica auctoritate doctrinam de fide vel moribus ab universa Ecclesia tenendam definit, per assistentiam divinam ipsi in beato Petro promissam, ea infallibilitate pollere, qua divinus redemptor Ecclesiam suam in definienda doctrina de fide vel moribus instructam esse voluit; ideoque eiusmodi Romani Pontifices definitiones ex sese, non autem ex consensu Ecclesiae, irreformabiles esse. (DS 3074)

> (Canon) Si quis autem huic Nostrae definitioni contradicere, quod Deus avertat, praesumpserit: anathema sit.

> And so faithfully keeping to the tradition received from the beginning of the Christian faith, for the glory of God our Savior, for the exaltation of the Catholic religion, and for the salvation of Christian peoples. We, with the approval of the sacred council, teach and define that it is divinely revealed dogma.

> That the Roman Pontiff, when he speaks *ex cathedra*, that is, when, acting in the office of shepherd and teacher of all Christians, he defines, by virtue of his supreme apostolic authority, doctrine concerning faith or morals to be held by the universal Church, possesses through the divine assistance promised to him in the person of Blessed Peter, the infallibility with which the divine Redeemer willed his Church to be endowed in defining doctrine concerning faith and morals; and that such definitions of the Roman Pontiff are therefore irreformable of

themselves, but not because of the agreement of the Church. (DS 3074)

(Canon).   But if anyone presumes to contradict this our definition (God forbid) let him be anathema. (DS 3075)

Our principal concentration has been to know Kung's mind, his "state of intellect," before he disavowed his former faith in the dogma of Petrine and papal infallibility. To look into his theologizing in the exposition of this basic article of faith and contrast this with his assault upon it in *Inquiry* in 1970. But central to this comparative study is the plain observation that the material is the same, the same revelational data, the scriptural exegesis unchanged, if any, rather reenforced by the new found theological persuasions of converts to Catholicism.   But Kung's conclusions are not simply different, they are contrary to one another. He puts forth no new "evidence" that would have invalidated his former faith. He points to no specific failing in his precedent creed that he could now correct. There is no increase or correction in his deposit of knowledge of Scripture and Church history that he had not known before. Yet *out of this same deposit of personal learning* he at one time adhered to the dogma of infallibility (and even called upon Protestants to reconsider their theological position on the Petrine and papal office)—and at another time, less than a decade later, he challenges the dogma of infallibility as being without warrant, without "proof, evidence, substantiation, demonstration," from Scripture and Tradition. The personal question that we may respectfully address to Hans Kung is: how does he explain his loss of faith; that is, how does he explain himself.

What does Kung say of infallibility in *Structures*? He patiently explains the "Catholic doctrine" according to the Fathers of the First Vatican Council and makes it his own. There are no disavowals, no rejections.

In the seventh chapter of *Structures*, Kung raises the question, *What does Infallibility mean*? In section (1) Kung discusses summarily *The Fallibility of Councils According to Luther and Calvin*, and more jejunely than this question desires. It would require a separate study to appraise accurately and critically weigh all of Kung's reflections on these two Reformers on this matter of infallibility and fallibility in the Church if a starting point of departure for ecumenical dialogue were to proceed without mutual misunderstanding. In section (2) *The Limits of Infallibility at the First Vatican Council*, the subdivision (a) *Karl Barth and Vatican I* holds our attention for two reasons; first, for Kung's response to Barth, and secondly, because we are persuaded that in *Inquiry*, Kung actually adopts the Barthian criticism and makes it his own mind on the matter of papal infallibility:

We choose these exerpts from 2 (a):

For Catholic doctrine in infallibility of the Church and the infallibility of ecclesiastical office (of the pope and of the councils) are essentially connected. For the reason that Christ in His Spirit promised to preserve the Church, as a whole, from apostasy through His eschatologically triumphant grace. He will also preserve office as a whole in the Church from apostasy: from falling away from faith, from a substantial error which would destroy Christ's message. No dilemma exists between the Church of the faith of the apostles and the Church of the office of the apostles. To the extent that it concerns the binding teaching of the whole Church and to the extent that the task of office (of the pope and of councils) is to serve the doctrine that is binding upon the whole Church, this office with and in the Church is an infallible norm for the faith of the individual Christian. Thereby the office does not raise itself above the Scripture as the apostolic witness to Christ, rather, in its authoritative teaching it actually exercises its own obedience with respect to the teaching of the apostles. This infallibility is not guaranteed by any kind of human characteristic or in a "competency" necessarily to be assumed in the bearer of the teaching office, but by the assistance promised to the Church by the Holy Spirit. The Spirit exercises His counselling and guiding power according to His pleasure. And this is precisely the way in which the Spirit prevents the office, in its ultimate doctrinal decisions, from introducing human inventions into the binding witness to Christ. (*Structures*, pp. 314-315)

This passage and what follows are clear and precise in the summary exposition of the Catholic doctrine and contrasts sharply with the ludicrous caricatures in *Inquiry* and the crudity of a figure of speech (cf. especially, p. 77) on the interrelationship between Tradition, Scripture, and the teaching authority of the Church. The focus on the promise of Christ, of the unfailing assistance of the Holy Spirit so manifest in *Structures* is not so evident in *Inquiry*. In this later work

Kung never inquires into the meaning and significance of this divine assistance, what could Our Lord have meant, what profoundly supernatural efficacy will be guiding the solemn and authoritative teaching of the Church wholly within the Truth committed to its deposit of faith in a visible way, with visible means, through the service of an uninterrupted, continuous apostolate instituted by God, Our Redeemer.

We continue with Kung:

> The opposition which Luther and Calvin ushered in against the "arbitrariness" of the Catholic teaching office has been continued by Karl Barth even more sharply.

After a compressed presentation of the Barthian criticism (315-321), Kung replies:

> As regards the relationship between revelation and the ecclesiastical teaching office, it was expressly established at Vatican I that the pastoral task (*munus pastorale*) of the Petrine office is responsible for spreading Christ's doctrine of salvation (*salutaris Christi doctrina*) among all peoples and for preserving it unimpaired and pure (*sincera et pura conservetur*). Hence, it is neither the task of the Church nor that of the Petrine office to produce revelation, to replace or to absorb revelation (as Barth contended). The task of the Church as well as that of the Petrine office is that of serving revelation through the protective and preserving care of the pure doctrine of the Gospel.

> Vatican I, however, did not state this only in this general way; the dogma of infallibility was expressly shielded against misinterpretations in the Barthian sense; the definition of a pope means precisely not a revealing; the Holy Spirit is not promised to Peter's successors so that they may reveal new doctrines through His revelation. Neque enim Petri successoribus Spiritus Sanctus promissus est, ut eo revelante novam doctrinam patefacerent .... The definition of the pope signifies only an authoritative bearing of witness to the revelation that has occurred, the Holy Spirit is promised to the successors so that with His help the revelation, transmitted through the Apostles, may be preserved holy and explained faithfully: "ut eo assistente, traditam per Apostolos revelationem seu fidei depositum sancte custodirent et fideliter exponerent."

The ground and, at the same time, the limit of the Church teaching authority is the word of God proclaiming itself in a human utterance. The exercise of Church teaching authority also can be understood only as an actualization of obedience *vis-a-vis* the superordinated word of God. God and His word above, the Church and her word below: hence no reversal is possible—all commissioning, authorization comes from above. (*Structures*, 321-323)

And so on and on in a lucid explanation and defense of the Vatican I doctrine against Barthian criticism. In each paragraph one senses Kung's own sincerity and deep theological persuasion about papal infallibility. Not the slightest qualm arises in his mind about the propriety of the definition and not even a minuscule footnote about alternate consideration and indefectibility. And he responds to misunderstanding of papal infallibility with complete theological reassurance. Contrast this exact intelligence of the papal office in *Structures* with the untheological distortions in *Inquiry* (c. II).

The whole of Kung's energetic exposition and defense of the First Vatican Council definitions (and their antecedent discussions) in *Structures* is always forceful, persuasive, and personally sincere. One would be hard put to select any particular segment as the best— they are all on the high level of theologizing. But if I must choose, this excerpt from Kung is my preference. On pp. 326-327 of *Structures*:

If we are not to fall victim to misunderstanding at the outset in this discussion, everything will depend upon an exact understanding of papal infallibility as it has been understood by Vatican I. All too often outside the Church the Vatican definition is considered as the insurpassable peak of the concentration of teaching authority in the pope and as the establishment of an unlimited papal infallibility. At the same time it is a fact that this very definition signifies a very clear *limitation* by contrast with what was frequently asserted about the infallibility of the pope in the Catholic Church before the council . . . . But as we shall soon see, the Council laid down very definite conditions against it which in fact very strongly limited the infallibility of the pope.

In *Inquiry* Kung "falls victim" to the very "misunderstandings" he labors zealously in *Structures* to dispel. Why? How come? We have earlier speculated whether Kung would have ever challenged infallibility in the Church, of the pope and councils, and of Scripture, if *Humanae Vitae* had never been promulgated, or, *ex hypothesi impossibili* if a moral doctrine contrary to a consistent and constant centuries old ban on artificial contraceptives had been proclaimed as the new morality (?). There may be, in addition to Kung's resentment of *Humanae Vitae*, a dim suspicion, unsubstantiated, that papal infallibility sat incongruously with Kung's latitudinarian ecumenism of *Inquiry*. The disparity to the point of contrariety between the doctrinal commitment of Kung in *Structures* and its abandonment in *Inquiry* in a narrow time period between 1964-1970 (earlier actually because thoughts and writing precede publication at least by two years) poses an intriguing study of the spiritual adventures of an intellectual process in theological invention. We cannot repeat too often that the "evidences," the material, so to speak, the revelational data of the New Testament, and Kung's own learning in ecclesiastical history is the same—but he argues to opposite conclusions, He never directly confronts his former faith in infallibility and points to the supposed faults he had not adverted to before and on what account he now justifiably disowns this dogma of Catholic faith. Nor, does he put forth some new "evidence" not known in his earlier works that now turns his mind to a new found conviction. Our methodology has been unmistakably clear—to let Kung speak for himself. We now come to our final selection of excerpts from *Structures* (pp. 328-329):

Absolute infallibility is ascribed to God exclusively: *in no respect is an absolute infallibility ascribed to the pope* (italics in the original). This was stated with all desirable clarity by the speaker of the Deputation on Faith, Bishop Gasser: "The question is in what sense the infallibility of the pope is absolute: I answer and firmly confess: in no sense is the pontifical infallibility absolute, for absolute infallibility corresponds to God only, the first and essential truth who can nowhere and never deceive or be deceived." Infallibility is communicated to the pope only with respect to a definite end. It is wholly subject to definite *limits* and *conditions*: "Any other infallibility ever communicated has a certain end and limits and conditions under which it is given. This is the case also for the infallibility of the pope." The infallibility of the pope is wholly limited to the pastoral ministry of the whole Church (Mt. 16:18; Jn. 21:13-17): "Outside this relation to the universal Church, Peter in his successors does not enjoy this charisma of truth, granted by Christ in that promise." Therefore, the infallibility of the pope is limited in a threefold way: in relation to the *subject* (only when the pope as the universal and supreme teacher and supreme judge of the Church speaks *in cathedra*); in relation to the *object* (only when he speaks on matters of faith and morals): in relation to the *act* itself (only when he defines what is to be believed or rejected by all Christians): "In fact, the infallibility of the Roman Pontiff is restricted in respect to the *subject* when the pope speaks as teacher of the universal Church and as supreme judge in the chair of Peter, that is, constituted at the centre. It is restricted in respect to the *object* in so far as it concerns matters of faith and morals and when he defines explicitly what has to be held or rejected by all the faithful."

Thus all conditions without exception must be fulfilled and securely established before one can talk of an infallible definition. Hence the CIC (can 1323 #3) also defines: "Nothing is understood as dogmatically declared or defined, unless it is clearly established."

Therefore, the pope is not *separate from the Church*. He is infallible only to the extent that he is representative of the whole Church: ". . . We do not separate the Pontiff from his well-ordered connection with the Church. The pope is infallible only when he exercises the office of teacher of all Christians and therefore representing the universal Church judges and defines what has to be believed or rejected by all." In no sense is a co-operation on the part of the Church excluded: "He must not be separated from the universal Church which he has to support as a foundation from the universal Church which he has to support as a foundation does a building. We do not separate the pope who defines infallibily from the cooperation and agreement of the Church, at least in this sense that we do not exclude this co-operation and agreement." (pp. 328-330)

All of the above is dutifully repeated in *Inquiry* within the economy of approximately half a page (pp. 102-103), but in an entirely different temper. His immediate comment in *Inquiry* after his contracted resume is:

But all this scarcely changes anything in the basic problem: the problem is still papal absolutism, as it has taken shape since the eleventh century and as it was exercised not only in the middle ages and the Renaissance, but also in modern times at the expense of the Church and the unity of Christendom. (p. 103)

The sudden catapulting to the middle ages, eleventh century, and the Renaissance is extraordinarily remarkable. Of the only two infallible papal definitions, *ex cathedra*, the Marian dogmas of the Immaculate Conception and the Assumption of the Most Blessed Virgin Mary, one was solemnly defined in the nineteenth century (1854) and the other in the twentieth century (1950). Each infallible definition was universally acclaimed in the Church throughout the world. And surely, neither the faithful, whose Marian piety was dependent upon and interacted with the ecclesial tradition about the Virgin Mary, Mother of Jesus, nor the bishops throughout the world, (and their *periti*) whom the Roman Pontiffs consulted, ever conjured up the notion of papal absolutism in the pontifical exercise of infallibility on these two Marian dogmas.

On the much discussed phrases—*ex sese, non autem ex consensu Ecclesiae, irreformabiles esse*—Kung observes:

According to Gasser's authoritative commentary these words —"irreformable of themselves,"—signify nothing more than an explanation of "*ex sese*"; the *ex cathedra* decisions of the pope have a binding character by themselves, not on the ground of the consensus of the Church or the episcopate. Only the ground of law from which the binding force derives, not the criterion on the basis of which the pope produces the decision, is specified here. The necessity of a simultaneous or subsequent consensus of the episcopate is to be excluded, yet it is not maintained that the pope can define a truth without having already in principle the agreement of the Church. No doubt the pope does not require the formal consent of the Church for the definition, nevertheless, he may not define without the mind of the Church. At the same time, what Gasser stated still holds; that the normal way (*medium ordinarium*) is the exercise of the teaching office together with the Church and with the episcopate. (p. 331)

And three footnotes are appended to this passage, two from

R. Aubert and one from G. Thils, neither of which is materially incorporated in the text of *Inquiry*, while, of course, these references are dutifully listed in the Appendix—Notes, p. 54, n. 25.

N. 50: R. Aubert, "L'ecclesiologie au concile du Vatican," in *Le concile et les conciles* (Paris, 1960) 271: "The whole context of the debates shows quite well that their idea involved excluding concomitant or further consent of the episcopacy and not that of claiming that the pope can define a truth without having previously received the agreement of the Church on its essentials."

N. 51: R. Aubert, *op. cit.* 281: "Undeniably, the serious discussions which the Vatican definition occasioned have allowed a clearer perception of the distinction between the *sensus Ecclesiae* from which the pope, the vicar of tradition, can never exempt himself, and the *consensus Ecclesiae*, which is not necessary to him."

N. 52: G. Thils, "Parlera-t-on des évêques au concile?" in *Nouvelle revue théologique* 93 (1961) 791: "A kind of separated infallibility, normally exercised *without* any relation to the episcopate or the testimonies of tradition, has been wrongly concluded therefrom. On the contrary, the pontifical magisterium is exercised *normally* with the Church, in union with her organs, in communion with the testimonies of tradition, and, certainly, in perfect fidelity to the sources of revelation. But— and here is the point of the conciliar declaration—the pope, in well-defined conditions, can appeal to the charism of infallibility. In this case, the act by which he defines is valid, infallible by itself, by virtue of this charism, and not by virtue of the consensus of the Church."

We consider this passage from Gustave Thils very enlightening, one that surely deserved open quotation in the body of *Inquiry*, as becomes a truly open inquiry. Kung in his work of 1970 writes of the "*notorious non autem ex consensu Ecclesiae*" (p. 102) and draws a foreboding picture of papal arbitrariness (pp. 103-108). If by some contrivance, the authorship of *Structures* and of *Inquiry* were successfully kept from one and the same reader, this writer seriously doubts that the reader would guess that the two books were by the same author. From the same material, the discussions of the Fathers of the First Vatican Council (Mansi edition, continued by Petit and Martin, t. 62. col. 1212-1317). Kung draws in *Structures* a theological understanding that is reassuring to him and to his readers; from the same material, he gives in *Inquiry* an interpretation that is ominous for the Church, one that justifies his distrust and rejection of pontifical infallibility. For example:

> But no one in the Church can prevent him (the pope) from acting willfully and arbitrarily (104).

> Presumably even the sun king, Louis XIV of France, would have had no objections to such theoretical-abstract restrictions on his own power. It must be recognized without any illusions that, according to Vatican I and II, no one can prevent the pope from proceeding arbitrarily and autocratically in questions of doctrine-fallible and infallible (105).

One would hardly believe the above passages (and others) were written by the theologically self-assured author of *Structures* published some five years before. The crude parallelism with Louis XIV discloses an untheological state of intellect. No divine promise of the assistance of the Spirit of Truth had ever been given to the French monarch and such a divine warrant cannot seriously, without the risk of impiety, be considered on a "theoretical-abstract" level. For the promised assistance of the Holy Spirit for the infallible transmission of Christ Jesus' salvific message and event is itself the principal restriction against any humanly contrived arbitrariness. For the divine guarantee against error *a fortiori* is itself a guarantee against "proceeding arbitrarily and autocratically in questions of doctrine." If the divine guidance against error in solemn and authoritative teachings of the Church, of the pope and of councils in union with the pope, does not preclude arbitrariness, then *cui bono* the divine assurance of inerrancy in faith and morals. When then Kung writes: "But the teaching of Vatican I really amounts to this: if he wants, the pope can do everything, even without the Church." This statement goes beyond the bounds of freedom of thought; it is an irresponsible, arbitrary exercise of freedom with thought, with faith, with theology. Herein lies Kung's most serious failing. Besides the dutiful acknowledgment of Christ's promise of the assistance of the Holy Spirit given in the Johannine evangel, Kung does not inquire into the telling significance of this divine promise of the Spirit of Truth as specially related to Peter and his successors. On the contrary, in his manner of speech in *Inquiry*, whatever the nature of the efficacy of that divine assistance, Kung writes as if the Roman Pontiff in a solemn act of defining an article of faith could by his "arbitrariness" neutralize the Holy Spirit into ineffectiveness. As an instance of the sharp contrast of tone, style, and content, the reader may compare questions, which in the actual order, present and future, are nonrelevant, are nonetheless raised by Kung tentatively and with academic propriety in *Structures* (pp. 333-334) and their reappearance as categorical statements in their crudest form in *Inquiry* (pp. 104-105).

And as for the credibility of the Catholic Church in the eyes of non-Catholics, for the man of faith, it is the divine credentials and not human conduct that established the credibility of the Catholic Church or His Church. It is the divine warrant that sets the Catholic Church uniquely apart from all other religious professions.

The employment of extensive quotations from *Structures of the Church* was for the purpose that Kung may be said to speak for himself on the hierarchical structure of the Church as discernible in the New Testamentary books, none excluded, and the dilemma that as a consequence confronts Protestants. In *Structures*, the insistence is on Scripture in its totality and on each of the books. But in *Inquiry*, in discussing the hierarchical structure of the Church, the *Pastoral Epistles* are passed over in silence. On infallibility, Kung accepts approvingly Bishop's Gasser's interpretation of the dogmatic definitions of the First Vatican Council.

A Critique, in Part, of Kung's Structures of the Church

However, the reader must not suppose that this author approves of all the contents of *Structures*. Kung's theological thinking is not always above question, and not infrequently he is misleading. As one who has studied many of Kung's books this writer gets the impression that Kung compares the Catholic Church to his own concept of what the church should be and then passes judgment on it; or, what amounts to the same thing, what the Catholic Church should be in order to be "credible"; that is, be ecumenically acceptable to other faiths. This approach, of comparing the Catholic Church to the Kungian ecclesial paradeigma, leads the Tubingen professor to theological exaggerations. His elastic, latitudinarian ecumenism of the future wherein the ecumenical credibility of the Catholic Church results from "a renewal within the Catholic Church to be effected by a successive realization of the justified demands of the Orthodox, Protestants, Anglican, and even the Free Churches" (p. 45), apart from its own dubious merits, can scarcely be paralleled as Kung does to the Council of Nicaea whose "catholicity" was recognized by the individual churches of the Catholic Church (pp. 40-41). This is to confound orthodoxy, schism, and heresies into an amalgamation of creeds. Kung's discussion of apostolicity (pp. 63 ff.) is within the general context of the common priesthood without the significant difference of the apostolic missions of the episcopacy and the ministerial priesthood. His advocacy of direct participation of the laity in councils (pp. 67-83) is a theological *tour de force.* A truly astounding statement on development in the Church appears on p. 84. All development must be subjected to "the discernment of spirits by the mature Christian who not only feeds on mild but can also digest solid food and thus train his faculties to distinguish between good and evil. It is not the question of holding fast to everything; rather must everything be shed and the good alone retained (1 Thess. 5:21). The testing standard is not the *status quo* (itself to be tested) of the Church, but the gospel of Jesus Christ." Kung's reliance on 1 Thess. 5:21 nearly offends its exegesis when Kung ignores the obvious Pauline intent to admonish against the dangers involved in "the discernment of spirit," and the reasoning based on that text and the conclusion are too broad ("everything") to be convincing. When Kung discusses apostolic succession (pp. 162 ff.), he raises some personal doubts about formal episcopal succession as the only way to transfer ministerial power and authority. There is much to distinguish between apostolic succession as appropriate (Lutheran) and objectively necessary (Tridentine). Indeed, he even suggests the possibility of *ordo in voto* of lay people in cases of absolute necessity celebrating Mass or hearing confession, an adventurous notion that he repeats in *The Church* (1967) and enlarges upon in *Why Priests?* (Doubleday, 1972).

Council of Constance

In *Structures of the Church* (p. 240 ff.) Kung discusses the "Ecclesiological Importance of the Council of Constance" (1414-1418). His principal positions are that the decree *Sacrosancta* (fifth session, April 14, 1415) with its conciliary concept of the Church is dogmatically binding (pp. 240, 251, 254, 255), and, secondly, that there is a dialectical tension between the Council of Constance and the First Vatican Council (pp. 270, 279, 280). With both of these positions we are in disagreement. Kung is far more self-assured about the uncertainties that enveloped the Great Western Schism and the *Acta* of the Council of Constance than the many scholars who are divided about facticity and interpretations. He weaves together a mosaic of alternate conjectures into a persuasion that is far from convincing.

There are many complex and troublesome questions about Constance that have not yet been resolved with any large concurrence by scholars, no conclusive assessment of all the important components of the totality of events, no firmly established synthesis that has won acceptance by theologians and historians of ecclesiastical history. At its core, prescinding from all the attendant historical factors, what is at issue is the legitimacy of the three claimants to the papal throne, the legitimacy of the council itself, and the authenticity of its decrees *Sacrosancta* and *Frequens* (with its provision for the periodicity of future councils).

When Angelo Guiseppe Roncalli took the name of John XXIII upon his election to the papacy on October 28, 1958, as successor by name to John XXII (1316-1334)), was he disavowing by implication the legitimacy of the Pisan pope who had convoked the Council of Constance (Nov. 5, 1414) and aligning himself with the Roman obediences from Urban VI to Gregory XII? Was Urban's election, the first to take place in Rome after Avignon, legitimate despite the intimidations of the Roman populace and the flight of the French cardinals? Was their return at his invitation and presence at his coronation a validating tacit consent? After their final rejection of Urban, the one and same college of cardinals elected Clement VII. There has never been an official papal pronouncement on the question of the legality of the Roman or Avignonese lines of popes, nor, for that matter, on the Pisan line. If John XXIII of Pisa was not a legitimate pope, could he legitimately convoke the Council of Constance? If not, then the much controverted decree *Sacrosancta* would be devoid of any dogmatic validity. Was the Council legitimized at its convocation by Gregory VII prior to his voluntary resignation? That still leaves the question of the authenticity of *Sacrosancta*, promulgated on April 16, 1416, unanswered because that decree had been promulgated before Gregory's intervention. The whole question of the authenticity of *Sacrosancta* ultimately revolves on whether it was subsequently confirmed by Martin V. All these and other questions about contestable validity are summarily disposed of by Kung: "there was no question from the very beginning of papal approbation" (p. 243). But Christendom as a whole did not know with certainty who was the true papal claimant of the three. The Great Western Schism was unique in that it involved no denial of the papal primacy. Europe was divided solely on a question of fact—*quoad personam, non quoad officium.* The action of the Council in deposing John XXIII (May 29, 1415), in effectuating the resignation of Gregory XII (July 4, 1415), and in the deposition of Benedict XIII (July 26, 1417) did not involve the admission of any conciliar supremacy *per se.* And so we pose the question, what meaning and understanding does the language of the decrees disclose on this precise issue?

For all the teutonic insistence on *sitz im leben*, it is unexpected that Kung should quote P. de Vooght: "It is not from the reason which motivated the fathers thereto that we shall ask the meaning of what they have defined, when this meaning leaves no doubt at all" (*Structures*, p. 242, n. 6). Of the extraordinary emergency situation that constituted the Great Western Schism there is no doubt that that very urgency set into motion the events at Constance and gave supreme direction to the conduct and conclusion of its proceedings.

Now, is it true that, in particular, the language of *Sacrosancta* "leaves no doubt at all" about its meaning?

At the fifth general session (April 6) the Council enacted the decree *Sacrosancta.* The crucial passage declares:

> This holy synod of Constance, constituting a General Council and lawfully assembled to root out the present schism and bring about the reform of the church in head and members ... declares that being lawfully assembled in the Holy Spirit, constituting a general council and representing the Catholic Church militant, it holds power immediately from Christ and that anyone of whatsoever state or dignity, even the papal, is bound to obey it in matters which pertain to the faith, the rooting out of the said schism and the general reform of the church in head and members. Further, it declares that any person of whatsoever rank, state or dignity, even the papal, who contumaciously refuses to obey the mandates, statutes, ordinances or instructions made or to be made by this holy synod or by any other General Council lawfully assembled concerning

the aforesaid matters or matters pertaining to them shall, unless he repents, be subjected to fitting penance and duly punished, recourse being had if necessary to other sanctions of the law. (Mansi 27:590)

to root out the present schism and bring about the reform of the church does this solemnly avowed purpose circumstance and circumscribe what follows wholly within the abnormal situations of three claimants to the papacy and to the resolution of three dubious obediences to one?

in matters which pertain to the faith, is the comprehensiveness of this statement without any limitations or is it restricted to the business at hand—"the rooting out of the said schism and the general reform of the Church?"

constituting a General Council and representing the Catholic Church militant, it holds power immediately from Christ and that anyone of whatsoever state or dignity, even the papal, is bound to obey it in matters which pertain to the faith

is this restricted to the Council of Constance and the critical affairs before it or was it intended as a general assertion of conciliar supremacy and religious omnicompetence?

be subjected to fitting penance and duly punished, recourse being had if necessary to other sanctions of the law.

If the law, the decree, is directly and principally concerned with very restricted and specific types of emergency situations, which in fact had prompted the promulgation of the law, that is ordained exclusively to the remedy of exceptionally abnormal historical situations, the uncertainty of popes, then its sanctions are coextensive with that law emergency situation—solely, they do not go beyond the remedial ordinations of that law. In such specified singular crisis, "another lawfully summoned general council" can cope with it.

We have not, nor is there any need to list the many questions that are much controverted by scholars about the composition of the Council, its organization, proceedings, manner of voting; when attendants participated or refused to do so *en bloc* in the fourth and fifth sessions; the variant mentalities on conciliar ecclesiology; the theological significance of Pope Martin V's prohibition of appeals to future councils—was this a universal decision of principle or a singular decision? Can the unpremeditated angry response of Pope Martin to the Polish representatives on the Falkenberg affair have dogmatic validity?   Our own reflections led us to observe that the decree *Sacrosancta* is on its face, ambivalent; that it is open to variant interpretations.   The decree is no less susceptible of an orthodox interpretation as it may be interpreted in another way. Is not Pope Martin's (and his successor's) conduct toward *Sacrosancta* (*and Frequens*) more revelatory of what he actually intended by any construed approval than the words he used? While there are expressions in *Sacrosancta* that may suggest a permanent definition of doctrine, there are other expressions that seem to point only to the immediate future—the end of the schism.

Kung makes an extensive and edifying display of learning, employing scholars distinguished for their studies on the Western Schism and the Council of Constance—Jedin, K. A. Fink, F. X. Funk, Hübler, Baümer, P. de Vooght, etc., and the highly important researches of Kuttner, Jacob, Ullmann, and especially, of Brian Tierney on medieval canon law and ecclesiology, that bore a major influence upon the fathers at Constance. Kung's own ultimate finding on the binding character of the decrees is in great part influenced by D. de Vooght's understanding of them. (Actually Kung goes beyond him.) P. de Vooght maintains that *Sacrosancta* did teach and formally defined the conciliary concept of the Church. Of themselves, the decrees claimed dogmatic validity.   But they had no binding force on the dogmatic level for the sole reason that the controverted confirmations of Pope Martin V in the Falkenberg disputation, "*in rebus fidei et conciliariter*," "*non aliter nec alio modo*" and in his Bull "*Inter cunctas*" (Feb. 22, 1418), "hold for certain all that it (Constance) decreed *in favorem fidei et pro salute animarum salute animarum*," despite their restrictive expressions did not fulfill the conditions necessary for an *ex cathedra* as required by the dogmatic pronouncements of Vatican I. Kung holds that the decrees are dogmatically binding. His understanding of the meaning of *Sacrosancta* is cautiously allowable. He firmly rejects the extreme radical conciliarism.   In his own words, "a definite kind of superiority of the council in the sense of at least moderately 'conciliar theory'" (*Structures*, p. 255).

Our position is in accord with that of H. Hollensteiner, H. Jedin, and A. Franzen that *Sacrosancta* (*Frequens* was a disciplinary decree) was at most an emergency measure for a clearly defined exceptional case and not a general statement of faith. At a time when first two and then three popes of dubious legitimacy reigned simultaneously, Constance was the only viable means of ending an obdurate schism.

Sacrosancta was the legalization of the Church's right to deal with emergencies, which medieval law developed from the heresy clause and which was now accepted by the Church as law. (See August Franzen, "The Council of Constance: Present State of the Problem" in *Concilium*, 29-68, vol. 7, Aug. 17, 1965.) Within this context of an emergency situation (heresy and its extensions) provided for in medieval canon law as the exception to the general principle of papal immunity—*prima sedes a nemine iudicatur*—and the conviction historical (Jedin), canonical (Franzen), and theological (Hellensteiner) that *Sacrosancta* was not a dogmatic definition of faith (as Kung maintains), we find ourselves in disagreement with Kung's supposition that there is a dialectical tension (pp. 270, 280), a polarity (p. 278 ff.) between the Council of Constance and the First Vatican Council with its dogmatic definition of papal primacy and magisterial infallibility. Kung has not proved that the former council defined anything with regard to the authority of any council *vis a vis* the authority of any pope.

Kung on Primacy and Infallibility

Since we quoted extensively from Kung's *Structure of the Church* on papal primacy and magistral infallibility to observe how his faith in the dogmatic definitions of Vatican I was still vital relatively shortly before he disavows it in *Inquiry*, we did not intend at the same time to communicate to our readers an unqualified endorsement of *Structures*. For all its accumulation of learning, there is much adventurous theologizing in it. We have already pointed to some notable instances and commented extensively on Kung's overworking of the Council of Constance. Others, such as apostolic succession (cf. Kung's favorable reflections upon the alternatives posed by the Protestant theologian, E. Schlink, to the Tridentine definition of formal succession, *Structures*, p. 168 ff.) would require a full study beyond the scope of our present objectives.

Kung's discussion of papal primacy of jurisdiction, correct in its conformity to the Vatican canons, is nonetheless circumscribed with discussions of decentralization, subsidiarity, and service that the reader is left wondering whether Kung has done full justice to the New Testament idea of authority as well as of service. And what he has to say of the freedom of the individual conscience and the teaching authority of the Church (pp. 341-344) leaves out of its account the office of the Church as the divinely appointed teacher and interpreter of the divine law and her informative and formative role of human conscience. (Much less is there any study of how a conscience can justify its opposition to a grave matter of morality taught by the Church.)

Even Kung's discussion of infallibility, as it hews close to the official interpretation of the Council's definition by Bishop Gasser, is followed by a series of questions (here raised with academic propriety and repeated crudely in categorical form in *Inquiry*) about providing means of effectively preventing the pope from making arbitrary definitions ("perhaps true, but under certain circumstance, nevertheless greatly harmful to the Church"), p. 333. Certain reflections are in order: To begin with, there have been only two papal definitions *ex cathedra*, the Immaculate Conception of the Blessed Virgin Mary by Pope Pius IX (*Ineffabilis Deus*, December 8, 1854) and the definition of the Assumption of the Blessed Virgin Mary by Pope Pius XII (*Munificentissimus Deus*, November 1, 1950). At both times, each pontiff consulted the universal collectivity of bishops and there was at each time a worldwide enthusiastic acclaim by the faithful whose Marian piety had in fact contributed to the better understanding of the Marian mysteries. As their consciousness of a Christian truth and reality developed and grew, they accompanied it with a living practice. Both Pontiffs were giving finality of formal and infallible expression to what had been an authentic Tradition of the deposit of faith. Secondly, Kung's proposal framed as a rhetorical question actually offends the efficacy of the abiding presence of the Divine Spirit of Truth who was promised by Christ Jesus to preserve the *kerygma* intact and inviolable, so that all mankind may know it as His. Kung confronts us with an intriguing speculation of a pope defining something that is "perhaps true" (p. 333), "even if it is true in itself" (p. 334), "but under certain circumstances, nevertheless greatly harmful to the Church" (p. 333), "*contra consensum ecclesiae*" (p. 334). For the moment, Kung answers in *Structures* (p. 334), "*Under no circumstances.*" Despite all emphasis on papal full authority Vatican I repeatedly attached a great importance to the fact that no opposition could arise between the pope and the Church (episcopate). Despite this rearguard answer, Kung repeats this consideration in *Inquiry* (pp. 103-108) with no doubt of the probabilities of such a conflict, despite Vatican II's reassurance that such a case is purely imaginary, since one and the same Holy Spirit directs the Pope, the episcopal college, and the universal body of the faithful:

"To the resultant definition the assent of the Church can never be wanting, on account of the activity of that same Holy Spirit, whereby the whole flock of Christ is preserved and progresses in unity of faith. (*Lumen Gentium*, c. 25)

But in his supposition, Kung does raise a question that *he* should answer. Should not the Roman Pontiff define what is true even *precisely because* in Kung's supposition, there were a contrary consensus among the faithful. This contrariety to a papal definition of what is true would obviously be heterodoxy. For longer than two centuries, Christianity in the heretical form of Arianism was all pervasive among the Visigoths, Ostrogoths, Vandals and Burgundians, no thanks to the zeal of Bishop Ulfilas and his unknown companions who began their missionary work beyond the Danube about 340. In such a historical situation would it have been arbitrary, improper, for a pope to have defined that the Son is consubstantial with the Father, if there had not been the first Council of Nicaea (325)? In the East, the religious phenomenon between the Council of Nicaea (325) and the First Council of Constantinople (381) was similar but in reverse. It was the faithful people and the local priests, under the leadership of Athanasius and the Egyptian bishops, who held fast against the Arians while numerous bishops opted for that heresy at the synods of Caesarea and Tyre (334, 335), at the Great Council of Dedication at Antioch (341), the seceder of the Council of Sardica (347), at Sirmium (351), at Arles (353), at Milan (355), at the Councils of Selucia and Arminum (359).

Did not St. Jerome exclaim "Ingemuit totus orbis et se esse Arianum miratus est" (*In Lucif.* 19)? John Henry Newman's explanation of the failure in orthodoxy on the part of so many hundreds of Eastern bishops is that "there was nothing after Nicaea of firm, unvarying consistent testimony for nearly sixty years." If a pope had defined then the divinity of the Son, "*contra consensum ecclesiae*" (the episcopacy)—as Kung's supposition reads—should he have not done so if Nicaea had never existed? As a matter of fact, has not the judgment of history been critical of Pope Liberious for not being more forceful and, in all appearances, entirely beyond all shadow of suspicion for wavering on Athanasius under tremendous pressure from Constantius, the emperor? Kung's proposal for a "juridical security" against papal absolutism, as he puts it, (*Inquiry*, p. 107) suffers from an inherent weakness. As such, Kung's proposal simply transfers the ultimate power of decision from the Vicar of Christ, the key-bearer and steward of His Church (Matt. 16:18, 19) and universal shepherd of His flock (Jn. 21:15-17) to another ecclesiastical agency of human invention without any of the unique prerogatives Christ gave His chief steward. In such a supposition—*quis custodiet ipsos custodes*? Who then will be the guardian of the guardians—this question was posed by a *prechristian* Roman who found his answer in civil law.

We have quoted at length from *Structures* with the purpose of manifesting to the casual general reader how supportive Kung was on the scriptural basis for ecclesiastical offices, for his supportive explanations of papal primacy and infallibility in a publication (1964) scarcely six years before his disavowal of the dogmatic definitions of the First Vatican Council in *Inquiry* (1970). Considering that the composition of a manuscript and its publication require the minimum of two years and allowing for some time for a change of mind to the novel stance, then Kung's disavowal of the unique prerogatives of the papal office (and of the infallibility of ecumenical councils and of the inerrancy of scripture), his defection of faith occurred in a shorter span of time.

Presentation of "Inquiry" in "The Church"

On December 8, 1965, The feast of the Immaculate Conception of the Blessed Virgin Mary, the twenty-first ecumenical council, the Second Vatican, solemnly closed. In 1967, appeared both the original German, *Die Kirche*, and English translation, *The Church*. In its *Foreword*, (xiii), we read that: "*Structures of the Church* (1962, English version 1964) is to be understood as a prolegomenon to this book."

On pp. 449-450, Kung recapitualtes (in small print) the dogmatic teaching of Vatican I on papal primacy and infallibility. He notes with emphasis: "Since the definition of primacy has often been misunderstood the elucidation of it emerging from the Council documents are of importance. They show that papal primacy, even in the view of Vatican I, is by no means an arbitrary absolutism, but rather that . . ." and he proceeds to say that the power of the popes is not absolute, not arbitrary; it has its limits.

It is limited actively by Christ, passively by the apostles and their successors. The pope is also limited as a matter of course by the natural law (*ius naturale*) and divine law (*ius divinum*).

The concrete limits of the exercise of primacy are: (a) the existence of the episcopate, which the pope can neither abolish nor dissolve as regards its position or its rights; (b) the ordinary exercise of office by the bishops; in no case may the pope, being as it were another bishop, intervene in the daily excerise of office by the bishops; (c) the aim of the pope's exercise of office: its constant aim must be the edification and the unity of the Church; (d) the manner of the papal office; it must not be arbitrary, inopportune or exaggerated, but must be dictated by the needs and the evident benefit of the Church.

Compare this brief summation with the phantasmagoria of *Inquiry* of an "arbitrary, autocratic, papal absolutism" (pp. 104-105).

There are, however, some presentations in *Church* of what will follow in *Inquiry*, and perhaps they may have been intended as the opening wedge for the negations of the later book.

On p. 342, we read: "Infallibility" therefore means a fundamental remaining in the truth, which is not disturbed by individual errors." This is taken bodily into *Inquiry* (p. 181) as Kung acknowledged (n. 8).

On p. 343, the second paragraph, titled *Fragmentariness*, is a summary statement of what will appear more expansively and more boldly in *Inquiry* (pp. 157-173) on the "problematic of propositions as such" and, in particular, "The problematic of ecclesiastical definition." Logically, Kung's whole challenge to papal infallibility, and of councils, and of the inerrancy of Scripture was rendered superfluous by his theory of knowledge, and the fundamental ambiguity of all propositions. The fourth chapter of *Inquiry* with his theological gnoseology would have sufficed by itself.

Fragmentariness: Every formulation of faith, whether made by an individual or by the whole Church, remains imperfect, incomplete, unclear, partial and fragmentary; these are the kind of expressions used by Paul in I Corinthians 13:9-12. This is often overlooked when the infallibility of an individual statement, where infallibility begins after a colon, is considered. The partial and incomplete nature of such statements is not only the result of the polemical bias and the narrowness of doctrinal formulations made by the Church. It is part of the necessary dialectic character of human statements of the truth. Any human statement of the truth, because of its human limitations, is very close to error, and one only has to overlook the human limitations of truth to turn truth into error. All human truth stands in the shadow of error. All error contains at least a grain of truth. What a true statement says is false; what it means but does not say may be true. It is a simplified view of the truth to suppose that every sentence in its verbal formulation must be true or false. On the contrary, any sentence can be true *and* false, according to its purpose, its context, its underlying meaning. It is much harder to discover what is meant by it than by what it says. A sincere, fearless and critical ecumenical theology, the only kind which can hope to be constructive, must give up throwing dogmas at the heads of the other side. Theology today must be actively concerned to try and see the truth in what it supposes to be the errors of the other side, and to see the possibility of error in what it itself believes. In this way, we would reach the situation which it is essential to reach; the abandonment of supposed error and a meeting in common Christian truth. (*The Church*, p. 343)

This all adds up to what Kung in *Inquiry* (p. 161) calls the fundamental ambiguity of all propositions. The entire passage is an untheological mélange of rhetoric, half truths and whole falsehoods, a misuse of a Pauline text, the rejection of the human capacity for formulations of propositional truths exempt from error, the indifference to the divine efficacy of the Holy Spirit of Truth to warrant an infallible declaration of revelational data, the implication of the futility of receiving Christian revelation as a secure human possession as Christ Jesus intended it to be, and lastly a dismal and cavalier confusion of partial, inadequate, and imperfect knowledge with error, with falsehood. Obviously, any knowledge of divine mysteries will always fall short of them. And in human sciences the advance has always been by a gradual achievement of partial truths and succeeding through them to additional truths. It is this possible and actual achievement that constitutes science.

And if this be true of human capacity for certitude in natural sciences, however frequently the human enterprise may fail in the pursuit and grasp of natural truths, how much more enhanced, elevated, protected and directed will the ecclesial magisterium be as it seek out from the *depositum fidei* (1 Tm. 6:20; 2 Tm. 1:12, 14) entrusted by Jesus to His Church through the Apostles a deeper, greater and clearer understanding of divine revelation through the promised abiding assistance of the Holy Spirit (Jn 14:16, 26; 16: 12-13). What is involved here is not only the human capacity to receive and understand God's communications to His People, but also—and far more so—, the divine efficacy to make good His guarantee that He will be heard and His salvific message understood. If Faith comes by hearing, it comes by hearing His word with His divinely guided assistance without error or distortion. Kung's concentration is solely on human capacity without consideration of the divine warrant to preserve the salvific reality inviolable.

In citing I Cor. 13: 9-12, Kung argues backwards from a predetermined conclusion to a premise of questionable exegesis of the Pauline pericope. All knowledge that we have *now* is imperfect because of the finitude of our intelligence. But not all imperfect knowledge is erroneous or fundamentally ambiguous. When Paul speaks of his knowledge as imperfect, even with the benefit of the vision of the Lord of glory, he knows and preaches Christ Jesus, crucified and risen, with certitude, with not the slightest admission of error in his propositional truths. In his First Epistle to the Corinthians, Paul is comparing the knowledge we have of God "now" on earth with the knowledge we shall have "then" in the heavenly presence of God "face to face." Paul employs metaphors—"in an enigma," and "face to face" taken from the Old Testament (cf. Nu. 12:6), and one—"in a mirror," is borrowed from the popular Cynic-Stoic philosophy. The first metaphor contrasts the privileged revelations given to Moses with those given to the prophets. The second metaphor refers to the indirect vision of an object seen in a mirror. And Paul's use of the metaphor of the mirror takes on not only the Cynic-Stoic meaning of indirection but also the poor quality of the ancient mirror in which the reflection was not as clear as in our modern ones. The Pauline text must be understood within the context given to a consideration of spiritual gifts. Paul is comparing with the "face to face" vision of God the knowledge possessed through the charismatic gifts of gnosis and prophecy. As Paul writes: "In short, there are three things that last: Faith, hope, and love; and the greatest of these is love" (v. 13). "Then I shall know as fully as I am known" (v. 12)—a contrasting parallel is drawn between the perfect vision or knowledge of God and the charity by which we love God even in this life. Faith and hope take on an effective meaning when conjoined to love. They remain in a perfect state at the consummation of this world—*now-then*.

Any comparison of earthly knowledge with heavenly knowledge

would obviously suffer by the enormous contrast. But Paul is raising no epistemological problem nor calling into question the validity of all propositional formulations including those of faith. Apart from Kung's exegetical misapropos, and taking his use of the Pauline texts as he intends them, Kung compounds his flight from the human capacity for propositional truths by asking his readers to believe that despite the "fundamental ambiguity" of all propositions, the Church will "persevere in truth." Such a faith commitment inserts a wide kantian wedge between the postulates of speculative reason and practical reason. (We shall discuss at considerable length Kung's theological gnoseology in volume III.)

On page 451, we read: "The pope, instead of being referred to as the "head of the Church," is called "the pastor of the whole Church." This *"instead"* is without any significance. In the Dogmatic Constitution on the Church, (*Lumen Gentium*), a cursory review numbers several instances of the pope as "head." In n. 22 alone, we read of the pope: "Together with its head, the Roman Pontiff, and never without this head"; "joined with their head"; "under one head"; "primacy and preeminence of their head"; "head of the college." In the Decree on the Bishop's Pastoral Office in the Church (*Christus Dominus*), n. 4, "with the head"; "together with its head, the Roman Pontiff, and never without this head"; and so on. These references to the pope as head is in relation to the episcopal college. True, but the reality of the Petrine-papal office is larger than any single word. The Roman Pontiff is spoken of as successor of Peter, as the "perpetual and visible source and foundation of the unity of bishops and of the multitude of the faithful"; his solemn definitions "of themselves, and not from the consent of the faithful"; his solemn definitions "of themselves, and not from the consent of the Church, are justly styled irreformable . . . they need no approval of others, nor do they allow an appeal to any other judgment"; the pope is declared by the Fathers of the Second Vatican Council to be "supreme shepherd and teacher of all the faithful"; "as the supreme teacher of the universal Church, as one in whom the charism of the infallibility of the Church herself is individually present" and so on. Peter and his successors are the rock-foundation of the universal Church, the key-bearer, the one Jesus singles out to strengthen the faith of his brethren, the shepherd chosen by the Risen Savior "to tend and feed" His flock. If there is any evidence of a put-down of the Roman Pontiff in the writings of Kung, it is in marked contrast to the very keen sense of the Petrine-papal office so repeatedly and widely manifest in the documents of the Second Vatican Council.

The Transition to "Inquiry"

In 1968, Hans Kung published his *Truthfulness: The Future of the Church* (Sheed and Ward, New York). It is in tone, style, methodology, and content the transition from the heavy accouterments of learning in *Structures of the Church* (1964) and *The Church* (1967) to the open-ended challenges of *Infallible? An Inquiry* (1970). It draws with magnetic pull every conceivable human failure of the Church within its book covers, half-truths, exaggerations, misconstructions, antipathies, aversions. Not only is the Catholic Church projected against Kung's own ecclesial paradeigma, but he is *the* judge of ecclesiastical conduct, of ecclesial authority, of popes, bishops, priests, theologians, the Curia, canon law, of the whole course of ecclesiastical history. Indeed, his *judgments* given without any self-awareness of "fundamental ambiguity" constitute at the same time *norms* of rectitude in every area of Church life. His judgments betray none of the "problematic inherent in propositions as such" (*Inquiry*, p. 159). His judgments apparently are above the five limitations that render them necessarily open to error (p. 158-161) and wholly free from the general rule of Kung's own theory of cognition that "every proposition can be true *and* false" (*Inquiry*, p. 172). In *Truthfulness* (and in *Inquiry*) we are in the presence of the most absolutist evaluatory judgment.

> We are taking part not only in the end of the Tridentine age but also in the end of ecclesiastical medievalism, insofar as it was scholastic, legalistic, hierarchical, centralistic, sacramentalistic, traditionalistic, exclusive and often superstitious (p. 1) . . . crisis of leadership, ambiguity of some conciliar decisions . . . curial minority, efficiently controlling and half-hearted measures (3) . . . there is a slowness, often an incapacity, attachment to an obsolete system, bureaucratic machinery (4) . . . The Italian Court mentality . . . Roman institutions . . . equivocal conciliar verbalism . . . unintelligent intervention of a hopelessly backward Roman theology against the Catechism approved by the whole Dutch episcopate . . . Some bishops' conferences more disappointing than Rome (p. 5) . . . . This is the result of insecurity, passivity, fear of Rome, persistence in long-obsolete ecclesiastical positions and privileges (especially in education and politics) of preconciliar mentality, theological ignorance, personal animosity towards persistent criticism, and irrelevant and ineffective reaction to suggestion for reform from their own Churches. (p. 6)

These are random selections from only the first six pages. Long concatenation of negative judgments, torrentially voluble, excited (but unexciting) become the general expectation rather than the exception in *Truthfulness*. Kung regurgitates all the human failures in the Church in a constant and seemingly endless review of her historical existence. Yet, Kung finds ground for hope for this "constantly failing and straying Church" (p. 107) in the evidences he lists for "the beginning of a change" (pp. 107-125). But these high expectations are somewhat dimmed in the sequent chapter "Change of Course in Doctrine?" Kung sees the change in Catholic *teaching* as the test-case for ecclesial truthfulness (p. 127). But such change can only be facilitated by a change in the doctrinal meaning of "infallibility." We are now brought to the theme that will become the major theme of *Inquiry*. In *Truthfulness*, infallibility is "a basic persistence of the Church in truth, which is not destroyed by errors and *through* all errors" (p. 136). Compare this with *Inquiry* (p. 175): *"The Church will persist in the truth IN SPITE OF ALL ever possible errors!* (the italics, large print, and exclamation mark in the original). And again—*"a fundamental remaining of the Church in truth, which is not annulled by individual errors* (*Inquiry*, p. 181. Italics in the original). "The Church . . . composed of human beings . . . can constantly and in a very human way deceive herself and others on *every* plane and in *all* spheres. Therefore, in order to avoid all mis-understandings, it is better to ascribe to the Church, not "infalli-bility,"—but—on the basis of faith in the promises—"indefectibility" or "perpetuity": an unshatterability and indestructibility; in belief, a fundamental *remaining* in the truth in spite of all ever possible errors" (*Inquiry*, p. 185)—"on every plane and in all spheres"— *cui bono* the Kungian indefectibility?

The sad irony is that "truthfulness" in the Church becomes the catalyst for doing away with the divine warrant against error in trans-mitting to all mankind to the consummation of time the salvific event and message of Christ Jesus in accordance with His divine mandate and commission. *Truthfulness: Future of the Church* (1968) is the bridge between *Structures of the Church* (1964) and *The Church* (1967) and *INFALLIBLE? An Inquiry* (1970).

There are no human failings in Kung's own ecclesial paradeigma except the divine failure to guarantee the preservation and trans-mission of His own divine revelations to men without admixture of error, without falsification, without misconstruction. There will be "truthful existence in the Church and truthful existence of the

Church (in Kung's own ecclesiology pp. 94-95), but there will be the divine failure not to have created man to His own image—a divine failure that will incapacitate all men, including the human authors of the scriptural books, the popes, councils—even theologians, leave alone believers and unbelievers—to formulate propositional truths. There are many presentations in *Truthfulness* of what will appear in *Inquiry*, for example, the errors of the ecclesiastical teaching office, an almost verbatim summation, in *Truthfulness* (pp. 133-134) in *Inquiry* (pp. 31-32); "the absolutist, authoritarian and often totalitarian system" (*Truthfulness*, p. 103, and *passim*, *Inquiry* pp. 18-28; 104-108; and *passim*); the ambiguity of all human propositions in *Truthfulness* (pp. 137, 138), in *Inquiry* (pp. 157-162); "fundamental remaining in the truth in spite of all possible errors" in *Truthfulness* (pp. 136-138), in *Inquiry* (pp. 175 ff.); the questioning of "primacy and infallibility" (p. 57) in the one, and their rejection in the other (pp. 79 ff.).

Concluding Reflections

We have noted Kung's untheological distempers toward all that Rome signifies: the Curia, Canon Law, theology, administration. We note his negative criticism of Pope Paul's VI's encyclicals on the Church (*Ecclesiam Suam*, 1963), on the Blessed Eucharist (*Mysterium Fidei*, 1965), on Priestly Celibacy (*Sacerdotalis Coelibatus*, 1967), on Human Life (*Humanae Vitae*, 1968), the *Credo* (1968, a summation of all solemnly defined truths), the papal directives on mixed marriages (*Motu Proprio* of March 31, 1970).

We have noted that Kung exploits an uprooted history in his glissade of "errors of the ecclesiastical teaching office." We have explained that these "errors" (?) were not errors touching upon ecclesial infallibility, papal, conciliar, and scriptural, and not infrequently it was a matter of prudential judgment. Kung's denial of the primacy of jurisdiction does not take adequate account of the scriptural concept of authority. He has failed to grasp the deeper understanding of Church jurisdiction as it is uniquely and preeminently situated in *Kepha* We have maintained that the primacy of service, understood in its fullest sense, the preservation and transmission of divine truths, and the means of sanctification, requires by a principled necessity in accordance with the Petrine texts primatial authority. Kung's antithesis between law and liberty is neither Pauline nor evangelical. Kung's employment of St. Autustine's *De Trinitate* (1,

3, 5) hardly accords with St. Augustine's own intentions and objectives.

All referrals to the natural law in *Humanae Vitae* are not an "inappropriate medley of platonic-aristotelian-thomistic ideas," but the existential natural law that is an integral constituent of evangelical morality, the *lex Christi*, by which man, through the redemptive merits of Christ and by the grace of God, may attain eternal life situated as he is from the moment of his being in the *de facto* supernatural status. It is *the* natural law which is within the scope of the commission of Christ to Peter and his successors to teach and interpret to all mankind without error.

Kung's credibility is not only gravely at fault but it is seriously handicapped by a number of intellectual *aporiae*. His adversary "state of intellect" disposes him to separate, to dichotomize what are integral religious realities, inseparable constituents of the Catholic dogmas. He disjoins the institutional from the charismatic Church; the Pope, the visible head of the Church, from the Lord of glory, the invisible Head; the Pope from the Church; the Church from the Mystical Body of Christ; the Church's teaching office from the abiding assistance of the Divine Spirit of Truth. He severs apart Tradition, Sacred Scripture, and the Magisterium and inserts an arbitrariness between them. The "clear passage to truth" is considerably dimmed by Kung's selective use of primary and secondary sources. Further, he misconstrues his sources, notably, the *False Decretals*, Verardo's *Introductio Editoris*, St. Thomas Aquinas' *Contra Errores Graecorum*. He uses authors selectively to suit his purpose and omits others whose theology is supportive of ecclesial infallibility, papal and conciliar, and the inerrancy of Scripture. Kung demands "proofs," "substantiation," "demonstration," but he never explains what precisely would constitute "proof" in dogmatic theology on an article of faith. And with all his insistence on "demonstration" in the area of fundamental theology, he incongruously cuts the ground from under his requirement since he does not hold for the inerrancy of Scripture, the source of biblical "demonstration." He compounds his own problem by maintaining the "fundamental ambiguity" of all human propositions, not exempting ecclesiastical definitions. With such an epistemological crisis of his own contrivance, neither Scripture, much less human intelligence can respond to his own insistent demands. His open-ended methodology cannot stand scrutiny. He never tells his reader what method, if any, appropriate to the various disciplines to which he has recourse, that he is following. Nor can one discern that he abides faithfully by the methodological exigencies of, say, ecclesiastical history, secular history, scriptural exegesis, dogmatic theology, fundamental theology, etc. The most startling omission is Kung's silence about his former adherence in faith to the solemn definitions of the First Vatican Council. At no time does he confront his present loss of faith in infallibility and disclose the flaws that he now sees, but had not seen before. He does not inform us of any new historical, scriptural, theoretic evidence that he had not known before and which he now possesses to warrant his defection in faith. John Henry Newman over a century ago and Heinrich Schlier in our own times, apparently felt compelled to give reason to their former co-religionists in faith (and to their new ecclesial communion) why and how they were converted to Catholicism. Kung is moved by no such moral urgency. The matter is the same, the historical and exegetical, but now Kung draws contrary conclusions from them. We have sought the reason for this turnabout on infallibility, and tentatively put down these three factors: The promulgation of *Humanae Vitae* (which Kung admits to be *infallibilis ex ordinario magisterio*. Cf. *Inquiry*, p. 58); the protestantizing of ecumenism which leads him to a latitudinarian Christianity; the new (old) theology of liberal Protestantism to serve that purpose. In the Decree on Ecumenism (*Unitatis Redintegratio*) the Fathers of the Second Vatican Council declared in solemn session:

> For it is through Christ's Catholic Church alone which is the all embracing means of salvation, that the fullness of the means of salvation can be obtained. It was to the apostolic college alone, of which Peter is the head, that we believe our Lord entrusted the blessings of the New Covenant, in order to establish on earth the one Body of Christ into which all those should be fully incorporated who already belong in any way to God's people. (c. 3)

In unequivocal terms, the successors of Peter and of the apostolic college, state that the principal and primary purpose of ecumenism, apart from its concomitant and secondary beneficences in charity, is to bring all, each and every one into the Catholic Church which has the "all-embracing means of salvation, the fulness of the means of salvation" for the Catholic Church is "Christ's Catholic Church."

Kung's use of ecclesiastical history is one-sided, partial, biased—

whatever subserves his predetermined purpose. And not the least misuse is to confound papal primacy of jurisdiction and magisterial infallibility with the enormous papal authority in temporalities in that unique historical phenomenon, christendom, which was a response to a special historical situation beginning with Gregory VII and culminating in the governance of Innocent III and Innocent IV. It is not exact theology nor correct history to identify the power of these popes in that most unusual coincidence of Church and Empire, with their distinct but interlocking functions working for the unity of the West on the basis of the Christian faith, through the complexities of the feudal system and the legal bonds of Canon Law, to a moral unification based on the religious and juridical substructure of Christendom, with their operations conceived as taking place within and not outside nor alongside the Church. It is not, nor was it ever a part of our Catholic faith to identify the nature, extent, and comprehensive reach of medieval papal authority in temporalities with the narrowly defined dogmas on papal primatial authority and magisterial infallibility in matters of faith and morals.

There has always been and there will always be a great need for scholarly studies of the dogmas of the Catholic faith, none excluded. At a time when the ecumenical movement demands that papal infallibility be studied intelligently and rendered intelligible to non-Catholic and non-Christians alike, not only within the terms of the *loci classici*, the three Petrine texts, but also within the totality of the New Testament books, indeed, of all of Sacred Scripture, when the human failures in the members of the Church should not be allowed to obfuscate the vision of the Lord (Jn. 21:7) nor of the shepherd chosen by Him to "tend" and "feed" His flock (vv. 15-17), Kung has published a book on infallibility that has not the scholarly care nor the extensive learning of his earlier and better books.

The forthcoming complementary volumes will be Volume II— *Catholic Ecclesiology and Hans Kung's Ecclesial Paradeigma*; Volume III—*The Theological Gnoseology of Hans Kung*.

As for this priest, *"I know whom I have believed"* (2 Tim. 1:12).

Credo in unam, Sanctam, catholicam, apostolicam ecclesiam.

A fallible Church, patterned on an errant Scripture, with a fallible foundation and a fallible shepherd "to feed and tend" His flock cannot be an object of faith.

BIBLIOGRAPHY

Acts of the Apostles. A commentary by Ernst Haenchen. Translated from the 14th German edition by Bernard Noble and Gerard Shinn, with the translation revised and brought up-to-date by R. McL. Wilson, Philadelphia, Westminster Press, 1971.

Aquinas, Thomas, *Contra errores Graecorum*, edition R. A. Verardo, *Opuscula Theologica I*, Turin and Rome, 1954. (I am greatly indebted to Miss Mary Bires, Reference Librarian, St. Louis University, for photostat copies of *Editoris* [Verardo's] *Introductio*, pp. 269-283; *Synopsis*, pp. 284-314; *Locorum concordantia iuxta Libelli De Fide S. Trinitatis ordinem*, pp. 284-309; *Auctoritatem series juxta opusculi Contra errores Graecorum*, pp. 310-313; *Nota Bibliographica*, p. 314; *Contra errores Graecorum ad Urbanum IV Pontificem Maximum*, pp. 315-346.)
Summa Theologia, II, II, q. 1, Art. 10 and 3.

Baldwin, M. W., *The Medieval Papacy in Action*, New York, 1940.

Barth, Karl, *Church Dogmatics*, trans. from the German by G. T. Thompson, New York, 1955.

Battifol, P., *Cathedra Petri, Etudes d'histoire ancienne de l'église, Unam Sanctam* 4, Paris, 1938.

Bea, Cardinal Augustin, "The Word of God and Mankind," *Franciscan Herald*, 1967.

Brucker, J., *Dictionnaire de Théologie Catholique*, 2.2:2364-91. (Chinese Rites Controversy), Paris, 1903.

Carlyle, R. W. and A. J. Carlyle, *A History of Medieval Political Theory*, 6 vols, Edinburgh and London, 1903-1936.

Cary-Lewes, C., *China and the Cross: A Survey of Missionary History,* New York, 1957.

Catechism of the Council of Trent for Parish Priests, issued by order of Pope Pius V, trans. into English with notes by John A. McHugh, O. P. and Charles J. Callan, O. P., 2nd rev. ed., London, Herder, 1923.

Cayre, F., *Manual of Patrology and History of Theology*, trans. from the French by H. Howitt, Paris, 1936.

Chapman, J., *Studies on the Early Papacy*, New York (n.d.).

Cohen, I.B., *The Birth of a New Physics*, Garden City: New York, Anchor, 1960.

Congar, Yves, *L'eccesiologie du haut moyen-age*. Paris, Les editions du Cerf, 1968.

L'eglise de saint Augustin a l'époque moderne, Paris, Les Editions.

Costanzo, Joseph F., S.J., "Graeco Roman Politeia," *Fordham Law Review*, XX, June 1951, pp. 119-155.

"Catholic Politeia I," *Fordham Law Review*, XXI, June 1952, pp. 91-155.

"Catholic Polteia II," *Fordham Law Review*, XXI, December 1952, pp. 236-281.

"Juridic Origins of Representation I," *Fordham Law Review*, XXIII, December 1954, pp. 296-322.

"Juridic Origins of Representation II," *Fordham Law Review*, XXIII, June 1954, pp. 123-146.

"Il principio agostiniano di egualità," *Humanities*, (Italy), IX, October 1954, pp. 1030-1039.

"Dottrina Agostiniana sul 'integrità della natura umana," *Giornale di Metafisica* (Italy), IX, October 1954.

"Lo studioso cattolico e la libertà scientifica," *La Civiltà Cattolica* (Italy), IV (2604), December 1958, pp. 549-581.

"Liberta scientifica e libertà sociale," *La Civiltà Cattolica*, (Italy), I (2609), March 1959, pp. 493-503.

"The Divided Allegiance of the Catholic," *Problems and Progress*, (Newman Press, 1962), pp. 17-39.

"Papal Magisterium and Humanae Vitae," *Thought*, Autumn, 1969.

"Academic Dissent: An Original Ecclesiology," *Thomist*, October 1970.

"Papal Magisterium, Natural Law and Humanae Vitae," *The American Journal of Jurisprudence*, Vol. 16, 1971.

Cullmann, O., *Peter, Disciple, Apostle, Martyr. A Historical and Theological Study*. Translated from the German by Floyd V. Filson, London, 1953.

Dawson, C., *The Making of Europe*. Ohio, World Publishing Co., 1952. (Originally published in 1932).

Religion and the Rise of Western Culture. New York, Sheed and Ward, 1950.

De Doctrina Concilii Vaticani Primi, Libreria Editrice Vaticana, 1969, studia selecta annis, 1948-1964, scripta denuo edita cum centesimus annus compleretur ab eodem inchoato concilio.

Constitutio Dogmatica De Fide "Dei Filus"

Alexander Kerrigan, O.F.M., Doctrina concilii Vaticani I de'sine scripto" traditionibus.

Robert Schlund, Zur Quellengrage der vatikanischen, Lehre von der Kirche als Glaubwürdigkeitsgrund.

Roger Aubert, La Constitution "Dei Filus" du Concile du Vatican.

Marc Caudron, Magistére ordinaire et infaillibilité pontificale d'apres la Constitution "Dei Filus."

Paul Anu, O.S.B., Le magistére pontifical ordinaire au premier Concile du Vatican.

George Paradis, S.J., Foi et raison au premier Concile du Vatican.
Constitution Dogmatica Prima De Ecclesia
Christi "Pastor Aeternus."
Lambert Beauduin, O.S.B., L'unite' de l'eglise et le Concile du Vatican.
Umberto Betti, O.F.M., Dottrina della, Costituzione dommatica "Pastor Aeternus."
Wilfred F. Dewan, C.S.SP., "Potestas vere episcopalis" au premier Concile du Vatican.
Walter Kasper, Primat und Episkopat nach dem Vatikanum I.
Giuseppe Columbo, Il problema dell'episcpato nella Costituzione "de Ecclesia catholica" del concilio Vaticano I.
Jerome Hamer, O.P., Le corps épiscopal uni au Pape, son autorité dans l'Eglise, d'aprés les documents du premier Concile du Vatican.
Ursicino Dominguez Del Val, Obispo y Colegio episcopal en el Concilio Vaticano I y en la patristica tradicion.
J. P. Torrell, O.P., L'infaillibilité pontificale est-elle un privilége "personnelle?"
Georges Dejaifve, S.J., "Ex sese, non autem ex consensu Ecclesiae."
Gustave Thils, L'infaillibilité de l'Eglise "in credendo" et "in docendo."
Antoine Chavasse, La veritable conception de l'infaillibilité papale d'apres le Concile du Vatican.
Dempsy, B. W., *Interest and Usury*. Washington, 1943.
Divine, T. F., *Interest. A Historical and Analytical Study in Economics and Modern Ethics*. Milwaukee, 1959.
Dizionario Dei Concili. 6 vols. Diretto da Pietro Palazzini. Instituto Giovanni XXIII Nella Pontificia Universita Lateranense, Citta Nuova Editrice, 1963-1967.
Documents of Vatican II, Editors, Walter Abbott, S.J. and Mgsr. Joseph Gallagher. New York, America Press, 1966.
Duchesne, L. *The Beginnings of the Temporal Sovereignty of the Popes A.D. 754-1073.* Translation from the French by Arnold Mathew, New York, 1908.
Early History of the Christian Church. Translated from the 4th French edition, London, 1950.
Dvornik, F., *Byzantium and the Roman Primacy.* A translation of Byzance et la primauté romaine. (Editions di Cerf, Paris, 1964) New York, Fordham, 1966.
The Photian Schism, History and Legend. Cambridge, 1948.
Enchiridion Symbolorum, Definitionum et Declarationum De Rebus Fidei et Morum. Denziger et Schonmetzer, S.J. Edito XXXII, 1963.
Fathers of the Church, New York, Christian Heritage, 1946.
Gospel according to John, I-XII. Translated with an introduction and notes by Raymond E. Brown, New York, Doubleday, The Anchor Bible, 1966. (XIII-XXI). 1970.

Grabowski, H., "St. Augustine and the Primacy of the Church of Rome," *Traditio*, IV, 1946, pp. 89-113.

Graham, S.J., R.A. *Vatican Diplomacy*. Princeton: New Jersey, 1959.

Greek New Testament, edited by Aland, Black, Martini, Metzger, and Wikgren, second edition. Wurtemberg Bible Society: Stuttgart, Germany, 1966.

Grelot, P., *Introduction to the Bible*. Translated from the French by G. Patrick Campbell. New York, Herder and Herder, 1967.

Harnack, A., Von. *History of Dogma*, 7 vols. English translation by N. Buchanan, et. al. London, 1896-99.

The Mission and Expansion of Christianity in the First Three Centuries, trans. and edited by James Moffat, second edition, 2 vols., New York, 1908.

Hefele, C. J., *A History of the Councils of the Church*, 5 vols, Edinburgh, 1896.

Hughes, P., *History of the Church*, New York, 1935.

The Reformation in England, 3 vols. New York, Macmillan, 1951-1954.

Hull, S.J., E.R., *Galileo and His Condemnation*. London, Sands, 1913.

L'infaillibilité. Son Aspect Philosophique et Theologique. Actes du Colloque Organise Par Le Centre International D'Etudes Humanistes Et Par L'Institut D'Etudes Philosophiques De Rome. Rome, 5-12 Janvier 1970 aux soins de Enrico Casyell, Audiber, Editions Montaigne, 1970.

Enrico Castelli Docétisme, linguistique et herméneutique de l'infaillibilité.

L'aspect philosophique et théologique du concept d'infaillibilite.

Sergio Cotta, Le droit á l'infaillibilité et la faillibilité du droit.

Vittorio Mathieu, Infaillibilité et autolegitimation d'un systéme juridique.

Karl Rahner, Quelques considérations sur le concept d'infallibilité dans la théologie catholique.

Claude Bruaire, Le Probléme de Dieu dans l'explication de l'erreur.

Roger Aubert, Motivations théologiques et extra-théologiques de partisans et des adversaires de la définition dogmatique de l'infaillibilité du pape á Vatican.

Raoul Manselli, Le cas du pape héretique vu á travers les courants spirituels du XIVe siecle.

Paul De Vooght, Les dimensions réeles de l'infaillibilité papale.

Ernst Benz, Vision et infaillibilité.

Joachim Jeremias, L'attente de la fin prochaine dans les paroles de Jésus.

Eberhard Jungel, L'autorité du Christ suppliant.

Jean-Louis Leuba, L'infaillibilité, necessite de la foi et probleme de la raison.

Henri Gouhier, Infaillibilité et Nature.

Jean Brun, Libérations et délivrance. Le seuil de l'infaillible.

Xavier Tilliette, La vérité de Galilee, la vérité de Giordano Bruno.

Stanislas Breton, "Lumen naturae" et "lumen gratiae" dans le concept theologique d'infaillibilité.

Evandro Agazzi, Foi dans le Verbe ou foi dans la proposition?

Rene Marle, Dogme infailliblé et herméneutique.

Germano Pattaro, Infaillibilité et Foi.

Karl Kerényi, Problemes sur la Pythia.

Ernesto Grassi, L'infaillibilité: un probléme philosophique, langage et vision.

Donald M. MacKinnon, L'irrévocabilité en metaphysique en ethique et en theologie.

Antoine Vergote, L'infaillibilité entre le désir et le refus de savoir.

Anphonse De Waelhens, Reflexions philosophiques sur l'infaillibilite.

Gabriel Vahanian, Ecriture et Infaillibilité.

Raymond Panikkar, Le sujet de l'infaillibilité. Solipsisme et vérification.

Johannes Lotz, Problématique du "semel verum-semper verum."

Giulio Girardi, Infaillibilité et liberté.

Luis Alonso-Schokel, L'infaillibilité de l'oracle prophétique.

Georges C. Anawati, Le probleme de l'infaillibilité dans la pensee musulmanne.

Renzo Bertalo, Quelques considérations sur la notion de conscience dans le protestatisme contemporain.

Rubina Giorgi, L'infaillibilité et le discours de l'espérance.

Italo Mancini, Une hereméneutique infaillible a-t-elle sens?

Pietro Scapin, Fidélité et infaillibilité dans l'attitude du croyant.

Boris Ulianich, L'infaillibilité chez Luther jeune.

Andre Scrima, L'infaillibilité: inscription conceptuelle et destinée eschatologique.

Jerome Biblical Commentary. Edited by Raymond Brown, S.S., Joseph A. Fitzmyer, S.J., Roland E. Murphy, O. Cam. Englewood Cliffs, New Jersey, Prentice-Hall, 1968.

Karrer, O., *Peter and the Church*. An examination of Cullmann's thesis.
    8 Quaestiones Disputatae. Translated from the German by Ronald Walls. New York, Herder and Herder, 1963.

Kloppenburg, O.F.M., B. *Ecclesiology of Vatican II*, translated from the Portughese by Matthew O'Connell. Chicago, Franciscan Herald Press, 1974.

Kummel. W. G. *The New Testament: The History of the Investigation of Its Problems*, translated from the German by S. McLean Gilmour and Howard C. Kee. New York, Abingdon Press, 1972 (German edition, 1970).

Kung, Hans. *The Council, Reform and Reunion*. New York, Sheed and Ward, 1961.
    Structures of the Church, translated from the German by Salvator Attanasio. Notre Dame: Indiana, 1964.
    The Church, translated from the German by Ray and Rosaleen Ockendeen. New York, Sheed and Ward, 1967.
    Truthfulness: The Future of the Church, translated from the German by Edward Quinn. New York, Sheed and Ward, 1968.
    Post-Ecumenical Christianity, The New *Conciliam* edited by Hans Kung. New York, Herder and Herder, 1970.
    Infallible? An Inquiry, translated from the German by Edward Quinn. New York, Doubleday, 1971.
    Why Priests? A Proposal for a New Ministry, translated by Robert C. Collins, S.J. New York, Doubleday, 1972.

On Being a Christian, translated by Edward Quinn. New York, Doubleday, 1974.

Langford, O.P., J.J. *Galileo, Science and the Church*. New York, Desclee, 1966.

Lebreton, J. and Zeiller, J. *The History of the Primitive Church*, trans. from the French by E. Messenger. New York, 1949.

Maccarone, M. *Vicarious Christi*. Storia del titolo papale. Rome, Lateranum, Nova Series, XVIII, 1952.

Maitland, F. W. *Roman Canon Law in the Church of England*. London, Methuen, 1898.

Mann, H. K. *The Lives of the Popes in the Early Middle Ages*. Second edition, London, 1925.

Matthew. Introduction, translation and notes by W. F. Albright and C. S. Mann. New York, Doubleday, 1971.

McKenzie, S.J., J.L. *Dictionary of the Bible*. Milwaukee, Bruce Publishing Company, 1965.

Neill, S. *The Interpretation of the New Testament, 1861-1961*. London, Oxford, 1964.

New American Bible. Translated from the original languages with critical use of all the ancient sources by members of the Catholic Biblical Association of America. New York, Benziger, 1968.

New Catholic Commentary on Holy Scripture. Editors: Rev. Reginald C. Fuller, Rev. Leonard Johnston, Very Rev. Conleth Kearns. London, Nelson, 1953.

Newman, J. H. *The Arians of the Fourth Century*. London, Longmans, Green, 1901.
    Certain Difficulties Felt by Anglicans in Catholic Teaching, Vol. II. London, Longmans, Green, 1907.

Noonan, J. T. *The Scholastic Analysis of Usury*. Cambridge, Massachusetts, 1957.

Pastor, L. Von. *History of the Popes from the Close of the Middle Ages*. Trans. from the German by E. F. Peeler, 40 vols. St. Louis, Herder and Herder, 1891-1953.

Pirenne, H. A. *History of Europe*, 2 vols. Translated from the French by Bernard Miall. Originally published by University Books, Inc. in 1956. New York, Doubleday, 1958, Anchor Books edition.

Pope John XXIII. *Journal of a Soul*. Translated from the Italian by Dorothy White. New York, McGraw-Hill, 1964.

Quasten, J. *Patrology*, three vols. Maryland, Westminster, 1950-53.

Rahner, K. and Ratzinger, J. *The Episcopate and the Primacy*. London, Freiburg, 1962.

Ricciotti, G. *The History of Israel*, 2 vols. Translated from the Italian by Clement Della Penta, O.P. and Richard T. A. Murphy, O.P. Second edition. Milwaukee, Bruce Publishing Company, 1955.
    Paul the Apostle. Translated from the Italian by Alba I. Zizzamia. Milwaukee, Bruce Publishing Company, 1953.

Riviere, J. Le probléme de l'eglise et de l'etat au temps de Phillippe le Bel. Louvain, 1926.

Sacramentum Mundi. An Encyclopedia of Theology. Edited by Karl Rahner, Cornelius Ernst, and Kevin Smyth. 6 vols. New York, Herder and Herder, 1968-1970.

Sellers, R. V. *The Council of Chalcedon*. A historical and doctrinal survey. London, 1953.

Sixteen Documents of Vatican II. N.C.W.C. translation. Boston, Daughters of St. Paul, 1966.

Serviére, J. de la. Les anciennes missions de la Compagnie de Jesus en Chine. 1552-1814. Shanghai, 1925.

Tawney, R. H. *Religion and the Rise of Capitalism*. New York, 1958.

Thils, G. *L'infaillibilité pontificale*. Gembloux, editions J. Duculot, 1969.

Tierney, B. *Foundations of the Conciliar Theory*. The Contributions of the Medieval Canonists from Gratian to the Great Schism. Cambridge University Press: 1955.

Tixeront, J. *History of Dogmas*. 3 vols. Translated by H. L. Brianceau. St. Louis, 1910-1916.

Ullmann, W. The Growth of Papal Government in the Middle Ages. A study in the ideological relation of clerical to lay power. New York, Barnes and Noble, 1953.

Vaux, R. de. *Ancient Israel, Its Life and Institutions*. Translated by John McHugh. New York, McGraw-Hill, 1961.

Watt. J. A. *The Theory of Papal Monarchy in the Thirteenth Century*. New York, 1965.

APPENDIX A

PAPAL MAGISTERIUM AND "HUMANAE VITAE"

By virtue of the mandate entrusted to us by Christ.

Humanae Vitae (6)

This article is one priest's reflection upon a constellation of arguments enunciated by the dissident clerics who have denied the obligatory force of the encyclical, *Humanae Vitae*, upon the conscience of spouses. I have arranged them in a sort of logical procession as follows: the "changing concept of authority"; episcopal collegiality and the papal magisterium; the controversial question of the historical and doctrinal validity of *Humanae Vitae*; the matter of conscience; religious freedom. I am not unaware that other considerations may be attended to but I have limited myself to those arguments which are pointedly related by the dissident clerics to the Second Vatican Council as if to say that Pope Paul has by his doctrinal teaching on birth regulation turned his back upon the documents and spirit of that Synod and beclouded the *aggiornamento* they augured so hopefully. In a careful scrutiny of the Council documents,[1] I noted an intriguing silence about "theologians" which I thought may be construed as a telling commentary upon the role the dissident "theologians" claim to be rightfully their own within the magisterium of the Church.

Reprinted from *Thought*, Fordham University Quarterly, Vol. XLIV, No. 174, Autumn 1969.

Humanae Vitae is a definitive teaching of the authoritative and authentic interpreter of the divine and natural law and is therefore gravely binding in conscience.

[1] All references to the official texts promulgated by the Twentieth Ecumenical Council are to *Documents of Vatican II*. Ed. Walter Abbott, S. J. (America Press, 1966). All citations will be either to Abbott by pagination or to specific document and section number.

I

The Changing Concept of Authority

Sociologizing clerics exceed the bounds of pardonable presumption when they endeavor to impose human experiential constructs of authority upon the divine provision for salvation history. They see the concentration of papal authority as a quotient of history, in the succession of strong popes who fought to salvage a Christian society from the irruptive assaults of barbarian invasions, as the emergence of papal supremacy at the apex of power in a pattern of feudal society during vacuums of secular strength, particularly during the pontificates of Gregory VII, Innocent III, and Innocent IV. They see historical parallelism during the reign of lesser popes with the rise of autocratic emperors and kings—Clovis, Charlemagne, the Otto's, and so on. These historicist perspectives confuse the fortunes and vicissitudes of institutional growth and involvement in human events with the papal office itself, its origin, and its scope, by adumbrating all human experiences within a naturalist monism. The papal apostolic mission, its teaching authority and jurisdiction, rests wholly upon a divine mandate. It is a supernatural fact. It is not a natural fact either as a response to the exigencies of the natural moral law nor is it the contrivance and resultant of purely conflicting and emergent historical forces. The papacy manifests itself in its institutional extension and multiplicity of auxiliary agencies in divers ways in history but the origin of the papal office itself and its divinely endowed empowerments are not the product of nor subject to the laws of historicism. It has no human equivalent or parallel among the wide range of social and political institutions. The papal office is unique in origin (immediate divine establishment), unique in its nature (divinely commissioned to teach the ways of eternal salvation and to administer the sacraments of sanctification), unique in character (a permanent office, enduring to the end of time), unique in its prerogatives (the warrant against errancy in matters of faith and morals), unique in the exercise and extent of its jurisdiction (plenary, universal, unconditioned by any dependency upon human agencies for the validity of its authentic and authoritative teaching).

Political authority is from God but in the absence of a divine revelation manifesting a direct designation by God, the recipient of authority, the manner and condition of its exercise, are constructs of human contrivance. It is human in the presuppositions of its actual exercise (the consensual and contractual basis), human in the definition, distribution, and assignation of offices (constitutionalism), human in the *de iure* extension of popular participation (democratization), human in enlarged popular accountability (representative governance), human in the delegation and limitation placed upon active governing authority (popular sovereignty). Centuries of political speculation and experience in the West have forged a variety of political and legal instrumentalities, to preclude the exercise of arbitrary power. The sociologizing clerics who look for analogous expansion and distribution of papal authority in the government of the Church delve into history but they do so without benefit of the Christian vision.

II

Episcopal Collegiality and Papal Magisterium

There is no distinction between the Roman Pontiff and the bishops taken collectively, but between the Roman Pontiff by himself and the Roman Pontiff together with the bishops (cf. Appendix to *Lumen Gentium*).

In the celebrated third chapter of the *Dogmatic Constitution on the Church (Lumen Gentium)*, the Second Vatican Council gave expression to the doctrinal formulation of the collegiality of bishops. The more one studies the document, the more firmly the conviction grows that in the act of affirming the collegiality of bishops, the Synod was reaffirming the primacy and infallibility of the Pope as Peter's successor with a greater sharpness—if that were possible —than had Vatican I. Two dogmatic professions emerge: one, the plenary, supreme teaching authority of the Roman Pontiff in matters of faith and morals, whether solemnly exercised infallibly *ex cathedra* or otherwise officially expressed rests wholly and exclusively upon the mandate entrusted by Christ to Peter and his successors as His vicars upon the earth. It is independent, unconditioned by any dependency upon the approval or consent of others within the Church. Second, the authenticity and authority of the magisterial functions of a bishop or severalty of bishops is wholly contingent upon union and agreement with the Roman Pontiff. I for one cannot completely suppress the deep lingering conjecture that the doctrinal formulation of the collegiality of bishops as successors to the Apostles in their union with Peter provided the occasion to remove whatever dim doubts may have endured about the definition of papal infallibility and primacy in the First Vatican Council. Repeatedly without exception as if to foreclose any faint supposition to the contrary that a strict literalist might seize upon, every mention of the episcopal college is conjoined with such expressions as "in union with," "in communion with," "joined together with," "unity with," "together with," "only with the consent of," "in agreement with," the Roman Pontiff. Those who would infer from episcopal collegiality a diffusion of papal authority among co-participants, a dependence of the papal magisterium upon a collective episcopal consensus, a diminution of its independence, are reasoning from prepossessions wholly at variance with the Council Fathers themselves to whose documents they make such facile rhetorical reference. The practical consequence logically inherent in the doctrinal formula of the college of bishops is to rein into unity with the Roman Pontiff the magisterium office of every bishop.

But the college or body of bishops has no authority unless it is simultaneously conceived of in terms of its head, the Roman Pontiff, Peter's successor, and without any lessening of his power of primacy over all, pastors as well as the general faithful. For in virtue of his office, that is, as Vicar of Christ and pastor of the whole Church, the Roman Pontiff has full, supreme, and universal power over the Church. And he can always exercise this power freely.

The order of bishops is the successor to the college of the apostles in teaching authority and pastoral rule; or, rather, in the episcopal order the apostolic body continues without a break. Together with its head, the Roman pontiff, and never without its head, the episcopal order is the subject of supreme and full power over the universal Church. But this power can be exercised only with the consent of the Roman Pontiff. For Our Lord made Simon Peter alone the rock and keybearer of the Church (cf. Mt. 16:18-19), and appointed him shepherd of the whole flock (cf. Jn. 21:15 ff.) (*Lumen Gentium*, 22).

The dependence of union and consensual agreement is always on the part of the bishop with the Vicar of Christ, and not vice versa.[2]

---

[2]Cf. Abbott, *op. cit.*, 98-101.

III
Humanae Vitae

We had no doubt about Our duty to give Our decision in
the terms expressed in the present Encyclical . . . . We hoped
that our scholars especially would be able to discover in the
document the genuine thread that connects it with the Christian
concept of life and which permits Us to make Our own the
words of St. Paul: "But we have the mind of Christ" (1 Cor. 2:
16) (General Audience at Castel Gandolfo, July 31, 1968).

Historical Conspectus

John J. Noonan, author of *Contraception, A History of Treatment
by the Catholic Theologians and Canonists*, and one who augured a
diverse papal pronouncement from *Humanae Vitae*, acknowledged
in 1965: "No Catholic writer before 1963 had asserted that the general prohibition of contraception was wrong."[3]
The early Church opposed the rampant practice of contraception
in Roman society, a practice usually in the form of *coitus interruptus*
or by crude drugs, as well as abortion and infanticide. In the catalogue of mortal sins listed under the way of Death in *Didache* 5. 2,
the first-century summary of the teachings of the Apostles for the
catechumens, is the extinction of life by contraceptive drugs (*pharmakeia*) and abortion ("child-murderers"). The same condemnation
reappears in the *Epistle to Barnabas* 20.2, an early second-century
document. Clement of Alexandria denounced contraceptive methods
in unmistakable language. "Because of its divine institution for the
propagation of man, the seed is not to be vainly ejaculated, nor is it
to be damaged, nor is it to be wasted" (*Paedogogus* 2, 10, 91, 2).
Marcus Minucius Felix strongly denounced the use by the pagan women of contraceptive or abortifacient drugs which "extinguish the
beginning of a future man, and before they bear, commit parricide"
(*Ocatvius* 30.2). Lactantius numbers among evil carnal acts those
with contraceptive effects (*Divinae Institutiones*, 6.20.25). St. Justin
wrote, "We Christians either marry only to produce children, or, if
we refuse to marry, are completely continent" (*Apologia*, 1.29).
Athenagoras wrote to Marcus Aurelius and to Commodus in defense
of the morality of Christians that they marry only to produce chil-

---

[3] John T. Noonan, *Contraception: A History of Its Treatment by Catholic Theologians and Canonists* (Belknap Press of Harvard University, 1965), p. 512.

dren and thereby implicitly excluded any marital act to the contrary (*Legatio pro Christianis*, 33). Opposition to Christian doctrine came mainly from the Gnostics in the second century, the Manichaeans in the fourth, and the Cathari in the twelfth and thirteenth centuries. Condemnations of contraceptive drugs do not, comparatively speaking, appear as frequently as those of carnal actions with contraceptive effects. But preventive interference with the life-giving process in marriage is often denounced together with abortion and murder to stress, it would seem, the moral depravity of such actions. On the other hand, there is absence of any evidence of an official and authoritative teaching of the Church that would permit on occasion for exceptional reasons a single contraceptive act as morally correct within a habitual and general commitment by the spouses to the procreative purpose of marriage. Lactantius does raise the problem of the Christian who cannot support a large family and the only alternative he points to is continence (*Divinae institutiones*, 6.20.25).

The sacrality of marriage and its carnal union was expressed in its most exalted terms in St. Paul's Epistle to the Ephesians, 5:25-33, wherein the spouses' love for one another is projected against Christ's love for His Church. The "inseparable connection" and essentially equal terms of the interrelationship between the "two meanings of the conjugal act," the unitive and procreative, which *Humanae Vitae* affirmed against the subordination of one to the other (*H.V.* 12), has its strongest scriptural basis in the Pauline Epistle and among patristic writings in St. John Chrysostom's *Homily 20 on Ephesians*. But the prevailing teaching of the Church for centuries to come—most likely in response to the heterodox concepts of marriage and procreation taught by the Gnostics, Manichaeans, and the Pelagians—was based on St. Augustine's threefold purposes of marriage—*proles, fides, sacramentum* (*De bono matrimonii* 29.32). The primary and principal purpose is procreation, then, a bond of mutual indebtedness to supply one another's needs, and thirdly, the indissolubility of marriage double reinforced by the Christian sacrament. This doctrinal teaching insisted on the sacral nature of the marital act even as it was posited, as indeed all of man was, within the mystery of Original Sin, the disobedient body and its consequences. In recent times, down to the Second Vatican Council, some moral theologians advocated the primacy of love in marriage which, while committed habitually to procreation, might allow single conjugal acts to be rendered intentionally infecund for exceptional reasons with full regard for the totality of the matrimonial good.

Humanae Vitae rejected the supposition of the subordination of one to the other by affirming categorically the equally essential inter-relationship of the meanings of the conjugal act, the unitive and the procreative.

Down to 1930, all Christian churches proscribed artificial birth regulation as a moral evil. Historically, it was the predominantly Protestant-controlled legislatures in some countries which enacted public laws against the manufacture, distribution, and sale of contraceptive devices. At the Lamberth Conference of 1930 the Anglican bishops were the first to break with its traditional opposition and to permit the artificial regulation of births. Since then, the Anglican Church and other Protestant churches have come to advocate planned parenthood as a duty and, through succeeding years, to allow a narrowly restricted permissiveness for permanent sterilization, and even under the most compelling reasons, abortion and infanticide. In England, these ecclesiastical relaxations of conjugal sexual morality have become embodied into public laws which on their face are sufficiently broad and elastic to withstand most objections to the contrary.

On December 31, 1930, Pope Pius XI promulgated the encyclical *Casti Connubii*, the most authoritative papal pronouncement on contraception since the bull, *Effraenatam*, of Pope Sixtus V in 1588. After discoursing about the divine institution of marriage, its beauty, and multiple blessings, Pius XI turns to the reasons generally given to justify the "criminal abuse" of the conjugal act by frustrating the generative intent of the act of intercourse.

> But no reason, however grave, may be put forward by which anything intrinsically against nature may become conformable to nature and morally good. Since, therefore, the conjugal act is destined primarily by nature for the begetting of children, those who in exercising it deliberately frustrate its natural effect and purpose, sin against nature and commit a deed which is shameful and intrinsically vicious.

After noting the action of the Anglican bishops, he contrasts the steadfastness of the Catholic Church to integrity of doctrine for which she had been divinely commissioned.

> The Catholic Church, to whom God had entrusted the defense of the integrity and purity of morals, standing erect in

the midst of the moral ruin which surrounds her, in order that she may preserve the chastity of the nuptial union from being defiled by this foul stain, raises her voice in token of her divine ambassadorship and through Our mouth proclaims anew: *any use whatsoever of matrimony exercised in such a way that the act is deliberately frustrated in its natural power to generate life is an offense against the law of God and of nature, and those who indulge in such are branded with the guilt of grave sin (AAS, 22:559-560)* (italics added).[4]

The general proscription—"any use of marriage whatever"— would seem to be all-inclusive of every act directly related to the coital act itself. However, in the constructive interpretation of a moral or legal prohibition, the moral agent is held to the narrow interpretation. The prohibition in *Casti Connubii* could be restricted to an action (*coitus interruptus*) or mechanical device used by either spouse so that seminal intromission or fecundation can be obstructed in the act of intercourse. Whatever doubts were entertained about the range of the prohibition were removed by Pope Pius XII when in his Allocution to the Italian Catholic Society of Midwives on October 29, 1951, he rephrased the doctrinal teaching of *Casti Connubii* so as to state explicitly the inclusion of postcoital interference with the natural prospects of fecundation.

Our predecessor, Pius XI, of happy memory, in his encyclical *Casti Connubii*, December 31, 1930, solemnly proclaimed anew the fundamental law governing the marital act and conjugal relations; that any attempt on the part of the married people to deprive this act of its inherent force and to impede the procreation of new life, either in the performance of the act itself *or in the course of the development of its natural consequences*, is immoral (*nello sviluppo delle sue consequenze naturali*);

---

[4]For the various theological notes ascribed to *Casti Connubii*, cf. Ford and Kelly, *Contemporary Moral Theology* (2 vols., Newman Press, 1964), Vol. II, 245-254. Of particular interest is Noonan's own appraisal, *op. cit.*, p. 428: "How great was that authority? By the ordinary tests used by theologians to determine whether a doctrine is infallibly proclaimed, it may be argued that the specific condemnation of contraceptive interruption of the procreative act is infallibly proclaimed. The encyclical is addressed to the universal Church. The Pope speaks in fulfillment of his apostolic office. He speaks for the Church. He speaks on moral doctrine that he says 'has been transmitted from the beginning.' He 'promulgates' the teaching. If the Pope did mean to use the full authority to speak *ex cathedra* on morals, which Vatican I recognized as his, what further language could he have used?"

and no alleged "indication" or need can convert an intrinsically immoral act into a moral and lawful one.

This precept is as valid today as it was yesterday; and it will be the same tomorrow and always; because it does not imply a precept of the human law, but is the expression of a law which is natural and divine (*AAS*, 43:843) (italics added).

The explicit proscription of postcoital frustration of the natural prospects of intercourse is stated calculatedly in such a manner as to indicate that the Roman Pontiff is not adding to the proscriptions of *Casti Connubii* but explicitating what was immanent within the comprehensive phrase "any use whatsoever of matrimony." Even more notable is the subsumption of both coital and postcoital abuses under one and the same precept, whose irrevocability is spelt out in an all-exhaustive temporal dimension, "valid yesterday, today, tomorrow, always." In a radio broadcast, March 23, 1952, Pope Pius XII referred to his earlier statement as an illustration of the Roman Pontiff "intervening authoritatively in moral questions" (*AAS*, 44:275).

A third question, a precoital action calculated to render the conjugal act temporarily infecund, was doubly compounded by the development of the prestigerone pill which was equally effective to induce contraceptive sterilization as well as correct an irregular ovulatory cycle. On September 12, 1958, Pope Pius XII in an Address to the Hematologists addressed himself to the new moral problem: "Is it licit to prevent ovulation by means of pills used as remedies for exaggerated reactions of the uterus and of the organism, although this medication, by preventing ovulation, also makes fecundation impossible?" His authoritative response was an application of the principle of double effect. The intake of the drug with the direct intent of preventing pregnancy was direct sterilization and therefore "illicit." But if the use of the drug is motivated primarily to the correction of an ovulatory irregularity it was permissible even if it interdicted temporarily the prospects of fecundation. In a word, the moral condemnation falls equally upon temporary contraceptive sterilization as in the case of anovulatory drugs as it does upon direct and permanent sterilization as with vasectomy and salpingectomy (*AAS* 50: 732-740).

Publication in 1963 of *The Time Has Come*, by Dr. John Rock, a Catholic and an eminent American gynecologist, brought to the surface a controversy that had seemingly quieted with Pope Pius XII's pronouncement of 1958. Dr. Rock contended that when a woman makes a conscious decision to swallow Enovid pills she is simply allowing the brain to start a natural suppressive process that other body systems bring about automatically in other circumstances, and like the rhythm method, not an unnatural means of birth regulation. The real difference, he maintained, between Catholics and non-Catholics was only over method rather than objective. But, as his own bishop, Richard Cardinal Cushing, noted, the qualifying word "only" was, in this instance, an absolute and not a comparative adjective.

On September 29, 1963, the second session of the Vatican Council convened. Publication of articles and books by the laity, clerics, and ecclesiastical authorities, and speeches by Melkite Patriarch Maximos IV, Cardinal Suenens of Belgium and Cardinal Leger of Montreal at the Council, urged reconsideration of the Church's teaching on birth control. Both Pope John XXIII and Pope Paul VI in the spirit of *aggiornamento* had stressed the need of baring, as it were, the place and role of the Church in the contemporary world to the broad daylight of view for all to see, and the fearless confrontation with the moral problems that weighed heavily upon all mankind. The highly sensitive nature of the question with its many complexities explains in part the withdrawal of it from general discourse by the Fathers of the Council and entrusting the problem for a thorough study to a papal commission. The ultimate and final judgment was to be given by the Roman Pontiff. Unfortunately, the open discussion of the moral question suggested in some quarters that birth control was at its inner core an open question. It was hardly a difficult step to advance to *lex dubia non obligat* and the cauistry of *probabilism*. When some confidently foretold a change in Church teaching, the Holy Father concerned over their effect upon the consciences of the faithful felt compelled to warn against such presumptive misconstructions placed upon the interlude of "study and reflection."

A controversy of sorts was generated on whether a practical doubt had been engendered prior to *Humanae Vitae*, a controversy which still is simmering.[5] After examining the succession of statements made by the Holy Father, we are persuaded that there never

---

[5]Cf. Ford and Lynch, "Contraception: A Matter of Practical Doubt?," *Linacre Quarterly*, August 1968, 159-171. For the opposing view, cf. "Notes On Moral Theology," *Theological Studies*, December 1968, 718-725, by Richard A. McCormick, S.J. cf. David Fitch, S.J., "*Humanae Vitae* and Reasonable Doubt," *Homiletic and Pastoral Review*, April 1969, Vol. LXIX, No. 7, pp. 516-523.

was any personal doubt in the mind of Pope Paul on the immutability of the norms set down by his predecessors, Pius XI and Pius XII. At the same time, we acknowledge that in one or two instances of categorical affirmation of the enduring obligatory force of those norms, Pope Paul also gives expression to a time dimension—"as long as," "until now," "not now in a state of doubt." Our own conclusions are that none of the categorical reaffirmations is weakened by these temporal allusions; that the time element must be related to the interlude of "study and reflection"; that the temporal waiting period preceding *Humanae Vitae* was not expressive of any personal hesitance but a necessary incidence of and a respectful attendance upon the studies which his predecessor, Pope John, and he had initiated. The doubts that were fostered may be attributed to two principal causes: first, to the awkward, unavoidable and circumstanced conjunction of declaring firmly adherence to the traditional norms and at the same time putting off the solemnity of a formal declaration until after the commission's reports were completed and studied. And, secondly, to the excessive confidence of those spokesmen who publicly foretold the novel direction of the papal teaching. It is to this latter factor that the major responsibility of engendering a practical doubt in the minds of the faithful must be attributed as well as the painful spiritual consequences that have endured to this day.

A word is in order about the facile reference to *probabilism* and to *lex dubia non obligat*. Probabilism simply points to the lack of conclusive persuasion that an alleged law is known with such certainty as to preclude some reasonable intellectual doubts. Probabilism admits that in choosing to act contrary to an alleged law, the individual may be materially if not formally violating the law. But the saving grace of probabilism is that the moral agent who chooses to act contrary to the alleged law does so prudently, not unreasonably. If, then, as we hold, Pope Paul held steadfast to the proscriptions against contraceptives set down in *Casti Connubii* and repeated by Pius XII, then reliance upon probabilism prior to *Humanae Vitae* seems to us unwarranted. A *lex dubia non obilgat* is a contradiction in terms. If it is a law it has some obligatory force. If it is doubtful, then obviously we have no law except by extrinsic connotation. The expression "doubtful law" is permissible in the philosophical inquest into the order of morality and its exigencies. Probabilism, on the contrary, allows that some hold to the existence of an alleged law and to its substantive meaning while others are not as fully convinced. Probabilism is related to the consensus of the professional moralist.

Papal Magisterium and the Natural Moral Law

> No believer will wish to deny that the teaching authority of the Church is competent to interpret even the natural moral law. It is, in fact, indisputable, as our predecessors have many times declared, that Jesus Christ, when communicating to Peter and to the Apostles His divine authority and sending them to teach all nations His commandments, constituted them as guardians and authentic interpreters of all moral law, not only, that is, of the law of the Gospel, but also of the natural law, which is also an expression of the will of God, the faithful fulfillment of which is equally necessary for salvation (*H.V.* 4).

The use of oral contraceptives was the specific issue upon which the general principle of *Casti Connubii* was brought to bear in *Humanae Vitae*. This was done by a fresh and authoritative insistence on the competency of the papal magisterium to be an authentic interpreter of all the moral law, by virtue of the mandate of Christ to Peter and his successors. We think that this forceful confirmation of what in fact had been also affirmed by previous Pontiffs will emerge as a principal doctrinal teaching of the encyclical no less than the specific ruling on the pill.

Historically, references to the natural moral law are more frequently found in Church documents since the pontificate of Pius IX than in earlier Church history. At the Synod of Arles (475 A.D.) Lucidus, the presbyter, submitted to a rejection of his erroneous teaching by admitting to the divine providence of salvation for those who lived before Christ.

> Assero etiam per tationem et ordinem saeculorum alios lege gratiae, alios lege Moysi, alios lege naturae, quam Deus in omnium cordibus scripsit, in spe adventus Christi fuisse salvatos (H. Denzinger, *Enchiridion Symbolorum*, ed. 1948, p. 76).

Medieval popes intervened in temporalities *ratione peccati, ratione justitiae* with practically illimitable powers of adjudication on the morality of every conceivable human activity. While the medievalists, William Auxerre, Albert the Great, and St. Thomas Aquinas, developed a natural-law philosophy solely within the purview of human reason, their contemporaries generally made mention of natural law either in terms of the theologians' hyphenation of the natural-revelational moral theology or the canonists' amalgam of natural-supernatural (scriptural), juristic constructs. There is notably greater reliance upon natural law in the papal encyclicals of the nineteenth and twentieth centuries. This was undoubtedly required by the very nature of the questions touching upon the political order (the State, education, communism, Nazism, fascism, conduct of war), social (racial relations), economic (labor conditions, wages, underdeveloped nations), familial (conjugal relations, indissolubility of marriage), and medico-moral problems. Invariably, mention of the natural law is accompanied by reference to "Christian wisdom," "Christian vision," "supernatural," "the teachings of Christ," "the evangelical," and so on. The competence of the magisterium to proclaim authoritatively not only in dogma but also on the entire moral law is affirmed repeatedly without restriction and unconditionally. In addition, necessity for the exercise of this ecclesial authority as an indispensable assist to human reason is explained with particular relevance to conjugal relations by Pope Pius XI in *Casti Connubii*.

This conformity of wedlock and moral conduct with the divine laws respecting marriage . . . supposes, however, that all can discern readily, with real certainty, and without any accompanying error, what those laws are. But everyone can see to how many fallacies an avenue would be opened up and how many errors would become mixed with the truth, if it were left solely to the light of reason of each to find out or if it were to be discovered by the private interpretation of the truth which is revealed. And if this is applicable to many other truths of the moral order, we must pay attention all the more to those things which appertain to marriage, where the inordinate desire for pleasure can attack frail human nature and easily deceive it and lead it astray. This is all the more true of the observance of the divine law, which demands sometimes hard and repeated sacrifices, for which, as experience points out, a weak man can find so many excuses for avoiding the fulfillment of the divine law.

On this account, in order that no falsification or corruption of the divine law but a true genuine knowledge of it may enlighten the minds of men and guide their conduct, it is necessary that a filial and humble obedience towards the Church should be combined with devotedness to God and the desire of submitting to Him. For Christ Himself made the Church the teacher of truth in those things also which concern the ruling and regulation of moral conduct, even though some things are not of themselves impervious to human reason. For just as God in the case of the natural truths of religion and morality added revelation to the light of reason so that these things which are right and true, "in the present state also of the human race may be known readily with real certaintly without any admixture of error," so for the same purpose He has constituted the Church the guardian and the teacher of the whole of the truth concerning religion and moral conduct (*AAS* 22:579-80. 1930).

In *Humanae Vitae*, the God-given authority to interpret the entire moral law, the invariable conjunction of the natural and supernatural, and the necessity for the papal teaching to provide certitude to a fallible reason are expressed with a stress and emphasis that goes beyond preceding encyclicals. This triple interrelationship is central to the full force of *Humanae Vitae*. We are not being invited to accept an argument based on natural law but to acknowledge that the teaching of the Church on birth regulation be accepted precisely because it is the divinely established teacher who is interpreting the law of God.[6] St. Matthew records an encounter of Our Lord with the Pharisees (19:1-12) that illustrates the moral necessity of Christian revelation that reason may know with certitude and free of all error those religious and moral truths which are not of their nature beyond its purview but which the passions of a disobedient body, the consequences of original and personal sin, and genuine burdens of the human condition, keep from admitting more readily. The Pharisees argued that a man could put away his wife because Moses had

---

[6]Cf. Pope Pius XII, *Humani Generis*: ". . . though absolutely speaking, human reason by its own force and light can arrive at a true and certain knowledge of the one personal God . . . and also of the natural law, which the Creator has written in our hearts, still there are not a few obstacles to prevent reason from making efficient and fruitful use of its natural ability. The truths that have to do with God and the relations between God and men completely surpass the sensible order and demand self-surrender and self-abnegation in order to be put into practice and to influence practical life. Now the human intellect, in gaining knowledge of such truths, is hampered both by the activity of the senses and the imagination, and by evil passions arising from original sin. Hence men easily persuade themselves in such matters that what they do not wish to believe is false or at least doubtful. It is for this reason that divine revelation must be considered morally necessary so that those religious and moral truths which are not of their nature beyond the reach of reason in the present condition of the human race may be known with a firm certainty and with freedom from all error" (*AAS* 42 [1950], 561-62).

permitted it. Our Lord replied that marriage was indissoluble ("What God hath joined together, let no man put asunder"), that Moses had granted permission for divorce "because of the hardness of your heart," but *from the beginning it was not so*." When His own disciples remonstrated that some marriages may be exceedingly difficult, Our Lord offered as an alternative to marriage an invitation to practice chastity for a supernatural motive ("for the kingdom of heaven"). So too, the Vicar of Christ, by virtue of that charisma that is the unique prerogative of his office may, like his Divine Master, authoritatively propound an authentic interpretation of the natural moral law that many may find difficult to accept and follow.

The Principle of Totality

> Each and every marriage act (*quilibet matrimonii usus*) must remain open to the transmission of life (11).

The prevailing tradition dating from patristic times that held procreation to be the primary purpose of marriage has in recent decades been counterbalanced by an increasing emphasis upon conjugal love as the principal objective of matrimony. Not every conjugal act results in fecundation and there are many marriages among the young and old that are sterile. The tendency to view these two essential meanings of matrimony as competing with one another found some reconciliation in the suggestion that the marital status be considered as a totality with an overarching good to which individual acts of conjugal relations be related. Within this principle of totality a way was thought to be found to correct certain deviations tending to elevate conjugal love to the detriment of the procreative end of marriage and, on the other hand, to explain more satisfactorily natural sterility, temporary or permanent, in accord with the connatural intent of procreation. The practical consequence of this concept of totality would warrant the hypothesis that an individual act of marital intercourse might be morally permissible even though the prospects of procreation were intentionally precluded by the spouses for grave considerations provided that the totality of married life was sincerely governed by a habitual intention to beget children. *Humanae Vitae* takes explicit cognizance of this question when it asks: "Could it not be admitted, that is, that the finality of procreation pertains to the ensemble of conjugal life, rather than to its single acts?" The dogmatic response is, in the words of *Casti Connubii* and of Pius XII, "each and every marriage act must remain open to the transmission of life." If marriage is not merely for procreation, it is not and cannot be merely for conjugal love. Each and every marital act is an inviolable and indissoluble totality in itself of true conjugal love.

That teaching, often set forth by the magisterium, is founded upon the inseparable connection, willed by God and unable to be broken by man on his own initiative, between the two meanings of the conjugal act: the unitive meaning and the procreative meaning. Indeed, by its intimate structure, the conjugal act, while most closely uniting husband and wife, capacitates them for the generation of new lives, according to laws inscribed in the very being of man and of woman. By safeguarding both these essential aspects, the unitive and the procreative, the conjugal act preserves in its fullness the sense of true mutual love and its ordination towards man's most high calling to parenthood (12).

A marital act is devoid of the fullness of true mutual love if it is not performed with the intent of the spouses to give by that very act the supreme gift of love to one another, the similitude of one another's being. In this, then, marital love is distinguishable pre-eminently for its superiority to other expressions of love between humans which are made manifest by loyalty, assistance, the exchange of material and spiritual gifts. Conjugal love intends to give without reservation what one is, his very being to the procreation of a similitude common to and generated by both spouses.

The Holy Father disallows the relevance of the principle of totality, which is applicable in medical surgery when a part of the body is sacrificed for the good of the whole, to matrimonial relations. Such a parallelism ignores the fact that the concept of nature is analogous. The conjugal act is itself a totality. It may not be trifled with; it can only be intentionally fulfilled connaturally or frustrated arbitrarily. Those dissident clerics who charge that the encyclical focuses upon the biological function of the marital act are less than fair in their criticism. The biological function of marital communion could hardly have been invested with greater spiritual significance, with a more personalist dedication of the spouses, with a more elevated cooperation of human providence with the divine.

One who reflects well must also recognize that a reciprocal

act of love, which jeopardizes the responsibility to transmit life which God the Creator, according to particular laws, inserted therein, is in contradiction with the design constitutive of marriage, and with the will of the Author of life. To use this divine gift destroying, even if only partially, its meaning and its purpose is to contradict the nature both of man and of woman and of their most intimate relationship, and therefore it is to contradict also the plan of God and His will. On the other hand, to make use of the gift of conjugal love while respecting the laws of the generative process means to acknowledge oneself not to be the arbiter of the sources of human life, but rather the minister of the design established by the Creator (13).

A Doctrinal Teaching

Amen, Amen, I say unto you . . . thou shalt, . . . thou shalt not. . . .

Between the faithful who have given "religious submission of will and mind . . . to the authentic teaching authority of the Roman Pontiff, even when he is not speaking ex cathedra" (*Lumen Gentium,* 25) and the dissidents who challenge the obligatory force of *Humanae Vitae*, as the principal informant of a correct conscience on birth regulation, a third group has been emerging. On the one hand, they insist that they do give deference and loyalty to papal authority and, on the other, they try to mitigate the literal and explicit absoluteness of the proscriptions of *Humanae Vitae*. They do this either by (i) refusing to take seriously the dogmatic language in which the doctrinal teaching is unambiguously expressed, or by (ii) weakening the binding force of the doctrinal propositions by an evaluation of the merits of the intrinsic argumentation of the encyclical, or by (iii) mitigating the condemnations of contraceptive intercourse in the light of the pastoral counsels set down by Pope Paul in the third and concluding part of the encyclical. This third group differentiates itself from the outright dissident clerics by maintaining that *Humanae Vitae* gave expression to a prudent, positive, ennobling ideal which the spouses should strive to realize in their conjugal relations. In other words, they seem to say, Pope Paul did not authoritatively propound an authentic doctrinal teaching on marital relations to be followed in the daily lives of the married. This ingenious construction, we respectfully submit, can work to an earnest self-deception. It does violence to the language of moral condemnations of the encyclical and, as a principle of interpretive exegesis, will work no less havoc with other doctrinal teachings of the Church.

(i) "manifest mind and will" (*Lumen Gentium*, 25)

> In conformity with these landmarks in the human and Christian vision of marriage, we must once again declare that the direct interruption of the generative process already begun, and above all, directly willed and procured abortion, even if for therapeutic reasons, are to be absolutely excluded as licit means of regulating birth.
>
> Equally to be excluded, as the teaching authority of the Church has frequently declared, is direct sterilization, whether perpetual or temporary, whether of the man or of the woman. Similarly excluded is every action which, either in anticipation of the conjugal act, or in its accomplishment, or in the development of its natural consequences, purposes, whether as an end or as a means, to render procreation impossible (14).

The language is so absolute and exclusionary as to fulfill every rigid requirement for a dogmatic and incontrovertible doctrinal teaching. There is no specific mention of the "pill" to avoid pregnancy but its proscription is undoubted. The malice of preventive contraception is underscored by equating its proscription with the moral condemnation of abortion. The all-comprehensive statement of *Casti Connubii*, "any use whatsoever of matrimony," which condemned at least coital contraception, and which Pope Pius XII explicitated to include postcoital defeat of the "natural consequences" of conjugal relations, now is elaborated to comprehend precoital preventive contraception, "in anticipation of the conjugal act." The spiritual malice of "the use of means directly contrary to fecundation" (16) is declared to be "intrinsically disorder," "intrinsically evil" (14), and "always illicit" (16). To construe these absolute, exclusionary moral propositions, however posited in a constellation of relevant considerations, into something less than doctrinal teaching is to do violence to "the manifest mind and will" of the Roman Pontiff.

(ii) "by virtue of the mandate entrusted to us by Christ" (*H.V.* 6)

It has been noted in some quarters that since the encyclical makes several references to the natural moral law, might not the faithful rightly raise epistemological questions which respectfully may challenge the intrinsic validity of the natural-law reasoning as embodied in the encyclical. But, reference to the natural moral law in *Humanae Vitae* is invariably conjoined with revelation, which, as we have already noted earlier, has also been true in the encyclicals of preceding Pontiffs. For example, "a teaching founded on the natural law, illuminated and enriched by divine revelation" (4), "human and Christian vision of marriage" (14), "the entire moral law, both natural and evangelical" (18), "natural and divine law" (23, 25), "the fullness of conjugal love" as illustrated by Christ's love for the Church (25), "to diminish in no way the saving teaching of Christ" (29), the "holiness of marriage, lived in its entire human and Christian fullness" (29), and so on. This conjunction of the natural moral law with the supernatural is not merely additive in the sense that in the present frail condition of mankind it is a morally necessary corrective to the discernments of reason alone of the exigencies of the natural law. The natural moral law is part of God's will for the salvation of mankind revealed through the Incarnate Word who designated Peter and the apostles and their successors to the end of time as guardians and authentic interpreters of all the moral law. The Church, then, may teach the requirements of the natural law with the assistance of Christian revelation authoritatively and provide the faithful with a more reliable moral doctrine than can be ascertained by unaided natural reason. This is not to deny that fallen man can by reason alone rationally demonstrate the existence of the natural law, nor to suggest that the Church is indifferent to the instructions of reason on the moral law. We are simply affirming that when the Church teaches authoritatively matters of natural morality, it does not do so as a master metaphysician any more than did Peter and the apostles. For centuries the faithful were guided by the authentic and authoritative teaching of the Church without benefit of philosophical systems and the science of theology, and until the Council of Nicaea, without solemn definitions. This is the profound significance of the repeated reference in *Humanae Vitae* to the Church's constant apostolic teaching through time. The validity of her teaching rests primarily on Christ's commission to her and on the abiding assistance of the Holy Spirit. The encyclical does make its appeal to reason, it discourses in part of the biological process, of demography, of the demoralizing consequences of contraceptive practices, of the nature of conjugal love. But the internal and external obedience of the faithful is directed to the doctrine propounded by reason "of the mandate entrusted by Christ" (6) to the Church. It is not dependent upon nor proportioned to the intrinsic merits of the encyclical as a philosophical argumentation, as a scientific treatise, as a sociological tract. Like his divine Master, the Vicar of Christ does make an appeal to reason (as well as to the Christian vision and the charismatic teaching authority of the Church). But also in the manner of his Lord, he too may teach, "Amen, amen, I say unto you. Thou shalt . . . thou shalt not. . . ."

There is more impression than substance in pointing to the distinction between the infallibility of a solemn *ex cathedra* definition and the authentic and authoritative teaching of the Roman Pontiff. The insinuating argument is that what is not formally infallible is fallible. It supposes that infallibility may not derive from another source than a solemn *ex cathedra* definition. Church documents and the "theologians" themselves have traditionally acknowledged an infallibility *ex ordinario magisterio*. This means more than mere longevity but a continuing active and constant witness of the teaching authority of the Church to the general moral principle that opposes all contraceptive practices, the novelty being only its authoritative application to specific problems as they emerged in time. Further, who could honestly question the gravity and solemnity of the historical occasion for *Humanae Vitae*? The world-wide expectation of the papal pronouncement by the faithful and non-faithful alike, the critical nature of the controversy, the largely predictable divisive consequences—all these attest to the awesome responsibility with which Pope Paul has spoken.

There was really no need for the formality of an *ex cathedra* definition.[7] The Roman Pontiff was giving witness to the constant

---

[7]In Church documents, the expression *sedes Apostolica* repeatedly appears to signify the supremacy of papal authority within the Church and when conjoined with *Petrus* and his successors, to signalize the unique and exclusive charism of infallibility with which the Roman Pontiff is invested upon succeeding to the "chair." The Greek form, *Cathedra* (the teacher's chair), obtains its most notable context in the definition of papal infallibility by the Fathers of Vatican I. The historical thrust of the 1870 phrase *cum ex cathedra loquitur* was to reject the separatism between *sedes* and *sedens* which the Gallicans of the 17th century employed to contend that the particular occupant of that supreme office shares in its unique prerogative of infallibility only in agreement with the Church—*nisi Ecclesiae consensu accesserit* (Denz. 1325). Both Vatican Councils repudiate that condition in identical terms—*defitiones ex sese, non autem ex consensu Ecclesiae, irreformabiles esse* (Denz. 1839; *Lumen Gentium*, 25). It seems, at least for the time being, that some critics of *Humanae Vitae*, while not formally resurrecting the Gallican consensual agreement, have fallen back to expect or even to require that condition for the authentic teaching authority of the Pontiff when he is not speaking *ex cathedra* by the more elaborate formula of the Modernists of a consensus theology between *ecclesia docens et discens* (cf. Denz. 2006 for its condemnation by Pope Pius X, *Lamentabili*, July 3, 1907).

teaching of the Church. The papal commission on birth regulation had been entrusted with the "gathering of opinions on the new questions regarding conjugal life" (5) but was devoid of all authority human or divine. Its majority report contained "certain criteria of solutions . . . which departed from the moral teaching on marriage proposed with constant firmness by the teaching authority of the Church" (6). The obligatory force of *Humanae Vitae* derives from the abiding assistance of the Holy Spirit which has through the centuries sustained the continuity of the Church's moral teaching on marriage and which Pope Paul, by virtue of the mandate entrusted to him by Christ, applied to the new question of the "pill." The faithful are bound to the doctrinal proposition affirmed, not to the persuasive cogency of the dialectical argumentation and collation of scientific evidences which may be brought to bear upon it. Fourteen years earlier, Pope Pius XII in his Allocution, *Magnificate dominum*, set this problematic into precise perspective:

> Therefore, when it is a question of instructions and propositions which the properly established Shepherd (that is, the Roman Pontiff for the whole Church and the bishops for the faithful entrusted to them) publish on matters within the natural law, the faithful must not invoke that saying (which is wont to be employed with respect to opinions of individuals): "the strength of the authority is no more than the strength of the arguments." Hence, even though to someone certain declarations of the Church may not seem to be proved by the arguments put forward, his obligation to obey still remains. (*AAS* 46:672. Nov. 2, 1954).

The technical formality of an *ex cathedra* definition would not add to the intrinsic validity, that is, its certitude, and the obligatory force of *Humanae Vitae*. The magisterium of the Church is no less "put on the line" by its constant and universal ordinary teaching than by the solemnity of a formal definition. Surely, no one would suggest that the papal teaching authority was in abeyance in matters of faith and morals for almost four centuries prior to the solemn definitions of the Council of Nicaea. Numerically, the aggregate of defined dogmatic and moral theology is very small indeed in comparison with the great majority of things to be held by the faithful. To the best of my ability to ascertain from an examination of H. Denzinger: *Enchiridion Symbolorum*, the generality of philosophical truths which the faithful must hold are not solemnly defined unless these verities are formally implied in revelational data. The doctrinal tenets of the spirituality of the soul, its immortality, the free will— these are formally implied in the Christian revelation of final judgment and eternal life. The proposition that human reason is capable of a natural theology to the extent at least that men may hold themselves morally accountable to God rests on St. Paul's Epistle to the Ephesians, 1. One would indeed be hard put to find a moral doctrine of the Church that has been solemnly defined which rests wholly on rational grounds. The overwhelming number of solemn definitions whether *ex cathedra* or by a council in union with the Roman Pontiff are divine mysteries, those verities most removed from reason; the Trinity, the Incarnation, the Eucharist, the sacraments, the Immaculate Conception, the Assumption, and so on. Put into perspective, *Humanae Vitae* propounds a doctrinal teaching which is of the natural moral law, but whose certain discernment and unambiguous formulation derive principally from the abiding assistance of the Holy Spirit that has sustained the constant and universal teaching of the Church on the moral principles on marriage and on the unique charisma of the papal magisterium which has applied those moral principles to specific acts of conjugal relations. It is precisely on this motive primarily that Pope Paul calls upon priests to teach "without ambiguity" (n. 28) the Church's moral doctrine on marriage.

That obedience, as you know well, obliges not only because of the reasons adduced, but rather because of the light of the Holy Spirit, which is given in a particular way to the pastors of the Church in order that they may illustrate the truth (n. 28).

(iii) "To diminish in no way the saving teaching of Christ constitutes an eminent form of charity for souls" (No. 29).

Unlike those who hold that the individual conscience and not the encyclical is the ultimate determinant of the morality of each conjugal act, the "mitigators" see in the pastoral directives of *Humanae Vitae* (III, 25, in particular) a diminution of the absolute ban on artificial birth regulation (especially II, 14). During the interlude of "study and reflection," a number of clerics told the faithful in advance what the forthcoming pronouncement of the Holy Father would teach. As a result many faithful were confused and others misled despite Pope Paul's repeated admonition not to ignore the traditional norms on marital relations which his predecessors Pope Pius XI and Pope Pius XII had authoritatively reaffirmed. The moral crisis within the Church was somewhat analogous to the situation that had obtained in sixteenth-century England when the pastors of the faithful led them out of, into, and again out of the Catholic Church, and then sat in judgment at the heresy trial of the flock that had trustingly followed their leadership. It is, then, with a keen sense of the tragic lessons of history and a profound compassion for the faithful who had been misled by the doctrinal confusion which in no small measure must be attributed to well-intentioned but ill-advised and premature predictions of the forthcoming papal pronouncement that Pope Paul encourages marital couples to repair frequently to the Sacrament of Penance and humbly by prayer and renewed effort disengage themselves from the binding hold of new-formed habits.

> Let them implore divine assistance by persevering prayers; above all, let them draw from the source of grace and charity in the Eucharist. And if sin should still keep its hold over them, let them not be discouraged, but rather have recourse with humble perseverance to the mercy of God, which is poured forth in the sacrament of Penance (25).

This is no more nor less than the merciful pastoral and ascetical theology which Our Divine Lord manifested in His own conduct toward sinners and made memorable by His parables of the Good Shepherd, the Prodigal Son, the gathering of the wheat and cockle. The patient latitude of forgiveness is illustrated by His prayer, the Pater Noster, and the exhortation to forgive seventy times seven. Like his Divine Master, Pope Paul condemns sin in absolute terms and exhorts sinners with enduring patience and compassion not to be discouraged but to strive to repent and amend their lives. These pastoral directives set down by the Roman Pontiff are as applicable to the sins of habits of impurity, of habits of defamation of character, of thefts, of lying, of marital infidelity, and so on, as to the habits of artificial birth regulation.

> To diminish in no way the saving teaching of Christ constitutes an eminent form of charity for souls. But this must ever be accompanied by patience and goodness, such as Our Lord Himself gave example of in dealing with men. Having come not to condemn but to save, He was intransigent with evil, but merciful toward individuals (29).

IV
Theologians

> Your first task—especially in the case of those who teach moral theology—is to expound the Church's teaching on marriage without ambiguity (28)

The Second Vatican Council has become a rallying point for the dissident clerics. The doctrinal formulation of episcopal collegiality (a doctrine whose status as a noninfallible teaching is no different from that of *Humanae Vitae*), is construed somehow to symbolize a democratization of the Church, at least to the extent that the Roman Pontiff ought to be the oracle of an ecclesial consensus contrary to the explicit reaffirmations of *Lumen Gentium* (esp. 22-25). The Roman Pontiff, it is said, should be guided by the findings of theologians. Also, much is made of the Council's several references to charisms which the Holy Spirit distributes as He wills to all the faithful.[8]

To begin with, it was the Roman Pontiff and the Synod of bishops who signed the documents of the Council, not the theologians. Vatican II is revered, not as the teaching of theologians, but as the official and authoritative teaching of the ecclesial magisterium, the Pope and the bishops in union and agreement with him. Secondly, throughout Church history, the highest theological qualification attached by the theologians themselves to a prevailing position among them is *opinio communis theologorum, consensus theologorum*, at the lower levels of the scale of theological notes.

---

[8]Cavalier references are occasionally made to the charisms which the Holy Spirit distributes "among the faithful of every rank . . . for the renewal and upbuilding of the Church" (cf. Abbott, *op. cit.*, 30, 492, 519, 613). These are no more nor less than the sufficiency of graces which God gives to all in order that each may do His will on earth according to the vocation to which he has been called, and they are appropriately called "special graces" by the Council. In addition, God gives "outstanding" or "extraordinary" charismatic gifts but of these the Council says that "Judgment as to their genuineness and proper use belongs to those who preside over the Church, and to whose special competence it belongs, not indeed to extinguish the Spirit, but to test all things and hold fast to that which is good" (*Lumen Gentium*, 12). We know from the Pauline Epistles that the infant Church was blessed with ordinary charisms (Romans, 1:11; 5:15; 6:23) and with extraordinary charisms (1 Cor. 12:4 ff.). But St. Paul also wrote that all charisms are to be judged by the Church authorities (1 Thess. 5:12; 19-21). Unfortunately, some dissidents have tried to insert a dichotomy between the charisms of the congregation of believers and authority with an implied or openly asserted depreciation of the hierarchical institutional Church. It is very difficult to see how God would grant an extraordinary charism, of a special competence in faith and morals to one who is in open, formal disobedience to the solemn and authentic teaching of the supreme magisterium of His Church.

The Documents of Vatican II are remarkably silent about theologians. In discoursing *passim* about the office, powers, responsibilities, the role, and appropriate charisms for all the members of the Church, the Documents never refer to theologians as a distinct class by virtue of what they currently conceive to be their part in the magisterium of the Church. The Council Fathers speak of the Vicar of Christ, of his unique charisma and of the binding force of his official and authoritative teaching without any *sine qua non* dependency upon the approval or consent of others (*Lumen Gentium*, 22-25); of the validity of the teaching authority of the bishops only when they act in union and agreement with the Roman Pontiff (*Ibid.*, 18-28); of the priests, and the laity. Not only are "theologians" never graced with a distinct classification, but the word itself rarely appears. There is one mention of the word in the Index (Abbott, *op. cit.*, 790); and, subject to correction, I found it mentioned in the text of the Documents in one exceptional instance: "Furthermore, while adhering to the methods and requirements proper to theology, theologians are invited to seek continually for more suitable ways of communicating doctrine to men of their times." (Abbott, *op. cit.*, 268) In none of the references but one listed in the Index under Theology are theologians mentioned. It is intriguing to observe that a universal Council of bishops, many of whom were accompanied by *periti*, never referred to "theologians," at least, surely, to eminent theologians as a separate group collectively designated to whom a special, however undefined, office of a particular deference, rights, or privileges, are ascribed by reason of their presumed or acknowledged *expertise* in theology. But there is no hint of any such apartness of theologians in the Dogmatic Constitution of the Church (*Lumen Gentium*), nor in the Pastoral Constitution On the Church (*Gaudium et Spes*), nor anywhere else. Let there be no misunderstanding of the direction of our discourse. We are simply pointing out that in the traditions and theology of the Catholic Church theologians are never set apart as a collective group with a particular office within the official and authoritative magisterium of the Church. Medievalists would hail their eminent theologians as *angelicus, subtilis, seraphicus,* yet of these St. Thomas wrote: "We must abide rather by the Pope's judgment than by the opinion of any of the theologians, however well-versed he may be in the divine scriptures" (*Quodl.* IX. Art. A, 16). "Against his authority, neither Jerome nor Augustine nor any other of the holy doctors defends his own personal views" (*Summa*, IIa, IIae). There is not the slightest supposition in the Documents that the Roman Pontiff in consulting whom he will must speak as the oracle of a consensus or be the accommodating agency of a correspondence between the *ecclesia discens et docens*. This very proposition was condemned by Pope Pius X's decree *Lamentabili*:

> Truths are defined by a collaboration between the learning and teaching church such that the teaching church has no function other than ratifying the common opinings of the learning church. (In definiendis veritatibus ita collaborant discens et docens Ecclesia, ut docenti Ecclesiae nihil supersit, nisi communes discentis opinationes sancire) (Denzinger, *op. cit.*, 2006).

By virtue, then, of what delegated authority or by reason of what divinely established office do the dissident clerics oppose the doctrinal teaching of *Humanae Vitae* and contrary to the absolute proscriptions of the encyclical and the Holy Father's repeated confirmations since its publication assert that it is not binding in conscience? It may be disconcerting to the pneumatic collegial dissidents to realize that they are not part of the magisterium of the Church, that they do not share in its teaching authority, nor may they with any authentic authority of their own offer the faithful an alternative of their own theological construction. The science of theology proper did not evolve for some centuries. The theologians' methodology is wholly a human enterprise, their learning, at best, a scholar's erudition, and in the absence of divine revelation to the contrary, not invested with any divine warrant against errancy. Their function is to teach, explain, defend, explore what the magisterium teaches. They are auxiliary forces in the service of the magisterium as becomes their high vocation. The Roman Pontiff is the Supreme Teacher, not a theologian among theologians, nor the supreme arbiter of contending theological schools of thought, nor the supreme executor of the majority report of a commission, nor the reconciler of opposing positions, nor the formulator of a doctrinal proposition that would adumbrate contrary moral decisions in the light of one and the same moral principle. He is not the recorder of a "total process" that gives expression to a prevailing consensus or to that communal congregationalist moral principle that each conscience is the final determinant of the morality of a specific act. The Roman Pontiff is the Vicar of Christ, and only of Christ, Our Lord. He is not the vicar of the universal Church, nor of any ecumenical council, nor of a group of bishops, nor of theologians. Perhaps in the realization that they are not a constitutive part of ecclesial teaching authority, the theologizing dissidents endeavor to downgrade the moral force of an encyclical by equating *Humanae Vitae* with the social encyclicals whose moral obligations upon the individual conscience seem not so compelling. To begin with, the value of a doctrinal teaching does not in any way depend upon its format, whether it be an encyclical, an allocution, a papal bull, a sermon, or a formal response to inquiries made by an ecclesiastical body, a metropolitan synod of bishops, for example. What is significant is the undoubted stated intent of the Holy Father to speak authoritatively on a matter of faith and morals to the universal Church as its supreme pastor and teacher, whatever the literary format and the particular occasion. The lean to noninfallible papal pronouncements is even for these dissidents a novel stratagem whose logical prolongation has already worked havoc on many Catholic doctrines in some quarters of the Church. Pope Pius XII took explicit cognizance of its implications and addressed himself directly to the issue:

> Nor must it be thought that what is expounded in encyclical letters does not itself demand consent, on the pretext that in writing such letters the Popes do not exercise the supreme power of their teaching authority. For these matters are taught with the ordinary teaching authority, of which it is true to say: "He who heareth you, heareth Me"; and generally, what is expounded and inculcated in encyclical letters already, for other reasons, appertains to Catholic doctrine. But if the Supreme Pontiffs in their official documents purposely pass judgment on matters up to that time under dispute, it is obvious that the matter, according to the mind and will of the same Pontiffs, can no longer be considered a question of open controversy among theologians (quaestionem liberae inter theologos disceptationis iam haberi non posse) (*Humani generis. AAS* 42 [1950], 568).

And the Pope of *aggiornamento*, John XXIII, wrote in *Mater et magistra*, the encyclical so enthusiastically hailed by many of the present dissidents:

> It is clear, however, that when the hierarchy has issued a precept or decision on a point at issue, Catholics are bound to

obey their directives. The reason is that the Church has the right and obligation, not merely to guard the purity of ethical and religious principles but also to intervene authoritatively when there is question of judging the application of these principles to concrete cases (*AAS* 53 [1961], 457).

The parallel between *Humanae Vitae* and the social encyclicals falters badly. The doctrinal teaching on the behavior to be observed by married couples specifically concerns particular acts of carnal relations. The moral obligations fall squarely upon, at most, two persons, the spouses. What is morally correct and what is condemned as moral evil is expressed in dogmatic, absolute, and exclusionary terms. Social encyclicals are addressed to social, political, and economic disorders. Their improvement involves a multitudinous number of moral agents—of the government, of public and private agencies, of the populace at large. The extent of cooperation and the degree of individual responsibility is unevenly distributed and diffused. Some of these problems of their very complex nature require not only a nation-wide collaborative effort but an international readjustment as well. The efficacy of the conscientious cooperator is so contingent upon a vast support that its fruition can be easily canceled. A parallel between *Humanae Vitae* and the social encyclicals that discloses more disparities than similitudes does not warrant an equation of moral obligatory force.

V

Religious Freedom and the Personal Conscience

Religious freedom, in turn, which men demand as necessary to fulfill their duty to worship God, has to do with immunity from coercion in civil society. Therefore, it leaves untouched traditional Catholic doctrine on the moral duty of men and societies toward the true religion and toward the one Church of Christ (*Dignitatis humanae*, 1).

Probably the most abused document of Vatican II is the Declaration of Religious Freedom (*Dignitatis humanae*) On the Right of the Person and of Communities to Social and Civil Freedom in Matters Religious.

The dignity of the human person (the first words of the Pontiff's statement) requires that men act "on their own judgment," with "responsible freedom," motivated by a sense of duty" and "not be driven by coercion." And to insure this immunity from coercion, "constitutional limits should be set to the powers of government, in order that there may be no encroachment on the rightful freedom of persons and of associations." This general proposition is then immediately made to bear upon those values most "proper to the human spirit" and principal among them is the "free exercise of religion in society," all the more so since God has made known to mankind the way in which men are to serve Him. And then suddenly, almost abruptly, Pope Paul identifies the one true religion.

> We believe that this one true religion subsists in the Catholic and apostolic Church, to which the Lord Jesus committed the duty of spreading it abroad among all men. . . .On their part all men are bound to seek the truth, especially in what concerns God and His Church, and to embrace the truth, come to know and to hold fast to it.
> This sacred Synod likewise professes its belief that it is upon the human conscience that these obligations fall and exert their binding force. The truth cannot impose itself except by virtue of its own truth, as it makes its entrance into the mind at once quietly and with power.
> Religious freedom, in turn, which men demand as necessary to fulfill their duty to worship God, has to do with immunity from coercion in civil society. Therefore it leaves untouched traditional Catholic doctrine on the moral duty of men and societies toward the true religion and toward the one Church of Christ.

Pope Paul identifies his statement with that of the Council: "First, this sacred Synod professes, . . . We believe. . . This sacred Synod likewise professes," and so on. The dignity of the human person derives from having been made in the image of God and redeemed by the Incarnate Word. The contrast is between coercion in civil society and a "responsible freedom" motivated by the "binding force" of "the moral duty" "to seek the truth" by which men are to worship and serve God. This moral imperative to seek out God's revelation is related specifically to the "one true religion" which "subsists in the Catholic and apostolic Church." The profound significance of Pope Paul's statement (and its implications for ecumenism) is further deepened by the fact that *Dignitatis humanae* is the only single conciliar document that is addressed to the whole world, to Catholics, to non-Catholic Christians, to non-Christians, to nonbelievers.

The Roman Pontiff's Declaration is followed by lengthier statements by the Council. The synod first considers religious freedom in the light of reason and declares it to be a right rooted in the very dignity of the human person and therefore inalienable. Certain observations are in order: nowhere does the vibrantly popular expression "freedom of conscience" appear. This calculated omission is consonant with the principal emphasis on the negative content to the right of religious freedom. All men are to be free from coercion "on the part of individuals, or of social groups, or of any human power" so that no one may be forced to act contrary to his own beliefs. This emphasis on the negative is correspondent to the repeated affirmations of the Council that all men are under the moral imperative to seek the ways of worship and salvation God has revealed to mankind. At no time in the Documents is the right to believe as one pleases ever affirmed. This bears significantly upon the Council's propositions on personal conscience, because both in the papal and episcopal Declarations on religious freedom the Catholic Church is explicitly pointed to as the Church which Christ established. For that reason, when the Council considers religious freedom in the light of revelation (9-15), the right of the Catholic Church to freedom, which she has in common with other churches, is declared to be unique because of the divine mandate conferred upon her by Christ Himself.

Among the things that concern the good of the Church and indeed the welfare of society here on earth—things therefore which are always and everywhere to be kept secure and defended against all injury—this certainly is pre-eminent, namely, that the Church should enjoy that full measure of freedom which her care for the salvation of men requires. This freedom is sacred, because the only-begotten Son endowed with it the Church which He purchased with His blood. It is so much the property of the Church that to act against it is to act against the will of God. . . . In human society and in the face of government, the Church claims freedom for herself in her character as a spiritual authority, established by Christ the Lord. Upon this authority there rests, by divine mandate, the duty of going out into the whole world and preaching the gospel to every creature (13).

It is therefore an obvious logical prolongation of the inalienable right of religious freedom in a Catholic for the Vatican Council to proceed directly in the next paragraph (14) to the proposition that the divinely established Church is the authoritative informant of the Catholic conscience not only in matters of Christian revelation but also in those matters concerning the natural moral law.

> In the formation of their consciences, the Christian faithful ought carefully to attend to the sacred and certain doctrine of the Church. The Church, is, by the will of Christ, the teacher of truth. It is her duty to give utterance to, and authoritatively to teach, that Truth which is Christ Himself, and also to declare and confirm by her authority those principles of the moral order which have their origin in human nature itself (14).

In the Pastoral Constitution on the Church in the Modern World (*Gaudium et Spes*), the Council Fathers related its propositions on religious freedom and personal conscience to the moral responsibilities of parents in the procreation and education of children. While on the one hand it upheld the obligation as well as the right of parents to make the ultimate decision as properly becomes every free moral agent, it insisted on the other hand on the divinely endowed right of the Church to form that conscience by its authentic interpretation of the divine law.

> The parents themselves should ultimately make this judgment, in the sight of God. But in their manner of acting, spouses should be made aware that they cannot proceed arbitrarily. They must always be governed according to a conscience dutifully conformed to the divine law itself, and should be submissive toward the Church's teaching office, which authentically interprets the law in the light of the gospel (50).

> Therefore when there is question of harmonizing conjugal love with the responsible transmission of life, the moral aspect of every procedure does not depend solely on sincere intentions or on an evaluation of motives. It must be determined by objective standards. These, based on the nature of the human person and his acts, preserve the full sense of mutual self-giving and human procreation in the content of true love. Such a goal cannot be achieved unless the virtue of conjugal

chastity is sincerely practiced.   Relying on these principles, sons of the Church may not undertake methods of regulating procreation which are found blameworthy by the teaching authority of the Church in its unfolding of the divine law (51).

It is difficult to find any support in the Documents of the Council that would warrant subordinating the Church's traditional and irreformable condemnation of contraception in all circumstances to overriding considerations of the individual conscience of a Catholic.

As we have already noted, the phrase "freedom of conscience" appears nowhere in the Council documents.   This we take to be a calculated omission but hardly an evasion.   The appeal to personal conscience may lead to opposing commitments.   There is the conscience of St. Stephen and those who stoned him to death (Acts 1:6, 7), of Henry II and St. Thomas à Becket, of Henry VIII and St. Thomas More, of Martin Luther and St. Ignatius Loyola.   Freedom of conscience may also connote in the judgment of many reasonable and prudent men tragically perverse conduct like that of deviates and head-hunters.   The generality of mankind acknowledges the profound gulf between objective truth and mere subjectivism, between moral right and wrong, between the true and the false.   The problematic does not infrequently arise as to what is objectively true and false. But it is precisely here that Catholics, at least, have the benefit of the obligation to form a right conscience in keeping with the authentic teaching of the Church as expressed by the supreme teacher, the Vicar of Christ who is guided by the Holy Spirit. It is misleading to suggest that an incompatibility or dichotomy intervenes between a responsible freedom of conscience and the obligation inherent in that responsibility to abide by the authoritative pronouncements of the papal magisterium because in fact they are both gifts of God. The continuity of Christ in His vicars is primarily intended as the primary informant and corrective of the consciences of the faithful. Conscience is not the teacher of morality but the guide of personal choice, and not infrequently conscience may be its own accomplice rather than its guide.   The criterion of a correct moral conscience is outside and superior to itself, namely, the moral law of God.   This may be known by reason alone to some extent, by reason and revelation, or by a fallible reason confirmed into certitude by revelation. This certitude Catholics may have by the "teaching authority of the Church in its unfolding of the divine law" (*Gaudium et Spes*, 51). To admit that "conscience is always binding" is not to say that a man's judgment and choice of action are invested with objective moral rectitude. The objectively erroneous conscience firm in its personal sense of moral correctness may excuse from the gravity of moral culpability. But religious and civil authorities may and do contravene objectively erroneous consciences. Public law and local ecclesiastical authorities have opposed racial segregation as both immoral and illegal against those who protest their freedom to follow their consciences in racial relations. The woman at the well was quite content in her conscience with her generous distribution of affections to a number of husbands but Our Lord corrected her conscience and for this she went about glorifying God. Man is not a law unto himself nor wholly autonomous in formulating his moral judgments.

The world-wide expectation of the forthcoming papal pronouncement, the gravity of the moral issue, the supreme apostolic authority which Pope Paul invokes in *Humanae Vitae*, the absolute and exclusionary terms in which the moral proscriptions are categorically stated, the appeal to the public authorities—"Do not allow the morality of your peoples to be degraded; do not permit by legal means practices contrary to the natural and divine law to be introduced into that fundamental cell, the family" (23)—the call upon men of science to demonstrate that "a true contradiction cannot exist between the divine laws pertaining to the transmission of life and those pertaining to the fostering of authentic conjugal love" (25), the appeal to priests and bishops to expound the Church's teaching on marriage "without ambiguity" (28)—all in all, in text and context, *Humanae Vitae* is a definitive doctrinal teaching binding in conscience.[9] Those who insist—only lately, on the occasion of the encyclical—on an *ex cathedra* definition would logically bring down crashing upon their heads much of the Church's moral and doctrinal teaching. At no

---

[9] I am personally persuaded that the theological note of *Humanae Vitae* is *infallibilis ex ordinario magisterio, irrevocabilis, irreformabilis* as to its substantial immutability. Whatever addendum may yet possibly take place, as with Pope Pius XII's and Pope Paul's explicitation of postcoital and precoital contraception, which they judged to have been immanent in the moral condemnations of *Casti Connubii*, such an addendum—whatever that may conceivably be—will leave the doctrine affirmed substantially immutable. It is in this sense that I call it irreformable. It is not infallible by an *ex cathedra* definition, a sort of definition which is generally prompted by extrinsic reasons, but which by itself adds nothing intrinsically to the validity of the truth affirmed. *Humanae Vitae* is a definitive teaching. It condemns contraception as intrinsically evil in absolute and exclusionary terms. The infallibility of the ordinary magisterium is scarcely a record of longevity but rather an active enduring and universal witness to a constant dogmatic and pastoral teaching of the authoritative teachers of the Church, the Roman Pontiff and bishops in union and agreement with him. *Humanae Vitae* is a solemn teaching—except to the dissidents—based on apostolic authority which Pope Paul invokes.

time prior to *Humanae Vitae* did the dissident clerics set down that requirement for the "internal and external dissent" to papal teaching nor for any of the documents of Vatican II. Conscience is ultimate in the sense that personal responsibility for the course of action ultimately rests with it but it is never absolute in the sense that it can subordinate the authentic and authoritative interpretation of the divine moral order to its own superior determination of the morality of an act. Since the publication of the encyclical, Pope Paul has repeatedly reaffirmed its grave obligatory force upon individual consciences in the face of opposition to it and contrary to such interpretations as would attenuate it.[10]

Two months before the public release of *Humanae Vitae*, His Holiness, Pope Paul, spoke, it seems, with prophetic anticipation of the revolt against the ordinary magisterium:

There are many things in Catholic life that can be corrected and changed, many doctrines that can be more profoundly

---

[10]Cf. Pope Paul's Address to the General Audience at Castel Gandolfo, July 31, 1968. And on August 4: "Once again we remind you that the ruling We have reaffirmed is not Our own. It originates from the very structure of life and love and human dignity, and is thus derived from the law of God. It does not ignore the sociological and demographic conditions of our time. Contrary to what some seem to suppose, it is not in itself opposed to the rational limitation of births. It is not opposed to scientific research and therapeutic treatment, and still less to truly responsible parenthood. It does not even conflict with family peace and harmony. It is just a moral law demanding and austere—which is still binding today. It forbids the use of means which are directed against procreation and which thus degrade the purity of love and the purpose of married life."

Note too Monsignor Lambruschini's commentary to Associated Press, *Osservatore Romano*, August 8, 1968: "The decision has been given and it is not infallible. But it does not leave the question of the regulation of birth in a state of vague uncertainty. Only definitions strictly so called command the assent of theological faith. But a pronouncement of the authentic Magisterium requires full and loyal assent—internal and not merely external—in proportion to the importance of the Authority that issues it (in this case the Supreme Pontiff), and the matter with which it deals (in the present case a matter of the greatest importance, treating as it does of the vexed question of the regulation of birth). This decision binds the consciences of all without any ambiguity. In particular, it can and must be said that the authentic pronouncement contained in the Encyclical *Humanae Vitae* excludes the possiblity of a probable opinion, valid on the moral plane, opposed to this teaching—and that notwithstanding the number and the authority (hierarchical, scientific and theological) of those who have in recent years maintained that it is possible to have such a probable opinion. The pretext of the presumed doubt in the Church owing to the long silence of the Pope is not consistent, and conflicts with the repeated appeals of the Pope and Council to abide by the previous directives of the Magisterium which were still binding. All those who have in recent years incautiously taught that it is lawful to use artificial contraceptives to regulate births and have acted accordingly in their pastoral guidance and in the ministry of the confessional, *must now change their attitude* and set an example by their *full acceptance* of the teaching of the Encyclical. This is not a case of servility to be shunned, but rather one of essential loyalty and consistency in the profession of Catholic doctrine and in the practice of the Christian life . . . " (italics supplied).

studied, integrated, and expressed in more intelligible terms, many regulations that can be simplified and better adapted to the needs of our time. But there are two things especially which cannot be made subjects of discussion: the truths of faith that have been authoritatively confirmed by tradition and by the *magisterium* of the Church, and the constitutional laws of the Church requiring obedience to the pastoral government which Christ established and which the Church has wisely developed and extended in the various members of the mystical and visible body of the Church for the guidance and strengthening of the multiform structures of the People of God.

Therefore: Renewal, yes—arbitrary change, no. The ever-new' and living history of the Church, yes; a historicism which dissolves adherence to traditional dogma, no. Integration of theology according to the teaching of the Council, yes; a theology conformed to free subjective theories often derived from hostile forces, no.

A Church open to ecumenical charity, responsible dialogue and the acknowledgment of Christian values among our separated brethren, yes;—an irenicism which renounces the truths of faith or which tends to conform to certain negative principles that have favored the separation of so many Christian brethren from the Catholic communion, no.

Religious freedom for all within the framework of civil society, yes, as well as personal adherence to religion according to the considered decision of one's own conscience, yes; freedom of conscience as the criterion of religious truths without support from the authenticity of a serious and authorized teaching, no (*AAS* 60, 328-329, June 28, 1968).

Whatever may be put forth as the complete explanation for opposition to the encyclical, *Humanae Vitae*, no part of it may rely upon the Documents of the Second Vatican Council.

APPENDIX B

ACADEMIC DISSENT: AN ORIGINAL ECCLESIOLOGY
A REVIEW ARTICLE

Two volumes[1] which spell out a well-publicized position on dissent bear extensive critical evaluation. The first volume, purports to repeat substantially the theological rationale which Charles Curran and his associates submitted to the Inquiry Board at the Catholic University in justification of their public dissent to *Humanae Vitae*. The companion volume, *The Responsibility of Dissent: The Church and Academic Freedom*, is a development of the written testimony presented to the Inquiry Board by counsel on behalf of the "subject professors" in vindication "of the propriety and responsibility of their actions in the light of accepted academic norms." The first volume contains its own history of the case.

Within thirty hours of the encyclical's promulgation a neuresthenic telephonic harvesting of signatures was activated with zealous vigor by Charles Curran and twenty associates of the Department of Theology of The Catholic University of America for subscription to their *Statement* of July 30, 1968 in opposition to the doctrinal prescriptions of *Humanae Vitae*. Some of the subscribers did admit that they had not yet read the text of the encyclical or, if they had, that it was hardly with benefit of those scholarly and meditative reflections that a broader expansion of time would have encouraged. Time has the numbing effect of dimming the memory of the asperities of this contestation of a solemn and definitive papal teaching but the spiritual wounds inflicted upon the faithful may be long in mending. The raw aching fact is that scandal was given. These dissidents did interpose their pastoral counsel between the Supreme Pastor of the

Reprinted from *The Thomist*, XXXIV, 4, October, 1970.

[1] *Dissent IN and FOR the Church: Theologians and Humanae Vitae*, by Charles E. Curran, Robert E. Hunt, Terence R. Connelly; *The Responsibility of Dissent: The Church and Academic Freedom*, by John F. Hunt and Terence R. Connelly with Charles E. Curran, Robert E. Hunt, Robert K. Webb. Search Book paperbacks. New York: Sheed & Ward, 1969.

Universal Church and the faithful in a grave matter of morality touching intimately the conscience of spouses. None of the numerous statements of Pope Paul subsequent to the promulgation of *Humanae Vitae* in any way had subtracted from the full original force of its doctrinal content, nor—more nearly to the nerve center of the sensitivities of academic freedom, its prerogatives and immunities in theological disciplines, as they are related to the grave responsibilities of Catholic theologians and priests to teach, preach, publish, and counsel in accordance with the authentic teaching of the Catholic Church—has there been any expression of disapproval from the Vatican on the correctness of Cardinal O'Boyle's stand on *Humanae Vitae*, both in his capacity as Chancellor of the University and as Ordinary of his priests.

My own religious and intellectual response to these two volumes is such that to dispense with them by the customary brief review would be less than fair to readers of the review. There is need for an article-length review in order that frequent referrals to the text may disclose the evidence for the critical appraisal.

The title, preface, and first chapter, *The Historical Context*, chronicle the events leading to the theological contestation of *Humanae Vitae* by the author and the "subject professors" with a faultless choice of words and expressions. The title is *Dissent IN and FOR the Church*, (italics in the original). The Preface spells out the refreshing liberalization and independence of priests and layman "of ecclesiastical direction" and "from the institutional Church" and notes that "Pope Paul VI has spoken frequently in a *fearful, and even reactionary*, manner about the contemporary tumult of the Church" (italics supplied). The defense of dissent is undertaken "with the hope that the Roman Catholic Church will thus be able to carry more faithfully its God-given mission in history." And the volume is dedicated "especially to those unjustly accused of disloyalty without benefit of due process." Their *Statement* did not constitute a "rebellion or revolution" but rather was inspired by a conscientious responsibility to do just what they did in the very manner they did it.

Summarily, my own appraisal of the *Statement* is that it is a supercilious pastiche of highly questionable postulates, such as the crude charge that the Roman Pontiff does not correctly understand orthodox catholic ecclesiology, the referrals to past reversals of authoritative papal pronouncements on matters about which even onetime militant Protestant scholarship has long since become too embarrassed to regurgitate, the position that *Humanae Vitae* is at variance with affirmations of Vatican II and demonstrates no advance upon *Casti Connubii*, etc.

The *Statement*—and the exposition of all that is implied therein in succeeding chapters—constitutes a bold and novel ecclesiology which, we respectfully submit, none of the Pontiffs, Councils, and Fathers of the Church have ever known, and surely one that might have drawn unusual interest had it been proposed to the Fathers of Vatican II as the Dogmatic Constitution on the Church.

Chapter Two, *Preliminary Consideration concerning the Nature of Theology and the Role of Theologians*, and Chapter Three, *Preliminary Consideration concerning the Nature and Function of the Magisterium*, represent the schema of the constitution of the Church which the authors are confident that the ever "ongoing" divine revelation will ratify and make incontestably clear to the community of believers in unearthing the original and authentic divine intent of Our Divine Lord from the historical incrustations of usurpations of ecclesiastical power and from uncritical deference and obedience to an "aggrandized teaching authority residing in councils and Church officers."

> In the face of this trend toward establishing an exclusive teaching prerogative in the hierarchy, recent historical studies have exercised a modifying influence by pointing out the presence of error by way of theological dissent. Dissent thus appears traditionally as one possible, responsible option in the theological task, and in its own way, is an intrinsic element in the total magisterial function of the Church. The entire Church, as truly magistral, can never be contained simply and exclusively in what has become known as the hierarchical magisterium (pp. 86-87).

The credibility of *Dissent IN and FOR the Church* then rests on the necessity of bringing the "theologians," dissenters as well as non-dissenters, within the magisterial authority of the Church as, supposedly, established by Christ, Our Lord. This is done by the employment of a concatenation of terms excised from Vatican II and at variance with their original meaning in text and context. The argument proceeds as follows: The People of God—all, without exception, are called upon to the *aedificatio Corporis Christi* which St. Paul proclaims (Col. 2:7; Eph. 4:16). Now surely within this all comprehensive sweep "theologians" are associated in a special way by a "coresponsibility," a notion that is in accordance with and is further reenforced by the full implications of "collegiality of bishops." Now, when we turn to *the* principal document of Vatican II, *Lumen Gentium*, the *Dogmatic Constitution on the Church*, the very first chapter is an unambiguous reaffirmation of the doctrine of the *Mystical Body of Christ* with eighty-four scriptural references to attest to this, and of the supplementary notes five are *nominatim* to Pius XII's *Mystici Corporis* and *Humani Generis* and others to the Fathers and Doctors of the Church, Conciliar documents, and papal encyclicals in support of it. Let the reader compare Chapter One of *Lumen Gentium* on the *Mystical Body of Christ* with the only two scant considerations of it by Curran:

> Pius XII, in *Mystici Corporis* (1943) and again with more emphasis in *Humani Generis* (1950), insisted that the mystical body of Jesus on earth was simply identical with the Roman Catholic Church. In *Humani Generis*, the Pope insisted that his teaching on the matter was to settle the discussion among theologians. Vatican II has produced a different teaching (p. 80).

Has It?

> In the twentieth century, the distinct and "official" recovery of a broader-based ecclesiology under one biblical image was brought about by the encyclical *Mystici Corporis* of Pius XII (1943). This encyclical marked an important stage in the development of ecclesiology—the end of one era (taking up the findings and themes of over a century of minority theological works) and the beginnings of another era. Ecclesial life-style, however, was not significantly changed by the issuance of *Mystici Corporis*. However, almost immediately, it was recognized that the doctrine and limits of the 1943 encyclical and the use of solely the "mystical body" image were inadequate to articulate properly an authentic churchly self-awareness, both domestically in terms of the internal componency and life-dynamics of the Church, and especially in respect to other Christian communities outside the Roman communion (p. 95).

Is this a valid reflection of Chapter One of the Dogmatic Constitution of the Church on the *Mystical Body of Christ*?

Chapter Two, *On the People of God*, follows upon without abrogating, the preceding and first chapter on the *Mystical Body of Christ*. It affirms the universal salvific will of God, the redemptive merits of Christ's passion, death, and Resurrection, the removal of ethnic, racial, national, and geographic barriers among the People of God, etc. Within this all comprehensive catholicity all the people are the people of God, and they are diversely related to the Mystical Body of Christ, his Church on earth. The Catholic faithful are "fully incorporated"; the catechumens are incorporated into the Church by intention; the baptized non-Catholic Christians are "linked" with the Catholic Church to the degree that they "share" by baptism and other sacraments, the acceptance of Scripture, and participation in prayer in the life of God. All these are "prompted" by Christ's grace to that unity by "faith in its entirety" and "union of communion with the successor of Peter" for which "Mother Church never ceases to pray, hope and work that this may come about." (15) If there is a fuller and more radiant bloom to the doctrinal formulation of the People of God, its roots are deeply embedded in medieval theologizing.

Chapter Three of *Lumen Gentium—On the Hierarchical Structure of the Church and in Particular on the Episcopate*—with its firm reaffirmation of the Petrine commission, its unique and exclusive prerogatives, its independent, plenary, and unconditioned magisterial authority, and the formal explicitation of the doctrine of the collegiality of the bishops (and of the bishops alone, not a collegiality of any other ministry) as a constitutive part of ecclesial magisterium in its union with, agreement with, and by consent of the Vicar of Christ, stands out with the full radiance of divine revelation against the congregationalist ecclesiology of Curran; it stands out fully authoritarian and unabashedly hierarchical. All this in one of the only two dogmatic constitutions of Vatican II.

But the college or body of bishops has no authority unless it is simultaneously conceived in terms of its head, the Roman Pontiff, Peter's successor, and without any lessening of his power of primacy over all, pastors as well as the general faithful. For in virtue of his office, that is, as Vicar of Christ and pastor of the whole Church, the Roman Pontiff has full, supreme, and universal power over the Church. And he can always exercise this power freely. The order of bishops is the successor to the college of the apostles in teaching authority and pastoral rule; or, rather, in the episcopal order the apostolic body continues without a break. Together with its head, the Roman Pontiff, and never without its head, the episcopal order is the subject of supreme and full power over the universal Church. But this power can be exercised only with the consent of the Roman Pontiff. For Our Lord made Simon Peter alone the rock and keybearer of the Church (cf. Mt. 16:18-19), and appointed him shepherd of the whole flock (cf. Jn. 21:15 ff.) (*Lumen Gentium*), n. 22.

As Oscar Cullman, the renowned Protestant theologian observer at the Council remarked, the formulation of the doctrine of the collegiality of the bishops left the full and plenary powers of the Roman Pontiff undiminished and unconditioned as before, and, if I may add, completely removed any lingering doubt to the contrary on the intent and meaning of the Vatican I definition. Square all this with the shabby historicism on p. 56 and following.

The insistence of the authors of *Dissent* that theologians are intrinsic to the ecclesial magisterium is the most rootless of all their protestations. There is no warrant for it in the mandate of Christ, neither explicitly, implicitly, or by any manner of prolonged inferential ratiocination. There is no evidence of such a role for theologians in the writings of the Fathers of the Church nor in any of the official documents of the Church, papal and conciliar. And for all the dissidents' facile rhetorical references to Vatican II, the Council Fathers never graced them with a distinct classification or separate consideration as they did with the Roman Pontiff, the bishops, the religious, laity, and priests. Indeed, the word itself "theologians" appears *only once* among the 103,014 words of the sixteen official texts promulgated by the Ecumenical Council. Considering the centrality of the dissidents' concept of the role of theologians as "an intrinsic element in the total magisterial function of the Church" (p. 87) to their ecclesiology, it seems that they have been slighted by a Council celebrated for its formulation of the collegiality of bishops by those very bishops who were accompanied by *periti*.

Undaunted, the dissidents manage to overcome this formidable accumulation of traditional ecclesiological barriers by several ploys. First, the absolutes and certitudes of Christian doctrine are brought within the changing concept of valid knowledge and subjected to the historical and cultural limitations to which most human science is heir.

The object of science has changed from the Aristotelian—Scholastic ideal ("certain knowledge of things through their causes")—and the resultant concern for university, necessity and certainty—to the contemporary scientific ideal (complete explanation of all data in terms of their intelligible relationships)— and the resultant concern for development, probability and matter-of-factness (p. 32).

In the light of an appreciation of historical growth and development, the theologian realizes he will never attain the older ideal of absolute certitude (p. 32).

(What a field day Gilbert K. Chesterton would have had with these new ecclesiologists and a pity we have been denied so much amusement.) What shall we say of the absolutes of "whatever I have taught you" that Christ Our Lord commanded his Apostles to teach to every man everywhere to the end of time unconditionally for eternal salvation? At this juncture of theologizing, there must be a denial to any empowerment on earth to definitive teaching—including the last Council.

With all reverence, theologians recognize that the documents of Vatican II were "dated" on the first day after solemn promulgation.

The *spirit* of Vatican II might be ignored in favor of the letter of officially promulgated formulations. Reference in the future to the letter of the pronouncements of Vatican II as the final norm for evaluating theological data would effectively bring Roman Catholic ecclesiological *progress to a halt*. This is not because Vatican II formulations are unsuitable; rather, it is because they are intrinsically limited to what the Council Fathers intended them to be—formulations which express, for the most part, the maximum capacity of that time but which do not preclude future, ongoing developments beyond the categories of Vatican II itself (pp. 100, 101) (italics supplied).

And if this be true of Vatican II, then it is no less true of all the ecumenical councils since Nicaea. Whether they realize it or not, the dissidents have extinguished the blaze of their fiery zeal to gray ashes. For, if Vatican II is "dated" on the first day after their solemn promulgation in an "ongoing" process of religious knowledge and understanding, then there really never is any dissent. How could one distinguish an orthodox from a heterodox (Catholic) theologian?

A negative book review is generally not likely to encourage its readers to peruse the volume, much less to advertise its sales. I for one earnestly urge all who were interested or troubled by the *Statement* of the principal and the "subject professors" and by succeeding events which brought into their train among other considerations the question of the prerogatives and immunities of academic freedom to read *Dissent IN and FOR the Church* studiously together with a copy of the Documents of Vatican II. We have noted how far apart are *Dissent's* referrals to the Mystical Body of Christ, the People of God, the papacy, the collegiality of bishops, and the hierarchical Church, as well as the role the dissident "theologians" claim to be rightfully their own within the magisterium of the Church from the doctrinal teaching of the Fathers of the Council as solemnly set down in *Lumen Gentium*. The reader of *Dissent* ought also to observe whether its referrals to the Council's teaching on religious freedom is based on a correct understanding and application of the authentic meaning of the *Declaration On Religious Freedom* (*Dignitatis Humanae*). One such provocative reference reads as follows:

> Vatican II, with its declarations on collegiality and religious liberty, has made every contemporary theologian particularly familiar with doctrinal development and with the implications of that process for his interpretative endeavors (p. 35) (see also p. 100).

Now, surely, it is not to the discredit of the Fathers of the Council nor is it a slight upon the Council's *Declaration On Religious Freedom* that neither their deliberations nor the document's content in any way were concerned even remotely with "doctrinal development and the implications of that process for (every contemporary) theologian's interpretative endeavors."

Religous freedom, in turn, which men demand as

> necessary to fulfill their duty to worship God, has to do with immunity from coercion in civil society. Therefore, it leaves untouched traditional Catholic doctrine on the moral duty of men and societies toward the true religion and toward the one Church of Christ (*Dignitatis Humanae*, 1).

The reader of *Dissent* ought earnestly to search the Council's document to note whether the "subject Professors" and their principal have based their ecclesiological theologizing on the teaching of the Council Fathers and further, in broader context, whether, in fact, the main thesis of *The Responsibility of Dissent: the Church and Academic Freedom*, the companion volume, has been virtuously exercised. Of course, the reader must also bear in mind that they have written:

> With all reverence, theologians recognize that the documents of Vatican II were "dated" on the first day after solemn promulgation (p. 100).

With such an escape hatch, it would be rather difficult to hold anyone of them to account.

The authors of *Dissent* exert much effort on distinguishing between infallible and noninfallible teachings of the magisterium. Their discussion, however, is inadequate and the emphasis misplaced. To begin with, the note of infallibility is attached to the solemn definitions of the Vicar of Christ, to the solemn definitions of an ecumenical council, not, however, without approbation and ratification of the Roman Pontiff, and to what has been traditionally recognized by the theologians themselves: *infallibilis ex ordinario magisterio*. Of this last, *Dissent* is completely silent despite the fact that Vatican II first speaks of this infallibility before expounding that of the Roman Pontiff, followed by the infallible pronouncements of a council acting together with the successor of Peter. *Dissent* does fix upon noninfallible teachings of the Church which are authentic but—as they will argue—not binding even if and when the Teaching Authority of the Church says that it is binding in conscience, as it did in *Humanae Vitae*. This is as necessary to the argumentation of *Dissent* as the necessity of inserting the "theologians" within the magisterium. Summarily, this necessitous course of logic proceeds as follows: Infallibility absolutely precludes the possibility of error. Anything less than an infallible teaching does not foreclose absolutely such a possibility of error. And herein is grounded ultimately the possibility of dissent (p. 40) and the recourse to probabilism whereby an alternate course of conduct becomes justifiably permissible. A number of clarifications are here in order. An authentic noninfallible teaching of the magisterium is invested with certitude, that is, with moral, practical certitude. Such a certitude precludes and, in fact, is unrelated to any consideration of a contrary probable opinion. It is not the absolute possibility of error that an authentic noninfallible teaching of the Church speculatively does not foreclose that establishes the justifying grounds for recourse to the principle of probabilism. Nor is such recourse dependent upon the acknowledgement of a "doubtful law does not bind," a popular axiom which presumes what it denies. Probabilism does not rely on the absolute possibility of error but rather, given the absence of certitude (which an authentic noninfallible teaching of the Church does provide), it is an exercise of the virtue of prudence to choose between two solidly probable opinions. No such claim on the absence of certitude on the Church's absolute ban against artificial contraceptives may be made as existing within the Magisterium, whatever doubts some private theologians may have entertained within their own persuasion after 1963. (At this point we may appreciate more fully why it was necessary for the "subject professors" and their principal to bring the dissidents into the authority of the Church.)

Of the universality of commitment prior to the Council John T. Noonan wrote:

> No Catholic theologian has ever taught, "Contraception is a good act." The teaching on contraception is clear and apparently fixed forever. (*Contraception: A History of Its Treatment by the Catholic Theologians and Canonists* [1966], p. 6.)

> No Catholic writer before 1963 had asserted that the general prohibition of contraception was wrong (p. 512).

And on *Casti Connubii*: whose validity and binding force the *Statement* called into question, Professor Noonan wrote:

> How great was its authority? By the ordinary tests used by the theologians to determine whether a doctrine is infallibly proclaimed, it may be argued that the specific condemnation of contraceptive interruption of the procreative act is infallibly set out. The encyclical is addressed to the universal Church. The Pope speaks in fulfillment of his apostolic office. He speaks for the Church. He speaks on moral doctrine that he says "has been transmitted from the beginning." He "promulgates" the teaching. If the Pope did mean to use the full authority to speak *ex cathedra* on morals, which Vatican I recognized as his, what further language could he have used? (*ibid.*)

In 1962, the year the Council opened, Cardinal Suenens declared:

What was condemned as intrinsically immoral yesterday will not become moral tomorrow. No one should entertain any confused doubt or false hope on the point. The Church has not decided that these (contraceptive) practices are immoral; she has merely confirmed what the moral law already said about them. (*Love and Control*, Eng. tr. Robinson. Burns Oates [1962], p. 103.)

And at the Vatican Council Cardinal Suenens chose to conclude his speech of November 7, 1964 on the Schema on the Missions pointedly to reject and dispel the misconstruction he claimed the press had placed upon his speech on marriage of the 29th of October with these unambiguous affirmations:

Allow me to take this opportunity and this method of replying very briefly to some reactions in public opinion which interpreted my speech on matrimonial ethics as if I had said that the doctrine and discipline of the Church in this matter had changed. So far as doctrine is concerned, my words made it quite clear that I was asking only for research in this whole area, not with a view to changing anything in the Church's doctrine which has been already authentically and definitively proclaimed, but only with a view to elaborating a synthesis of all the principles which are relevant in this domain. So far as discipline is concerned, it is clear that the conclusions of the Commission to which I have referred have to be submitted to the authority of the Sovereign Pontiff and adjudged by his supreme authority. I said this explicitly. It is obvious that any decisions regarding the functioning of the Commission rest exclusively with that same authority. I say these things now in order to remove all misunderstanding in public opinion.

There is nothing in the Encyclical itself nor in any of the numerous declarations about it since its promulgation by Pope Paul that dimly suggests any legitimate doubt about the absolute obligatory force of the doctrine which is propounded "by virtue of the mandate entrusted to us by Christ."

I have noted earlier that the stress which the authors of *Dissent* place upon the distinction between infallible and authentic noninfallible teaching is misplaced as far as the controverted issue is concerned. What matters is the deliberate, formal, calculated, purposeful intent of the Vicar of Christ teaching, as he undoubtedly did in *Humanae Vitae*, as Supreme Pastor of the Universal Church on a grave matter of faith and morals, a doctrine that is binding in conscience upon the spouses and the grave obligation of acceptance in teaching, preaching, and counselling "especially in the case of those who teach moral theology" (*H. V.* n. 28) and of the pastoral duty of the episcopate on this matter "as one of your most urgent responsibilities" (*H. V.* n. 29).

Two days after the promulgation of *Humanae Vitae* His Holiness said:

> We had no doubt about Our duty to give Our decision in the terms expressed in the present encyclical . . . . We hoped that scholars especially would be able to discover in the document the genuine thread that connects it with the Christian concept of life and which permits Us to make our own the words of St. Paul: "But we have the mind of Christ" (I Cor. 2:16) (General Audience at Castel Gandolfo, July 31, 1968).

The pretext of a presumed doubt during the interlude of "study and reflection" was largely the confection of private theologians who actively engaged in teaching contrary to the repeated admonitions of Pope Paul not to ignore the traditional norms on marital relations which his predecessors, Pius XI and Pius XII, had authoritatively reaffirmed. Let there be no misunderstanding on the precise issue before us. If there was any doubt about the absolute ban on contraceptives in any private theologian, there was none in the Magisterium.

What, then, of a sincere doubt in a theologian? No one can be so presumptuous as to preclude such a subjective state of mind in a private theologian of piety, erudition, and good intentions. But such a supposition, we respectfully insist, is in the light of the historical testimonials unrelated to a *lex dubia* or the principle of probabilism. We simply posit it as a sincere and genuine intellectual difficulty in one who, while not denying the Teaching Authority of the Church to bind in conscience by an authentic noninfallible doctrine, would want to be more rationally satisfied intellectually. We hope to have supposed the case of a doubting or even contesting private theologian with the best of human credentials. (Ultimately, it is the problem of the relationship of faith and reason, a matter to which we will dedicate our energies in a subsequent study.)

In regard to personal external conduct, that is, preaching, teaching, publication, and counselling in the confessional, the obligation, to communicate the moral doctrine of the Church is no less absolute than in matters of dogma even if they are of the authentic noninfallible description. This would preclude the presentation of alternate positions in good conscience on an *a pari* basis with the teaching of the papal and ecclesial Magisterium by some recourse to the principle of probabilism. Further, the obligation not to contest the Church's teaching in public, for example, via the communications media, is unconditional. This does not forbid private theologians to discourse together and raise all sorts of questions about the doctrine propounded if it is done discreetly, in places and in a manner and with such fellow discussants as not to give scandal. There is no incompatibility between the absolute obligation to teach in accordance with Church doctrine and, at the same time, to try to resolve sincere intellectual difficulties by collective discourse. Reconsiderations, restudies, repeated intellectual probings are of ancient vintage in the Church. One need only recall the wild revelry in medieval *quaestiones, controversiae, disputationes, ego autem contra, sic et non* wherein every theological and philosophical verity was challenged in order to plumb the full dimensions of a question and to conclude to a richer knowledge of a truth that had already been professed. The *Statement* of the "subject professors" and their principal, the telephonic solicitation of signatures, the speed of their response to *Humanae Vitae*, the subsequent contestation shown in a variety of ways in order to organize and galvanize additional public opposition to the Encyclical, in effect, to interpose their pastoral counsel between the Supreme Pastor, of the Universal Church and the Faithful, hardly comport with the exigencies of scholarly discourse.

Even within the internal sanctuary of his own mind there is a *per se* obligation for the private theologian to assent especially where the obligation of acceptance is stated so unambiguously as in *Humanae Vitae*. The obligation of acceptance as related to personal conduct remains absolute. The obligation to personal internal intellectual agreement with the doctrine propounded may become conditional in exceptional instances of an eminent theologian truly noted for his erudition and devotion to the Church. This extraordinary hypothesis will hardly cover the generality of priests and nuns who teach theology. All of us are accountable to God and not, as it is popularly said, to personal conscience, and, for Catholics at least, the Church's role in the formation of conscience is not diffused by private magisteria of theologians, prestigious and nonprestigious. It is not left to the conscience of the Catholic to subordinate the authentic and authoritative interpretation of the divine moral order to its own superior determination of the morality of an act. Conscience may speak with many tongues and not all of them are always reliable, nor are all the persuasions of conscience above the strongest urges of human passion, burdensome inconveniences, and rationally appealing self-interest.

The argument of the right to dissent, based on the possibility of error that an authentic noninfallible teaching by definition does not absolutely preclude, is finally given anchorage in the ominous "possibility of a

> pope becoming a heretic or a schismatic. Popes, canonists, and theologians have acknowledged the possibility of papal heresy or schism, and some nine centuries of theological and canonical discussion have included consideration of what the Church at large could do in such a case (pp. 46-47).

Well, that ought to do it, if nothing else will!

Dissent abounds with casual teases, employment of words, expressions, and brief allusions, all calculated like psychedelic lights to induce a new consciousness of the Church. To "community of believers," "collegiality," and "religious liberty" harnessed to "co-responsibility of theologians," now add, "historically and culturally conditioned views of authority and truth," "the very notion of teaching is ambiguous," "post Vatican II self-awareness," "post Vatican II mentality," "entire Church as magistral," "sensus fidelium," "Charisms," the need for a "theology of compromise," etc. All of these are mentioned or stated in such a manner as to diffuse *The Hierarchical Structure of the Church, With Special Reference to the Episcopate*, c. 3, of *Lumen Gentium* and to suggest a latitudinarian magisterium (there is more than one way to insert the "theologians" into the magisterium. If they cannot make it on their own, then, surely, through an all inclusive congregationalist ecclesiology). Consider for example, *Dissent's* treatment of *sensus fidelium* (p. 56) with what Vatican II says of it:

> The body of the faithful as a whole, anointed as they are by the Holy one, cannot err in matters of belief. Thanks to a supernatural sense of the faith which characterizes the People as a

whole, it manifests this unerring quality when, "from the
bishops down to the last member of the laity," (cf. St. Augustine,
De praed. sanct.) it shows universal agreement in matters of
faith and morals (*Lumen Gentium*, n. 12).

The stress on complete unanimity of all the laity with the entire
episcopacy is not so apparent in *Dissent*. The Council statement is
tautological. Everyone is without error or everyone is in error. But
God will not fail his Church in such unanimity. *Dissent* accustoms
its readers by the sheer force of frequency to the employment of
terms and expressions of the Council documents with a meaning
at variance with their original source and context. The purpose is
unmistakably clear. By appealing to a "post Vatican II mentality"
and the inevitability of an "ongoing" process of doctrinal "development" the right of theological dissent becomes more than an exercise
of academic freedom; it is a necessary beneficent catalyst in doctrinal
"development" the right of theological dissent becomes more than
an exercise of academic freedom; it is a necessary beneficent catalyst
in doctrinal adjustment and reformulation. In a word, there are no
absolutes in creed and morality. The "subject professors" and their
principal have wandered blithely into the wastelands of relativism
simply by their insistence that orthodoxy be saved from itself. And
all this is by the providence of a pneumatic imperial demiurge that
moves the community of believers by graces and special charisms
through a variety of ministries to the "theology of compromise."
The Montanists never exercised the Holy Spirit with such relentless
vigor.

But surely it is bad grace when the authors of *Dissent* quote Pope
Paul VI on conciliar decrees as a witness to their novel ecclesiology.
On p. 101 we read:

> As Paul VI reminds us: The conciliar decrees are not so
> much a destination as a point of departure toward new goals.
> The renewing power and spirit of the council must continue to
> penetrate to the very depths of the church's life. The seeds of
> life planted by the council in the soil of the church must grow
> and achieve full maturity.

One is hard put not to wonder whether a deliberate, calculated
deception is here intended or some intellectual incapacitation
accounts for this unwarranted juxtaposition of the "dynamic inter-

pretation" of *Lumen Gentium* which the authors espouse with the transitional developments through change initiated by decrees. *Constitution* is the general term for statements concerning the Church itself. Of the sixteen official texts promulgated by the Ecumenical Council four of them are constitutions, dogmatic, pastoral, and liturgical, each expressive of theological propositions. Three of the documents are Declarations (On Christian Education, Relationship of the Church to Non-Christian Religions, and On Religious Freedom). *Declarations* are "policy statements" or statements of particular principles on relations with those who do not belong to the Church. (Note that the declaration is on Christian, not just Catholic, education.) *Decrees* are documents of practical significance. They are affirmations of the Council on modern problems and their solutions. They are essentially opportune, prudential directives to cope with contemporary problems in their wide diversity and to effectuate appropriate adjustments and progressive changes in accordance with the soteriological continuing mission of the Church. Thus, when the authors of *Dissent* quote Pope Paul VI on the intent of conciliar decrees—"not so much a destination as a point of departure towards new goals"—in approbation of their "dynamic interpretation" of the *Dogmatic Constitution On the Church* in accordance with their own novel ecclesiological prepossessions, they are being less than reverent with His Holiness and with the Fathers of the Council.

The authors of *Dissent* dust off some allegedly historical instances of papal doctrinal failings and reversibility of which Protestant scholars have long since been too embarrassed to have cited against the validity of papal authority. There are the cases of Popes Liberius, Vigilius, and Honorius, and, of course, the popular referrals to Galileo and usury, and the more recent "reversals" of *Quanta Cura* and *Mirari Vos* by the Vatican II's *Declaration on Religious Freedom*. An occasion other than a lengthy book review should consider these allegedly doctrinal failings and reversals; thus it is understandable that we direct our limited comments to the following issues:

(1) The *Galileo* case illustrates what hazards are risked when the Roman Pontiff acquiesces in the findings and recommendations of an ecclesiastical commission. This aspect of the Galileo case and its relevance to Pope Paul's exercise of papal authority independent of the majority report of the papal commission has strangely been given the silent treatment by critics of *Humanae Vitae*. Further, the *Galileo* case becomes less intolerable, if not more understandable, when projected against the condemnation of Kepler by the Protestant theo-

logical faculty of Tübingen in 1596 for affirming the identical scientific truth for which thirty-seven years later Galileo was condemned. The unanimous decision of the Protestant divines was that Kepler's book, *Prodromus Dissertationum Cosmographicarum*, was heretical because it contradicted the Old Testament's story about Joshua's command to stay the sun in its cyclical course around the earth. Kepler's scientific thesis, his explanation and defense before the Academic senate of Tübingen, is substantially identical to that of Galileo before the Roman commission. It may not cast light upon the problem, but perhaps it may engender a sympathy for the times and their shortcomings to observe that Luther, Melancthon, and the generality of Protestant university professors and preachers strongly opposed the Copernican theory as contrary to the teaching of the Bible while, by contrast, the Copernican system was favorably considered and received by many of the Roman ecclesiastics even in high office. Further, what is generally overlooked is that the condemnation of Galileo was by virtue of a scriptural interpretation then prevalent among theologians who could not tolerate Galileo's challenge of their scriptural exegesis.

It seems to me that when the authors of *Dissent* fault the papal teaching authority in the Galileo case and pass over their favorite theme on the "coresponsibility of theologians" whose scriptural exegesis provided the major premise for Galileo's condemnation by the Roman commissions, they are looking to theological self-interest rather narrowly.

(2) On usury we may consider some second thoughts and reflections by two scholars of the science of economy.

I was brought up to believe that the attitude of the Medieval Church to the rate of interest was inherently absurd, and that the subtle discussions aimed at distinguishing the return on money-loans from the return to active investment were merely jesuitical attempts to find a practical escape from a foolish theory. But I now see these discussions as an honest intellectual effort to keep separate what the classical theory has inextricably confused together, namely, the rate of interest and the marginal efficiency of capital. For it now seems clear that the disquisitions of the schoolmen were directed towards the elucidation of a formula which should allow the schedule of the marginal efficiency of capital to be high, whilst using rule and custom and moral law to keep down the rate of interest. (Lord Keynes,

The General Theory of Employment, Interest and Money
[1946], p. 351.)

The very simple formula in which ecclesiastical authority
expressed its attitude to the question of profit-making is this:
Interest on pure money loan in any form is forbidden, profit
on capital in any form is permitted, whether it flows from
commercial business or from an industrial undertaking...
or from insurance against transport risks, or from share-holding
in an enterprise or however else.

This is at bottom by no means so astonishing when we consider more closely the men whom we are used to call Scholastics.
We have been accustomed to do them a great injustice in regarding them as unpractical, abstruse-minded book-worms,
treating of unreal topics, through endless repetitions and with
intolerable prolixity.... If one attentively pursues the writings
of the Scholastics, especially the wonderful work of the very
great Thomas Aquinas, the monumental quality of which was
equalled only by the creations of Dante and Michaelangelo,
one gains the impression that the work of education which they
had at heart was something different from our education in
middle-class respectability; that it was the education of their
contemporaries to be upright, intelligent, courageous and
energetic men. (Werner Sombert, *The Bourgeois* [1920], p. 314.)

(3) *Dissent* sees a reversal of doctrine of "freedom of conscience"
as stated in *Quanta Cura* of Pius IX and *Mirari Vos* of Gregory XVI
by the *Declaration On Religious Freedom* of Vatican II. The simple
fact is *Dignitatis Humanae* of Vatican II never discourses about
"freedom of conscience." The expression itself does not even appear
once in the entire document. The Declaration treats with immunity
from coercion in civil society on matters of belief and worship;
not a word or even an oblique reference to "freedom of conscience."
Further, there is nothing in any of the documents of Vatican II that
diminishes the condemnations of the egalitarian value of all beliefs
and nonbeliefs which is the essence of the indifferentism proscribed
by Pius IX and Gregory XVI. On the contrary, the *Declaration on
Religious Freedom* identifies the Catholic Church as the one true
religion which all men are bound in conscience to acknowledge but
freely, with responsible freedom and with immunity from coercion
in civil society.

(4) There are endless occasions for critical comment; referrals to "auctores approbati" without saying approved by whom, "charisms" without noting the ancient Pauline doctrine on the sufficiency of grace for every vocation, and the gift of extraordinary charisms such as abounded in the early Church and the persecuted Church of martyrs but with no mention of Council's repetition of St. Paul's admonition that only Church authorities may judge competently about the extraordinary graces.

(5) Even an article-length book review has its limits, and so we conclude with this last animadversion on *Dissent*. On p. 162, there is initiated a discussion of the *Failure to Admit Plurality of Natural Law Theories* (in *H.V.*). I must confess that after repeated study I still fail to appreciate the thrust of the authors' complaint. In the history of moral philosophy there have been a wide variety of natural law theories whose diversities extend from similarities to contraries and even to contradictories. There is the cosmological necessitarianism of the Stoics' naturalist monism and its variations by Cicero, Gaius, Ulpian, and Seneca. There is the Aristotelian natural law severed from its Platonic metaphysical moorings. The early Christian formulations of the natural moral law by Lactantius and St. Ambrose are followed by the natural law theories of medieval civilists, canonists, and theologians. Within the Protestant ethic, the range has extended from outright rejection to a modified acceptance of the scholastic basic doctrine to substantially identical concurrence with (Catholic) natural moral law teaching (especially among the Anglicans, as Bishop Gore, Dr. Kirk, and Dr. Mortimer). Be it noted and reflected upon that all the Christian Churches held unanimously to the absolute ban on contraceptives until the first breach by the 1930 Lambeth Conference. The preceding Lambeth Conferences of 1908 and 1920 explicitly condemned contraception by appealing to the natural law. There is, too, the moral situationalism or contextualism which has gained wide acceptance among non-Catholics and even among some Catholics, and lately, love morality (Fletcher). Among some contemporary Catholics, there is evidence for revised versions of traditional natural moral law (Grisez, Bockle, Fuchs, and by such who are inspired by the evolutionary cosmology of Teilhard de Chardin, Monden), and lastly, the personalists. The generality of Catholic revisionists are, with some heterodox exceptions, really emphasizing one or other element of the traditional natural moral law which they are convinced would redress the balance of total perspective of the human act that they fear has not been maintained.

There are, too, theories of natural law of human conduct of realists (not excluding Marx) quite contrary or even contradictory to the above enumerated variations, that is, empiricist, mechanist, behaviorist, etc.

All referrals to the natural moral law in *Humanae Vitae* are, as in every Church document, not to a theory of natural law that is explicitly and exclusively identified with a particular system of philosophical speculation in the history of moral philosophy but pointedly to the existential natural law that is an integral constituent of evangelical morality, the *lex Christi*, by which man, through the redemptive merits of Christ and by the grace of God, may attain eternal life situated as he is from the moment of his being in the *de facto* supernatural status. That is why every mention of it is always in conjunction with the supernatural. It is *the* natural law (unlike that of the philosophers) which is within the scope of the commission of Christ to Peter and his successors to teach, interpret, and transmit to the faithful to the end of time without error. This may explain why in none of the Church official and authoritative documents, papal and conciliar, do we ever find a systematic corpus of natural law doctrine formulated, much less the development of argumentation as to its existence, the demonstration of its general and particular principles, and the rationale vindicating the application of the principle to a particular moral act. Put into perspective, *Humanae Vitae* propounds a doctrinal teaching which is of the natural moral law but whose certain discernment and unambiguous formulation derive principally from the abiding assistance of the Holy Spirit that has sustained the constant and universal teaching of the Church on the moral principles on marriage as they are existentially integral to the evangelical morality, the *lex Christi*, and subsequently on the unique charism of the papal magisterium which has applied those moral principles to specific acts of conjugal relations. It is as Vicar of Christ,—"by virtue of the mandate entrusted to Us by Christ" as successor to Peter and not as a venerated and world-renowned moralist, that Pope Paul VI teaches in *Humanae Vitae* (would it have mattered if he had?).

The companion volume, *The Responsibility of Dissent: The Church and Academic Freedom*, might not inappropriately be titled *The Primacy, Not of Peter, but of AAUP* in the teaching of Catholic faith and morals by Catholics at a Department of Catholic Theology in an American Pontifical University. Involved is a very serious issue, the question of academic freedom. Historical studies of academic freedom in universities in Europe and America do not disclose a firmly settled and definite doctrine. Many affirmative admissions are made but they are in the nature of general libertarian aspirations and immunities for the pursuit of truth and correspondingly severe negative declarations against suppression and constraints placed upon freedom of expression. Academic freedom is a very complex and complicated problematic. To begin with, is it a univocal or analogous notion when applied to diverse institutions of higher learning, state-owned, privately owned, church affiliated colleges and universities? Secondly, is the exercise of academic freedom and the conditions attendant upon it the same for all disciplines—natural sciences, social sciences, aesthetics, history, law, philosophy, theology, etc.? Thirdly, do challenges to or experimentation of received or established propositions of the various sciences relate equally to applied science and the speculative and under the same or different conditions? But not every question will receive the same answer nor every answer resolve every question. In suggesting a new title for the second volume I was not being facetious. The question of teaching religious orthodoxy is, in my judgment, a unique consideration and deserves a different approach and different standards of academic freedom than may apply to other studies. As for myself, I have no hesitance in stating that the norm of orthodoxy in matters of Catholic faith and morals is the solemn definitive teachings of the papal magisterium whether *ex cathedra* or not and of the Councils approved and ratified by the Roman Pontiff.

As for the "subject professors" and their principal at the Catholic University, what really matters is what they did in the name of academic freedom and in invoking their rights of conscience. As a contemporary witness of the events *via* the various communications *media* I found them scandalous. They did do grave spiritual harm. They interposed their spiritual counsels between the faithful and the Supreme Pastor of the Universal Church and offered the faithful an *a pari* (they went beyond that, actually) alternative moral evaluatory judgment. And little to their credit they exercised themselves vigorously in galvanizing an opposition to the teaching authority of Pope Paul in *Humanae Vitae*. I found the incandescent indefectibility and radiant rectitude of *everything* that the dissidents said and did as detailed and "documented" in the companion volume a frightening example of edification.

John Henry Newman wrote while still a Protestant in 1829:

It is said that a man may go on sipping first white (wine) and then port, til he loses all perception which is which: and it is very great good fortune in this day if we manage to escape a parallel misery in theology. ("The Anglo-American Church, October 1839" in *Essays Critical and Historical*, vol. I, p. 372.)

When after much spiritual searching and by the grace of God, John Henry Newman came to recognize what was the difference and how it is discerned, he chose to Consent Within and For the Church.

APPENDIX C

PAPAL MAGISTERIUM, NATURAL LAW, AND HUMANAE VITAE

We examine the supposition, openly or implicitly avowed by some critics of *Humanae Vitae*, that when the Roman Pontiff teaches a moral doctrine that is based on the divine natural law, he is philosophically accountable to the faithful. Or, in other words, when the Vicar of Christ presents a rational argumentation, acceptance and submission by the faithful depends on its conclusive demonstrative force. This supposition, we shall explain, is a misconstruction of the nature and function of the papal teaching authority, and, besides, proceeds from overweening rationalist pretensions.

I. Integrality of the Supernatural: A Historical Conspectus

From the first centuries of Christianity almost down to modern times, official Church documents record scant mention of the natural law. In 473 A.D., Lucidus, the presbyter, recanted in a letter submitted to the Synod of Arles (473 A.D.) errors of the universality of the salvific will of God and the redemptive merits of Christ by confessing to the divine dispositions of salvation for those who lived before Christ by twice referring to the "law of nature" but not without relating it to the coming of the Redeemer: "*per primam Dei gratiam, id est per legem naturae, in adventum Christi esse salvatos,*" (DS 160a), "*alios lege naturae, quem Deus in omnium cordibus scripsit, in spe adventus Christi fuisse salvatos*" (DS 160b). But substantive verities of the natural law of human nature were implicitly and unavoidably affirmed during the great Christological controversies of the fourth and fifth centuries: against Arius (Nicaea I, 325 A.D.), Nestorius (Ephesus, 431 A.D.), Eutyches (St. Leo, the Great, 449 A.D.), the Monophysites (Chalcedon, 451 A.D.). Implications on the

Reprinted from *The American Journal of Jurisprudence*, Vol. 16 (1971), An International Forum for Legal Philosophy, Notre Dame Law School, Notre Dame, Indiana.

natural law of human nature are also to be found in papal and conciliar teaching against Pelagius and the Semipelagians on Original Sin, Grace, and Predestination. In the Late Middle Ages, we find documentary condemnations of carnal impurities and perversions by the unmarried and the married because they are in contravention of the natural law and not sinful because of divine or ecclesiastical will which could have otherwise arbitrarily decreed their moral liceity.

In the middle of the nineteenth century, the rationalist denigration of the supernatural, the miraculous, of divine revelation, the Church itself, prompted in reaction Pius IX's pronouncements on the capabilities, and limitations, and liabilities of human reason, of the concordance between faith and reason, and of the compatibility of faith and science. (*Qui pluribus*, 1846; *Singulari quidem*, 1854; *Eximiam tuam*, 1857; *Gravissimas inter*, 1862; *Tuas libenter*, 1863; *Quanta cura*, 1864). The First Vatican Council pronounced on the authentic dynamism and ordination of human reason to accord with revelational verities, i.e., on the natural law governing the operation and functions of human intellection. And in turn, the Council taught that for the present condition of fallen mankind, revelation is by moral necessity an indispensable auxiliary to reason, even within areas of its own competence.

From Leo XIII to John XXIII, the Second Vatican Council, and Paul VI, there is an increasing frequency of referrals to the natural law motivated in part by the modern insistence on reasonableness apart from religious pronouncements—(a *riposte* to the rationalists. Was not the Medieval Age of Faith an Age of Reason more truly than the Age of Enlightenment?). Besides, the social, economic, and political inequities and disorders were to be righted hardly because of the faith of the people. The encyclicals were to the whole world. The problems of peace and war, the confrontation with totalitarian regimes, social justice, ethnic and racial relations, underdeveloped countries, marital relations, medical-moral questions—all these were to be answered in terms of the natural dignity of man and the inherent rights of human nature.

In the generality of papal pronouncements there is one constant— the natural law is authentically existential as a constituent of evangelical morality. There is no dichotomy, no separatism between the two except as a methodological requirement of the philosopher's speculation. The distinction of the moral realities endures authentically through a gradation of orders, in the unity of one final end of man. Patently, the supernatural means a superiority of status to the merely natural. But it is in relating properly in conceptual terms the two orders that constitutes the classic opposing perspectives of Augustinians and Thomists, on nature and grace, and correspondingly, philosophy and theology, reason and faith. Be that as it may, grace does not absorb nature but grace does penetrate its inner being; grace is not opposed to nature, but on the contrary, besides elevating and sanating it, grace facilitates human understanding (illumination, an Old and New Testament term) and confers *power* to the will (a Johannine and Pauline term) in order that men may become sons of God. Human nature without grace will never attain the beatific vision of God. Grace without the employment of the spiritual and moral capabilities of man does not sanctify. The evangelical morality presupposes and perfects the natural law even as it goes beyond it.

The early apologetes and Fathers of the Church who perforce had to philosophize with their contemporaries gave expression to this integration of the supernatural in a logical succession of bolder affirmations. St. Justin's *Dialogus cum Trypho*, Lactantius' *Institutiones*, St. Ambrose's *De Officiis Ministrorum*, and, to a lesser degree, Minucius Felix's *Octavius*, Athenagoras' *Legatio pro Christianis*, Irenaeus' *Adversus Haeresis*, and Clement of Alexandria's *Stromates* insisted on the compatibility of reason and Christianity, then, on the beneficent effects of Christian revelation on reason, further—reason finds its own fulfillment and highest achievements in the Christian truths—indeed, classical wisdom itself—Plato, Aristotle, the Stoics, had been providentially motivated by the advent of Christ. Had not St. John written that the "Word enlighteneth every man who comes into this world"? The Petrine exhortation to give reason for the faith, an invitation to apologetics, is given a new development best epitomized by St. Augustine's *De Utilitate Credendi*. St. Anselm made more forceful affirmations—*fides quaerens intellectum, credo ut intelligam*.

The conceptual history of the natural law began with the Greeks who saw it as an immanent entelechy at work within the natural processes striving towards self-fulfillment. The Romans projected this connatural teleology against the overall design of the *cosmos* where the *logos* conferred on each being its "due" place in a hierarchical structure of the universe. This natural order was to find its counterpart in the harmony and rectitude of human conduct.

The Catholic canonists, civilists, and theologians strove with scholastic vigor to systematize the various categories of law—natural, eternal, civil, and ecclesiastical into a coherent pattern of obediences.

But for all their zeal for definitions and distinctions, the moral problematic was compounded by the status of man before and after the Fall. Gratian's *Concordia Discordantium Canonum* was successful in forging considerable order out of the mass of disparate laws, but even he could not avoid hyphenations between the natural, divine, and human laws. The canonists gratefully took their cue from Gratian and identified natural law with scriptural commandments. They were thus able to ignore Ulpian's all-comprehensive definition of the natural as inclusive of the instincts of the animal kingdom and accentuate at the same time the rationality that sets man uniquely apart from it. Aquinas' masterly treatise in his *Summa Theologica* defined four categories—eternal, natural, human and divine positive law with a separateness that eliminated hyphenations, but withal affirmed a harmonious and orderly interrelationship between them. By prescinding from Original Sin which had complicated the problem for his predecessors and contemporaries, Aquinas could distinguish animal appetites from sinful *concupiscentia.* By this method he was able to show a spiritual continuity of the natural appetites of man—all of human biology, with the rational and moral, and thus affirm their authentic goodness and capability to be infused with grace despite the wounds inflicted by Original Sin. Plato's heavenly *paradeigma* had become Augustine's eternal law of the all-provident God which neither the Platonic Absolute Good nor the Aristotelian Unmoved Movers could even dimly suggest. God's will entered into the realm of human conduct *per modum cognitionis*, not merely by being subjected to it without choice, *per modum actionis et passionis.* For what is the natural law of human nature but the eternal law brought into human psychology. With this the decisive philosophic break with cosmological necessitarianism was accomplished. Yet even Aquinas for all the neatness of definition could not shunt off his philosophical speculations entirely from revelational data. He held, reluctantly, no doubt, that the institution of slavery was justifiably permissive as a result of sin.

The difficulty of the pre-Thomists in disengaging the various classifications of law from one another ought not to be attributed simply to a less ingenious philosophical acumen than that of Aquinas. Rather it took root from the existential integration of the natural in the supernatural. And this in turn explains the mutual reliance of philosophy and theology, of reason and faith. This found its classic expression in Vatican I. The existence of God can be known by reason in accordance with Paul's *Epistle to the Romans* (1:20).

God nonetheless revealed Himself to the human race "in another and supernatural way" (Heb. i:iff.) (DS 3004). Then, the Council proceeded further to affirm the moral necessity of divine revelation in the present condition of mankind that those religious truths which are by their nature not impervious to reason may be known more readily by all, with firm certitude, and without any admixture of error (DS 3005). This proposition has been repeated practically verbatim by our natural law Pontiffs and Council (Pius XI, *Casti connubii*, AAS 22 [1930] 579-80; Pius XII, *Humani generis*, AAS 42 [1952] 561-62; Second Vatican Council, *Dei verbum*, n. 6).

There are certain discernible characteristics in the referrals to the natural law in official Church documents: (i) papal and ecclesial teaching authority (*there is no other teaching authority in the Catholic Church*) has identified a natural law precept as deriving from a natural law principle as distinguishable from the evangelical ethic; (ii) the particular concrete application is warranted by a moral obligation proceeding from that same source; (iii) the designation of the natural law invariably (as best as I have been able to ascertain) appears in context related to the *lex Christi*. This is done in one of three ways: (a) Either by general all-comprehensive terms that in context preclude the exclusion of one or the other—"all his (man's) actions, insofar as they are morally good or evil," "the moral order," "the entire moral law," "moral issues," "the total deposit of truth," etc. (b) By explication—"the entire moral law, both natural and evangelical," "authentic interpreters of all moral law, not only, that is, of the law of the Gospel, but also of the natural law," etc. (c) And by conjunction: "natural law and divine law," "a teaching founded on the natural law, illuminated and enriched by divine revelation," "moral and religious," etc. (iv) In none of the pontifical and conciliar documents do we find a systematic corpus of natural law doctrine or an identification of the Church's traditional natural law with any particular system or theory of a school of natural law— (save the pontifical counsels that seminaries follow St. Thomas as a guide in philosophical and theological inquiries, not, however, as Pius XI admonished without that "honorable rivalry with just freedom from which studies make progress," cf. Leo XIII, *Aeterni Patris*, DS 3135, Pius X, *Doctoris Angelici*, DS 3601, Pius XI, *Studiorum Ducem*, DS 3665). (v) The competence and authority to declare what is contained and the extent of the deposit of truth committed to it belongs to the *magisterium* solely. Private "theologians" are free to opinionate on the matter but what they say that is at variance with papal and ecclesial doctrine should have no validity with the faithful. They have received no apostolic mandate from Christ. Indeed, for centuries theologians in the technical sense did not exist. (vi) Whenever the Church teaches natural law doctrine or a specific application of it to a concrete moral issue, it does so by virtue of the Petrine commission, and not as eminent philosophers or world-renown metaphysicians. We cannot too strongly stress these propositions because it explains why we have said critics of *Humanae Vitae* who require a philosophically conclusive demonstration as a condition for acceptance are misconstruing the scope and function of the divinely established *magisterium*. The Church does give reasons for its condemnations of totalitarianism, abortion, artificial contraception, of economic exploitation, racial discrimination, etc. But the motive for submission to the Church's doctrinal teaching by the faithful is the divine investiture of the *magisterium* with Christ's promise of inerrancy, and not the intrinsic merits of its arguments, the persuasiveness of its ratiocinations or the conclusiveness—as each may judge—of its demonstration. But even these philosophic expectations are unwarranted.

II. Rationalist Pretensions

The *natural* law is so called not because it is discernible by a natural faculty, human reason, but because it is the law of the nature of man. Nor is it called natural *law* because it is the law of human reason—but because it is the will of the divine legislator made manifest in the exigencies of human nature as an obligatory norm of moral conduct. To speak of the "appeal to reason" and the "law of reason" in the context of natural law should not suggest more than a methodological approach. No human reason has the power or the authority to legislate its own morality.

The *naturalness* of our nature's moral law is unaffected by the cognitive process by which we come to know it. It may be known by natural information (rational speculation, philosophy, synderesis) and by a divine didactic (revelation). God may reveal philosophical truths, doctrinal and moral, as well as supernatural. If the knowledge of these truths is necessary to salvation, then God must will a way by which men may come to know them with certitude and without error. It is within the boundaries of these propositions that we situate the natural law doctrine of *Humanae Vitae* as taught by virtue of the apostolic authority of the Roman Pontiff.

It has been customary to speak of philosophy as the knowledge of reality by "unaided reason." This may be misleading. Who, for example, can preclude the hidden action of grace in human thought? Who will deny the influence of religious faith on philosophical inquiry? Did not St. Thomas Aquinas, the philosopher, succeed where Plato, Aristotle, and the Greek and Roman Stoics had failed because of the undoubted assistance of his Catholic Faith on the nature and existence of a personal God, on the divine attributes— eternity, infinity, omniscience, omnipotence, universal and specific providence—and on the personal immortality of every man? "Unaided reason" may mean no more than a conscious, deliberate effort of the Christian believer who philosophizes, not to admit an authoritarian proposition as an intrinsic element in the process of reasoning. Even here, we encounter an intriguing experience. In his classic treatise on Law (*Summa Theologica*, I-II, *Quaestiones* 90- 109), in discoursing on the *Essence of Law*, the *Various Kinds of Law*, on the *Effects of Law*, on the *Power of Human Law*, on *Change in Law*, St. Thomas Aquinas, the philosopher, totally dedicated to a purely rational approach to natural law ethics, frequently cites and quotes Aristotle—"according to the Philosopher," "as the Philosopher teaches," "as is stated in *Metaphysics*," "according to *Ethics*," This is not unexpected. What is striking are St. Thomas' more prolific citations and quotations from the Old and New Testament. A cursory review numbers at least eighty-nine biblical references. A more attentive check might yield a higher count. Not only are the number and frequency of scriptural texts impressively notable but even more so the wide diversity of scriptural sources employed in a philosophical treatise on Law: *Exodus, Leviticus, Deuteronomy, Kings, Psalms, Proverbs, Ecclesiastes, Isaiah, Osea, Matthew, Luke, John, Acts, Romans, Corinthians, Galatians, Timothy, Hebrews, Peter.* Though they are hardly quoted as authoritative supports—they are used under *Objection* as well as under *Reply*—surely they are brought into the flow of philosophic argument for the content and cogency of expression and, will it or not, as respectable propositions worth noting even in an inquiry of "unaided reason." When a Christian reasons, it is a Christian who reasons. "Unaided reason" is not so "unaided" after all.

The second rationalist pretension is even more unwarranted than the first. Should not a natural law precept, one that is grave and necessary for salvation within the subsumption of the higher evangelical law, be demonstrable and compelling upon each conscience?

Such an expectation is unfounded. In maintaining the existence, intelligibility, and obligatory force of the law of human nature, philosophers within and outside the Church have never affirmed that all men, or the generality of men, or the majority of men— are possessed by the same knowledge and convictions on the same moral precepts and on identical practical applications. Further, we may well question how many "proofs" and "demonstrations" which are conclusive to a philosopher are equally so for the generality of philosophers—not to mention the non-philosophizing minds. We may go yet further and ask whether there is any one "proof" that has won general acceptance. How many proofs are there, for example, on the existence of God and personal immortality that is beyond contestation among all philosophers? We are speaking of Catholic philosophers who hold firmly to the same doctrinal propositions but who challenge one another's demonstrations. One need only recall what vicissitudes have befallen the *quinque viae* of St. Thomas. What is most intimate to our very being is not necessarily more readily evident to general acceptance. The philosopher's "proof" is not as appealing as the empirical evidence of the scientist nor does it appear as conclusive as the mathematician's Q.E.D.

Another rationalist pretension bears the credentials of reasonableness. It is supposed that by collective and collaborative discourse a general consensus might be reached on a moral norm and its practical application. Here the history of human experience dispels any such hopeful expectations. It is naive to believe that human consciences would be held bound in a grave matter of morality by a general consensus, that a majoritarian determination would be subscribed to and acted upon by the dissenting minority, an expectation most unlikely in an atmosphere of the inviolability of the individual conscience. Compromise and general consensus belong to the political process which knows no political absolutes, but expediency, opportuneness, effectiveness, in the choice of any number of *morally good means and goals.* These political choices are reversible according to preestablished procedures but the specific determination must ever accord with the exigencies of the moral order.

Philosophic consensus is no less a myth than theological consensus. The history of philosophy as well as the history of theology and religion discloses a centrifugal tendency to division, and proliferation. When we speak of *philosophia perennis*, we are referring to a constellation of basic philosophical propositions which thinkers have held in common across the span of centuries. *Philosophia perennis* may or may not prevail at different periods in history but it is never beyond challenge and rejection.   Theological consensus within Christianity has been a derivative of the Teaching Authority of the Catholic Church. Outside its fold, theological doctrinal differences and ecclesial divisions have multiplied to the hundreds especially since the sixteenth century.

In place of these rationalist pretensions that seem unwarranted to us, ought not the *reasonable expectation* to be the divine provision of an unfailing Teaching Authority to interpret and apply the moral imperatives of the natural law which are not so easily discernible by "unaided" human reason?   The philosophizing dissidents have required of the Vicar of Christ what philosophers have never achieved themselves. With benefit of the Christian vision, reason can have no illusions as to its limits. Least of all should the philosopher forget the indebtedness of reason to revelation and on certain natural verities its moral necessity. This moral necessity is fulfilled by the ecclesial Magisterium, *iure divino*. There is no other Teaching Authority of divine revelation on earth.

> The task of authentically interpreting the word of God, whether written or handed on, has been entrusted *exclusively* to the living teaching Church, whose authority is exercised in the name of Jesus Christ (*Dei verbum*, n. 10, italics supplied).

"Lord, that I may see" is a prayer which the philosopher and the theologian no less than the blind may sincerely utter.

III. Christian Pedagogy

Our Divine Lord did not establish a Platonic Academy, an Aristotelian Lyceum, the Stoic's Porch, nor a Schoolmen's university where reason, the appeal to reason, and the intrinsic merits of an argumentation were the principal warrant for acceptance through personal persuasion and conviction. *Our Divine Lord did not say, "He who agrees with you agrees with me," but, "He who hears you hears Me."* The expectation that the faithful should have of the successor of Peter is not a philosophical accountability when as Supreme Pastor of the Universal Church he teaches a moral doctrine of the natural law to be binding in conscience. The solemn definitive teachings of the popes and of the councils in union with him are not surprisingly similar to the pedagogy of the Divine Master.

When Our Lord is discursive, it is to illustrate by means of similes, metaphors, parables, and examples drawn from daily experience the necessity of a prudential judgment which is no less necessary to the spiritual life than to earthly concernments. But when He teaches truths, doctrinal and moral, i.e., His divinity, the Trinity, the Blessed Eucharist, the indissolubility of marriage, charity, compassion, forgiveness, etc., He does so by simple declaration. "The Father and I are One," "Unless you eat My Body and drink My Blood, you shall not have life in you," "What God has joined together let no man pull asunder." His auditors were "scandalized" at His "hard sayings" and many "walked no more with Him." He did not call them back and reason with them—save in exceptional instances of the briefest apologetics. "If you do not believe what I say, believe My works." "If I do the works of Beelzebub, then his kingdom is divided against itself." Nor will it do to counter that Our Lord could not explain divine mysteries adequately in human terms whose acceptance depended wholly on faith in His divinity. The issue before us is whether there are not some natural verities (*opus creationis*) which are necessary to salvation (*opus recreationis*) which are not easily within the capacity of all to discern clearly and with certitude. Whether this general intellectual incapacitation constitutes the moral necessity for the exercise of the Teaching Authority of the Church in such moral matters. If human reason has been auxiliary to revelational theology, it is no less true that revelation has been not only auxiliary to reason but also in certain issues, doctrinal and moral, an indispensable associate—by the grace of divine provision.

The pedagogy of Scripture is *Kerygma*, proclamation, and *didache*, teaching. When St. Peter exhorted the early Christians "to give reason" for their Faith, he gave impetus to apologetics—the pedagogy of rationally explaining the credentials of Christianity. But this was hardly an educational exchange of philosophical accountability. The four Gospels and the Epistles are declarative, authoritarian, affirmatory and prohibitory in their pedagogy. We are considering the nature and manner of "teaching" by the Roman Pontiffs and the councils. In none of the solemn definitions of the councils from Nicaea on were the arguments—even these were in considerable part authoritarian in kind—of the controverted doctrine ever inserted into the ultimate formulation of the doctrinal proposition. This is no less true of Vatican II. Though given more to discursiveness than any of the preceding ecumenical councils, its discursiveness is addressed to those who already hold to certain beliefs and convictions. Its discursiveness is expository, hardly demonstrative. Two of the Council's documents which may be described as uniquely modern, The Declaration on Religious Freedom (*Dignitatis humanae*) and the Pastoral Constitution on the Church in the Modern World (*Gaudium et spes*) are resonant with such authoritarian phrases as "this Vatican Synod declares," "Synod further declares," "Religious bodies also have the right," "the Council affirms," "this sacred Synod likewise professes," "the Church sincerely professes," "the Church recognizes"—when speaking of the natural law explicitly or by implication, when discoursing about the dignity of all men (created in the image of God) and their connatural rights as being rooted in their very being, or when teaching about conjugal love. The occasional "therefore" and "hence" are but concatenations in a continuity of progressions of judgments and not the conclusion of a syllogistic demonstration nor may they be construed as such.

Both the clarity and certitude of the natural verities, doctrinal and moral, taught by the Council are put beyond all rational challenge not by an irrefutable philosophic demonstration but by reliance upon biblical revelation and principally upon Christian revelation. The Decree on Ecumenism (*Unitatis integratio*) with its practical norms for promoting the restoration of unity among all Christians is immediately situated in the Introduction and Chapter I within the boundaries of Catholic dogmas: the divine establishment of the Church; the Petrine commission; the primacy and universal jurisdiction of his successors, together with a repetition of those scriptural texts upon which the infallibility of Peter and his successors is based (here, too, note the recurrent theme underlying collegiality of *Lumen gentium*—"the bishops with Peter's successor at their head"); "the unity of the Church of God"; non-Catholic Christians are brought through Baptism "into a certain, though imperfect, communion with the Catholic Church"; "*it is through Christ's Catholic Church alone, which is the all-embracing means of salvation, that the fullness of salvation can be obtained*"; "that unity of the one and only Church which Christ bestowed on His Church from the beginning. *This unity, we believe, dwells in the Catholic Church as something she can never lose*"; "*the Catholic Church has been endowed with all divinely revealed truth and with all the means of grace*"—all these dogmatic affirmations are made in advance before the Council Fathers proceed to express their reverence for the sincerity and piety of non-Catholic Christians with whom they exhort the faithful to join to charitable discourse and mutual understanding as a practical program that may hopefully and prayerfully conduce to the unity of faith of all Christians within the Church of Christ. Much is professed because far more is presupposed. It is not without significance that the Decree on Ecumenism was promulgated on the same day as the Dogmatic Constitution on the Church, November 21, 1964. One can search in vain for any philosophic proof or demonstrations in any of the sixteen official documents of the Second Vatican Council. (Italics supplied.)

All of our preceding reflections may best be pursed together by a passage from the Declaration on Religious Freedom:

> In the formation of their consciences the Christian faithful ought carefully to attend the sacred and certain doctrine of the Church. The Church is, by the will of Christ, the teacher of truth. It is her duty to give utterance to, and authoritatively to teach, that Truth which is Christ Himself, and *also to declare and confirm by her authority those principles of the moral order which have their origin in human nature itself* (n. 14, italics supplied).

The Fathers of the Council state that the Church is divinely established to teach truth. The Fathers draw no distinction between papal *ex cathedra* definitions, solemn definitions of councils with the approval of the Roman Pontiff, definitions of the ordinary, i.e., constant and universal teaching of the Church, and the authentic and authoritative noninfallible pronouncements. The prefatory phrase, "sacred and certain doctrine," should in context be understood in all its comprehensive meaning. The Church has "the duty to give utterance to, and authoritatively to teach, that Truth which is Christ Himself" and on that same level of authoritative teaching—"*also to declare and confirm by her authority* those principles of the moral order which have their origin in human nature itself." The omission of the distinctions noted can scarcely be considered an oversight.

It is notable that only in three paragraphs of the sixteen official documents do the Fathers speak of infallibility (*Lumen gentium*, n. 25). Everywhere else the texts read, "the teaching office of the Church," "teaching authority of the Church," "duty to give utterance to truth," "authoritatively to teach," and of itself, this Sacred Synod "declares," "professes," "proclaims." If ecumenical councils of the past were noted for their solemn definitions, the Second Vatican Council is uniquely renowned for elevating the demands of the authentic and authoritative "teaching" of the Church not formally characterized as infallible upon the religious submission of the mind and will of the faithful. It is *such* authoritative "teaching" not formally avowed as infallible that is to be the spiritual instrumentalities of achieving the council's triple objective: giving witness to God in the modern world; to build up the Mystical Body of Christ, His Church on earth; and to restoring the unity of faith among all Christians within the fold of the Catholic Church. The dissidents have missed the forest for the tree.

IV. The Natural of the Supernatural

Historians of philosophy within the Church might ponder with profit how much more we have come to know about the nature of man through revelation of his supernatural vocation than was known in the pre-Christian period or since the advent of Christianity in ignorance or rejection of it. This would in no small measure point to the moral necessity of revelation for natural verities about man (and God) and explain, too, why natural law principles of morality are within the deposit of truth committed by Christ, Our Lord, to the Teaching Authority of the Church to teach all men to the end of time. Before looking into the biblical basis of the natural law tradition, we ought to note that the early Church carried out its evangelization of Jews and Gentiles for a span of years without any written Gospels and Epistles. It underscores the unique charism with which the *magisterium* of the Church was invested by its Divine Founder.

In his *Epistle to the Romans* (1:19-21; 2:14-15), St. Paul declares the knowability of God from creation (1:19) and then abruptly states the Gentiles actually had knowledge of God (1:20). The Apostle does not say by what specific manner of reasoning, i.e., analogy, causality—man can come to know God from the contemplation of the universe—if he averted to the question at all. But their acknowledgement of the existence of God by the use of reason is such as to hold them inexcusably guilty for failing to worship Him as they ought. In *Romans* (2:13-15), St. Paul points to a second source of rational cognizance of God, the human conscience, through "the law written in their hearts" (i.e., synderesis) (an expression that will reappear repeatedly in Church documents). Moral depravity darkens both man's intelligence and his conscience. Certain reflections are here in order. When St. Paul speaks of natural law morality, he is far from admitting to a natural morality. The validity of the existence, intelligibility, and the obligatory force of the natural law does not constitute natural morality. Within the context of the supernatural its authenticity is preserved, "taken up," so to speak, within the Gospel ethic. Historically, natural law morality alone more often than not fails. The Church since the days of Augustine taught the necessity of divine grace for the integral fulfillment of the natural law. As a salvific force it is completely insufficient and ineffective. There is only one way of salvation for all men—through the redemptive merits of Jesus Christ, Our Redeemer. There is only one saving morality, the evangelical, of which the natural law moral precepts are existentially a constituent part.

When St. Paul preaches natural law morality he is far from teaching a duality of moral orders. He makes it clear in his other epistles that natural law precepts are taken up within the *evangelium*. This is clearly evident in his first Epistle to the *Thessalonians* (4, 1-12), where natural law morality is contributory to sanctification within the Christian dispensation. *Philippians* (4, 9) summarily purses together the totality of human conduct. ". . . all that is true, all that deserves respect, all this is honest, pure, admirable, decent, virtuous, or worthy of praise." 1 *Corinthians* (7, 10) affirms the indissolubility of marriage, a natural law precept, and speaks of it as "the Lord's commandment."

In the apostolic Church we find recorded evidence of natural law proscriptions in the *Didache* or *Teaching of the Twelve Apostles*, the first-century summary of the teachings of the Apostles for the catechumens. In the category of mortal sins listed under the *Way of Death* (5, 2) is the extinction of life by contraceptive drugs (*pharmakeia*) and abortion ("child-murderers"). The identical condemnations are to be found in the *Epistle to Barnabas* (20, 2), Clement of Alexandria (*Paedagogus*, 2, 10, 91, 2), Marcus Minucius Felix (*Octavius*, 30, 2), Lactantius (*Divinae Institutiones* 6, 20, 25), St. Justin (*Apologia* 1, 29) Athenagoras (*Legatio pro Christianis* 33). Neither contraception nor abortion is explicitly mentioned in the New Testament writings, yet they, as no one doubts, are human acts under the governance of the moral law. Nearer to our modern times, during the pontificate of Alexander VII, we find in the *Errores doctrinae moralis* (*Propositiones Decreti*, 24 Sept. 1665, DS 2021 ff.), condemnations of duelling (n. 2), killing by private judgment and authority (ns. 17, 18, 19), unnatural sexuality (n. 24), concubinage (n. 41). A decade later, Pope Innocent XI condemned *Erroes doctrinae moralis laxioris* (*Decr. S. Officii* 2 Mar. 1679. DS 2101 ff.): that there is no moral obligation to love our neighbor by internal as well as formal, external acts (ns. 10, 11); denial of the need to give alms from superfluities (n. 12); satisfaction on the misfortunes of others because of personal advantage accruing therefrom (ns. 13, 14); oathtaking without intention of meaning to do so (n. 25); false witness, concealment of truth, lying (ns. 26, 27); Killing on private judgment and personal execution (n. 30); killing as an excessive punishment disproportionate to the offense (ns. 31, 32); abortion (ns. 34, 36); stealing (ns. 36-39); usury (ns. 40-42; false testimony (ns. 43, 44); fornication (n. 48); the denial of the intrinsic evil of immoral sexuality (n. 49); collusion in illicit sexuality (ns. 50, 51). If someone should object that some of these proscriptions have a biblical origin, the objection is prompted by a misconception. A natural law precept does not lose its naturalness because it is divinely revealed. The naturalness is not transmuted by the cognitive process. God may choose to reveal His will by a divine didactic other than by its evidentiary manifestations in the works of His creation.

V. Incarnation and the Natural Law

The truth is that only in the mystery of the Incarnate Word does the mystery of man take on light. For Adam, the first man, was a figure of Him who was to come, namely Christ the Lord. Christ, the final Adam, by the revelation of the mystery of the Father and His love, *fully reveals man to man himself* and makes his supreme calling clear. It is not surprising, then, that in Him all the aforementioned truths find their root and attain their crown . . . . Since human nature as He assumed it was not annulled by that very fact it has been raised up to a divine dignity in our respect, too. For by His Incarnation the Son of God has united Himself in some fashion with every man. He worked with human hands, He thought with a human mind, acted by human choice, and loved with a human heart. Born of the Virgin Mary, He has truly been made one of us, like us in all things except sin (*Gaudium et spes*, n. 22, italics supplied).

In the Pastoral Constitution on the Church in the Modern World, the Council addressed itself "to the whole of humanity" and concerned itself principally with "man himself, whole and entire, body and soul, heart and conscience, mind and will" (n). The central theme is that the natural dignity of man is better understood through the revelation of the supernatural dignity of man and above all and much more so by the Incarnation whereby the Son of God in the awesome mystery of the hypostatic union assumed an unblemished human nature in the unity of one divine Person. Apart from the requirements of Redemption, the Incarnation is the greatest compliment paid to human nature. In *Genesis* God created man in His image. In the "fulness of time" the Son of God became the Son of man. In a paraphrase of the Second and Third Councils of Constantinople, the Council Fathers affirm dogmatically that the Son of God assumed a truly human nature—and this is what constitutes the unitive likeness between the Incarnate Word and every man. Its authenticity is further confirmed by the fact that Christ, Our Lord, taught natural law obligations: redemption of debts, payment of taxes, obedience to civil authorities, the duty to alleviate our neighbors' burdens, daily sustenance for services rendered, etc. Our Divine Lord and St. Paul spoke of recompense for spiritual ministries, 1 Cor. 9: 4-18.

We cannot repeat too often that natural law is inseparable from the being of man and secondly, that natural law morality is not natural morality but within the supernatural status of man takes on a salvific force *only* as part of the *lex Christi*. It is in this light that exigencies of the natural law become part of that total deposit of truth committed to Peter and His successors to teach, interpret, and apply for the salvation of our eternal souls.

VI. Christian Vocation and the Natural Law

The invitation to the Christian vocation is intelligible in a twofold way, in its human articulation and in its resonant response in human capacity and experience. The *lex Christi* not only supposes the intelligibility and knowledge of the connatural exigencies of human nature but is built upon it as well as it incorporates and elevates it. The evangelical morality is communicated to man in that same human language within which the *lex naturae* is discerned and formulated judiciously. When God speaks to man, He speaks in human terms; there is no other way of communicating with man unless by the exceptional way of infused knowledge and even then God must do so within human conceptual intelligence. "If faith comes by hearing," as St. Paul wrote, what is heard must in some way be verbally cognizable so that auditors may "walk away" because of the "hard sayings" or follow Him because He is "Christ, the

Son of God." Our Lord's parables are drawn from immediately felt experiences: the calculating sagacity of wise stewards; vigilance of shepherds against the thief in the night; reenforcement of garrisons against enemy assaults—the centrality of prudence against deception; true life is union with God—"I am the vine, you are the branches. Abide in Me and I in you"; the characteristic of love is above all unity of wills: "If you love Me keep My commandments"; "Not everyone who calls out, Lord, Lord, will enter into the kingdom of heaven, but he who does the will of my Father"; "Not My will but Thine be done." St. Paul's exhortation for husbands and wives to love one another as Christ loved His Church and gave His life for it can only be intelligible in terms of human ardor and total fidelity. Some Romans who admired courage were converted to Christianity by the example of martyrs in the Coliseum. The invitation to be a personal follower of Christ, Our Lord, does not exempt but presupposes the fulfillment of existing obligations. The rich young man was told to keep the commandments if he would attain eternal life. "All these have I kept; what is yet wanting to me?" *Then,* Our Lord answered, "If thou will be perfect, go, sell what thou hast, give to the poor, and follow Me" (Matt. 19, 21 ff.).

VII. The Supernatural and the Natural Law

Few words are self-definable as supernatural: that to which human nature is elevated, presupposes, conserves, and reveals human nature; otherwise it would be a contradiction in itself etymologically. The Supernatural does not miraculously transubstantiate us from the natural to a status of being that eliminates the authentic exigencies of human nature. The First Commandment calls upon man to love God "with all your heart, with all your soul, your whole mind, your whole strength" (Deut. 6, 4 and Levit. 19, 18). The summons to grace, the gratuitous gift of supernatural life and the beatific vision cannot be earned *de condigno*. It must nonetheless be worthy *de congruo*. The natural law is part of the whole moral order. The God of salvation is the God of creation and it is one and the same divine will which legislates the *lex naturae* and the *lex Christi*. Revelation on the Decalogue which the moral consciousness of man already prescribed bore the instruction that the natural moral law is divine law. As such, natural law is no less the object of theology, natural and revelational, as it is of philosophy. Every natural truth is *revelabilia* without losing its naturalness. When revealed or inextricably bound up with the way of salvation it belongs to the deposit of truth entrusted to the Church.

To repeat a caution: there is not a natural morality and a supernatural morality but only one salvific morality, evangelical morality of which natural law morality is existentially a part and as such is necessary to and leads men to their ultimate end, God, by sanctifying them through obedience to its moral precepts, and to those of the Gospel ethics. They are not separate or separable in the present dispensation except as a philosophical methodology. Christian revelation then, as Vatican II repeatedly affirms, adumbrates the whole of humanity, the natural dignity and its supernatural dignity. Rather, human nature as illumined by the Incarnation, restored by the Redemption, revealed as never before or since by the humanity of Christ, has been entrusted as a treasure "bought by a great price" to the care of His Church for its sanctification and salvation. The natural capability for virtue requires the supernatural as its necessary complement if it is to have any authentic relevance for the supernatural destiny of man. The connatural law of human nature is contained within the deposit of revealed truth either explicitly—as we have seen in the teaching of Our Lord and in St. Paul—or implicitly, or obscurely, of which the abiding presence of the Holy Spirit will give clearer and deeper understanding to the custodians whom Christ, Our Lord, has set over His Church "fully reveals man to man himself."

VIII. Human Biology Is of Human Life

A recurrent theme of *Humanae Vitae* that is stated by a rich variety of expressions and iluminating insights is that man's sexuality is never merely biological. Carnal communion of the spouses is an act of "total love," "fully human" whose "biological laws . . . are part of the human person." It is preeminently personalist because it is expressive "of the reciprocal personal gift of self." This is unalterably true whether the spouses are young or old, fertile or sterile, whether the marital act is consummated during periods of natural sterility or during the brief intervals of fecundity. The Encyclical rejects as morally justifiable by whatsoever motivation the human initiative and complicity in artificial contraception.

It borders on the facetious to object that the Encyclical bases its morality on the biological process. Should it have ignored it? The biological structures, the organic functions and the course of the development of the natural consequences of carnal communion are a divinely designed pattern expressive of the divine will. When spouses refrain during the fertile period (and they may freely abstain at any time with mutual consent) and resort to the naturally infertile period, they are acting in conformity with the totality of God's will which has defined the whole ovulatory cycle of the woman. Artificial contraception is not part of that divine design.

Human biology is of human life. The marital act is procreative in "intent," in "ordination," in "meaning" whether fruitful or not. Conjugal love is not love plus sexuality but conjugal love is uniquely expressed in the totality of the marital act. It is never merely reproductive as an animal breeding. The natural moral law is not restricted to the rational which is intellect, to the spiritual as opposed to the physical. The natural moral law covers the whole man. His instincts are human instincts to subserve human purposes, his emotions are human emotions to enrich a human life, his intelligence is human reason to give richness and unity to human life, his physical composition—the senses, the physical organs and functions, all these while serving partial purposes, all unite in the life-giving process. That is why Pope Pius XII forbade artificial insemination. Such conception is devoid of the fullness of human desire, the communion of beings, the one-in-flesh. In the Allocution of May 19, 1956, Pope Pius XII had anticipated the high synthesis of *Humanae Vitae*

> The child is the fruit of the conjugal union, when it is expressed in its fullness through the simultaneous functioning of the organic functions, of the sense emotions connected with it, and of the disinterested and spiritual love that animates it. It is in the unity of this human act that the biological conditions of procreation must be situated. It is never permitted to separate these different aspects to the point of positively excluding either the procreative intention or the conjugal relation.

> It is evident that the scientist and the doctor have the right to concentrate their attention to its purely scientific elements and to resolve the problem in function of these data alone. But when we enter into the field of the practical applications to man, it is impossible not to consider the repercussions that the methods proposed will have on the person and his destiny.

The morality of human sexuality is biologically grounded, very much so. But it is a biology that is human and its morality derives from man's total humanity and his eternal destiny.

It is surprising that anyone should want to challenge a natural law morality that is biologically based at a time when so much of our moral anguish is about biological needs: material aid to underdeveloped countries, distribution of the earth's resources, nourishment, clothing, decent residence, employment, just wages, restrictions on the conduct of war, treatment of prisoners, etc.

IX. *Constancy and Universality of Human Nature*

A two-pronged effort has been initiated in some quarters to weaken certitude in religious belief and moral imperatives. For example, we are told that Semitic and Hellenic categories divide biblical anthropology and patristic and scholastic anthropology. Besides the conceptualization, the verbal articulation is not so reliable a medium for the inviolate transmission of the Word of God. Were not the Hebraic, Greek, and Roman theological propositions "historically and culturally conditioned" and their verbal formulations captive in Platonic conceptions and Aristotelian categories? (What Ayer had done for logical positivism, the theologues would do for the new theology.) All this is further compounded by an "ongoing process" of doctrinal development wherein doctrinal conformity and dissent interact much like the Hegelian triad to a synthesis that in turn is subject to the multiple variants of time, place, semantics, culture, historical circumstances and motivations. As for articles of religious creed, suffice at this time to ask, is it not possible for God to speak in time, place, and local language the same way of salvation to all men to the end of time without the hazards of serious distortion of His word? Could Christ Jesus, true God and true man, effectively guarantee that His Gospel can be preached to all men to the end of time inviolably as He promised, whatever the language, the attendant historical circumstances, the cultural differentiation? Ultimately the question is, is God the Redeemer capable of speaking to all men through His Church?

The assault upon the traditional natural moral law has the unenviable advantage of word appeal and a motivation that is sensitively humane. The traditional natural law is "static," "archaic," "closed-in," prevents "progress," does not "keep up with the times."

Let us look at the traditional natural law which was above disfavor as recently as Pope John's *Pacem in terris* and *Mater et magistra.*

Human nature bears within itself the purpose of its existence for itself and for others. It is predetermined by its Maker what it ought to be and endowed with connatural energies and capacities, physical and spiritual, by whose exertions it may realize its own fulfillment or deviate from it. In a word, human nature is both normative and perfectible. We do not conceive of it as did the eighteenth century *philosophes* in a state of pure nature. Rather, it is an existential human nature constant and universal—of the savage, the barbarian, the civilized, the saintly, the wicked. Abstraction from particularities of each individual existence, and historical circumstances, does not reduce our human nature to a state of pure nature but is simply a philosophical method so that we may correctly answer the question, "is it a human being or an animal who was slaughtered?" The rational formulations of the exigencies implanted in man by God go appropriately by the name of the natural law, being at one and the same time, the law of the nature of man and a divine law. The constancy and universality of human nature and its laws are the ultimate basis why men in every generation have felt righteous anger against man's inhumanity to man, whether Nordic, Latin, African, Oriental. Looking at it in a brighter light, it is the reason why we take pride in Socrates, St. Francis of Assisi, Dante, Michelangelo, Shakespeare, Newton, etc., because they are one of us. We wonder at and pray to angels but we do not take pride in them because they are not one of us. Because of this constancy and universality of human nature, we condemn contraception, abortion, infanticide, euthanasia, genocide, slavery, human exploitation, etc. Constancy and universality are properties of the moral absolutes which envelop all men with immunity from the arbitrary, with inviolability of life and those accompanying liberties that are necessary for man's pursuit of temporal and eternal happiness. It is this transcendental referral that invests man with a unique dignity—to have been made in the image of God in a manner that no other earthly creature is and to be destined with eternal union with Him. This likeness to God is preeminently manifest in the human intellectual capacity to reach out to all truth, including God, and the ability to will all goodness, including God. By these capacities men have developed a variety of natural sciences astounding in their achievements and a rich diversity of arts wonderful to contemplate. Human nature is constant and universal, normative, perfectible—and progressive. Collective intellectual and spiritual maturity—as the history of "justice" among men testifies—is exceedingly slow and sluggish. But individual intellectual brilliance and heroic sanctity are to be found in every generation.

One is hard put to understand the charge that traditional natural law is static, archaic, unprogressive, when in fact, historically, men's struggle for rights and liberties was in the name of the inviolable law of their nature, newborn nations proclaimed their right to be, to originate in natural law, and so much of international law has advanced under the inspiration of the natural law. The capacity for perfectibility is not vitiated by the malicious ability to be perverse, the absoluteness of natural law moral imperatives is not compromised by the capricious arrogance to defy them. But if men are to respond to equality, fraternity, liberty for all, then the human struggle to actualize as much of these moral absolutes into historical realities as possible must make its appeal to a human nature, and its law that is identical, that affirms thereby the equality of all men, the inviolability of that human dignity that is connatural. We cannot consistently condemn Dachau—or any other human perversity of the past or foreseeable future without acknowledging these moral absolutes of man. When St. Paul taught there was no difference between Greek and Jew, Gentile and barbarian, he was not speaking only of his contemporaries.

X. Principle of Totality

The "positive" basis on which the dissidents rest is an expansionist interpretation of the principle of totality. An individual act of matrimonial intercourse might be morally permissible, they argue, even though the prospects for procreation were artificially precluded by the spouses for grave reasons provided that the totality of married life was sincerely governed by a habitual intention to beget children. These "grave reasons" are summarily a conjectural calculus of the total family good.

The papal principle of totality is substantially different. When a part of the body endangers the well-being or survival of the whole, that part is disposable. It was on such a principle of totality that surgical operations of incurably diseased organs were morally justified. Pius XI for the most part applied the principle to the physical organism. The moral principle of totality indirectly denied absolute dominion over the body but affirmed a justifiably limited one. The excision of the incurably diseased organ was an exercise of a direct but restricted dominion over one's own body. The sexual organs and functions were never to be impaired.

The excision of an incurably diseased sexual organ would be morally justifiable by the same principle of totality in the exercise of a direct dominion. The excision of sexual organs or loss of their functions which are not physically disabled is morally allowable only as an indirect and unavoidable incidence of a directly intended surgical removal, i.e., of a cancerous womb. While the principle of totality warrants the direct disposition of individual members and functions of the body for the sake of the survival and well-being of the total person, the disposability of procreative faculties falls under a second moral principle, that of double effect. That is why directly intended sterilization, temporary or permanent, is morally forbidden. Contraceptive artifices and contraceptive uses of the anovulants are direct sterilization and as such are morally illicit means of restricting conception. The direct dominion over members and functions of the body is a limited one. It can never be morally arbitrary and as regards surgery a sufficiently justifying reason must exist. The direct dominion of spouses over their procreative faculties is restricted to their choice to engage in carnal communion or not. But once the marital act is begun (*opus hominis*), this limited direct dominion ceases. Thereafter the course of natural development and consequences (*opus naturae*) is totally inviolable against any human interference or frustration.

The principle of totality safeguards the human body against mutilations. Pius XII enlarged upon his predecessor's application of the principle and applied it to the totality of human personality. Questions beyond mere surgery, i.e., spiritual benefits, intellectual and emotional, that may ensue from sound psychiatric treatment were adjudged worthy of moral justification. The temporary arrest of the patient's free will and the facile disclosure of innermost thoughts, desires, fears, frustrations, and haunting memories to another's prying interrogations and temporary mastery are justifiable only if thereby the intent and conduct of the psycholanalysis were such as to release the patient from psychic disorders and perturbating indispositions. Pius XII's broadened principle also provided moral justification for transplants of organs from a donor to another not only to the advantage of the recipient but also as a profound expression of fraternal charity. The donor does not deprive himself of a biological function but rather shares it with another: blood transfusion, kidney transplant, skin and bone grafting, transplant of arteries and veins. The Second Vatican Council in the Pastoral Constitution on the Church in the Modern World (*Gaudium et spes*) stressed the unity and totality of man in body and soul to reaffirm that all of man is preeminently spiritual in his biological needs, in conjugal sexuality, in social relations.

Central to the papal principle of totality is the basic notion that nature is analogous. There are bodily organs which structurally and functionally exist to be, *bonum esse,* and whose reason to exist is to subserve other bodily organs and collaborate with the multiplicity of biological functions to the principal benefit of the entire human organism. They achieve partial goods and they are contributory participants in a superior all-enveloping good. When they threaten the survival and well-being of the whole person, they are disposable. Their activities are contingent; once initiated they may be interrupted. The marital act is uniquely different. The procreative faculties are not expressive of a partial good. They do not subserve a good higher than their own specific immanent "intent," "ordination," "essential and inseparable meanings" of the conjugal act. It is a totality in itself, expressive of a totality of being. This is the mystery of love revealed by God, that human love be an analogue of the eternal divine generation. The conceivable would be consubstantial with the father and mother, one with them in the unity of human nature, distinct from each. It is for these reasons that "each and every marriage act (*quilibet matrimonii usus*) must remain open to the transmission of life."

XI. Unprincipled Totality

At no time prior to the contraceptive controversy—neither in Pius XI, Pius XII, nor in the Pastoral Constitution (*Gaudium et spes*) of Vatican II—was the principle of totality ever extrapolated beyond the physical person to the collective or corporate personality of the family. Pope Paul analyzed this "so-called principle of totality" (H. V. n. 3) (which he contrasts with the correct understanding of the "principle of totality," n. 17), as follows:

> ... could it not be admitted that the intention of a less abundant but more rationalized fecundity might transform a materially sterilizing intervention into a licit and wise control of birth? Could it not be admitted, that is, that the finality of procreation pertains to the ensemble of conjugal life, rather than to its single acts? It is also asked whether, in view of the increased sense of responsibility of modern man, the moment has not come for him to entrust to his own reason and his will,

rather than to the biological rhythm of his organism, the task
of regulating birth (H.V. n. 3).

This conceptual innovation, together with studious inattention to the
analogy of nature and unrestricted by the principle of double effect,
rests on several questionable suppositions.

The first supposition suggests that each and every sexual act is not
intrinsically valued morally and that a "materially sterilizing intervention" may be transformed into a morally acceptable act by virtue
of a superseding principle of family calculus. But the point is that an
intentionally contrived act of artificial contraception can scarcely be
considered as "a materially sterilizing intervention." It is, morally, a
formal act of intervention and as such intrinsically illicit. Further,
the theory of moral conversion or transformation supposes that the
act in itself is either invested with moral import or is morally indifferent until ennobled by a prudential calculus of family providence.
The first meaning would entail a moral contradiction. As for the
second meaning, this writer, for one, disallows the indifference of
means. There is a coordinate correlation between the goodness of
the means and the goodness of the end. Every means anticipates
the end. The choice of a means is never *in vacuo*. There is a mutuality of goodness between means and ends. God's goodness is
participated in no less by means than by ends. That said, we affirm
that the carnal communication of the spouses is not a means but an
end in itself. And any relationship between marital intercourse and
the totality of family good is not a relationship of subordination but
a logical relationship of time and consequences.

The second supposition denies at least implicitly the uniqueness of
the matrimonial act as a totality in itself as an end in itself. Nor is
the connotation of habitual intention to beget children in "the ensemble of conjugal life" relevant. A habitual intention is one which,
if at a particular time it is not thought of, is nonetheless extant.

The third argument is one for responsible and providential parenthood, an end which the Encyclical itself commends. But planned
parenthood is presumptive when it will not conform to God's own
provision for natural limitation of family. While the lengthy period
of natural sterility is for the benefit of recuperating the woman's
energies and resettling her physical faculties, nonetheless this natural
disposition provides that facility for corresponding human dominion
with God's dominion over the bodies of spouses for regulation of
families during infecund periods as well as for corresponding to God's

will during the brief interval of fertility. This is collaboration, cooperation with God whensoever the spouses choose to join in carnal union.

It is much too facile to have recourse to the choice of the lesser of two evils. This principle is inapplicable to marital relations. Correctly understood, the lesser of two evils refers not to the personal commission of the lesser of two evils but to the tolerance—say, by the state for houses of prostitution—for the protection of individuals against rape. God never intends anyone to be placed in a forcible choice of one evil or another. In marital relations, the spouses are never confronted with such a choice. The underlying rationale for this unwarranted recourse to the lesser of two evils is that abstention during the short interval of fertility may be hazardous to marital fidelity. We think such fears to be unduly excessive.

Abstention is much a part of married life. The generality of doctors counsel abstention during the time of advanced pregnancy and for a time after the birth of the child. These acts of abstention are acts of tender regard for the child to be born and for the mother. Not infrequently spouses are hospitalized for lengths of time in their youth as well as in later years. There are many occasions of geographic separation—business trips, visiting sick relatives, times of bereavement, military service. Continence during these interludes of separation are acts of fidelity and unfailing devotion. And what of excessive fatigue or that moderating restraint which a heart condition would strongly commend? A carnal act that is selfishly imposed would scarcely be expressive of conjugal love and may be deeply resented. And what of young widows and widowers— ought they not bear witness to God's commandments and the life of grace? Abstention is part and parcel of married life. It is hardly unnatural; rather, it fosters its own virtuous advantage, conjugal chastity. For those who abstain during the fertile period—even with the addition of days to minimize miscalculation—grow in that discipline of strength so necessary to them when occasions will occur for their temporary separations. Not every act of abstention is an act of frustration; rather it may be the manifestation of a deep compassionate love, a tender concern, a thoughtful unselfishness that cultivates a greater conjugal love and belief in one another's fidelity.

There has evolved in modern times a meaning of love that stresses affection more than devotion, the varieties of romantic expressions more than fidelity, thoughtfulness, daily providence—it stresses enjoyment more than sacrifice, the temporal context of love almost to the exclusion of its eternal dimension. In antiquity love between spouses was not a consciously definable experience nor did it ever inspire a Greek or Latin *Romeo and Juliet*. The Pauline exaltation of conjugal love to the likeness of Christ's love for His Church and His self-expenditure for her sake does not readily suggest an accentuation upon the romantic or passionate. It may be that the most poignant remembrances of married life which constitute the *humanitatis solatium* in advanced age or after separation by death are those acts of tenderness, compassionate understanding, mutual trust, and the countless courtesies. Those who insist on recourse to artificially induced contraception during the brief periods of fertility rather than to abstinence motivated by a prudential calculus of the "total family good" are unduly overstating the urgencies of marital intercourse.

There is a totalitarian hazard, real and actual, immanent in the expansionist "principle" of totality that finds its justification in the name of communal, regional, and national interest. In our times, not a few public officials and some prominent citizens have advocated legally imposed fiscal restraints for families beyond a fixed limit. Pope Paul took full measure of a conjectural calculus of communitarian totality of self-interest that is regulated by artificially controlled procreation. He lays bare the inescapable logic of an *a fortiori* rationalizing moralism that takes as its premise and point of departure the permissiveness of artificial contraception for the sake of the family "good."

> Let it be considered also that a dangerous weapon would thus be placed in the hands of those public authorities who take no heed of moral exigencies. Who could blame a government for applying to the solution of the problems of the community those means acknowledged to be licit for married couples in the solution of a family problem? Who will stop rulers from favoring, the method of contraception which they judge to be most efficacious? In such a way men, wishing to avoid individual, family, or social difficulties encountered in the observance of the divine law, would reach the point of placing at the mercy of the intervention of public authorities the most personal and most reserved sector of conjugal intimacy (H.V. n. 17).

XII. Bona Matrimonii

Critics of the Encyclical point to the absence of any mention of the primary and secondary ends of marriage in the text on Marriage and Family (*Gaudium et spes*, ns 42-52). They infer that such a silence connotes a de-emphasis on procreation as the primary end of matrimony. They are correct in that *ex litteris* these terms do not appear at all in the Council document. But the inference they draw is baseless. At least twice the Council expressly states:

> By their very nature, the institution of matrimony itself and conjugal love are ordained for the procreation and education of children (n. 48).

> Marriage and conjugal love are by their nature ordained toward the begetting and educating of children (n. 50).

And again, God

> wished to share with man a certain special participation in His own creative work. Thus He blessed male and female, saying: "Increase and multiply" (n. 50).

> Parents should regard as their proper mission the task of transmitting human life and educating those to whom it has been transmitted (n. 50).

Indeed, the Council adds that "those merit special mention ... who bring up suitably even a relatively large family" (n. 50). It is our considered judgment that the substantive content of the primary and secondary ends of marriage are stated unequivocally in the Council doctrine even if the terms do not appear *verbatim*. In fact, neither does *Humanae Vitae* use the traditional terms primary and secondary ends of marriage, yet who could doubt that if each and every marriage act must remain open to the transmission of life (H.V. n. 11) the procreative purpose is the primary end of marriage? Still the question bears examination. What may have been the reasons why these terms, primary and secondary ends, were not mentioned in the Council document and later in *Humanae Vitae*?

Let us first note the Fathers did not intend a comprehensive doctrinal presentation. They concentrated on "certain key points" of the Church doctrine (n. 47) and addressed themselves to those Christians *and other men* ". . . to keep sacred and to foster the *natural* dignity of the married state and its superlative value" (n. 47, italics supplied). The Council in a word addressed its teaching on all valid marriages, of Christians and non-Christians, of the young and old, of the fertile and the infecund. This catholicity of vision while hardly minimizing the procreative purpose of marriage focuses on the ensemble of conjugal love, the "various ways" of "fostering this community of love," "this many-faceted love," which will endure "with unbreakable oneness" and "perpetual fidelity." It is "an intimate parternership," an "intimate union," of "mutual help and service to each other.'" Christ's love and union with His Church are the model of matrimonial love and total dedication of the spouses to one another. This devotion is manifest "in bright days or dark" and bears the qualities of prayerfulness, "large-heartedness, and the spirit of sacrifice." In the marital act which "uniquely"—but not exclusively—is expressive of conjugal love— there is so much more to the daily providence of matrimony than the marital act—the spouses become cooperators with God. What seems to this writer to be the principal emphasis in this document of traditional doctrine on matrimony is that it is a way of sanctification. The spouses "increasingly advance their own perfection, as well as their mutual sanctification, and hence contribute jointly to the glory of God" (n. 48). It is a recurrent theme that weaves through every consideration: "growing in perfection day by day," "caught up into divine love," "this love can lead the spouses to God," "penetrated with the spirit of Christ," "human maturity, salvation, and holiness," "love, merging the human with the divine, strengthened by grace for holiness of life." Matrimonial love that is in the likeness of Christ's love and which cooperates with the love of the Creator could not but sanctify. The undoubtedly calculated omission of the terms "primary and secondary ends" does not constitute any novel doctrinal stance but is an act of prescinding completely in accord with the catholicity of perspective. "The work of mutual sanctification" pervades the totality of conjugal love. Those who marry in advanced age and those young whose marriage is barren of progeny are not inferior in the Christian vocation of marriage to those who are blessed with children. The matrimonial life of Elizabeth and Zachary is illustrative of the stirring aspirations and community of love of spouses.

XIII. A Historical Summary

Commentators point joyfully to the advance of the Second Vatican Council on preceding traditional teaching of the Church on marriage. Whatever may be this advance, this newness—how much of it is indebted to traditional teaching?

From the first centuries of Christianity, we find condemnation of contraceptive purposes, and occasionally the similitude of the love of the spouses for each other to Christ's love for His Church (*Ephesians* 5:25). Clement of Alexandria, changing gender, used I Timothy (2:25): "*He* shall be saved by childbearing" (*Stromata* 2, 12, 19). St. John Chrysostom gave a more expansive attention to *Ephesians* (5) than any of the early Fathers. In Irenaeus, Jerome, and Ambrose marital intercourse is for procreative purpose. And among the apologetes, use of the Pauline *loci classici* on natural law struck a welcome resonance among the Roman adherents of Stoicism. But it is to St. Augustine (and later to St. Thomas) that we must turn for that language and the substantive doctrine on matrimony that prevailed unchallenged to our times in the generality of moral theology texts. The title of his work, *The Good of Marriage* (*de bono conjugii*) sets the tone. *Proles, fides, sacramentum*, these constitute the good of marriage. The primary and principal purpose is procreation, then, a bond of mutual indebtedness to supply one another's needs, and thirdly, the indissolubility of marriage doubly reenforced by the Christian sacrament. The Augustinian stress is on procreation, a higher and more intimate partnership of the spouses with God than in mere reproduction. And even procreation has a more extensive meaning. "The receiving of them (progeny) lovingly, the nourishing of them humanely, the educating of them religiously" (*On Genesis* 9, 7). Procreation is an expression of the natural "capacity for friendship" (*de bono conjugii* 1). And for the Christians there is the unique benefit of generation of the faithful. Procreation, not merely reproduction, rebirth, not merely birth. Augustine also taught that marriage is for an affectionate and compassionate companionship—*humanitatis solatium*—(*de bono viduitatis* 8, 11), a notion that goes beyond the basic *remedium concupiscentiae*. Some historians have suggested that the positive values implied in St. Augustine's *bona matrimonii* are not directly related to marital intercourse, or, put in another way, the positive meaning of marital coitus itself is not expatiated on. Further, they say the teaching of St. Augustine on marriage was forged as a polemic response to the Gnostics and Manichaeans' teaching on marital sexuality. The course of doctrinal development might have centered more on the centrality of love in carnal union of spouses had St. John Chrysostom's teaching prevailed instead. The insinuation is that St. Augustine's doctrine was historically conditioned, that is, directed to a specific objective, and formulated not as an exposition of the entire objective nature of marriage according to its natural institution and its Christian sacramental character. There is much to distinguish between a historically *provoked* moral teaching and a historically *conditioned* one. In a predominantly pagan society given to sexual degradations and perversions and even to a religious cult of sexuality which a darkened intelligence and stultified conscience had come to accept as moral (cf. *Romans* 1, 24-28), the Augustinian stress on procreative purpose is the necessary corrective of the pagan, Gnostic, and Manichaean distortion of human sexuality. But it is far from correct to suppose that Augustinian doctrine itself has been corrected by Vatican II and by *Humanae Vitae.* On the contrary his essentials, his very terminology prevail through succeeding centuries, passed on by St. Thomas, and incorporated in *Casti Connubii, Gaudium et Spes,* and *Humanae Vitae; proles, fides, sacramentum, amicitia conjugalis, pacto conjugalis, mutuum adiutorium.* Latter-day criticism has placed St. Augustine in the exceptional company of St. Paul who has been faulted because of *redditio debiti* (1 Corinthians 7, 3) despite the highest exaltation of conjugal love in *Ephesians* (5, 25). The critics see *redditio debiti* as a cold legal exaction on the part of one spouse of the other. But the full context discloses that St. Paul is teaching against the selfish, capricious one-sided choice, the mutuality of marital rights and the union of consensual disposition on carnal communion or abstinence between the spouses, an astounding affirmation of equality in marital sex relations to a pagan society wherein the wife was in an inferior status *sexually.* The patristic *bona matrimonii* were analytically singled out by Schoolmen with a passion for distinction and systematization through hierarchy of ends. The distinction between primary and secondary ends of marriage could express—as it etymologically does—the concomitant sexual affectivities and consequent human solaces attendant upon a truly desirous procreative intent—whether fruitful or not. "Delight follows operation," "Delight is the perfection of operation," so wrote Aquinas specifically of sexual pleasure (cf. *On the Sentences* 4, 31, 2; 4, 49, 3). When moralists discussed the *bona* in a context of conflict, the numerically suggestive terminology resolved the problem in a hierarchy of ends. This in no small part was historically *prompted* by the polemics against the Cathars, Albigensian, and Patarine's advocacy of sexual pleasure without seminal intromission. True human love, the most intimate human capacity of man, paradoxically had to wait for divine revelation of its nature in the advent of the Incarnate Word. It took centuries for our sluggish human nature to enlarge upon our concept of spiritual love to a noble and gallant romanticism and to incorporate it within married life itself. But this slow process belonged to human experience itself of all mankind and was not the resultant of restrictions of a moral doctrine on love in marriage.

XIV. Humanae Vitae

The substantive context of the primary and secondary ends of marriage is in *Gaudium et spes* and in *Humanae Vitae*. The absence of these terms in both these documents may be justified on the ground that they are no longer suitable to signify that fullness and richness of the *bona matrimonii* as enunciated in *Humanae Vitae*. Pius XI had expressed it earlier:

> This mutual interior formation of husband and wife, this persevering endeavor to bring each other to the state of perfection, may, in a true sense, be called, as the Roman Catechism calls it, the primary cause and reason of matrimony, so long as marriage is considered, not in its stricter sense, as the institution destined for the procreation and education of children, but in the wider sense as a complete and intimate life-partnership and association.

This much-ignored passage from *Casti Connubii* (ns. 24, 25) may rightly be considered a summary *precis* of numbers 47-51 of the Pastoral Constitution.

In *Humanae Vitae* we have a radiant synthesis of the traditional teaching of the Church on marriage. It is ironical that his sublime document which give expression to the essential humanity of the biological processes of man, to the companionship in salvation, to mutual personal perfection, to total self-donation, to responsible parenthood in collaboration with God's design both in the fertile and the nonfertile period, a total love which is "a very special form of personal friendship," to a totality of conjugal love that of its very nature cries out for similitude of the spouses—whether fruitful or not—that finds this totality in an openness to the transmission of life should have been criticized by the dissidents as too biological, unprogressive, nonpersonalist, etc. St. Thomas had written that

God "has imparted His own goodness to created things in such a way that each of them could transmit to others what it has itself received. Consequently those who withdraw from things their own operations, do wrong to the goodness of God" (*detrahere ergo actiones proprias rebus est divinae bonitati derogare" Contr. Gent.* III. 69). This comprehensive principle is no less applicable to man's disposition of his own natural faculties as to his use or abuse of the operations of other beings.

The supernatural status of man, the assumption of human nature with all its connatural exigencies as well as its supernatural gifts in the mystery of the Incarnation, the undoubted teaching of natural law precepts by Our Divine Lord, the teaching of natural law precepts by St. Paul as part of the evangelical law, the presupposition of natural law obligations in the Christian vocation, the necessary ordination of certain grave natural law precepts to salvific dispensation, the papal and conciliar teaching of natural law precepts without ever designating any limitation of competence and authority to do so without error—all these considerations point to the inclusion of natural law precepts within the total deposit of truth committed to Peter and his successors for communication to all mankind, interpreting it, and applying it to concrete issues. Conversely, there is no evidence in any of the Church official documents that explicitly states or even implicitly suggests that there is an area of morality outside the teaching mission of the Church as divinely mandated. Nor is there any evidence in any official Church document that in natural law verities the ecclesial magisterium is philosophically accountable. Papal and conciliar magisterium rests wholly upon the Petrine commission and the obligation for acceptance on the part of the faithful relies primarily and principally upon the divine warrant of inerrancy. "He who hears you hears Me"—not—"He who agrees with you agrees with Me." What the Church may teach *iure divino* and with what degree of authoritative affirmation belong exclusively to the teaching authority of the Church to declare.

* * * * *

On the last day of the year when the Church of England decided by majority to vote to reverse its centuries-old moral ban on artificial contraception, December 31, 1930, Pope Pius XI promulgated the encyclical *Casti Connubii*. We conclude with his assessment of the Church in the modern world:

The Catholic Church, to whom God had entrusted the defense of the integrity and purity of morals, standing erect in the midst of the moral ruin which surrounds her, in order that she may preserve the chastity of the nuptial union from being defiled by this foul stain, raises her voice in token of her divine ambassadorship and through Our mouth proclaims anew: any use whatsoever of matrimony exercised in such a way that the act is deliberately frustrated in its natural power to generate life is an offense against the law of God and of nature, and those who indulge in such are branded with the guilt of grave sin.

Each and every marriage act (quilibet matrimonii usus) must remain open to the transmission of life (AAS, 22, 559-560).

SCRIPTURAL TEXTS AND REFERENCES

INDEX

Alexander VI, pope, 93
Ambrose, St., 14
Antioch, council of, 172
Apocrisarius, 19
Aporia, 127-129
Aquinas, Thomas, 72, 81, 84, 95, 115, 129, 148, 210-217
Arian and Nicaean assemblages, 137 ff.
Aristotle, 82, 84
Assertio Septem Sacramentorum (Henry VIII, 1521), 197-198
Astruc, 96
Athanasius, St., 136, 140
Aubert, Roger, 256
Augustine, St., 14, 72, 81, 95, 109, 131, 147, 148

Barth, Karl, 150, 227, 250
Basle, Council of, (1431), 199
Ballarmine, Robert, St., 70, 72, 81
Bible, critico-historical exegesis, 95-102
Blake, Carson, 41

Canon 1543, 86
Canonization, 17-23
Carlyle, A. J., 89
Cassiodorus, 167
Casti Connubii (Pius XI, 1930), 123-124
Celibacy, 34-39
Certain Difficulties Felt by Anglicans in Catholic Teaching (Newman) 91-92, 107
Chalcedon, council of, 106, 184, 188-191
Christus Dominus (Vat. II), 12
Church, a teaching, 49 ff., 129-130
Cicogni, Amleto, Cardinal, Secretary of State, 124-125
Civilta Cattolica, 17
Comma Johanneum, 100-101
Congar, Yves, 77, 205
Conscience, 121-123, 217-218, 263
Constance, council of, (1414), 201, 258-263
Constitutio Constantini, 93
Contra errores Graecorum, 210
Credo of Paul VI, 39
Cullmann, Oscar, 50, 56, 222, 227
Cyprian, St., 193

Cyril, St., Patriarch of Alexandria, 14, 188

Daniel c.7, 51
Danielou, Jean Cardinal, 12, 26-29
Dante, Alighieri, 226
Dawson, Christopher, 89, 162
Declaratio Collectiva Episcoporum Germaniae (Jan.-Feb. 1875) 227-230
De Fide Sanctae Trinitatis, 210-217
De Genesi ad litteram (Augustine, 401-414), 82
De sancta virginitate (Augustine, 401), 14
De Trinitate (Augustine, 399-422), 109-110
Divino Afflante Spiritu, (Pius XII, 1943), 102, 157
Dutch Catechism, 15-17
Dvornik, Francis, 67, 77, 79

Ecclesiam Suam (Paul VI, 1963), 31, 32
Ekklesia-qahal, 50, 51
Enchiridion Biblicum, 100
Ephesus, council of, 13, 14, 102
Eusebius, 61, 95
Eutyches, 178, 188
Ex illa die (Clement XI, 1715), 87
Expositio evangelii sec. Luc (Ambrose, 390), 14
Ex quo singulari (Benedict XIV, 1742), 87
Ex sese, non autem ex consensu Ecclesiae, 254-256

Faith, 70-71, 141, 149, 268
False Decretals, 161-169
Ferrera, council of (1430), 200
Florence, council of (1439), 11, 97
Franzen, August, 262
Fuhrmann, Horst, 168

Galileo, 81-83
Galot, Jean, 17
Gundry, R. H., 56

Haering, Bernard, 36
Henotikon, 180, 182, 189
Henry VIII, 197-199
Historia ecclesiastica tripartita (560), 167